THE
ILLUSTRATED ENCYCLOPEDIA
OF
WORLD
GOLF

Chris Plumridge

WHSMITH
EXCLUSIVE · BOOKS ·

Foreword

It has been said that golf is a game at which you may exhaust yourself but never your subject. From the millions of shots struck every year throughout the world, that statement seems particularly appropriate. The game has never enjoyed such sustained popularity as it does now and it is difficult to imagine the sort of conditions it was played under by those hardy Scots over two centuries ago.

The Illustrated Encyclopedia of World Golf *makes a vibrant contribution in recounting the details of those past 200 years from the early golfers' first tentative steps onto the natural links to the development of clubs and balls. Inevitably, as the game grew in popularity, so the appetite for competition grew and this led to the establishment of the Open Championship, first staged in 1860 and the forerunner of championships everywhere. Of these, four championships stand as the ultimate challenge for any golfer — the Open Championship, the United States Masters, the United States Open and the United States PGA Championship. The history of these four championships is closely examined along with the dramatic moments which meant victory for some of the most famous names in the game.*

In my career as a professional golfer, I have been fortunate to win two of these four major championships and the memories of those victories will stay with me for ever. There have been other outstanding memories and many of them are captured within the pages of this book which, I believe, makes a valuable contribution to the literaturé of this endlessly fascinating game.

Tony Jacklin OBE

Left: Tony Jacklin's successes on the golf course did not end with his playing career. One of his greatest moments was as non-playing captain of the victorious European Ryder Cup team at The Belfry in 1985, where he is being chaired by a member of his team, Sam Torrance.

Author's dedication: To Joanna and Jessica

House Editor: Donna Wood
Editor: Peter Arnold
Art Editor: Gordon Robertson
Production: Craig Chubb

Produced exclusively for
W. H. Smith and Son Limited
by Marshall Cavendish Books Limited,
58 Old Compton Street,
London W1V 5PA

Typeset in 10/11 pt Times by Quadraset Limited

Printed and bound in Hong Kong

Contents

Below: The picturesque 10th green at Pebble Beach, California.

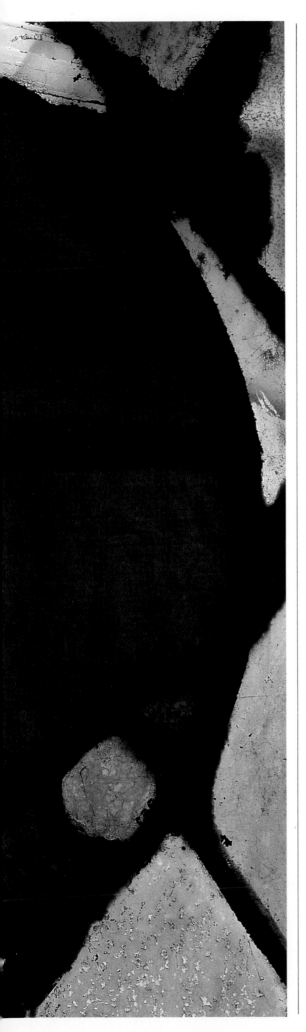

The History of Golf

The origins of golf are shrouded in mystery with many countries claiming to have invented the game. It is indisputable, however, that the Scots popularized golf and were responsible for spreading its gospel throughout the world. The formation of societies such as the Honourable Company of Edinburgh Golfers and the St Andrews Society led to the establishment of golf clubs which, in turn, began the administrative processes for the playing of golf and its rules. As golf took a hold, so the Open Championship came into being, which was then followed by the Amateur Championship. The foundation stone of American golf was laid by a Scot who, unwittingly, was to create the most powerful golfing nation on earth within the space of a century. From these early beginnings, golf has spread to the four corners of the earth to become an almost universal language.

Left: This figure in a stained glass window in Gloucester Cathedral is claimed by some to be the earliest picture of a golfer. The great east window was built in the 1340s. Is this really golf or a game more like hockey?

Millions of golfers of all ages pace the world's fairways every year, but how many of them even think how and when the game started? That it is an ancient game is undeniable, but its actual beginnings have always been open to debate, claim and counter-claim. Suffice to say that its origins go back several centuries but are unlikely ever to be pinpointed to one particular time or place. Almost certainly, golf was not a sudden invention. More likely it has been a game that has evolved down the years from similar activities.

We can go back to the Romans, who are credited for so many of today's inventions, for they are known to have spent some of their leisure time knocking a stone or other object around with a stick. The game was called *Paganica*. Later the Germans, the Icelanders, the French and the Dutch were involved in other ball games where a stick or the like was employed. In France the game was called *chole*, while an early English version was cambuca, played with a wooden ball. But many claimants to have 'invented' golf can be dismissed because they do not conform to a main characteristic of the sport which is to play with a club standing sideways to the ball. Most evidence points to the origins of golf being in Scotland and you will not convince anyone from north of the Border otherwise. But the Dutch make the biggest arguments against this, pointing to their own pastimes of the Middle Ages, *kolf* or *kolven*, names closely akin to golf.

The claims of the Dutch

The old Dutch game of *kolf* and golf differ by only one letter, but from there the similarities disperse. For while golf is played on rolling acres across many different terrains, *kolf* is, as far as the modern game is concerned, played indoors on a court not too dissimilar to a cricket pitch in dimensions. However, both games have evolved from lowlands by the sea while *kolf* was once played in the same manner as golf, outdoors and with ball and clubs. The Dutch also argue that early records show that *kolf* was being played earlier than Scottish records of golf. It is an argument which is certain to go on unless undisputed evidence is found to back the respective claims.

Much of the history of ball games in Holland has been researched by Dutch golf historian van Hengel. He traced the beginnings of golf in Holland back to 1296 at the village of Loenen-on-the-Vecht which had four holes for the playing of golf. He cites numerous records of the game being played during the 14th century. The Dutch also point to Albert, Duke of Bavaria, who conferred in 1398 on the citizens of Brielle, an ancient town near Rotterdam, the right 'to play *kolf* outside the ramparts of the town'. Similar rights had already been granted to the inhabitants of Haarlem in 1390 when the game of *kolf* was played in churchyards, on

the highway or on ice during the winter months. There are Flemish paintings which show a game being played on frozen rivers or lakes but this could also be taken as a forerunner of hockey or ice hockey.

Van Hengel also finds that this game ceased, apart from the one course at Loenen, around the beginning of the 18th century to be replaced by the indoor version already mentioned. The Dutch also argue that golf didn't originate in Scotland but was taken there by merchants who had played *kolf* in Holland and took it back with them. But again there is no hard evidence that this happened or that it was the forerunner of golf as we know it today. But there were certain similarities. Both games used a pile of sand to 'tee-up' the ball, the Dutch name being *tuitje*, while the Scots had an early club known as the cleek and in Holland they had their *klik* which was sometimes weighted with lead. The early Dutch game was played to a target such as a door while later it was played to different 'goals' which is taken as an early version of holes.

The Dutch are also credited with playing from one post to another and there is some evidence that they erected more than one post. They have also produced a marvellous volume, *The Book of the Hours*, now in the British Museum, which shows figures playing a game with implements faintly resembling

Right: 'Skaters' by Wilhelm Kool (1608–66), at the Alan Jacobs Gallery, London, includes figures who might be playing golf. It is well recorded that as early as the 14th century the Dutch played kolf *on ice.*

golf clubs. This book is the ace in the Dutch pack, but unfortunately it was produced around 1530, almost 100 years after the Scottish Government (Scotland being a separate country in those days) passed its famous Act of Parliament banning 'golfe' or 'the gouf' because it had grown in popularity to such an extent that it was interfering with archery practice. This action was taken by King James II of Scotland, who was concerned for national defence as his country was frequently at war with the English. However, this edict was not taken seriously by the populace and 'golfe' continued to be played, even though two more Acts were issued. Some 40 years after the original Act was issued it was revoked, and from then on the sport grew in popularity although still in a somewhat rudimentary style.

The influence of royalty

It could be said that the game had its turning point in the Middle Ages when royalty took an interest. Indeed, royalty also took an active part and in 1502 King James IV of Scotland secured a set of clubs and balls from a bowmaker in Perth. A year earlier the King had signed a peace treaty with England which allowed him more time to partake of golf, but in 1513 came the Battle of Flodden, James was slain and the two countries were at war again.

Golf soldiered on and it is known that James V was a frequent visitor to Gosford in East Lothian where he set up a private links. It must have been here that his daughter, Mary, Queen of Scots, learned the game at an early age, and when she was at school in France she continued to play. Later, in 1567, she was rebuked for playing on Seton Fields soon after the death of her husband, Lord Darnley. The game seems to have spread south of the Border when James VI of Scotland became James I of England in 1603 and moved to Blackheath, then a little way outside London. In 1608, a course, consisting of just seven holes, was laid out there mainly for the Scottish courtiers who wished to continue with their native pastime.

Before leaving the subject of foreign influences over the invention of golf, the Italians also claim an early form of the game called Pall Mall, *jeu de mail* or *pele mele*. It closely resembled golf and was later taken up by the French. When it turned up in Scotland it must have been Mary, Queen of Scots, who imported it from her schooldays. It arrived in England at the start of the 17th century and in 1717 a Monsieur Lauthier wrote a treatise on how the game was played and its rules. It was played with a mallet-shaped wooden club, not unlike today's polo mallet, and the object was to loft the ball through iron hoops. However, again it seems that it was

Above: 'The Start: Striking Off' is the title of this print from the Illustrated Times *showing golf in Scotland in 1865. There appears to be a lot of activity going on on the course.*

played in the confines of a court with specific boundaries. When the original course in Pall Mall, in London, was established is not known. The game was certainly played by King Charles I around 1629 and by Charles II around 1660, but it lost its appeal in the early 18th century although it retained a grip in southern France where it was played mainly along roads to a definite target.

References to golf during these times are sketchy but there is evidence of 'commoun golf ballis' being ordered in 1585 while in 1603, on James' accession to the English throne, a certain William Mayne was appointed the royal clubmaker. Then in 1618 James Melvill, a student at St Andrews University, was appointed golf-ball maker on a 21-year lease. That same year, by royal proclamation, the ban on Sunday golf imposed in Edinburgh in 1592 was lifted, providing players attended service first. Originally it was the Archbishop of St Andrews who had given permission to the local population to play golf over the local links, but following the 1592 ban the Sunday closure of the St Andrews courses remains to this day,

unless there is special dispensation such as when the Open Championship or any other major event is played over the Old Course with a Sunday finish.

Nevertheless, the game flourished in some form or another without too much documented evidence until 1687 when a diary written by one Thomas Kincaid describes quite colourfully how to swing a 'golve' club, the stance adopted and the materials used for making clubs and balls. It is arguably the earliest manual in existence but it doesn't say anything about the game itself, the course it was played on, or how far the players struck their shots. Neither did it make mention of any foreign influence. Clearly the Dutch played a significant part in golf-like games, as is proven by the numerous pieces of evidence apparent in many early paintings still in existence. But while the Scots were taking decisive steps to put the game on a more permanent and organized basis with the establishment of golf societies, which were the forerunners of golf clubs as we know them today, the Dutch were turning to *het kolven* which was a form of simplified mini-golf.

The Scots take over

Whatever claims are made over the introduction of golf, Scotland saw it blossom. By 1650 it was being played from Musselburgh and Bruntsfield in the south to Dornoch in the north, almost exclusively along the eastern seaboard where the land was most suited. The Scottish game was played on 'links', a name which has become synonymous with seaside courses, for it was often the thin strip of low land between the agricultural areas and the sea which was used: in other words, the link between the two. In those days it was a game for all classes and often wagers were laid on matches. But there were no official rules nor a limit to the number of holes, which varied depending on the amount of land available for the game.

Great strides were made in the 18th century. In 1735, by which time many influential people were being attracted to the game, a society was formed at Bruntsfield, near Edinburgh, for the purpose of meeting together, arranging matches and dining. Meanwhile at nearby Leith, a port through which much of the trade with Europe, and par-

ticularly Holland, would have passed, the enthusiasts who played on the links there decided to form a society which was to be called the Company of Gentlemen Golfers. That was in 1744 and they managed to persuade the Town Council of Edinburgh to put up a silver cup to be played for each year over the links. Apparently they got the idea from the archers, who had donated a Silver Arrow in 1709 for which they shot annually over the same links. The Cup came complete with a set of rules for the competition and it was played for the first time in 1745, the year of Scotland's tragic rebellion. The winner of the competition had the honour and privilege of appending a gold or silver piece to the prize and of being captain the following year.

The Company of Gentlemen Golfers played over Leith Links for almost half a century, despite the fact that the course consisted of only nine holes. In 1800 a charter was granted to the Company and it took on a new name, the Honourable Company of Edinburgh Golfers, but in 1831, when some alterations were made on the links, the course ceased to be attractive to the members so it

Above: 'Holeing the Ball at the Finish' is the companion print to that opposite. The semi-rough appears to extend right to the hole, and the man putting appears to be stymied.

was deemed advisable to dispose of the club-house and furniture. Many pictures, painted expressly for the club, were not reserved but sold to parties unconnected with the club. The Company was therefore wound up, but five years later in 1836 it was revived at Musselburgh, thanks to some of the original members. Gradually it outgrew its accommodation there and in 1865 it moved to its present home at Muirfield.

The original Bruntsfield society formed in 1735 also gained its charter in 1800 and became the Edinburgh Burgess Golfing Society.

In 1754 an event occurred which was to prove significant for the game worldwide. The Gentlemen of Fife invited the Gentlemen Golfers of Leith to join them in forming the St Andrews Society. This was almost 200 years after golf was first played on the links at St Andrews and not a day too soon as the Society was later to become the Royal and Ancient Golf Club of St Andrews. The 22 noblemen and gentlemen involved in the Society's formation drew up certain rules under which they wished to play. From then on the R & A developed as the governing body for the rules of golf. Among those early rules were the stipulations that the ball was to be teed-up within a club's length of the hole, the player whose ball lay further from the hole played first and the ball was not to be changed once it had been played off the tee. There were also rules about hazards and penalty strokes while any dispute not contained within the rules was to be settled by the captain.

The Royal & Ancient Golf Club

Certain changes took place from time to time. In 1834 King William IV became the Society's patron and conferred the title of Royal & Ancient Golf Club of St Andrews. As time passed St Andrews became accepted as the home of golf, a title which is recognized today throughout the world. By the end of the 18th century there were some seven societies or clubs in existence including Musselburgh (1774), Glasgow (1787) and Blackheath, the first in England. As previously stated, the Scots introduced golf to Blackheath as early as 1608 but although play continued there for many years it wasn't until 1766 that competitive golf was introduced, with a Mr Henry Foot presenting a silver driver to The Honourable Company of Golfers at Blackheath. This makes it the oldest club in England. But Blackheath appears to have been a different world to Scotland in that it was only the upper classes of the day who were privileged to play, and they wore a distinctive uniform of long red coats and white breeches.

The Scots also seem to have been active around the Manchester area because there is documented evidence of golf having been played there in 1815. The soldiers of the Royal Scots are believed to have played on Kersal Moor and when they departed the local businessmen of the area carried on and formed the Manchester Golf Club in 1818. Originally there were 12 playing members but many more on the social side, and it seems they were not averse to the odd flutter even at those times. It is documented that one wealthy businessman, and he needed to be of some substance, wagered £50 on a match in July 1821. Members were keen, and on one occasion eight years later they played in four inches of snow. As time passed the Manchester golfers began to play against other clubs, and in 1869 there were home and away events with the Royal Liverpool club which had just become established at Hoylake.

The Manchester club flourished until the 1880s when the demanding needs of the industrial revolution and the expansion of housing developments gobbled up more and more land. The club were caught up in this and when encroachment occurred on the course in 1882 the club suspended its activities. That same year another club was formed in a different area of the city and adopted the name Manchester Golf Club, while after a nine-year gap the original club re-formed in the Chorlton area and took the title of the Old Manchester Golf Club. Again progress was made and play continued until the later stages of the 1950s, when development again threatened its existence. New housing gnawed at its boundaries until, in 1959, the local council took over the course, from which date the club has been in a state of suspended animation. Many of the members joined other clubs while retaining their membership of Old Manchester, which now stands at 30 playing members. These still meet twice a year, to play in the Spring and Autumn Medals when the prizes are the original club trophies, including the Gold Medal presented to the first club by Alexander Bannerman in 1837. At present it doesn't seem that the Old Manchester club will achieve its own home, which is all the more concerning because the course they left almost 30 years ago is still there in parts, yet overgrown and neglected.

The influence of the Blackheath club was instrumental in spreading the golfing gospel in England as well as overseas. In 1864 the Westward Ho! Club was formed, the first links course in England, thanks to active support from Blackheath. The club, Royal North Devon as it is now known, still plays on the original links at Northam Burrows which covered 1,000 acres and 'commanded exquisite views of the Atlantic, Bristol Channel, Exmoor, Lundy Island, Hartland Point and the estuary of the twin rivers Torridge and Taw' as early books said. In 1864 Westward Ho! boasted 277 members who paid an entrance fee of three guineas (£3.15) and an annual subscription of ten shillings and sixpence (52½p).

A year after Westward Ho! was formed,

Left: The Royal & Ancient
Golf Club at St Andrews has
collected a number of trophies
and souvenirs over the years.
This is a section of the trophy
cabinet.

THE FIRST GOLF CHAMPIONSHIP MEDAL.

HIS medal is the first Championship Golf Medal of all time.

The Championship Belt, a very handsome trophy, which it replaced, was won outright by Young Tommy Morris, in his successive wins of 1868-69-70. His record was 77 strokes, made on the St. Andrew's Course in 1869.

It was fitting that a Morris should win it, as Old Tom had come within an ace of securing it in 1863, having won successively in 1861 and 1862.

He again won in 1864 and 1867 when Young Tommy's star appeared, which only set with his lamented death on Christmas Day, 1876.

After Old Tom's death the grandchildren presented the Belt to the Royal & Ancient Golf Club, where it occupies the place of honor in their famous collection of Golfing Relics.

This first Championship Medal represents an epoch in the game.

The change from a Belt to a money prize and medal possibly lies in the fact that the belt cost "a heap o' Siller" and, as there was no championship in 1871, the four societies subscribing for it were somewhat nonplused at its being won outright.

In 1872, therefore, a money prize and this medal were offered - and won by Young Tom.

(of a very interesting life of Tom Morris will be found in the Club Library.)

Above: The first Open Championship winners medal. It replaced the belt which Young Tom Morris won outright after his three victories from 1868 to 1870. After a break in 1871, Young Tom was the first to win the medal. The photographs are of Old Tom and Young Tom, and the statuette is of Old Tom Morris.

Opposite: Some of the early rules displayed in the Royal & Ancient Museum. The top booklet is dated 1873.

the London Scottish came into existence at Wimbledon while Royal Liverpool, Hoylake, was formed in 1869. By this time the Open Championship had been under way for nine years, while the spread of golf in Scotland had become a steady stream with clubs springing up all over the country. At that time few clubs owned their own courses while the number of holes constituting a golf course hadn't been standardized. This came about in 1858, when the Royal & Ancient issued new rules for its members. In Rule One it is stated that 'one round of the Links or 18 holes is reckoned a match unless otherwise stipulated'. This didn't appeal to everybody because at that time courses had anything from five to 12 holes, but by the 1870s more courses had 18 holes and a round was recognized as consisting of 18 holes, even if it meant playing nine holes twice or six holes three times.

The 18 holes at St Andrews

All that still doesn't explain why the number 18 was arrived at. After all, at one time seven holes was the norm, although Prestwick, formed in 1851, stuck to its 12. To find the answer we must take a closer look at the history of St Andrews and particularly the Old Course. Also it is worth considering the contruction, if it can be so described, of some of the old links courses. They certainly weren't constructed in a manner we would recognize today. They were created by nature — shaped by natural forces — on waste or reclaimed land close to the sea. Down the years the sea around Britain, particularly on

the eastern side and near river estuaries, receded, leaving behind mudflats, sandbanks and channels of salt water that gradually dried out. Furrows and ridges were also created and in time these became eroded by the wind and weather, leaving humps and hollows that are the characteristics of the links courses of today. These areas gradually became covered with grasses and other plants as the wind, birds and animals transported seeds, and this in turn attracted the rabbits. Where you have rabbits you also have foxes who pursued their prey along regular tracks and trails which over a period of time became worn into hollows. These hollows gradually got deeper and as the grass became scuffed or non-existent, the sand took over and thereby created today's bunkers.

The first record of golf at St Andrews occurs on 25 January 1552 and is contained on a licence granted by John Hamilton, 'archebischop of Sanctandros', to the inhabitants of the city permitting them to 'plant and plenish cuniggis (rabbits) whithin the north part of their common Links next adjacent to the water of Eden', and covenants within the City to accept the community's right 'inter alia to play at golf, futball, schuting at all gamis with all uther maner of pastime . . .' Because this grant was confirmation of right previously established it is clear that golf was played before that date and a primitive layout existed before the University was founded in 1413.

Returning to the subject of the number of holes, despite the varying numbers at other clubs, St Andrews settled for 12, which later became 22. However, the narrowness of the land ruled out separate holes for going out and returning, so in fact there were only 11 holes which were played twice using the same fairways and greens. At least one of the holes, if not more, was actually in the town, behind where the R & A clubhouse now stands, and the start was near the Martyrs' Monument. However, in 1764 the Royal & Ancient resolved that the first four holes should be converted into two, thereby reducing the course to 18 holes (nine played twice) which was to prove the norm throughout golf.

Later, six of the nine greens were extended laterally to allow two holes to be cut in them, which brought into being the enormous double greens for which the Old Course is famous. Several other changes took place mainly concerning the playing order of the holes, but by 1842 the general layout of the links was as it is today. However, up to the First World War there were right-hand and left-hand courses, used alternately week and week about. This led to a curious incident in the 1886 Amateur Championship, which was won by Horace Hutchinson. The tournament was played on the left-hand course, although according to the rota it shouldn't have been used. Play had started before officials realized what had happened so the tournament was completed over the left-hand course for the first and last time.

The story behind the number of holes wasn't the only mystique surrounding golf. Another was the size of the hole dug in the green, and why it became 4¼ inches in diameter. Apparently at some stage of its formative years the Westward Ho! club sent to Scotland for a hole-cutting tool. Before that, holes were cut using an ancient dinner knife or clasp-knife and the turf was cut around the circle of a gallipot or flower pot placed on the ground. When the cutting tool arrived it made a hole 4¼ inches in diameter but no reference has been found as to why the tool should have been that size.In 1894 St Andrews finally decreed that 4¼ inches would be the uniform size of the hole, which should be not less than four inches deep.

Of course, the early golfing pioneers didn't use holes. They used posts as targets but they soon found that because of the roughness of the grass they were unable to get the ball near the post. So the grass was cut close and this was the forerunner of today's greens. Then another area was cut nearby from where the ball was struck to the next target. Thus the teeing area was born. It is all very logical, but those early courses, like those of today, needed maintenance and eventually someone was detailed to care for them. This resulted in the appointment of keepers of the green who combined their work with clubmaking, playing with members and teaching and were, in fact, the first professionals.

With the progress of time, golf was reaching other parts of the country and spreading its appeal. From those early beginnings of seven clubs or societies in the 18th century, another ten came along in the first half of the 19th century, and the total rose to 36 in 1866 and to 59 in 1880. The overall membership was then around 5,000. But the real golf explosion took place between then and 1900 when the number of clubs reached 1,300. Just how many golfers there were is not known because many were not members of clubs, while others belonged to more than one. Certainly numbers had increased quite sharply, a fact confirmed by the ever-growing order books of the club and ballmakers.

Formation of the Laws

The development of golf in Scotland went on at a brisk pace but any reference to it must include the history of the game at St Andrews. When the formation of the Society of St Andrews Golfers was completed in 1754 little did the organizers realize what a revolutionary move they had made or what would come of their deliberations. However, the founder members soon adopted, with minor alterations, 'The Articles and Laws in playing the Golf' which had been formulated 11 years earlier by the Company of Edinburgh Golfers for play on the Leith Links. These 13 rules are worth noting as in several

cases they are virtually unchanged to this day. They read like this:

1. You must tee your ball within a club-length of the hole. (This refers to the hole just played or in the case of the first a starting point.)

2. Your tee must be upon the ground.

3. You are not to change the ball which you strike off the tee.

4. You are not to remove stones, bones or any Break Club for the sake of playing your ball except upon the fair green and that only within a club length of your ball.

5. If your ball come among water, or any watery filth, you are at liberty to take your ball, and throwing it behind the hazard six yards at least. You may play it with any club and allow your adversary a stroke for so getting out your ball.

6. If your balls be found anywhere touching one another you are to lift the first ball till you play the last.

7. At holeing, you are to play your ball honestly for the hole and not to play upon your adversary's ball, not lying in your way to the hole.

8. If you should lose your ball by its being taken up or any other way you are to go back to the spot where you struck last and drop another ball and allow your adversary a stroke for the misfortune.

9. No man at holeing his ball is to be allowed to mark his way to the hole with his clubs or anything else.

10. If a ball be stopped by any person, horse, dog or anything else, the ball so stopped must be played where it lies.

11. If you draw your club in order to strike and proceed so far in the stroke as to be bringing down your club; if then your club shall break in any way, it is to be accounted a stroke.

12. He whose ball lies furthest from the hole is obliged to play first.

13. Neither trench, ditch or dyke made for the preservation of the Links not the scholar's holes or the soldier's lines shall be accounted a hazard. But the ball is to be taken out, teed and played with any iron club. (Scholar's holes referred to a piece of ground where children played and in doing so made holes. Soldier's lines are not so clear,

to it suitably engraved with his name. The first winner was Bailie William Landale, a merchant in St Andrews, who became the first captain of the Club. However, the Club had no permanent meeting place and members gathered at various inns in the town.

However, in 1835 the Union Club was inaugurated for the benefit of both the St Andrews Archers Club and the Golf Club in premises called the Union Parlour. This was on a site later occupied by the Grand Hotel and now Hamilton Hall, part of the St Andrews University. This arrangement proved satisfactory until 1853 when it was agreed new premises should be built. By now the Club had had the title of Royal & Ancient conferred upon it by King William IV and in 1854 the R & A Clubhouse was officially opened, dominating the Town end of the Links as it does today. Four years later the R & A issued new Rules for its members which included the ruling over the number of holes constituting a round of golf.

The Club's original Silver Club trophy was played for every year until 1819 when it was replaced by a replica because after 65 years there was no more room to add further silver balls. It was decided that the original trophy would not be played for again but would go hand in hand with the Captaincy.

In 1806 a Gold Medal was played for as part of the Autumn Meeting, William Cook being the first winner with a score of 100. Many other trophies for competition were bestowed on the Club over the years, including a Silver Putter which was the result of a survival bet struck between Sir David Moncrieffe and John Whyte-Melville of Strathkinness in 1820. The terms of the wager were that on the death of one of them, the other should donate a Silver Putter, bearing the arms of the two parties, to the Club. This was duly done by Whyte-Melville in 1833, and subsequently the Gold Medals won at successive meetings were attached, as with the Silver Club.

In 1837, three years after William IV became the patron, he donated a Gold Medal, and a year later Queen Adelaide donated another in her name to be worn by the Captain on all public functions while he was in office. The person instrumental in these moves was Major J. Murray Belshes of Buttergask, who had earlier given the Club the Silver Cross of St Andrew which became the main Scratch medal at the Spring Meeting.

More trophies were presented as the 19th century progressed, including the George Glennie Gold Medal from the Royal Blackheath Club, to mark this player's long and active membership with both clubs, and a Silver Cashmire Cup from the Calcutta Club. Most were used for competition. In 1922 when the Prince of Wales became Captain of the Royal & Ancient he presented another replica of the Silver Cup to mark a new series of hanging balls.

Left: St Andrews in 1798. The burn is clearly a hazard on this green, which still looks fairly rough. The gentlemen players' headgear is elaborate, while the caddies all wear tam-o-shanters.

but could refer to entrenchments, etc, made in training.)

An amendment was added at a later date: 'The fifth and 13th Articles of the foregoing Laws having occasioned frequent Disputes, it is found convenient that in all time coming the Law shall be that in no case whatever a ball shall be lifted without losing a stroke except it is in the scholar's holes when it may be taken and teed and played with any iron club without losing a stroke and in all other cases the ball must be played where it lyes except it is at least half covered with water or filth when it may if the player chuses be taken out teed and played with any club upon losing a stroke.'

With a little modernizing of the language, it is easy to see how those early golfers played the game in simple terms while we are still beholden to these conditions today, although the number of Rules now total 41. But back at St Andrews. Having put their Society on a firm footing, the members subscribed to a silver club for competition, entry being open to players from all parts of Great Britain and Ireland with the winner attaching a silver ball

Above: Some of the great players of the early Open days, including two early winners. From the left: James Wilson, a clubmaker, Bob Andrew, known as 'The Rook', Willie Dunn, Willie Park, the first Open champion in 1860, Allan Robertson, the greatest player of his era, D. Anderson, known as 'Daw', Tom Morris, the second Open champion, and Bob Kirk.

Right: Allan Robertson, the great player and ballmaker, who refused at first to countenance the gutta-percha ball as he made a good living from manufacturing the feathery.

The first R & A professional

Another landmark at St Andrews was the appointment in 1864 of Tom Morris as the R & A's first professional. Tom and his equally famous son, Young Tom, were synonymous with St Andrews, and their successes on the fairways brought much credit on the old town. Tom was born on 16 June 1821, the son of a letter-carrier, and grew up in a golfing atmosphere. He began playing with a roughly carved club at the age of six and was schooled at Madras College. Golf was always going to be his trade and at the age of 18 he was apprenticed to Allan Robertson in the trade of ballmaking. This association worked well until the advent of the gutty ball when Robertson forbade any of his workforce to play with it in preference to the feathery which was their stock-in-trade. However, Tom used the new arrival which led to a bitter row and his setting up on his own.

In 1851 Tom was offered the job of looking after the Links at Prestwick which he accepted and stayed for 14 years. During that time the Prestwick Club inaugurated the Open Championship in 1860 with a Championship Belt as the prize. The first winner was Willie Park but Tom won the next two and was victorious twice more in 1864 and 1867. In fact, he played in every Open up to and including 1896 but by then he was back at St Andrews. In 1865 he took over as professional at the Royal & Ancient, taking charge of the golf course on a salary of £50 a year. His duties were spelt out and he could employ a man to do the heavy work on two days a week. He was handed the tools of the

trade — a barrow, a spade and a shovel.

Tom was to remain for the next 44 years, gaining a reputation throughout the golfing world. He resigned as greenkeeper in June 1903 but was made Honorary Greenkeeper with the assurance that his salary of £50 per annum would remain for the rest of his life. Over £1,000 was taken in a collection to buy an annuity of £80 a year. His portrait still hangs in the clubhouse.

Unfortunately Tom lived only five more years. One fateful day in May 1908 he went to the New Club, where he was a member, and after a period in the clubroom, got up intending to go to the toilet. However, it is believed he mistook the door, opened the one immediately next to it, and fell into the cellar eight feet below. He was still alive when found but died soon after being taken to hospital. He was a month short of his 87th birthday. To say that St Andrews was stunned would be an understatement and one local inhabitant was heard to say: 'They may toll the bell and shut up their shops in St Andrews for their greatest is gone.' Tom died on Sunday 24 May; his funeral was the following Wednesday and as a mark of respect there was no play on the Links. All St Andrews turned out to pay their last respects to their departed hero, shops were shut and everything came to a halt. After the service Tom was laid to rest beside his son Young Tom, who had passed away 33 years earlier at the age of 24.

Young Tom's death hit his father hard. And it was a tragic story which occurred just when it seemed Tom Junior was set for a long and successful life. He was a fine golfer, winning his first major tournament at the age of 16 when he beat Willie Park and Bob Andrews, two top men of their day, in a play-off at Carnoustie. That same year, 1867, Young Tom played his first Open Championship, finishing fourth behind his father. A year later Young Tom won the Belt by 11 strokes from Tom Senior and it was the same the following year. In 1870 Young Tom made the Belt his own with his third victory, this time by 12 strokes over three rounds of the same 12-hole Prestwick course. Over those three wins, Young Tom averaged 74½ shots per round, a record unequalled in the Championship while the gutty ball was used, even by later giants such as Harry Vardon, J.H. Taylor and James Braid.

The Championship wasn't played in 1871 but Young Tom won again in 1872 and seemed set to continue his domination. But late in 1875 he was playing alongside his father in a challenge match at North Berwick against the brothers Willie and Mungo Park when a telegram was delivered saying that Young Tom's wife was dangerously ill. However, Provost Brodie decided not to hand it over until the match was ended when a yacht was put at the Morris' disposal, thereby saving them a longer journey by train through Edinburgh. When they docked the other side another telegram was delivered which stated that Young Tom's wife had died in childbirth. He never recovered from the shock and three months later, on Christmas Day, he passed away in his sleep.

Another milestone in St Andrews' history was the formation of the first Ladies' Club in 1867, some 110 years before the Ladies' Golf Union moved its headquarters to the town. In 1897 the Royal & Ancient was given sole con-

trol of the Rules of Golf Committee, a major step in the control of the game. In 1919 it assumed the management of British Championships and ten years later legalized steel shafts in Great Britain. It may seem strange, but gate money was not charged until 1933. In 1946, soon after the end of the Second World War, St Andrews ended the facility of free golf. There have been two American Captains of the R & A, Francis Ouimet in 1951 and Joe Dey in 1975 but a third, Bill Campbell, is due to take over in 1988.

With the passing of the Morrises, the next to lord it over the Open Championship was another St Andrews man, Jamie Anderson. He won three consecutive Opens from 1877, the last being at St Andrews. The son of a famous caddie, he was noted for his accuracy rather than his power and length and became a putter of rare skill. He was succeeded by another hat-trick man, Bob Ferguson, born in Musselburgh, who won the Open in 1880, 1881 and 1882. He almost made it four but tied with Willie Fernie the following year and lost the play-off. Ill-health forced him out of the game but he is remembered in a fountain erected beside the Musselburgh Links.

Below: Young Tom Morris' grave at St Andrews. The inscription says that he held the Champion's Belt 'without rivalry yet without envy' and that his 'amiable qualities' were 'no less acknowledged than his golfing achievements'. The monument was erected with contributions from 60 golfing societies.

Above: A golfer and his caddie at Royal Blackheath in the early 19th century. Blackheath is the oldest club outside Scotland, and its members wore the distinctive red coats.

The biggest event on the amateur calendar in Britain is the Amateur Championship, which has just celebrated its centenary. It was back in 1885 that it was played for the first time, at Hoylake, the winner being A.F. MacFie. But the runner-up was Horace Hutchinson, who was to exercise considerable influence over the development of golf in England in the latter part of the 19th century. Born in London in 1859, Hutchinson learned his golf at Westward Ho! While his swing was not classic, it was nevertheless effective. He won the Amateur in 1886 at St Andrews and again the following year back at Hoylake, beating the redoubtable John Ball, but despite one more final appearance and three semi-final places he could not find a third success. However, he spent over 20 years active in golf and in 1908 became the first Englishman to captain the R & A. Hutchinson, a flamboyant character, was also a prolific writer on many subjects, not the least golf.

The game goes overseas

The spread of golf beyond Scotland's shores is a story in itself. While Blackheath enjoys the honour of being the oldest club outside Scotland, Pau in southern France was the first continental society, founded in 1856. According to legend Scottish soldiers under the command of the Duke of Wellington, who halted there on the march home from the Peninsula War, loved the area and some returned to live and build the golf course. Invariably it was immigrants from Scotland who were responsible for introducing golf to many parts of the world at different times, their departure from their homeland being precipitated by the quest for work and better opportunities in the late 19th century.

The first club in Australia was at Adelaide in 1871 while the Scots in Canada formed clubs in Montreal in 1873, Quebec a year later, in Toronto and Ottawa in 1876 and at Niagara in 1882. Canada even stole a march on the United States, for with just 25 members, the Royal Montreal club engaged the first professional golfer in North America when W.F. Davis arrived from Hoylake in April 1881. His duties were to keep the course in good order, for which he was paid five dollars (or just over one pound in the currency he was used to) per week while he could earn extra selling or repairing balls and clubs, as well as teaching. His additional earnings were to be made in the mornings and from 1.30pm each day his time was strictly for the benefit of the club. This arrangement doesn't seem to have gone down too well, for when the greenkeeping side became neglected the club complained about the state of the course. Shortly after this Mr Davis departed, but in 1889 he was back selling equipment and giving lessons. This stay too seems to have been only temporary, as in 1893 he helped lay out nine holes at Newport near Boston in the USA, and was engaged as clubmaker and instructor.

By this time golf had gained a foothold in other parts. In fact as far as the Indian continent was concerned it was very much part and parcel of everyday life for the British. The Calcutta Club claims to be the mother club in India, having been established in 1829, and further proof of the Scottish influence can be traced to a large collection of brass buttons in the club's possession which bear the Scottish thistle. Bombay got its first club in 1842 while other centres such as Bangalore, Madras, Mysore and Nagpur got theirs at the end of the century.

Cape Town in 1885 was the first base for golf in South Africa, where the first professional was a W.D. Day from Musselburgh, while within six years clubs were also in existence in Johannesburg, Kimberley and Port Elizabeth. There was a strong army and navy influence in the first officials of the Hong Kong club in 1889 while other parts of the Empire arrived on the golfing map with Aden (1890), Cyprus (1894), Malta (1888), New Zealand (1892), Mauritius (1893) and Gibraltar (1891). Golf's foothold in Hong Kong inevitably sparked interest in the Far East, which is a vast stronghold today, with the game spreading to Thailand and Japan.

COPYRIGHT, 1900 BY FRANK FOWLER

Left: John Reid, a Scot who went to America and, having sent for some golf equipment from Old Tom Morris' shop, founded the St Andrews Golf Club, New York. This portrait of 1900 is by Frank Fowler.

The beginnings in America

These days, the power base of golf from the standpoint of numbers, is the United States of America. Its vast area houses thousands of the most marvellous courses, on which millions play each year. But the beginnings of golf in America were small indeed. Again the influence was Scottish, with many emigrants sailing there to build lives in the New World. Scots were shrewd enough to believe America a land of opportunity and many who settled were golfers. Once they had established themselves in their various communities they turned their attention to the game and how they knew it back home. There is little doubt that America owes much to those immigrant Scots for although organized golf, albeit on a small scale, didn't start until late in the 19th century, there are reports that golf was played in isolated parts of the United States in the middle of the 18th century.

Records from the Port of Leith show that a large shipment of golf equipment — 96 clubs and 432 balls — was sent to Charleston, South Carolina, in 1743. This was about the same time societies were being formed in Scotland. That early delivery led to the formation of the South Carolina Golf Club in 1786 and this was followed by the Savannah Club in 1795. But whether the latter was anything more than a social meeting place is uncertain as records do not show if the game was actually played.

What we do know is that despite these early claims the first real organized golf in America was in the north-east, and that Yonkers in New York was the first significant club established. Again the move came from an immigrant Scot, John G. Reid, a Fifer born in Dunfermline, who soon became immersed in golf activities in New York. Reid had arrived in America some years earlier

and had made a reasonable amount of money. He was an active man and soon turned his attention to golf, suggesting to a close friend, Robert Lockhart, who happened to be travelling to Britain in 1887, that he buy a supply of clubs and balls during his visit. Lockhart agreed and journeyed to St Andrews to Old Tom Morris' shop where he made his purchase.

The consignment is believed to have consisted of a driver, brassie, spoon, cleek, sand iron and putter as well as two dozen gutta-percha balls. In due course these were delivered to Reid who, in February 1888, invited some friends to his home in Yonkers, Westchester County, New York, where three holes, albeit of a somewhat rustic nature, were laid out in a cow pasture. In fact, Reid is believed to have played against John B. Upham, who was to become the first secretary of the United States Golf Association, America's equivalent of the Royal & Ancient. The result of the match has been lost in the mists of time but such was the success of this first pioneering venture that soon a move was made to more spacious grounds where six holes were built on land belonging to a German butcher. However, whether a club was formed at the time of the three or six-hole course is not clear.

Nevertheless Reid and his friends, who by now had ordered more clubs and balls, enjoyed themselves throughout that summer, and in the following November, after a somewhat agreeable dinner at Reid's home, moves were made to form the St Andrews Golf Club in Yonkers. There were only a handful of members while the club still hadn't found a true home. When it was proposed to drive a road through the course, the club moved again. This time it was just a quarter of a mile away to a 34-acre apple orchard, after which the club's members became known as 'The Apple Tree Gang'. By then a few more clubs were springing up and another in the New York area was the Tuxedo in Tuxedo Park. Still the St Andrews club hadn't thrown down strong roots and as the membership rose, so did the problems as they outgrew their accommodation. So in May 1894 they were on their way again, three miles up the road to Grey Oaks where a farmhouse became the clubhouse. With more room, the club grew significantly, which was again somewhat counter-productive because they were soon looking for yet further space. The fourth and last move came in 1897 when the club moved to Mount Hope, where it has remained with its own 18-hole course.

Enthusiasm in America knew no bounds around the early part of the 1890s, and by 1894 there were 42 clubs, among them the famous Shinnecock Hills, which first saw the light of day in 1891. Shinnecock, at the eastern end of Long Island, has always been regarded as the first 'true' course in America because it was originally laid out by a course architect, unlike the method of holes being roughed-out on course land. The architect was a Scot, Willie Dunn, who constructed a 12-hole layout which was opened in June 1891 with 44 members buying $100 shares.

The members were also treated to a handsome architect-designed clubhouse, while a nine-hole course was soon added exclusively for the ladies. Around the same time another course was contructed at Newport, Rhode Island, at a place called Brenton's Point but this was only nine holes. It was the brainchild of 'Sugar King' Theodore Havemeyer, who was to become a legendary figure in United States golf.

Charles Blair Macdonald

The introduction of the game in Boston was thanks to a lady, Miss Florence Boit. She came from Pau in France, where she played golf, to stay with her uncle, Arthur Hunnewell, a member of the Country Club at Brookline, Massachusetts. She brought with her a set of clubs and balls and was soon introducing her relatives to the new pastime. As a result it was recommended that the club should include golf among its facilities and a seven-hole course was constructed. By now the ripples from the golfing waves on the Eastern seaboard were reaching out and they lapped at Chicago in 1893 when the first 18-hole circuit in the United States was laid out. The pioneer was Charles Blair Macdonald, a forceful and remarkable man, who was born in Scotland and who spent his schooldays in St Andrews. With that sort of grounding, he was a staunch disciple of the Royal & Ancient and all it stood for, so he was determined that those principles and rules would be adhered to in his adopted country.

Macdonald's Chicago Golf Club chose many good points and features of the Scottish game, its traditions as well as the layout of some of the great courses. But he was also a man who courted controversy. If there was a dispute then Macdonald was almost always at its centre. Therefore he attracted many enemies while gaining many staunch friends. With so much controversy abroad, there was a need for some sort of governing body, and when two clubs proclaimed different amateur champions in the same year, a move was somewhat overdue.

Macdonald was the central character in both championships. In 1894 the St Andrews Golf Club, having completed its links at Grey Oaks in Yonkers, decided to stage a tournament for the Amateur Championship of the United States, the dates selected being 11–13 October. Invitations were sent to the various golf clubs throughout the country, the tournament to be played according to the rules of the Royal & Ancient and the prizes being diamond and gold, silver and bronze medals. But they were suddenly upstaged by the Newport Golf Club, who decided to hold a Championship on 3–4 September with a silver cup at stake. The competition was to be over 36 holes of medal play.

Neither club would give way so there were two so-called championships in the same year. The Newport club's match was held at their newly extended Rocky Farm course where somewhat bizarre features were stone walls which straddled some of the fairways. Some felt these were splendid additional hazards while others were not so impressed, among them Macdonald. When his ball rolled under one of these walls he was even less impressed as it cost him a two-shot penalty which, in the end, was to prove decisive. He lost by one shot to W.G. Lawrence from Newport, a victory Macdonald refused to accept, saying that the walls were not legitimate hazards and that Amateur Championships shouldn't be decided by medal play.

When the St Andrews Club held their Championship they invited other clubs to a match-play tournament. But again Macdonald was a loser, being beaten this time by Laurence Stoddard of St Andrews, Yonkers, and formerly of Hoylake, 5 and 4 in the final. This time Macdonald claimed sickness and again refused to recognize Stoddard as the champion.

Clearly this sort of squabbling could not go on and in that same year, 1894, a major development occurred which was to prove decisive. On 22 December the Amateur Golf Association of the United States was created, later to become the American Golf Association and then the United States Golf Association. Five clubs were involved at that inaugural meeting held at the Calumet Club. They were the St Andrews Golf Club of Yonkers; the Shinnecock Hills Golf Club of

Left: The beautiful clubhouse at Shinnecock Hills, which claims to be the first true course in America, as it was laid out by a course architect, Scot Willie Dunn, in 1891, previous courses having been merely holes dug out on unaltered terrain.

Southampton, Long Island; the Country Club of Brookline, Massachusetts; the Newport Golf Club of Newport, Rhode Island; and the Chicago Golf Club. The first President was Theodore Havemeyer, although John Reid must have been disappointed at not receiving the honour for he had done much to kindle the enthusiasm for golf in the United States.

The new body was not slow in making sure its Amateur Championship was organized along the right lines. On 1–3 October 1895 there were 32 entrants, and this time Charles Macdonald was to realize his finest hour. He met Charles Sands of Newport in a somewhat one-sided final over 36 holes. Sands had taken up the game only three months before and was no match for Macdonald, who romped to a 12 and 11 victory and became the first official US Amateur Champion. Macdonald failed to manage another victory, although he was twice a medallist. He had a vested interest in the following two tournaments, which were won by an English journalist, H.J. Whigham, who married his daughter. There was a 'foreign' winner again in 1898 when exiled Scot Findlay Douglas took the title, and it needed the intervention of Herbert Harriman the following year to rescue the trophy for America with a surprise victory over Douglas.

Despite Macdonald's somewhat abrasive ventures in those early championships and the fact that he gained a reputation for being a difficult character, he was nevertheless passionately devoted to the game and the maintenance of tradition. Some of his battles may now seem bizarre and overdone yet he kept the game intact when the Americans might so easily have gone their own way with disastrous consequences. Because of his early links with Britain and his many visits, he retained close associations with St Andrews and Hoylake.

The rapid development of golf in America brought a fairly speedy requirement for courses on which the many new recruits to the game could learn the skills. This gave an opportunity for Scots with knowledge and experience of course design to take the chance of a new life in America. Some of the early courses were laid out by Willie Dunn and other immigrant professionals but Tom Bendelow's progress into course design was by another route. Tom was indeed a Scot, who went to America to work as a printer and was employed in the composing room of the *New York Herald* when Spaldings made him their course consultant. According to the story, his only recommendation was a Scottish accent, but that was enough to convince people that he had the right qualifications for the job. Based in Chicago, he began laying out courses in 1895 and at the time of his death in the 1930s he is credited with creating over 600 courses.

Bendelow's name might not be a household word in Britain when it comes to course design and there were others who were virtual novices in this new occupation. However, they began to take a back seat when more recognized course architects began to arrive from Scotland. One such immigrant was Donald J. Ross, who made the switch in 1899 and who subsequently laid out over 250 courses — many of today's recognized masterpieces — and remodelled others.

Apart from the Amateur Championship, the USGA also launched the US Open Championship as well as the US Women's Amateur in 1895. The winner of the inaugural US Open was a British professional, Horace Rawlins, an assistant at the Newport Club, who beat Willie Dunn, winner himself of an Open Championship a year earlier at St Andrews, Yonkers, before the event came under the USGA umbrella. Dunn was only 19 at the time and remains the youngest ever winner of the title. The first winner of the Women's title was Mrs Charles S. Brown.

Scots emigrate to the States

Towards the end of the 19th century it wasn't only course designers who were crossing the Atlantic for a better and more lucrative life. More and more Scottish professionals realized there was the time for opportunity in a developing country where they could speed the progress of the game to the ever-increasing number of recruits. Some went as individuals, some as whole families, like the Smiths from Carnoustie. Alex emigrated in 1898 and within a short time was joined by Willie, George, Jimmy, their parents and Macdonald. Not only did they flourish in the New World but most of them enjoyed a remarkable run of success on the American fairways. In 1899 and not long in America, Willie won the US Open by 11 shots in Baltimore. Then in 1906 it was Alex who took the title, becoming the first man to break 300 in the Championship, with Willie second as he was again two years later. Alex also won in 1910 in Philadelphia, beating his younger brother Macdonald and John McDermott. Alex had been runner-up at Shinnecock Hills, his first year in the States, and again in 1901 and 1905, both at Myopia. In his 50th year, in 1921, he was still good enough to finish fifth in a tie with the rising star Bobby Jones. But nine years later, in 1930, he died at the age of 58.

Beside his US Open successes, Willie won several other professional tournaments to enhance the Smith reputation, but after being professional at the Midlothian club he switched to Mexico City. Unfortunately he got caught up in the Mexican revolution of 1914–15 and when the clubhouse at his County Club was shelled he was found in the cellar in such a poor condition he died soon after, aged just 40.

Macdonald Smith was probably the best

*Left: Harry Vardon, one of the
Great Triumvirate of golfers
who dominated golf around
the turn of the century, won
Open Championships on both
sides of the Atlantic.*

Finish of a Mashie Shot

Finish of a Drive

Top of Swing with Mashie

Finish of a Brassey Shot.

Top of Swing with Driver

'Bunkered'

An Iron Shot.

Driving

Swing with 'Cleek'

Cleek' Shot

Finish with Driver

Arnaud Massy.

Reinhold Thiele

of the Smith brothers yet he never managed to win a major championship.

The early years of the 20th century saw the US Open in the hands of either immigrant Scots or a visiting Englishman Harry Vardon. Vardon won in 1900 on his first visit to America to promote Spalding's new gutty ball, the 'Vardon Flier'. At the Chicago Club, he beat travelling compatriot J.H. Taylor by nine shots. The following year brought the first of four wins in five years by another ex-Scot, Willie Anderson. Born in North Berwick, he emigrated in 1895, and his record in the US Open has never been bettered. He was runner-up in 1897, third in 1898, fifth the following year, then 11th when Vardon won. He broke through in 1901 with his first success then repeated the feat in 1903, 1904 and 1905. Dour and uncommunicative, Anderson saw his run ended by Alex Smith in 1906 and four years later he was dead from a fatal lung disease. He was then 32.

The Great Triumvirate

By this time Britain had embarked on the era of the 'Great Triumvirate' — Braid, Vardon and Taylor — that was to last until the start of the First World War. It seems to have had its birth in the Open Championship of John Henry Taylor at Royal St George's in 1894. Notably it was the first time the Championship had been held in England while Taylor's success was the first by an English professional. The victory also began the sequence that saw Braid, Vardon and Taylor win the Open 16 times between them over the 21 years before hostilities began in 1914, their dominance being denied only five times and by five different players. But on each occasion one of the famous trio finished runner-up.

Braid, Vardon and Taylor were giants of that early era of the game and each left a legacy for modern golf that keeps their names to the fore whenever and wherever the sport is discussed. Vardon, because his revolutionary style of grip is adopted by the great majority of today's players, is perhaps the best known. Born in Jersey, Channel Islands, in 1870, he was one of seven children of whom Tom and Fred also became professional golfers. Harry won the Open a record six times. His first taste of golf was as a seven-year-old caddie at the newly laid-out Royal Jersey course at Grouville. But it was after his younger brother Tom became a professional that Harry's golfing career blossomed. With Tom's help, Harry became professional and greenkeeper at a new nine-hole course in Ripon, Yorkshire, but didn't find fame until moving to Ganton after a spell at Bury St Edmunds.

Vardon's first Open appearance was at Prestwick in 1893 but he made little impression. Ironically that was also Taylor's first Open. The following year Taylor won and Vardon was fifth while in 1895, when Taylor retained his crown, Vardon was ninth. However, in 1896, when the two tied at Muirfield, Vardon denied his rival a hat-trick by winning the play-off.

Braid's first Open was in 1894 as an amateur. He was an apprentice joiner and clubmaker at the Army and Navy Stores in London. A Scot, he was born at Elie, Fife, in 1870 and after success in local competitions became nationally known by halving a match in 1895 with the then Open champion Taylor. Soon after that he became professional at Romford Golf Club where he was based when he won the Open in 1901, the first of his five successes. He moved to Walton Heath in 1904 where he remained for 45 years until his death in 1950.

Braid was a man of few words. He let his golf do the talking and he had the most perfect golfing temperament; cool and calm, little would ruffle him. In his early days he was known as a furious yet not a long hitter. However, he suddenly found his length 'out of the blue'. What probably happened was that he found a driver that suited him and it transformed his game. He still couldn't putt, yet that also seems to have been 'found' overnight. Using a cleek in the 1900 Open, he repeatedly three-putted but after switching to an aluminium-headed club he suddenly found his touch which led to his winning the title the following year.

That may not be quite as it happened with some of the facts becoming blunted with the passing of years. Yet it has become reality in golfing lore and adds colour to the happenings of those fascinating years around the turn of the century. Braid lost his title the following year, 1902, when finishing joint second with Vardon behind the winner Sandy Herd, the first man to use a rubber-wound ball in the Open. After three successive runner-up spots, Vardon won again in 1903 from his brother Tom, then in 1904 Braid became the first man to break 70 in the Open and was one ahead of the eventual winner, Jack White of Sunningdale, going into the final round. However, White equalled that feat to finish one in front of Braid and Taylor. The title went to Braid in the next two years, 1905 and 1906, with Taylor second on each occasion, so the Open tally by this time read Vardon four wins, and Braid and Taylor three each.

In 1907 the Open went overseas for the first time when Frenchman Arnaud Massy won but the Triumvirate were in business again in 1908 at Prestwick when Braid took his fourth crown after dominating the event. At the halfway stage he was 15 shots ahead of Vardon and eventually won by eight over Tom Ball, despite himself recording an eight in the third round. Braid and Ball were joint second at Deal in 1909 as Taylor took his fourth Open victory and his first since 1900 but Braid was back in the winner's circle a year later at St Andrews, making it four wins in six years for the determined Scot. It was

Left: 'How to do it' by Arnaud Massy, the first overseas player to win the Open. Frenchman Massy took the title in 1907, and it was not won again by a golfer from the Continent until Seve Ballesteros in 1979.

perhaps appropriate that he should collect his fifth and final Open success at the home of golf in 1910. That year he also crossed the Channel to win the French Open. Not that Braid was finished with the Open. He finished well up in the following two years, but it was the other members of the famous threesome who were to complete the Triumvirate's supremacy up to the First World War.

Taylor, who was a year younger than his fellow champions, having been born in 1871, was a Devonian from Northam, the home of the Westward Ho! course. He contrasted with both Braid and Vardon in that he possessed none of Braid's fierce hitting nor did he have the graceful swing that was Vardon's hallmark. But he was easily the best putter and a fine iron player, particularly in bad weather. Bernard Darwin wrote of Taylor that he was 'a natural leader who would have made his mark in any walk of life', yet Taylor was rejected by the Army, Navy and the police because of flat feet and poor eyesight. But for this he might never have been a professional golfer at all and what a loss that would have been to the game. After leaving school at the age of 11, his father having died when young Taylor was an infant, he worked at the Westward Ho! club until 1891, when as a 20-year-old he went to the Burnham club in Somerset as greenkeeper and professional.

By now he was a fine player and after his Open victories of 1894 and 1895, he was deserving of the title the best player in Britain. However, Vardon was just around the corner and when the two met in a challenge match at Ganton, where Vardon was pro, Taylor was hammered 8 and 7. When they clashed again a month later at Muirfield in the Open, Taylor led going into the final round only to be caught by Vardon who went on to win the play-off by four shots.

After Taylor's third Open win in 1900, he and Vardon embarked on a promotional tour of the United States during which they entered the US Open in Chicago. The British players showed their prowess with Vardon winning by two shots from Taylor with the third place man another seven shots back. Although not winning the Open Championship again until 1909, Taylor was nevertheless consistently in a challenging position, finishing runner-up in four successive years. After Braid's fifth and final victory in 1910, Vardon gained his fifth success in the 1911 Open at Sandwich ahead of Massy but had to give way to Ted Ray the following year at Muirfield. Taylor's fifth and final Open triumph came in 1913 at Hoylake and was reckoned by many to have been his greatest victory. He only just qualified — in those years everyone played through qualifying rounds — and then had to play in appalling conditions of wind and rain. Ray, who had featured in a tough play-off with Vardon and

Francis Ouimet in the US Open that year which Ouimet won, led Taylor by one shot at the end of the first day's two rounds. On day two a storm struck Hoylake and left the course devastated with tents blown flat. But Taylor, with his coat collar turned up, battled against the elements to card a 77 followed by a 79 to beat Ray by eight shots, proving once and for all that he was unmatched in such conditions.

The 1914 Open, the last before the First World War, returned to Prestwick and, like so many previous tournaments, was another battle of the big three. This time Vardon came through for his record sixth win, just ahead of the other two. Because of the war, this Open signalled the swansong of the Great Triumvirate for when peace returned they were each in their late forties. They played in further Opens, but with the arrival of a new breed of professional, particularly from America, they were never able to assume their earlier supremacy. Taylor and Vardon played in the 1922 Open at Sandwich, won by Walter Hagen, finishing sixth and eighth respectively while Taylor was fifth in 1924, again behind Hagen. Taylor also played in the 1926 Open, when Jones triumphed at Royal Lytham, but then announced his retirement at the age of 55. However, having been a guiding light behind the foundation of the Professional Golfers' Association in 1901, Taylor continued to support that body, serving as captain and chairman. He also played in the inaugural Great Britain v the United States match in 1921 and was captain of the victorious Ryder Cup team in 1933. Another award was made to him in 1949 when he became an honorary member of the R & A and when, in 1957, he retired to his native Northam he was made president of the Royal North Devon club. He survived to the age of 91, outliving the other members of the Triumvirate by several years.

The Vardon grip

Vardon's lasting bequest to golf is his famous grip which is generally regarded as the basis of a sound game. He certainly passed it on during his tours of America, which were so strenuous that they contributed to the breakdown of his health. He spent some time in a sanatorium in Norfolk in 1903 but such was his fighting spirit that he recovered to win more titles and set that Open record. He was the first of the Triumvirate to pass on, in 1937 at the age of 67.

Braid didn't venture to America but was still a force to be reckoned with even after passing the age of 50. In 1927, aged 57, he reached the final of the PGA Match Play Championship, only to be beaten by Archie Compston, then perhaps the best player in the country. Another remarkable feat saw Braid record a 74 on his 78th birthday in 1948 at Walton Heath, although he beat his age quite regularly. He had also been a member of the PGA Executive Committee in his time,

Right: 'The Great Triumvirate'. Harry Vardon, six times Open Champion, drives, watched by five-times winners J.H. Taylor (seated) and James Braid. Vardon's grip was used by many subsequent players and is the basic grip of most golfers today.

Above: Walter Hagen driving at Troon in 1923, when he finished second in the Open, winning it in 1922, 1924, 1928 and 1929. This was the year that Hagen invited the crowd for a drink at the local rather than enter the clubhouse, where professionals were normally barred.

was the author of three books on golf, and much sought after as a course designer. He died in 1950.

We have already seen that the development of golf in America was Scottish-orientated, from the early pioneers through the first club professionals to course designers. The early champions were invariably Scottish born, but men who had moved to the New World where opportunity was a commodity not readily available back in the land of the tartan. Therefore the likes of the Smith brothers, Alex, Willie and Macdonald, Willie Anderson and Laurie Auchterlonie were all finding fame and a little fortune in their adopted country and passing on their skills to those Americans who were grateful for the knowledge. But once the game had become established on a firm base America gradually began to produce its own champion players, who didn't have Scottish accents or ancestry.

If the immigrant Scots weren't winning those early titles in America then it would be such as Harry Vardon who would cross the Atlantic to plunder the prizes from under the noses of the Americans. But soon those Americans were showing the benefit of the knowledge passed on and were developing their own skills not only to win their own Championships but gradually to reverse the trend and cross to Britain to reap a rich harvest. The Open Championship has long been their greatest goal, but the famous tournament was over 50 years old before the Americans became a force in the game. The Championship was the sole property of the Scots, and rightly so, from its inception in 1860 until 1890 when John Ball, an amateur

from the Royal Liverpool club and Hoylake, broke the Scottish monopoly at Prestwick. Two years later another Hoylake member, Harold Hilton, gained the first of his two Open titles which paved the way for the era of the Great Triumvirate — Vardon, Braid and Taylor — who were to stage their own monopoly of the event until well beyond the turn of the century.

But in 1907 the Open went out of Britain for the first time when Frenchman Arnaud Massy won at Hoylake and he remains the only Frenchman to have carried off the famous old trophy. Massy's victory was something of a watershed for it proved that foreigners had the ability to come and beat the British in their own backyard. In those days that was a shock to the golfing system of the islanders, but now Britons have become accustomed to it so much that a home winner is a rarity of some distinction.

The Yanks start coming

After Massy's victory — in celebration of which he christened his daughter Hoylake — home-bred players soon regained their grip on the Open but the first American winner was not long in arriving, while others were waiting in the wings. In 1921 Jock Hutchison, an emigrant from St Andrews, returned to Scottish shores and in particular his home town, to wrest the trophy for America. He was involved in a play-off with elegant amateur Roger Wethered after the two had tied on 296. At first Wethered was not sure he could stay on for the extra day because he was due to play in a cricket match and did not want to let his team-mates down. But he was persuaded to stay and in the

36-hole decider it was Hutchison who ruled the day by nine shots, 150 to 159.

If the Americans were not fully convinced that their day had arrived with Hutchison, they were more than sure the following year at Royal St George's with Walter Hagen. In 1920 Hagen had played his first Open at Deal and finished last but one as George Duncan took the title. But in 1922 he was back to take the Championship and open the floodgates to American domination of the tournament that was to last another 11 years, with just one exception. Nothing like Hagen had been seen before. He was an extrovert who attracted fans more than any other player until the arrival of Arnold Palmer in the 1950s. Hagen, from New York, was a man for style and colour. He could be said to have invented the pullover or cardigan as the garb for golf and was often seen dressed that way, invariably in colours either matching his plus-four stockings or contrasting with them. He took golfing fashion out of its parochial ways and virtually banished the coat forever as attire on the fairway. He also popularized black-and-white golf shoes, and was the first to employ a manager.

When Hagen won the first of his four Open titles in 1922 he had much to criticize in the British game. What particularly annoyed him was that professionals were not allowed to change or eat inside the clubhouse. He countered this by hiring a Daimler limousine, parking it in front of the clubhouse and using it just for changing his shoes and eating in. When he saw the size of his winner's cheque he immediately handed it to his caddie. A year later Hagen finished runner-up to Arthur Havers at Troon and although this time he was invited into the clubhouse for the prize-giving, he refused, inviting many of the crowd for a drink at a local pub instead.

Havers' victory in 1923 was the last by a Briton until Henry Cotton's first success in 1934. The 25-year-old professional from Coombe Hill hit the front after three rounds of 73, one ahead of Australian Joe Kirkwood and two in front of Hagen, but the American was favourite to retain his title. Havers shot 76 in the final round with only Hagen near enough to beat him. But the American bunkered himself on the 18th and his chance was gone. However, when the Open returned to Hoylake the following year Hagen restored America's grip, pushing Ernest Whitcombe into second spot.

The 1925 Championship was to be the last held at Prestwick. The famous old course that had given birth to the Open and staged it 24 times in all, had been overtaken by the progress of time and of golf's appeal. Vast crowds proved that the Ayrshire course was no longer suited to the event as they made play extremely difficult. The occasion called for a 'home' victory and if that wasn't available then for one by an emigrant from the 'old country'. At one stage it looked as if Scottish-born Macdonald Smith, then

resident in America, would provide the Scots with some cheer as he led by five shots going into the final round. But the ocasion proved too much and he slumped to an 82 to finish fourth behind Long Jim Barnes, a Cornishman from Lelant who had moved to America in 1904.

Jones' famous shot

By this time a young amateur was making a name for himself in America with a string of victories. Robert Tyre Jones was just 24 in 1926 but had already won the United States Amateur Championship twice and the US Open once. He first played in the Open in 1921 when Hutchison won, but five years later he returned for the Championship's first playing at Royal Lytham & St Anne's and won with an aggregate of 291, which equalled James Braid's Open record set at Prestwick in 1908. It was during the 1926 event that Jones played his famous shot from a bunker to the left of the 17th fairway in the final round. Jones was tied with his playing partner, Al Watrous, at the time but he struck a 5-iron from the sand some 170 yards over rough and gorse to the green to achieve his par. Such was the impact on Watrous that he three-putted and the Championship was lost. A plaque now stands in that bunker to mark the feat while the iron used hangs in the Royal Lytham clubhouse.

A year later the Open was back at St Andrews and, as defending champion, Jones was not that enamoured about returning to the Old Course. His dislike of the famous links stemmed from his first Open there in 1921 when he fared so badly that he tore up his card in frustration. It all happened in the

Above: The plaque off the 17th fairway at Royal Lytham & St Annes which commemorates the famous shot played by Bobby Jones in the 1926 Open, when he found the green from an impossible position and demoralized his challenger Al Watrous.

third round when Jones was out in 46 then took six at the tenth. When he was bunkered on the 11th and run up another six it was the last straw. He tore up the card and returned to the clubhouse completely exasperated with his game. But what a different story six years later. He and the course were soon reconciled and with the weather kind throughout Jones proceeded to show his true skills. His first round 68 equalled the course record and gave him a four-shot lead over the field. He then added rounds of 72, 73 and 72 for a Championship record aggregate of 285 to win by six strokes from Aubrey Boomer, after leading from start to finish. From then on Jones formed a fond relationship with St Andrews town and the Old Course, so it was perhaps fitting that it should be St Andrews that staged the 1930 Amateur Championship when Jones won again on his way to the 'Grand Slam'.

By now the Americans seemed to be in complete control of the Open Championship. Hagen won again in 1928 at Royal St George's, then tamed the winds at Muirfield a year later for his fourth and final success in the event. It was indeed his swansong as

he never won another major title, although remaining a threat until the mid-1930s. It was the 1930 Open at Hoylake that saw history made. Jones had just captured the Amateur Championship with a 7 and 6 victory over Roger Wethered and was keen to see if he could win 'everything' — the Amateur and Open Championships on both sides of the Atlantic — that year. But his Open form wasn't that good, mainly because he was not happy with his putter. He opened with a 70 then added a 72 and a 74, after dropping eight shots in the first three holes. That left him one behind Britain's Archie Compston and two ahead of countryman Leo Diegel going into the final round. Jones then looked as if he'd lost his chance when he took seven at the par-five eighth hole without straying from the fairway. It is a fairly straight-forward hole and Jones didn't look in trouble as he was short of the green in two. But he fluffed two chip shots then three-putted to give heart to the many club golfers among the spectators who recognized this as a regular occurrence in their game.

Jones then had to wait a full ten minutes on the ninth tee while the vast crowds were brought under control, but he steadied himself over the rest of the round to finish with 75. That was beaten by others but not by those who mattered, so Jones took the title by two strokes from Diegel and Macdonald Smith as Compston slumped to a last-round 82.

The Grand Slam

So the 'Grand Slam' was still on and Jones returned to America and the US Open at Interlachen, Minneapolis, where he was the defending champion. His opening 71 and 73 left him well in the hunt, then his third-round 68 gave him a five-shot lead. Again his final round left something to be desired as he double-bogeyed three of the short holes. But his 75 was again good enough, leaving Jones two ahead of the unfortunate Macdonald Smith with the rest of the field at least three shots further back. The final act of the 1930 drama unfolded at Merion, and it once again brought the game to the pinnacle of the public imagination with newspapers detailing teams of reporters and photographers to cover every shot of the drama. Jones gave them just what they wanted, equalling the record with 69 and 73 in the qualifying rounds, despatching opponents with ease as the match-play series unfolded. His first round 5 and 4 success was his closest winning margin before Jones won 6 and 5 then 10 and 8 to reach the final against Eugene V. Homans. There was no stopping Jones and he sealed the Grand Slam with an 8 and 7 success.

The Jones act was hard to follow but still the Americans came to the Open and still they conquered all. In 1931 at Carnoustie the Scots had something to cheer about when one of their own, Tommy Armour, took the title,

Below: American golfers arriving on the SS Mauretania *in 1924 to play in the Open. On the stairway are Walter Hagen, who won, and Gene Sarazen. The other players are John Farrell, Gil Nicholls and W. V. Baxter.*

although he had left Scotland as a youngster and had lived in America for the previous 11 years. Armour, known as the Silver Scot, played steadily for two rounds then sank to a 77 to go into the last circuit five shots behind Argentinian Jose Jurado and two adrift of Macdonald Smith. But he played almost flawless golf on that final afternoon to return a 71, to win by one from Jurado.

When the Open returned South again in 1932 it was Gene Sarazen who maintained America's grip on the Championship, leading from start to finish at Prince's, Sandwich. Again the unfortunate Macdonald Smith was runner-up to earn the unenviable title as the best player of his time never to have won a major championship, as Sarazen zipped home in a new aggregate record of 283. It was Sarazen's finest hour in Britain and his only Open Championship victory. His success appears to have hinged on being reunited with his old caddie Daniels, who had also carried for Hagen. Sarazen had earlier decided not to use Daniels' services as he felt he was too frail for 72 holes. But this proved totally untrue as Daniels played a major part in helping the little American to a place in Open history.

When Great Britain won the Ryder Cup in 1933, every British golf fan must have been hoping that that success would lead to a blooding of the American noses in the Open which followed shortly at St Andrews. The whole American team stayed on to play and they made their presence felt by filling five of the first six places, the title going to Densmore Shute from Ohio. He had suffered a disaster in the Ryder Cup, losing to Syd Easterbrook by one hole after three-putting the final green. But he turned it around on the Old Course, although only after a play-off with fellow countryman Craig Wood, whom he beat by five shots in the 36-hole battle.

Cotton names a ball

It is worth noting that Shute's win was the last by an American for 13 years, albeit in six of those years the Second World War intervened and there was no Open Championship contested. The long wait for a British victory ended in 1934 at Royal St George's when the redoubtable Henry Cotton put a brake on the American domination. By then Cotton had earned himself a high reputation as well as a string of tournament victories and he had been in contention in 1933 with rounds of 73, 72 and 71 only to slip away with a final round of 79. At Sandwich he opened with 67 and 65, the latter round giving a name to the golf ball 'Dunlop 65' which remains to this day. At that stage Cotton had a nine-shot lead which he increased to 12 after a 72 on the morning of the final day. In the afternoon the crowds grew large, ready to cheer him to a famous victory, but he went down with an attack of stomach cramps as he waited to tee off.

Needless to say he began to drop shots

and his uncertainty was reflected in his outward 40 that included three short holes. As he turned for home, Cotton recorded three fives and the Open was beginning to slip away. But a birdie restored his balance and put him back on the rails, thus avoiding what would have been a major collapse in Open history. He covered the last six holes in level fours to finish in 79 which was still five shots better than anyone else. For the remaining Championships prior to the Second World War and those immediately after, Cotton was always in contention, winning twice more. Until the outbreak of hostilities the title remained in Britain thanks to a group of illustrious British golfers, although it must be said that the number of entries from America was lessening with every passing year.

In 1935 Alf Perry, born in Surrey, took centre stage at Muirfield and succeeded Cotton as champion. He carded rounds of 69, 75, 67, 72 to equal the record aggregate of 283 and win by four shots from another Alf, Padgham. But Padgham, another Surrey man, has his revenge the following year at Hoylake, finishing one shot in front of Jimmy Adams and Cotton. Padgham nearly

Below: Henry Cotton, on the left, and Alf Padgham at Roehampton in 1934. Cotton's 1934 Open victory was the first by a Briton for 11 years. Padgham was to win in 1936 and Cotton again in 1937 and 1948 in a period of British ascendancy.

didn't make it to the tee the final day. His clubs were locked in the professional's shop and he had to break the window to retrieve them in time to march to the title. In 1937 Cotton won again at rain-lashed Carnoustie while gales hit the 1938 event at Royal St George's but didn't stop Reg Whitcombe from adding his name to the Championship's immortals. Conditions were so tough that only Whitcombe, Adams and Cotton broke 300. It was a Lancastrian, Richard 'Dickie' Burton, who won in 1939 at St Andrews with a two-stroke margin over American Johnny Bulla. Because of the outbreak of war, he was to become the longest reigning Champion in

Below: Alf Perry, outside his shop which advertises him as the Assistants Champion of 1924 and 1925. Perry was to do much better than this, for he won the Open Championship at Muirfield in 1935.

A. PERRY
PROFESSIONAL
Winner Assistants Championship
1924 AND 1925

Open history, seven years until the Championship resumed in 1946.

When it did it was a similar story of the Stars and Stripes out in front, this time with Sam Snead by four shots from South Africa's Bobby Locke and Bulla as a new era of Open golf evolved. That year the prize money had advanced to £1,000 and Snead received £150. The explosion in the popularity of the Open with prize money rising in tandem was still over a decade away. The famous old trophy was lifted next, in 1947, by Irishman Fred Daly at Hoylake, then Cotton completed his third success in 1948 at Muirfield with Daly in second spot, five shots back. It was Cotton's last Open victory, although it poses the question of how many he might have won but for the war years. However, he remains the only British golfer to have won three Opens since the days of Vardon, Braid and Taylor.

With the end of Cotton's reign it was Locke and Peter Thomson from Australia who took over. Locke, the artist from Johannesburg, won in 1949 at Royal St George's after the famous episode of the ball in the bottle which many feel deprived Harry Bradshaw of the title, and in 1950 at Troon. Another British victory came in 1951 when Max Faulkner triumphed at Royal Portrush but that was the last home success until Tony Jacklin became everyone's hero in 1969. In 1952 the Championship returned to Royal Lytham for the first time since Bobby Jones' famous 1926 victory and it was Locke who rattled up win number three in just four years. This time he left Thomson in second spot, which almost underlined how these two commanded the Open stage almost continually in the 1950s. Even the Americans found it difficult to break in at that stage, although there weren't that many who felt inclined to leave their own tour and cross the Atlantic for what was then a small carrot. One who did was Ben Hogan, who ventured to Carnoustie in 1953 to win the hearts of the British golfing public, who remembered the horrific car crash a few years earlier involving Hogan and his wife which almost cost them their lives.

Such was Hogan's remarkable recovery that he fought back into top-class golf and on his arrival at Carnoustie he had pocketed both the Masters and the US Open that year. He was clearly the man of the moment and arguably playing better than before his accident and he arrived in Scotland in good time to plan his strategy. He not only familiarized himself with the course in all weathers but also with the smaller British ball that was compulsory in the Championship at that stage. He was delighted by the extra length he achieved with the small ball and qualified easily but was not overjoyed by the lack of pace in the greens. Hogan began with a 73 but progressed well with rounds of 71 and 70 to put himself in the box seat. Then in the final round a 68 assured him of the title. His aggregate of 282, although the second lowest in history, was still three more than Locke's record 279 set three years earlier. Nevertheless he became the first player to win three majors in a single season but a clash of dates meant he had to miss the US PGA.

Hogan's victory was to be the last by an American for eight years. It was a time when Thomson took over to write another chapter in the Championship's long ·history, the Australian winning for the next three years, 1954 to 1956 at Birkdale, St Andrews and Hoylake, on his way to five Open successes in the space of 11 years. Thomson's second success in 1955 made him the first player to earn a £1,000 first prize as the total purse

reached £3,750, while he and Locke maintained a stranglehold until 1959 at Muirfield when another South African, Gary Player, broke through on his way to making a major impact on the game. Two years earlier at St Andrews, when Locke collected his fourth and final Open victory, the Championship took on a now familiar look in that the leaders went out last for the first time, while the concluding stages of the tournament were televised live, another first. Today we take these and many more items for granted. But 30 years ago they were very new and something of a departure from the normal course of events.

Left: Snappy dressers Bobby Jones and Gene Sarazen at the National Championship in 1923. Jones retired early from golf after winning everything in 1930, but Sarazen performed outstanding feats as a veteran.

The Centenary Open

If these changes were looked on as revolutionary then those that occurred within a year or two were nothing short of sensational. The Centenary Open at St Andrews in 1960 attracted many players who were conscious of the occasion, while the prize money had reached £7,000, with the winner receiving £1,250. He was another Australian, Kel Nagle, who finished one in front of Arnold Palmer, like Hogan seven years earlier bidding for his third major of the year, after having already landed the Masters and the US Open. Palmer missed by a shot but more significantly he rejuvenated the Championship by persuading his countrymen that they should support the Championship, the Americans having been reluctant to enter since the Second World War. Palmer was approaching the height of his powers and he exercised considerable influence off the course. His efforts achieved their objective.

He was back in 1961 at Royal Birkdale to take the title by a shot from Dai Rees, the third time the little Welshman had been runner-up. Palmer's popularity in Britain knew no bounds and his followers were quickly dubbed 'Arnie's Army' as he exercised something of a Pied Piper influence over golf fans. There is little doubt that the man from Latrobe, Pennsylvania, was a major influence in restoring the Open's popularity and esteem not only with his own countrymen but also with the British public, who responded to his power, flair and showmanship. Not only did he help put the Open back alongside the Masters, US Open and PGA but his success made him golf's first superstar in the modern idiom.

Golf's first millionaire

Palmer was also the first golfer to top one million dollars in winnings but his Open victories in the early 1960s must have seemed small beer as a contribution to this sum. In 1961 he earned £1,400 as the total purse rose to £8,500, but before long the financial rewards were to climb in ever-increasing amounts with each passing Championship. As the event's popularity grew with the fans flocking to see America's expanding group of fairway heroes, the revenue generated was reflected in the prize money. Having tamed a gale to win at Birkdale, Palmer was back the following year at fast-running Troon to retain the Championship with a record low aggregate of 276, and finish six shots in front of Nagle with the rest another seven strokes further back. Incidentally, 1962 saw the first Open appearance of Jack Nicklaus who had won the US Open that year as a rookie.

New Zealander Bob Charles prevented another American victory at Royal Lytham in 1963 when he beat Phil Rodgers by four shots in a 36-hole play-off after they had tied on 277. But Uncle Sam's boys were back in their glory again at St Andrews in 1964 with Nicklaus and a Californian named Tony

Lema. Of Portuguese descent, Lema had been a veteran of the Korean war with the US Marines after which he tried his hand at golf. But he didn't find much success until Horton Smith cured his putting faults. He soon gained confidence on the greens and when he arrived at St Andrews he was on the crest of a wave, having won four of the previous five tournaments in the United States. But he still had to win a major championship. His late arrival left time for only two practice rounds over the Old Course so he wasn't a fancied performer against the likes of Palmer, Nicklaus, Player, Thomson and Charles.

With the experience of such a tried and trusted caddie as Tip Anderson, Lema went into battle as the gales lashed St Andrews and sent the scores soaring into the 80s. Thomson and Charles shot 79, Nicklaus 76 but Christy O'Connor from Ireland and Frenchman Jean Garaialde shared the lead on 71. Lema was handily placed with 73. Easier conditions on the second day saw Lema add a four-under-par 68 which gave him the lead by two. The final two rounds were still played on Saturday in those days and it was Nicklaus who stole the show. He began nine behind Lema but a morning 66 cut that to seven as

the Californian returned another 68 with his usual style and elegance. In the afternoon Nicklaus was almost as irresistible as he had been before lunch but despite a 68 he could only trim the gap to five shots at the finish, Lema carding a 70 for 279 and his first major title.

A year later Lema defended his title at Royal Birkdale but finished tied fifth behind Thomson, who collected his fifth Open by two shots from the twin home challenge on O'Connor and Brian Huggett. Whether Lema would have added to his 1964 success is open to speculation because tragically he and his wife were killed when their light aircraft crashed in America on the way to a pro-am after the 1966 US PGA Championship. He was just 32.

Nicklaus majors

By this time Nicklaus was knocking on the door of the Open and ready to reinforce America's claim to the crown. When the Championship returned to Muirfield in 1966 it brought Nicklaus back to familiar territory as he had played there seven years earlier in the United States' victorious Walker Cup side. That certainly stood him in good stead

Opposite: Arnold Palmer practising at Birkdale for the Open of 1965. Palmer was the most charismatic golfer of the 1960s and his raids on the British Open in the early 1960s revived interest in the event among fans and players on both sides of the Atlantic.

Left: Bob Charles established two firsts in 1963 — he was the first New Zealander to win the British Open and he was the first left-hander to win a major tournament of any kind. Often described as the best-ever left-hander, Charles' main strength was his great putting.

Above: Probably the greatest golfer who ever lived, Jack Nicklaus has won 20 major titles, a record unlikely to be beaten.

although the rough had been allowed to grow sufficiently to impose a severe penalty on the wayward drivers. But it didn't worry the man from Ohio who shared the first-round lead with 70 then added a 67 to edge in front. Solid iron play in preference to the wooden clubs had given Nicklaus his advantage but towards the end of his third round he began to let shots slip and finished in 75 to slide two behind fellow countryman Phil Rodgers. After one hole of the final round they were level as Nicklaus gained a birdie to Rodgers' bogey. Nine holes later Nicklaus led by three from Britain's David Thomas and four from Rodgers and another American, Doug Sanders.

Suddenly Thomas was level and Nicklaus knew he had to pull something from his repertoire to restore his lead. He did it on the long 17th when a 3-iron, 5-iron and two putts secured the birdie that proved enough to give him a one-shot victory over Thomas and Sanders. In winning Nicklaus joined the handful of illustrious players who have captured all four majors and he had achieved it in the short span of four years.

Nicklaus was strongly fancied to hang on to the title at Hoylake in 1967, particularly after he had secured the US Open crown that year for the second time. He began confidently with 71, 69 but a third round 67 from Argentinian Roberto de Vicenzo left Nicklaus three behind. De Vicenzo had been competing in the Open for 19 years without too much success and few would have included him among their favourites before the Championship got under way. But although Nicklaus was breathing down his neck with Player also handily placed, the popular South American kept his cool and played some marvellous golf after a shaky start to his final round. Nicklaus made up ground with a closing 69 but de Vicenzo climaxed his performance with some magnificent driving to finish in 70 for 278 and a two-shot victory. At just over 44 years of age, he became the oldest Open champion of modern times.

Nicklaus, anxious to get his title back, turned in another fine performance at Carnoustie in 1968 but had to be satisfied with the runners-up spot again, this time with Bob Charles. That year the prize money topped £20,000 for the first time with the winner pocketing £3,000, and it was Gary Player who emerged victorious for his second Open after a gap of nine years. The little South African was remarkably consistent over Carnoustie's massive 7,252 yards with rounds of 74, 71, 71 and 73 for 289 and a two-shot margin. Nicklaus was one of the few players to break 70 but his hopes were undone by a first-round 76 in the wind.

Jacklin's blow for Britain

By now it was 17 years since a British player landed the Open crown so when the 1969 event unfolded at Royal Lytham hopes were ever high, if not overwhelmingly so, that the trophy could be brought back to these islands. In the intervening years several home players had come close to pulling it off but always they were pipped at the post. Yet while the odds against a British win were reasonably long, some were wondering if the Americans could achieve their first success at the Lancashire links since Bobby Jones' victory there 43 years earlier. In fact, strange as it may seem, no American professional had been victorious in a Lytham Open.

Most of the British hopes lay with Tony Jacklin who had gained experience on the

American circuit and achieved his first win there the previous year in the Jacksonville Open. At Lytham he shot a first-round 68 to lie two behind Charles yet seven ahead of Nicklaus. A second-round 70 saw him stray three behind Charles and two adrift of Christy O'Connor at half-way yet maintaining his advantage over Nicklaus. Another 70 was vital as Jacklin hit the front by two as Charles shot 75, and when the final day dawned British fans wondered if this was indeed going to see an end to the foreign domination. Jacklin was unperturbed as he carded a 72 to maintain his two-shot margin and become a national hero with 280 to Charles' 282. He became the first British Open champion for 18 years. The following June he reversed the trend again, taking the US Open crown at Hazeltine.

St Andrews again played host to the Open in 1970 and having just been crowned US Open champion, Jacklin was strongly fancied to do it again. He certainly began his defence well with an outward 29 but when the heavens opened that first day play was suspended. When the round was resumed the next day the magic had deserted him and he finished with 67 instead of a possible record. Neil Coles led the British challenge with 65 but added a second round 74 while Jacklin carded 70 to be one behind Lee Trevino. On day three the weather was atrocious. Rain and wind swept the Old Course but Trevino, with a level par 72, kept his lead by two shots over Sanders, Nicklaus and Jacklin, who shot 73. On the final day conditions were even worse. Jacklin's challenge faded with a 76 and it came down to a straight duel

between Nicklaus and Sanders and remained that to the last two holes.

Sanders wins immortality

Both parred the 17th which left Sanders one ahead. He required only to par the 18th to take the title. He drove well and although his second was too strong his first putt finished only a couple of feet away. The rest seemed a formality. Sanders took his time and even stepped away from the putt once. When he resumed disaster struck as the short putt stayed out, thereby joining the long list of shots that have lost tournaments. Sanders'

Above left: Neil Coles playing in the 1969 Open Championship. Coles was the most consistent player in Britain for many years and is now enjoying success as a Senior.

Above: David Thomas, another consistent golfer of the 1950s and 1960s, who came very near to winning the Open in 1958, when only 24, but he lost in a play-off with Peter Thomson.

Left: Tony Jacklin, whose achievements in 1969 and the early 1970s marked him out as the best British golfer for many years.

Above: Tom Weiskopf possesses one of the most fluent swings of all golfers, and conquered an initial waywardness to become one of golf's elite, winning the Open in 1973.

Liang Huan Lu, quickly christened 'Mr Lu' by the fans, who took him to their hearts, was also well in the hunt.

It was Trevino who triumphed on 278, one ahead of Mr Lu and two in front of Jacklin. The following year at Muirfield, Nicklaus was on the trail of a modern Grand Slam, having won the Masters at Augusta and the US Open at Pebble Beach. Muirfield was his favourite British course and he began a firm favourite while British hopes again lay with Jacklin. But Trevino was not going to give up the title easily and he was to produce some outrageous scoring that had to be seen to be believed. Yorkshireman Peter Tupling was the first round leader with 68 with Jacklin on 69, Nicklaus 70 and Trevino 71. At halfway Jacklin and Trevino shared the lead on 141 with Nicklaus one behind with Sanders and Gary Player. Trevino and Jacklin were out together the next day when the American turned on a spectacular finish of five successive birdies to shoot 66 including twice chipping in, once from the sand. But for such fireworks, Jacklin's 67 would have led while Nicklaus drifted out with a 71 to start the final day six behind Trevino and five behind Jacklin.

Then the Golden Bear staged one of his famous charges and by the 11th had taken the lead. However, Trevino still had Lady Luck in his bag and although Jacklin stayed with him, the people's hero of 1969 was to have his heart broken by the American's audacious play which once again saw him chipping in from seemingly impossible positions and producing birdies when bogeys were the order of the day. In the end Trevino's incredible play was to win him the title again by a shot from Nicklaus while Jacklin, shell-shocked from Trevino's actions, was third again, two shots back.

In 1973 another American, Tom Weiskopf, overcame some dreadful weather at Royal Troon to win the Open and equal Palmer's record of 276, although perhaps the most memorable item of that Championship was the hole-in-one by veteran Gene Sarazen at the Postage Stamp eighth. Sarazen was making a nostalgic return to the event at the age of 71. Player took the title again in 1974 at Royal Lytham but the American influence was back in 1975 at Carnoustie when the reign of Tom Watson began. It was a close-run affair with five players separated by just one shot at the finish but Watson and Australian Jack Newton were out in front. This brought an 18-hole play-off which Watson won by one shot, 71 to 72 for the first of his five Open Championships.

Watson may have been the sensation of the 1975 Open but the following year's battle at Birkdale brought the emergence of a 19-year-old Spaniard who was to stamp his mark on world golf in a comparatively short space of time. Severiano Ballesteros, a professional for only two years, led for three rounds until American Johnny Miller

chance had gone. In the play-off Nicklaus shot 72 to Sanders' 73 to land his second Open. The following three years also saw the trophy cross the Atlantic. In 1971 Royal Birkdale played host for the 100th Open and Trevino arrived with the US and Canadian Opens already in his grasp. He was in top form but Jacklin again mounted a solid challenge, while the little known Taiwanese

Left: Lee Trevino, one of golf's great entertainers, who defied a bad back and being struck by lightning to win major tournaments on both sides of the Atlantic.

steamed through with a closing 66 to win by six shots from Nicklaus and Ballesteros. But the Spaniard would make up for his disappointment by lifting the trophy three years later. The Open broke new ground in 1977 when it was staged at Turnberry for the first time. And what a magnificent contest it proved to be. At the halfway mark four Americans headed the leaderboard on 138 — Watson, Nicklaus, Trevino and Hubert Green. But from then on it was strictly a two-horse race as Watson and Nicklaus, one and two in that year's Masters, slugged it out shot for shot. They both shot third round 65s, then in a majestic final round of what was in effect match-play golf, matched each other hole by hole until the 17th, when Watson's birdie put his nose in front. On the 18th

Nicklaus sank a putt almost across the length of the green for what looked like a play-off securing birdie. But Watson followed him in for another 65 to take his second Open by one shot with 268, a record. Green was third, eleven shots back.

Nicklaus had his revenge the following year at St Andrews, although Watson was in the hunt for three rounds only to slip with a 76. It was left to Simon Owen of New Zealand, and fellow Americans Ben Crenshaw, Ray Floyd and Tom Kite to make their bid, but in the end Nicklaus came through to snatch his third Open, his second at St Andrews, by one shot. In 1979 at Royal Lytham, Nicklaus was a strong bet to keep the title until Ballesteros scorched round in a second round 65 to be two behind Hale Irwin. The American still led going into the last round but he crumbled under the magic of the Spaniard's play and the title went to the continent for the first time since Massy in 1907. Nicklaus still managed to be joint second to complete an amazing record of having finished in the top three 13 times in 18 years.

Ballesteros was destined to win again in 1984 but the intervening years saw further American successes. In 1980 at Muirfield, the first Sunday finish to the Championship, brought Watson to the throne again. It was a year for low scoring with Japan's Isao Aoki equalling Mark Hayes' 1977 Open record low round of 63 while Watson shot 64 on his way to a four-shot victory and Open victory number three. In 1981 the Open returned to Royal St George's after an interval of 32 years and it was another American, Bill Rogers, who came through to take the title by four strokes from Germany's Bernhard Langer.

Watson misses the record

Watson's three previous victories had all been on Scottish courses so when the Open returned to Royal Troon in 1982 he must have felt his chances were better than good. Those feelings were fully realised as he won his fourth Open, this time over Britain's Peter Oosterhuis and Nick Price of South Africa. The spotlight moved to Birkdale again in 1983 where Watson again showed his pedigree, although for a time it looked as if Irwin or fellow American Andy Bean might earn their first Opens. But Watson was the master of the situation. Needing a four at the last, he got home for a one-shot win to equal James Braid, J. H. Talyor and Peter Thomson as a five-times winner.

Watson came close to making it six at St Andrews in 1984 to match Harry Vardon's record but he lost out in the battle with Ballesteros over the final two holes as the Spaniard went par, birdie to Watson's bogey, par to triumph by two. So to Royal St George's in 1985 and at last the foreign domination was broken as Sandy Lyle secured Britain's first win since Jacklin's

1969 success and Scotland's first victory since George Duncan in 1920. In 1986 at Turnberry, when the wind blew, the rain fell and the temperatures dipped, Greg Norman earned Australia's first win in the event for 21 years.

Then it became the turn of another Briton, Nick Faldo, whose one-stroke victory at Muirfield in 1987 recorded the second British win in three years, the best spell since 1948.

International team events

The Open Championship has been the cornerstone of competitive golf and is now a truly international event. International matches between Britain and America were instigated in the 1920s but the first official international match took place at Muirfield in 1903 between Scotland and England. In 1953, the World Cup, formerly the Canada Cup, was founded as an international team event for professionals. Each country is represented by two players with aggregate scores over 72 holes to count. The competition enjoyed a successful run until the early 1980s, when many of the top players lost interest because of the low level of prize money. There was no competition in 1981 or 1986 but the Cup was restructured in 1987 and looks to have a brighter future. The World Cup has been played only once in Britain, in 1956, and once in Ireland, in 1960, the United States winning on both occasions.

There are now several other international competitions apart from the Ryder Cup, the Walker Cup, the Curtis Cup and the World Cup, the most notable of these being the Eisenhower Trophy for men amateurs and the Espirito Santo Trophy for lady amateurs.

Golf becomes international

Today, golf is played in most countries of the world, although there are still a few exceptions, mainly in Africa and Asia. China now has a few courses while the game has also penetrated behind the Iron Curtain. Golf has also reached some unusual places so that it can truly be called an international sport. It is played in the deserts of Africa, among the Arabs of the Middle East and by the Red Indians of North America. The highest course is believed to be the Tuctu Club at Morococha, Peru, at 14,335 feet above sea level, while Bolivia has two courses at over 12,000 feet. In the northern hemisphere, Iceland has several courses which enjoy a comparatively short season but with the help of the midnight sun, play is possible for 24 hours.

There have been a host of bizarre feats such as members of a British Army unit climbing 16,000 feet in the Andes as part of an exercise and hitting balls to claim a golfing altitude record. But the greatest achievement must surely go to astronaut Alan Shepherd, who hit two golf balls on the moon after landing there in 1971.

The belt having been won thrice by young Tom Morris it became his... Championship remained in ab... when the present cup was offer... competition.

Winner—Tom Morri...
June 14...

Championships, Cups and Tournaments

There is an almost countless number of tournaments held during the golfing year but four have emerged as the ultimate prizes. They are the Open Championship, the United States Open, the United States Masters and the United States Professional Golfers' Association Championship. These four are known as the major championships and a golfer's career is measured by how many of them he wins. In bygone days, the amateur championships of both Britain and America were also considered major titles and it was in 1930 that American Bobby Jones achieved his incredible feat of winning both the Open and Amateur Championships of Britain and America, known as the Grand Slam. Such a feat could not be contemplated in the modern game since it is the professionals who hold sway, so the modern Grand Slam is held to be victory in the four major championships in the same year, something that has yet to be achieved. There are other tournaments with pedigree, such as the World Match Play Championship, while international team encounters such as the Ryder Cup and Walker Cup also enjoy high status and have added to the tradition and folklore of the game.

Left: The new and the old in Open Championships. In the foreground Young Tom Morris' Championship Belt, on an album which contains his photograph and scorecards of Open victories. Behind is Greg Norman, the 1986 Champion, on the picturesque 9th tee at Turnberry during his winning Championship.

THE OPEN

The first Open Championship was staged on 17 October 1860 when eight professionals gathered on the links at Prestwick to battle for the title over three rounds. Since there was no amateur involvement, the title 'Open' was incorrect but the main aim of the event at that time was to find a successor to Allan Robertson of St Andrews who, until his death the previous year, had proved to be virtually unbeatable. Seven of the eight competitors were from Scotland with the odd man out being George Brown from Blackheath, and they played three rounds of 12 holes apiece on the day. Willie Park of Musselburgh covered the 3,799-yard course in rounds of 58, 59 and 60 to take the Moroccan Leather Championship belt by two strokes from Tom Morris Snr.

For the first seven years of the Championship, Park and Morris took a virtual stranglehold on the belt with Morris winning in 1861, 1862, 1864 and 1867 and Park in 1863 and 1866, with the only player to break this domination being Andrew Strath in 1865. By now amateurs were competing regularly but the professionals still held sway and if they hadn't had enough of one Morris, they were about to become thoroughly acquainted with another. In 1868 Young Tom Morris followed in his father's footsteps and

at the age of 17 set a new record of 157 for the 36 holes. This youthful prodigy, who still remains the youngest winner of the Open, then lowered that record in winning the next year and in 1870 made it three wins in a row with an aggregate of 149, his first 12-hole round of 47 being one under fours and quite extraordinary considering the equipment at his disposal and the gutty ball.

The championship belt, presented by the Earl of Eglington, now became Young Tom's property and because there was no alternative trophy available, the Championship was suspended in 1871. Prestwick then approached the R & A and the Honourable Company of Edinburgh Golfers and the three clubs agreed to take it in turns to stage the Open. They purchased the silver claret jug as a permanent trophy. The Open returned to Prestwick in 1872 and once again Young Tom emerged the winner to make it four wins in a row, a record which has never been equalled. St Andrews hosted the event in 1873 for the first time and the winner was Tom Kidd with Young Tom finishing joint third, and the following year he was second at Musselburgh to Mungo Park. Tragedy then struck as Young Tom's wife died in childbirth and, broken-hearted, he too expired aged only 24.

Had Young Tom lived there is little doubt he would have added to his record of Open victories, but as it was the reins were taken up by Jamie Anderson of St Andrews and Bob

Below: Bobby Jones on the 18th green at Royal Lytham & St Annes in 1926, the first year in which he won the Open. This was also the first time that the Open was played at this course.

Ferguson of Musselburgh. Each won the title three years in a row, Anderson from 1877 to 1879 and Ferguson from 1880 to 1882, with the latter narrowly missing making it four in a row when he lost the Championship's first play-off in 1883 to Willie Fernie.

Scottish golfers continued to dominate the Championship over the next six years, but with the field expanding annually it was only a matter of time before the tide was turned. In 1878 an English amateur, John Ball from Hoylake, had finished fifth when aged only 14, and 12 years later at Prestwick he made the important breakthrough. Ball's success was quickly emulated by another Hoylake amateur, Harold Hilton, who won in 1892 at Muirfield, the first time the Open was held over 72 holes, and also the first time entry fees were levied. Prize money was tripled to more than £100.

The next significant milestone occurred in 1894 when the Championship was first staged in England. The Kentish links of St George's saw J.H. Taylor become the first English professional champion, and this victory heralded a new era of domination as Taylor was joined by James Braid and Harry Vardon to form the 'Great Triumvirate'. Between them they won the title 16 times in the space of 20 years, with Vardon just edging out the five victories of the other two with his sixth win in 1914. Their influence on the game was immeasurable, with Vardon in particular bringing a new dimension to a game which

hitherto had been one of crude lunge and bash. In 1898, Vardon became the first player to break 80 in all four rounds when he won at Prestwick and the next target was to break 300 over the 72 holes. This honour fell to a little-known English professional, Jack White from Sunningdale, whose last round 69 gave him a total of 296. This Championship also saw play being extended over three days, with the last two rounds on the final day, and the following year, in an attempt to ease the congestion of entry, a qualifying figure of 15 strokes behind the leader after two rounds was introduced. This, in fact, only removed four players from the scene while 99 continued.

In 1907 Frenchman Arnaud Massy became the first overseas champion, winning at Hoylake, and four years later he nearly won again, tieing with Vardon at the now Royal St George's. The subsequent play-off ended in curious fashion with Massy picking up his ball on the 35th hole of the stroke-play encounter in deference to the fact that Vardon was several strokes ahead.

The reign of the Triumvirate came to an end with the outbreak of the First World War and the suspension of the Championship.

Two pre-qualifying rounds were staged prior to the 1914 Open and the leading 80 players advanced to the Championship proper but increasing entries were making it clear that the event needed administrative leadership. A letter from Herbert Fowler,

Below: A montage of pictures of George Duncan driving, pitching and putting at the Royal Cinque Ports Club links at Deal in 1920. The Championship was described as the most dramatic in the annals of the game. Duncan's first two rounds were 80 and 80, leaving him 13 strokes behind the leader, Abe Mitchell. Duncan's following rounds of 71 and 72 nevertheless won the title with a total of 303, Mitchell subsiding to 307.

Right: Henry Cotton with the trophy after his fabulous win in 1934 at Royal St George's, Sandwich, when he began with rounds of 67 and 65 and won by five strokes despite a last-round 79, when he was unwell.

Below: Harry Bradshaw came close to an Open victory in 1949 when he tied with Bobby Locke after 72 holes, but lost the play-off.

architect of such courses as those at Walton Heath, Saunton and The Berkshire, advocated that since the R & A governed the rules of the game, it should also govern the game's most important Championship.

This suggestion took effect in 1919, and the first Open under the R & A's jurisdiction was the first after the war, in 1920, when George Duncan won at Deal. Duncan was nicknamed 'Miss 'em quick' because of the speed he executed each shot, an admirable philosophy but one which was to let him down two years later. By now the Championship had international appeal and in 1921 the

old silver claret jug took the first of many subsequent journeys across the Atlantic when Jock Hutchison, a St Andrean who had emigrated to America, won at St Andrews after a play-off with amateur Roger Wethered. The tie was made possible by Wethered incurring a penalty stroke for inadvertently treading on his ball while walking backwards from studying the line of a shot in the third round. The Corinthian spirit of the amateur game in those days was exemplified by Wethered having to be persuaded to remain for the play-off because he felt that his commitment to a cricket match in England was more important!

Bobby Jones and Walter Hagen

The 1921 Championship saw the first appearance of Bobby Jones, who tore up his card on the 11th hole, vowing never to return. Thankfully he did and over the next nine years he and Walter Hagen formed the spearhead of the American assault. Hagen broke through to win in 1922 at Royal St George's by one stroke from George Duncan, who needed to get down in two from the hollow on the left of the 18th to tie. Duncan's quickness over the chip almost deceived the eye and he fluffed it. Hagen, who was to win again in 1924, 1928 and 1929, epitomised the mood of the age. Flamboyantly dressed and darkly good-looking, he was the lounge lizard of the links. He lived life to the full, spending as he earned in the knowledge that another buck was always round the next corner. He had an ungainly, lunging swing but was a master of the short game and the chief exponent of rolling three shots into two.

In contrast, Jones was a quiet, somewhat introverted character who suffered nervous agonies during a Championship but whose lovely, drowsy swing rarely let him down. His first victory came at Royal Lytham & St Annes in 1926, the first time the Championship was staged there, and was notable for his legendary mashie shot from the scrubland to the left of the 17th in the final round. A plaque now marks the spot from where Jones struck that epic shot to demoralize completely his playing companion and nearest challenger, Al Watrous, although witnesses now swear that the plaque is several yards out of place.

Jones returned to St Andrews in 1927 and reconciled his relationship with the Old Course by setting a new record for the 72 holes of 285. Three years later he won again at Hoylake, but much more tightly this time due to a ridiculous seven at the 8th, when he was by the green in two, fluffed a couple of chips and took three putts. This was the second leg of his Grand Slam and it earned him a ticker-tape welcome in New York on his return.

The only interlopers in the Hagen/Jones domination were Arthur Havers at Troon in 1923 and Jim Barnes at Prestwick in 1925, the latter being that course's last Open due to its incapacity to cope with the crowds which swarmed across the links and effectively destroyed the hopes of Macdonald Smith who led by five strokes going into the last round but, swamped by the mob, crashed to an 82.

The American grip on the Championship continued into the new decade with Tommy Armour winning at Carnoustie in 1931, Eugene Saraceni, who changed his name to Gene Sarazen, in 1932 at Prince's and Densmore Shute at St Andrews in 1933 after a play-off with fellow American Craig Wood, the only man to lose a play-off in all four of the major professional Championships.

Henry Cotton's famous 65

That darkest hour for British golf, however, brought in a new dawn. Through sheer hard work and dedication, Henry Cotton had developed into a golfer whose striking was flawless. In 1934 at Royal St George's he converted that control into the two lowest opening rounds the Championship had ever seen, or has seen since. His first round was 67 and he looked like matching that in the second except that he finished with two threes for a 65, a score of such historic minimum that it gave birth to probably the most famous golf ball of them all, the Dunlop 65. His third round of 72 left him ten strokes clear of the field and new record aggregate looked likely. But prior to the final round he was assailed by stomach cramps and eventually limped home with a 79, still good enough to give him victory by five strokes and tie the low aggregate score of 283 that Sarazen had set two years earlier.

Left: Bobby Locke of South Africa driving. Locke was well-known in his later career for his plus-fours, his bulk, his general stately demeanour around the course and his brilliant putting.

Cotton's victory gave Britain a national hero and ushered in an unprecedented spell of home triumphs. The little-known Alf Perry won at Muirfield the next year, hitting woods out of bunkers like a man in a weekend knockabout, Alf Padgham won at Hoylake in 1936, the year he swept all before him and then it was Cotton's turn again. Carnoustie in 1937 saw the full might of the victorious American Ryder Cup team assembled, but with another display of sublime striking, Cotton produced a final round of 71 over the rain-lashed links to win by two strokes over Reg Whitcombe. The latter was the man of the moment at Royal St George's in 1938 when he stood foursquare in the tempest which swept the links to win by one shot from James Adams, who had also been runner-up to Padgham in 1936. In 1939 at St Andrews, Dick Burton unwittingly became the Champion who was to hold the title for the longest spell, due to the more pressing matters of the Second World War.

The Championship resumed in 1946 at St Andrews when German POWs helped prepare the course. The story goes that Sam Snead was travelling there by train in company with a bucolic Brigadier and glancing out of the window, Snead remarked that he thought he saw an old, disused golf course.

'That, Sir,' spluttered his companion, 'is the Old Course at St Andrews!'

Snead, no respecter of reputations, added insult to injury by winning the first prize of £150 by four strokes. Ulster's Fred Daly became the first Irish winner in 1947 at Hoylake, to be followed by Cotton who took his third title at Muirfield and laid on a second round of 66 in front of King George VI.

Bobby Locke and Peter Thomson

The Championship now entered an era that could loosely be described as the age of the Commonwealth. In fact, it was a ten-year period of domination by two players, Bobby Locke of South Africa and Peter Thomson of Australia. Between them they won the title eight times in that spell with only Max Faulkner (1951) and Ben Hogan (1953) breaking the sequence. Locke was an extremely unorthodox player in style, hitting every shot over cover point and bringing the ball back on target, but as a putter he had few equals and this, coupled with an imperturbable temperament made him a fearsome competitor. His first victory came at Royal St George's in 1949 when he defeated Ireland's Harry Bradshaw after a play-off. This was the Championship when Bradshaw hit his drive to the fifth during the second round and the ball finished in a broken beer bottle. Unsure of his rights, he elected to play the ball and the hole cost him a seven and the round 77.

Locke repeated his victory at Troon the following year and became the first man to break 280 for the 72 holes. Royal Portrush became the only Irish Club to stage the Open in 1951 when Max Faulkner won despite

tempting the fates by signing autographs as 'Open Champion' before he went out for the last round. Locke won again at Royal Lytham & St Annes in 1952 and then it was 1953, the year Ben Hogan bestrode the world. He arrived at Carnoustie a week early and plotted a path to the title in relentless fashion. Rounds of 73-71-70-68 in descending order of brilliance sealed his place among the immortals and made him the only professional to win three majors in a single year.

Peter Thomson won the first of his hat-trick of titles in 1954 at Royal Birkdale. A master tactician, Thomson's strength lay in accurate driving coupled with an astute golfing brain, qualities which have since held him in good stead on the US Seniors Tour. His victory in 1955 earned him the first £1,000 winner's cheque and he became the fourth man in Open history to win three in a row in 1956. The 1957 Open was switched from Muirfield to St Andrews because of the Suez crisis and petrol rationing, and Locke won from Thomson. Controversy arose when, on the final green, Locke marked his ball and moved the marker a putter-head's length away to allow his partner to putt. He then replaced his ball without moving the marker back to the original spot, and holed out. After much deliberation, the Committee decided that Locke's score should stand since he had gained no advantage.

There was a chance of a British victory in 1958 at Lytham when David Thomas tied with Thomson, but it was not to be as Thomson won the play-off by four strokes. The end of the decade saw Gary Player perform the first of his miraculous recoveries when he made up eight strokes over the last two rounds at Muirfield to win, despite taking six on the final hole.

The arrival of Arnold Palmer

Australia's Kel Nagle secured a popular victory in the 1960 Centenary Open at St Andrews but this Championship is perhaps best remembered for the dynamic presence of Arnold Palmer. The man who had taken American golf by the scruff of the neck was about to do the same for the Open. He finished second to Nagle by a single stroke on his first appearance but was not to be denied at Birkdale in 1961 when he powered his way through some of the foulest weather imaginable to win by a stroke from Dai Rees, the irrepressible Welshman who had also been runner-up in 1953 and 1954. Palmer put the field to flight in 1962 at Troon over a course that was baked hard by a prolonged dry spell, winning by six strokes and setting a new Championship record of 276 for 72 holes. This year also saw the first appearance of Jack Nicklaus who only just qualified for the last two rounds.

Led by Palmer, the American challenge was now in full cry. Bob Charles halted it in 1963 at Lytham when he became the first left-

hander and first New Zealander to win as he out-putted America's Phil Rodgers in a play-off, but 1964 at St Andrews saw one of the most remarkable victories in recent times. Tony Lema arrived at the Old Course with only enough time for one full practice round but his style and elegance captured not only the hearts of the spectators but also the title, by five strokes from Nicklaus. Peter Thomson took the fifth and most satisfying of his Opens at Birkdale in 1965 against the full might of the American invasion and then Nicklaus, after near misses in 1963 and 1964, finally broke through at Muirfield in 1966 over a course whose rough was formidably high.

Hoylake in 1967 witnessed one of the most popular victories when, after 19 years of trying, Roberto de Vicenzo held off Nicklaus to win but the size of the crowds sounded the death knell for Hoylake as an Open venue. Gary Player took his second Open at Carnoustie in 1968 after a thrilling battle with the ubiquitous Nicklaus and then came the spark that ignited the first European golf explosion.

Tony Jacklin's great win

Eighteen years without a British victory had left the populace hungry for a hero. It found him in Tony Jacklin, a player who had won in America the previous year, and who had the charisma and personality to accompany an aggressive mode of play. At Lytham in 1969 he ended the British drought of victories with a two-stroke margin over Bob Charles and launched himself into the hearts of millions. A year later, Jacklin also won the US Open, an unprecedented feat by an Englishman, but the next three Opens saw fate deal him some of the cruellest hands in Open history. In 1970 at St Andrews Jacklin covered the first nine holes of the opening round in 29 strokes and he appeared set to break all kinds of records before a thunderstorm halted play. The next day the magic had gone and although he finished with a 67, it was a question of what might have been as Jack Nicklaus and Doug Sanders tied after 72 holes.

Sanders had pre-qualified for the Championship and performed magnificently to come to the final hole needing a par four for victory. In an agonising sequence of indecision he contrived to take five, ultimately missing a putt of three feet which would have avoided the play-off in which Nicklaus eventually beat him.

In 1971 Jacklin gallantly harassed Lee Trevino at Birkdale but there was no stopping the American as he added the Open to the US and Canadian Opens he had won in the previous two weeks. Trevino's defeat of Jacklin in the 1972 Open at Muirfield was a tragedy

Above: Gary Player of South Africa is famous for his bunker play, but he is a good player from any difficult position on the course. This shot from the Muirfield rough was made during the Open of 1959 when he won from Belgium's Flory Van Donck.

for the Englishman. In the third round Trevino holed a chip and a bunker shot which struck the pin half way up and dropped, and then in the last round on the 71st hole chipped in again just when Jacklin looked as though he would take the lead. The events at Muirfield signalled the end of Jacklin as an Open challenger.

The tall, soldierly figure of Tom Weiskopf marched to victory at rain-sodden Troon in 1973 and then Gary Player became the only man to win the Open in three different decades when he led from start to finish in 1974 at Lytham, the first Open when the large ball was made compulsory.

Tom Watson's dominance

Carnoustie in 1975 saw the beginning of Tom Watson's domination as he captured the title five times in nine years. He defeated Australia's Jack Newton in a play-off in 1975 and then went on to win at Turnberry in 1977, Muirfield in 1980, Troon in 1982 and Birkdale in 1983. His battle with Nicklaus at Turnberry was an epic as the two of them went at each other like bare-knuckle prizefighters over the final 36 holes. Playing together, nothing separated them until Watson birdied the 71st hole and Nicklaus didn't. Watson's aggregate of 268 was eight strokes better than the previous record set by Palmer and Weiskopf at Troon in 1962 and 1973 respectively.

The Watson period also saw the emergence of Severiano Ballesteros, who first captivated audiences with his audacious play at Birkdale in 1976 when he led after three rounds. Slashing his way through Birkdale's dunes, Ballesteros finally succumbed to Johnny Miller's greater experience but his hour was not long in coming. Following

Below: Seve Ballesteros looks happy with his envelope at Royal Birkdale in 1976 but in fact he had been beaten after an exciting duel with Johnny Miller, seated centre, whose last round rally won him his only Open.

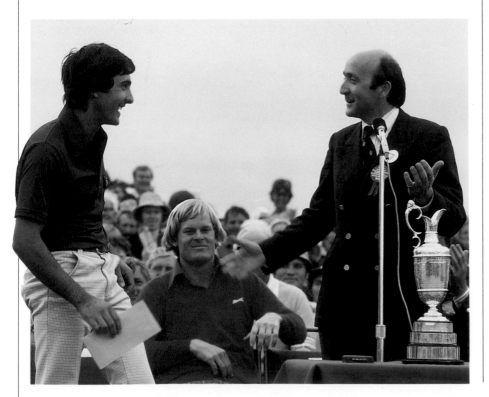

Nicklaus' third Open at St Andrews in 1978, Ballesteros thrust himself to the centre of the world stage with a cavalier performance at Lytham in 1979. Rarely on the fairway, the young Spaniard overhauled the third round leader, Hale Irwin, to become the first Continental winner since Arnaud Massy in 1907 and ignite a new European golf explosion which culminated in the Ryder Cup victory of 1985.

In 1981 the Championship returned to Royal St George's after an absence of 32 years and America's Bill Rogers won handily, with the growing European strength being emphasized by Bernhard Langer finishing runner-up. Watson won at Troon in 1982 after Zimbabwe's Nick Price squandered a three-stroke lead with six holes to play and the chunky American won again at Birkdale in 1983, hitting a superlative 2-iron to the final green to win by a stroke from Americans Andy Bean and Hale Irwin, the latter having suffered an inexplicable lapse in the third round when he went to tap in a one-inch putt and missed the ball altogether.

Left: *Tom Watson plays out of the rough trodden down by spectators at Royal Birkdale in 1983. In this tournament Watson registered his fifth Open victory, much the best record since Peter Thomson's five wins in the 1950s and 1960s.*

Now sitting on a hat-trick and a chance to equal Harry Vardon's record of six Open titles, Watson came to St Andrews in 1984 as clear favourite. An unknown Australian, Ian Baker-Finch, made the early running but the final round developed into an intense struggle between Watson, Ballesteros and, to a slightly lesser extent, Langer. The denouement came at the infamous Road Hole, the 17th, where Ballesteros made a par four and Watson, playing immediately behind, was betrayed by that same 2-iron which earned him victory the previous year. His second shot with that club to the 17th flew over the green to finish up against the wall and while Watson was taking five, Ballesteros was clinching victory with a birdie three on the last green. Record crowds of 187,753 attended during the week and prize-money was raised to £451,000.

Sandy Lyle wins for Britain

The £500,000 barrier was broken in 1985 when Royal St George's was the venue for the second time in five years. The extraordinary talents of Sandy Lyle, who had played three rounds of the Open as a 16-year-old school-boy in 1974, finally came to fruition as he grabbed a title nobody seemed to want to win by dint of two birdies over the final five holes. Lyle's victory ended a 16-year barren period for British wins and earned him £65,000, compared with the £4,250 Jacklin won in 1969.

Turnberry got the nod again in 1986 and the way the course was set up showed that the Championship Committee were keen on preventing any repeats of the 1977 low-scoring Watson/Nicklaus spectacular. The Committee needn't really have bothered since the weather did the job pretty effectively. High winds and lashing rain squalls found most of the field struggling in the thick, cloying rough. But no matter what the examination paper, one student always seems to have the answers, and in this case it was Greg Norman, in the midst of his *annus mirabilis*, who, in the second round, nearly scored 100 per cent. Norman fired a 63 in that round to tie the Championship record set by Mark

Hayes in 1977 and Isao Aoki in 1980. Norman could have set a new record but for three-putting the final green but his score gave him a lead he never relinquished.

In 1987 prize-money rose to £650,000, with Nick Faldo receiving £75,000 — not the largest prize in world golf in these inflated times but one which every competitor would give their eye teeth to win, for the title of 'Champion Golfer of the Year' means an elevation to immortality.

THE MASTERS

The United States Masters is the youngest of the four major championships, having been founded in 1934. Despite its youth, the Masters provides a tangible link with the past solely because of the event's creator, Bobby Jones. It was Jones who demonstrated the qualities of sportsmanship coupled with a playing record that has no parallel, and when he retired from competitive golf to build his own course and start his own tournament, American golf was destined to have a classic championship.

Although the Masters is a major championship, the Augusta National Club which stages and organizes it every year does not refer to the event as a Championship but simply as a 'tournament'. That may be regarded as inverted snobbery but it is all part of the Masters' philosophy of running the tightest ship in world golf. For a start, the Masters is not an open tournament. Players qualify through various successes but still have to receive an invitation.

Spectators' tickets are limited and cannot be bought at the gate but are handed down from generation to generation. There is no advertising on the course and no tournament programme. The atmosphere at the Masters is one of genteel Southern hospitality that is fiercely protected by a steely, quiet authority. Above all, the Masters is a week for the players. They play in twos rather than the more general three-balls, the crowds never spill over onto the fairways and the course is prepared to such an extent that even the water in the hazards is dyed blue.

The glories of Augusta are more fully described in the chapter on courses. Suffice to say here, the course's design is such that it has inspired some of the most heroic, breathtaking and stunning finishes in the history of the game. From Horton Smith's win in the first Masters in 1934 to Larry Mize's holed chip in 1987, the tournament has always drawn out something extra from each winner's repertoire of strokes.

The first resounding shot came in 1935 when Gene Sarazen stood in the middle of the par five 15th needing three birdies to tie with Craig Wood. He disposed of that requirement by the simple expedient of hitting his

4-wood second shot straight into the hole for an albatross two. Sarazen won the play-off to become the first professional to win all four of the major titles.

The pattern of dramatic turn-rounds continued over the next two years when, in 1936, Horton Smith made up six strokes on Harry Cooper to win for the second time and, in 1937, Byron Nelson played the 12th and 13th in two, three while the leader, Ralph Guldahl, played them in five, six.

Guldahl finished second again in 1938 to Henry Picard but took the honours in 1939. The Masters continued well into the Second World War with Jimmy Demaret winning in 1940 and Craig Wood making amends for previous disappointments in 1941. Byron Nelson and Ben Hogan tied in 1942 and the play-off produced a scintillating spell of scoring from Nelson, who trailed by three strokes after five holes but then overhauled Hogan to win by one stroke.

The reign of Hogan and Snead

It seemed that Hogan was never to win the Masters for when it resumed in 1946 after a

Opposite: Sandy Lyle, well protected by the Law, on his way to the presentation of the Open trophy at Sandwich in 1985. The precious claret jug is in the hands of Michael Bonallack, the Secretary of the Royal & Ancient.

Above: British wins appeared to be coming thick and fast in the mid-1980s. Nick Faldo, seen putting at Muirfield in 1987, was the second British winner in three years. Faldo had spent three years remodelling his swing, and was most impressive during the last-round pressure.

break due to the war, he three-putted the final green to lose by a stroke to Herman Keiser. But Hogan and also Sam Snead were both too accomplished to be denied the green jacket for much longer. After Demaret joined Smith and Nelson as a double winner in 1947, and Claude Harmon set a new record aggregate of 279 in 1948, it was their turn. Between them, over the next six years, they won five times with only Demaret interrupting the sequence with his third win in 1950. Snead won in 1949, 1952 and 1954, the latter after a play-off with Hogan, while Hogan won in 1951 and 1953.

The 1954 Masters was notable for the excitement created by amateur Billy Joe Patton, who holed in one at the 6th to take the lead on the final day but he came to watery grief at the 13th and finished one stroke out of the play-off.

Amateur representation at the Masters has always been a feature but no amateur has ever won. Following Cary Middlecoff's comfortable seven-stroke win in 1955, it looked like an amateur would win in 1956 as Ken Venturi stood four strokes clear after 54 holes. A combination of nerves and a blustery wind got the better of Venturi, and he stumbled to a last-round 80 as Jack Burke made up an eight-stroke deficit to win. Speedy Doug Ford, a player who often holed out before his partners had even reached the green, whipped in a last round 66 to win in 1957 but the time had now come for the Masters to be hauled into the limelight of one man's charisma.

Palmer takes over

The Augusta pines echoed to the cries of 'Charge!' as Arnold Palmer made it his habit to win and lose the title in alternate years. The broad fairways and tantalizing pin positions eminently suited Palmer's attacking style as he won in 1958, 1960, 1962 and 1964. In between his instincts betrayed him as he lost out to Art Wall in 1959, who fired five birdies in the last six holes for a 66, to Gary Player in 1961, a most memorable collapse when Palmer took six at the final hole from a greenside bunker when a four would have won, and in 1963 when Jack Nicklaus caused further consternation in 'Arnie's Army' by taking the first of his six Masters.

Nicklaus' second win was not far away either for in 1965 he obliterated the field to win by nine strokes from Player and Palmer in a scoring exhibition (67-71-64-69:271) that prompted Bobby Jones to comment that the winner played a game with which Jones was not familiar. Now the joint-holder of the lowest round and also the lowest aggregate, Nicklaus set another record in 1966 by becoming the first player to win in successive years when he defeated Gay Brewer and Tommy Jacobs in a play-off. Brewer's loopy swing did the business properly in 1967 and then came the Masters the Augusta committee would rather forget.

Right: Charles Coody won the Masters in 1971 after having led in 1969, only to collapse and blow his chances with bogeys at the last three holes.

Tragedy for de Vincenzo

Bob Goalby was the winner but the tragedy centred upon Roberto de Vicenzo. Roberto finished his final round with what he thought was a 65 and, mobbed by excited well-wishers, signed his card without really checking it. He failed to notice that his marker, Tommy Aaron, who was to win in 1973, had put down a four on the 17th when the world had witnessed the Argentinian make a birdie three. The higher score had to stand and de Vicenzo's restated 66 left him one stroke behind Goalby. The next year a small tent was erected at the back of the 18th for players to attend to their scorecards in peace.

At 6ft 6in, George Archer became the tallest Masters winner in 1969, to be followed by Billy Casper in 1970, after a play-off with Gene Littler, and Charles Coody in 1971. Nicklaus equalled Palmer's record of four victories in 1972 and Tommy Aaron won in 1973, the year when Britain's Peter Oosterhuis went into a rain-delayed final round with a three-stroke lead but could only manage a 74 to Aaron's closing 68. Gary Player took his second Masters in 1974, a 9-iron second to within inches of the hole on the 71st hole being the decisive stroke.

Now the Masters moved up an extra gear with a series of thrilling finishes. In 1975, Nicklaus was locked in titanic struggle with

Tom Weiskopf and Johnny Miller over the closing holes and it was a putt of 45 feet by Nicklaus on the 16th green which edged him a stroke ahead. Arriving on the final green, Miller and Weiskopf both had putts to tie but missed. It was Weiskopf's fourth runner-up finish.

Nobody could live with Ray Floyd in 1976 as he opened with rounds of 65-66 and ended eight strokes clear in equalling Nicklaus' record aggregate of 271. Tom Watson confronted Nicklaus over the final nine holes in 1977 and withstood the pressure to win by two strokes and then Gary Player wrote another unbelievable chapter in Masters history. Seven strokes behind leader Hubert Green with ten holes to play, Player birdied seven of those holes for a round of 64 to set a target only Green could match. On the final hole Green faced a putt of around three feet to tie but missed to make the diminutive South African Gary Player the oldest winner at that time.

More drama occurred in 1979 when Ed Sneed squandered a three-stroke lead with three holes left to play to end in a tie with Tom Watson and Fuzzy Zoeller. It was the first sudden-death play-off and, much to his own surprise, Zoeller won it on the second extra hole to become the first to win, apart from the inaugural winner Horton Smith, at his first attempt.

Ballesteros proves his worth

Following his victory in the 1979 Open, Severiano Ballesteros had been branded a slasher by the Americans, but exhibiting a controlled and fluid swing he laid waste to Augusta in 1980 to establish a ten-stroke lead with just nine holes to play. He stumbled on the homeward run to see that lead evaporate to two strokes but pulled himself together to become the second overseas player to win after Player, the first European winner and, at 23, the youngest. After Tom Watson and Craig Stadler won in 1981 and 1982, Ballesteros secured his second green jacket in 1983. The Spaniard trailed by one stroke at the start of the final round but an eagle and two birdies in the first four holes put the rest of the field to flight. Frequently a runner-up in major championships, Ben Crenshaw putted quite beautifully in 1984 to win by two strokes from Tom Watson.

European golf was given further impetus in 1985 when West Germany's Bernhard Langer took advantage of some costly errors from Curtis Strange over the last nine holes to win. Strange had opened with an 80 but followed that with rounds of 65 and 68 to stand on the threshold of the greatest recovery in history. He found water on the 13th and 15th to allow Langer a chance which he took with a decisive birdie putt on the 17th. Ballesteros finished second.

Above: A feature of the Masters is the presentation of the Champion's green jacket (it always fits, whoever wins) by the Champion of the year before. Seve Ballesteros, a multiple winner, gets helped into his first jacket by Fuzzy Zoeller in 1980.

Old Nicklaus returns

As long as golf is played, the events of the 1986 Masters will be remembered. American golf was smarting from the loss of the Ryder Cup and the fact that Sandy Lyle had won the Open and Langer was defending Masters champion. It needed a new hero. Instead it had to fall back on an old one as Jack Nicklaus came through with a final round of 65 to hold off the challenges of Greg Norman and Ballesteros. Ballesteros looked a likely winner when he eagled the 13th with a searing second shot to the green but he struck an un-characteristically awful second shot to the 15th into the water and his challenge was sunk. Norman needed a par four at the final hole to tie but put his second into the crowd on the right to finish in second place, along with perennial Masters runner-up Tom Kite, who missed a shortish birdie putt also to tie. The victory made Nicklaus, at 46, the oldest winner and his sixth Masters gave him a total of 20 major championships, including two US Amateur titles.

In the modern game there has never been a player like Nicklaus and it is entirely appropriate that his latest major title — one hesitates to say his last — should occur at the shrine of Bobby Jones, indisputably the greatest player of a previous era.

So the Masters provides a standard of excellence that is rarely matched anywhere else in the world. For golfers everywhere, the Masters heralds the start of a new season and as long as the azaleas and dogwoods continue to bloom round Augusta National, that feeling of anticipation will remain.

Right: Ballesteros and Bernhard Langer shake hands on the 72nd hole of the 1985 Masters, won by Langer. These are the only two Europeans so far to win the Masters.

Far right: The beauty of the Augusta course is well shown in this photograph from the Masters of 1987. The hole is the 11th in the play-off, where winner Larry Mize (right) chipped in and defeated Greg Norman, seen walking off the green.

US OPEN

Golf was still in its infancy in America when the first United States Open Championship was staged in 1894 and as the American Amateur had been held a year earlier as a match-play event, the US Open followed suit and was also a match-play tournament. It was won by Willie Dunn by two holes over W. Campbell at St Andrews, New York.

The Championship became stroke-play the following year and it is generally acknowledged that the winner, Horace Rawlins, was the first US Open champion. It was played over the nine-hole course at Newport, Rhode Island, and Rawlins, a British emigrant, set the pattern for a series of victories by other British-born players.

It was not until 1900, however, that the title was won by a player coming from overseas and he was Harry Vardon, who won by two strokes from J.H. Taylor at Wheaton, Chicago. Vardon and Taylor were engaged on a year-long tour of America at the time, spreading the gospel of golf to an enthusiastic public. Four of the next five years were the preserve of Willie Anderson, another Scottish-born resident, and his hat-trick of victories (1903–05) has never been matched, although Bobby Jones, Ben Hogan and Jack Nicklaus joined Anderson with four wins apiece.

Still the Scots dominated as Alex Smith, brother of the luckless Macdonald Smith, won twice in 1906 and 1910, but in 1911 America had its first home-bred winner when Johnny McDermott won at Wheaton and then repeated the next year at Buffalo.

Ouimet beats the British

The shock waves of the next Championship are still reverberating round the world. The Country Club at Brookline, Massachusetts, saw Vardon and Ted Ray looking set to take the title back to Britain again as they tied for first place. They were joined, however, by a young amateur, Francis Ouimet, and in the biggest upset in the game at that time, Ouimet beat them both in the play-off and the graph

Above right: Bobby Jones playing out of a bunker. His total of four victories in the US Open in the 1920s was not equalled until Ben Hogan scored his fourth win in 1953.

Right: Five former winners of the US Open are in this 1929 photograph. They are Walter Hagen (1914 and 1919), Jim Barnes (1921) and Ted Ray (1920), who are respectively second, third and fourth from the left in the front row, and Harry Vardon (1900), who is on the left in the back row, and Fred Herd (1898), who is third from left in the back row.

of American golf was set for its continuing upward path.

Home players took up the reins with Walter Hagen winning in 1914 and 1919 and amateurs Jerome Travers and Charles Evans taking the two titles prior to the suspension of the Championship for the First World War. The 1920 Championship was significant not so much for the victory by Ray, the last Englishman to win until Tony Jacklin in 1970, but for the first appearance of the 18-year-old Georgia prodigy, Bobby Jones. Jones finished eighth that year at Inverness, Ohio, which was the first club to open its doors to professionals, a gesture which prompted Hagen to make a collection to present a grandfather clock which now stands in the main lobby bearing the message:

> God measures men by what they are
> Not what they in wealth possess
> This vibrant message chimes afar
> The voice of Inverness.

Bobby Jones' long run

The first of Jones' four victories did not come until two years later as Jim Barnes and Gene Sarazen interceded. After his initial win in 1923, he never finished lower than second in seven attempts with the wins coming in 1926, 1929 and 1930 — a record of staggering consistency. His final and most important win came at Interlachen when he made three birdies in the last five holes to edge home by a stroke and complete the third leg of his 'Impregnable Quadrilateral'.

By 1931 the prize fund had risen to over $2,000 and that year's Championship at Inverness produced a unique play-off marathon between Billy Burke and George von Elm. Tied after 72 holes, they were still locked after 36 more and had to play yet another 36 before Burke ended a stroke in front. Flushing Meadow, New York, was the site of a remarkable spell of scoring in 1932 by Gene Sarazen, who came from seven strokes behind in playing the last 28 holes in exactly 100 strokes — made up of a two at the ninth in the third round, a 32 home and a final 66. It made Sarazen the second man after Jones to win two Opens in one year and his aggregate of 286 tied the record set by Evans in 1916.

Jones having departed the scene in 1930, amateurs were becoming less of a force and Johnny Goodman's victory in 1933 remains the last time an amateur triumphed. Olin Dutra, Tony Manero and Ralph Guldahl (twice) won over the next four years with Guldahl's victory in 1937 setting a new 72-hole record of 281.

The most quoted fact about Sam Snead is that he was the best player never to win the US Open but this should not detract from his status as one of the great figures in the game. Nonetheless, he never did win the title and his performance on the last hole at Spring Mill, Philadelphia, in 1939 was enough to scar a man for life. Standing on the last tee, Snead

needed a par five to win although he thought he needed a birdie four. Gambling on hitting the green with his second shot he instead found a plugged lie in a bunker and on reaching the green in five shots, three-putted for an eight. It was one of the most notorious collapses in golf and Snead did not even get into the play-off between Byron Nelson, Craig Wood and Densmore Shute which Nelson won for his sole US Open title.

Lawson Little and Craig Wood completed the list of winners prior to the Second World War. On the Championship's return in 1946 at Canterbury, Ohio, the prize-money had climbed to $8,000. Lloyd Mangrum, a veteran of the Normandy landings and winner of the Purple Heart, outlasted Nelson and Vic Ghezzi in the play-off to take the first prize of $1,500. Snead was unfortunate in 1947 when he tied with Lew Worsham at St Louis, Missouri. On the final green the two were still tied and both balls lay almost equidistant from the hole. Snead was about to putt from around three feet when Worsham stepped forward to query whether it was in fact Snead's turn to play. It transpired that it was, but Snead, disturbed by the interruption, missed and Worsham holed.

Above: Julius Boros won the US Open in 1952 and again in 1963, when he beat Jacky Cupit and Arnold Palmer in a play-off.

Above: Typical Arnold Palmer. A swash-buckling shot moves the gallery to cheers. Palmer's US Open record was strange — he came from way behind to win at Cherry Hills in 1960, but thereafter lost three times in play-offs.

Ben Hogan takes over

Ben Hogan won the first of his four titles at Riviera, Los Angeles, in 1948, smashing the Championship record in the process with a score of 276, but he was unable to defend in 1949 because of his horrific car accident. Cary Middlecoff stepped into the breach with Snead once again second. Hogan returned in 1950 and, hardly able to walk due to his extensive injuries, hauled himself round Merion to tie with Mangrum and George Fazio, his 2-iron second to the final hole of the 72 becoming part of the game's legend. Hogan won the play-off.

The legend continued in 1951 at Oakland Hills when Hogan destroyed one of the toughest courses in the Championship's history with a final round of 67. The course had been specifically made harder by amendments from architect Robert Trent Jones and the players decried it to a man. At the end of his final round, Hogan, not noted for his quotability, made the memorable comment: 'I'm glad I brought this course, this monster, to its knees.'

Julius Boros interrupted the Hogan sequence in 1952 but the little man from Texas had no peers in 1953 as he won at Oakmont to make it three major titles for the year. Following Ed Furgol's win at Baltusrol in 1954, the question on everybody's lips was could Hogan capture a record fifth US Open at Olympic, San Francisco? It seemed he could when he finished the 72 holes with only the unknown Jack Fleck still on the course with a chance. Unperturbed by the moment, Fleck coolly holed a putt of seven feet on the final green to tie. The legacy of his accident

was taking its toll on Hogan's legs and although he stood only one stroke behind on the 18th tee of the play-off, his foot slipped on the drive and his ball finished deep in the rough. Hogan finished with a flourish by holing a long putt for a six but Fleck had won the day.

That, however, was not to be Hogan's last challenge for the title as five years later in 1960 at Cherry Hills he was very much in the hunt and only a flirtation with water on the 71st hole kept him out. This Championship marked the dawning of another era for the preceding four winners, Cary Middlecoff (1956), Dick Mayer (1957), Tommy Bolt (1958) and Billy Casper (1959), never captured the imagination in the same way as the 1960 champion.

Arnie builds his army

Arnold Palmer never did things by halves. His swashbuckling swing with the whiplash follow-through sometimes put the ball in no man's land but his powers of recovery were astonishing and this approach won the hearts of the nation. Starting that fateful last round at Cherry Hills, Palmer lay seven strokes off the pace but then proceeded to birdie six of the first seven holes for an outward 30 and an eventual round of 65. It gave him victory by two strokes over a talented amateur named Jack Nicklaus. Over the next six years, Palmer challenged three more times for the title but each time lost a play-off. Gene Littler won in 1961 and then Nicklaus tied with Palmer at Oakmont in 1962 and the younger man won. In a rugged Championship at The Country Club in 1963, Palmer again tied, this time with Boros and Jackie Cupit, but lost to Boros and in 1966 he suffered a crashing defeat at the hands of Billy Casper, having led by seven strokes with nine holes to play at Olympic.

In between these traumas occurred one of the most emotional victories in the game as Ken Venturi finally won a major title that had so often been denied him. He had twice lost the Masters, once as an amateur in 1956 when he crumbled in the last round, and again in 1960 when Palmer birdied two of the final three holes to pip him. Wilting in the oppressive heat of Congressional, Washington, Venturi fired a third-round 66 and then staggered to a 70 to win by four strokes.

The 1965 Championship was held over the longest ever course, Bellerive in Missouri, and it resulted in victory for perhaps the smallest of champions, Gary Player, who defeated Kel Nagle in a play-off. Player thus became the third man after Sarazen and Hogan to win all four of the big ones and he donated $25,000 from his prize of $26,000 to cancer research and the development of junior golf.

Jack Nicklaus won at Baltusrol in 1967, firing a last round of 65 to beat Palmer by four strokes and lower the record aggregate to 275 as an unknown Mexican-American,

Lee Trevino, finished fifth. He wasn't unknown after the next Championship at Oak Hill as he became the first man to break 70 in all four rounds with a swing which made the purists shudder. Trevino's victory was followed by another shock winner in the shape of Orville Moody, a part-Indian who won at Champions, Texas.

Jacklin's easy win

Tony Jacklin gave a tremendous fillip to British golf with his seven-stroke victory at Hazeltine in 1970. The course was extremely long and weather conditions poor, but Jacklin thrived as his opponents complained about the course, with runner-up Dave Hill likening it to a cow pasture, a remark which

Below: Ray Floyd with the trophy and his daughter after his victory at Shinnecock Hills in 1987.

Above: A huge crowd round the 18th green to watch Seve Ballesteros putting in the 1987 Open at the Olympic Club course in California. The winner was the comparatively 'unknown' Scott Simpson.

cost him a heavy fine. Trevino defeated Nicklaus in a play-off at Merion in 1971 but the great man was not to be denied at Pebble Beach a year later as he took his third title in ten years.

Johnny Miller's amazing last round of 63 in 1973 at Oakmont lowered the individual round record as he erupted from nowhere to win, but scoring at Winged Foot a year later was considerably higher as the USGA pursued its policy of letting the rough grow right up to the edges of the greens. Hale Irwin's aggregate winning score of 287 was seven over par. Lou Graham and John Mahaffey competed the 25th tie in history at Medinah in 1975 which Graham won and in 1976, Mahaffey was again robbed of the title by Jerry Pate's magnificent 5-iron shot to the final hole of the Atlanta Country Club, Georgia, which finished a few feet from the hole.

Hubert Green won at Southern Hills, Oklahoma, in 1977 playing the last few holes with an armed guard, following a telephoned threat on his life, and in 1978 Andy North bravely holed a putt of four feet on the last green at Cherry Hills to win. Hale Irwin captured his second title at Inverness in 1979 as prize money rose to $300,000 and then it was the turn of that man again. All sorts of records fell to Jack Nicklaus at Baltusrol in 1980, including a Championship record-equalling 63 in the first round, the lowest

36-hole and 54-hole totals as well as a new record aggregate of 272. His four titles tied the records of Willie Anderson, Bobby Jones and Ben Hogan and the 18 years between his first and last victories was the longest winning span.

The perfection of David Graham's winning last round of 67 at Merion in 1981 has never been matched as the Australian did not miss a fairway or a green in regulation figures while in 1982, Tom Watson attained his own personal state of nirvana in winning at Pebble Beach by chipping in for a birdie at the 17th and birdieing the last hole to win by two strokes from Nicklaus. Watson was at his zenith and should have won at Oakmont in 1983. Play had been suspended overnight during the final round with four holes left for Watson and three for his closest challenger, Larry Nelson. Nelson resumed on the par three 16th and hit his first shot 65 feet from the hole. Incredibly, with his second shot of the day, he holed the putt to give him the vital edge over Watson.

Fuzzy gives in but wins

The carefree attitude of Fuzzy Zoeller belied a steely interior as he and Greg Norman fought out an epic duel at Winged Foot in 1984. Norman, playing just ahead of Zoeller, holed a monstrous putt on the final green which Zoeller, standing in the middle of the 18th fairway, thought was for a birdie three.

tough but this is unlikely to change, for the aim is to examine every aspect of a player's game to the fullest extent. While there have been a few 'streaky' winners of the US Open, generally the race has gone to the most competent and for a national Open, that is how it should be.

US PGA CHAMPIONSHIP

The last of the four major championships making up the modern Grand Slam, the United States Professional Golfers' Association Championship is younger than the Open Championship and the US Open but older than the Masters. It was first staged in 1916, the year the American PGA was formed, which makes it the second oldest tournament on the US Tour behind the Western Open which began in 1899.

The PGA's standing in world golf was certainly greater in the days when it was a match-play event, which made it unique among the four championships. The vagaries of match-play, which are in fact its very essence, are not popular with modern professionals who are weaned on an exclusive diet of stroke-play, and the demands of television have made the 18-hole sprint an unsaleable item. Thus it was that in 1958 the PGA succumbed to these pressures and abandoned the match-play format.

In its match-play years, the PGA produced many exciting finishes and was the perfect arena for the recovery skills of Walter Hagen. He became the first American-born winner in 1921 as Jim Barnes (1916 and 1919) and Jock Hutchison (1920) were both British-born immigrants. Hagen was the supreme match player whose devastating ability to roll three shots into two broke the hearts of his opponents. His first victory was followed by two in a row from Gene Sarazen, the latter in 1923 coming after an epic final with Hagen at Pelham, New York, which went to 38 holes, but after that Hagen was invincible for the next four years. His run of 22 victorious matches came to an end in 1928 when he was defeated by the eventual winner, Leo Diegel, in the third round. In typical Hagen fashion, he said he had mislaid the trophy in a taxi but it was eventually recovered and Diegel put his name on it a second time in 1929.

Tommy Armour, Tom Creavy and Olin Dutra took the next three titles with the last producing one of the most amazing turnrounds in the history of championship golf when, in an early round, Al Watrous stood nine up on Bobby Cruickshank, all matches being played over 36 holes. Watrous then conceded a putt to Cruickshank which, if missed, would have put Watrous 10 up with 12 holes remaining. Cruickshank started nibbling away at the lead and squared the match

In a memorable gesture, Zoeller waved a white towel in mock surrender but Norman's putt was only for a par four and moments later, Zoeller matched Norman's total and went on to win the play-off comfortably.

The amazing thing about Andy North's victory in 1985 at Oakland Hills was that it was only the third professional victory of his career, two of which were US Opens. For some time it looked as though the title would be won by an Asian player, T.C. Chen, who led the field by four strokes going into the final round. Chen suffered the unusual penalty of hitting the ball twice while chipping from thick rough on the fifth hole in the final round and North stepped in.

The Championship returned to its roots in 1986 when it was staged at Shinnecock Hills, site of the second US Open in 1896. Rough and blustery weather swept the course, which is the nearest to a links-type lay-out in America, but Ray Floyd played cannily to win and bring his total of major titles to four (US Open, US Masters and two US PGA Championships) and leave him on the threshold of being the fifth man to win all four majors as he just needs the Open Championship to complete the set.

Prize money for the Championship now stands at over $700,000 and, for an American player, it represents the ultimate victory. The USGA has faced a constant barrage of criticism for setting up the courses to be too with a long putt on the 36th green. He then defeated poor Watrous at the 41st.

Sarazen took his third title in 1933, and in 1934 Craig Wood completed his double of extra hole defeats when he lost to Paul Runyan at the 38th hole. The sand-wedge specialist Johnny Revolta won in 1935 and then Densmore Shute became the last man to win two in a row. The 1938 final was billed as being no contest as the diminutive Runyan took on the power of Sam Snead. It was no contest as Runyan, with some dazzling short game expertise, demolished Snead by 8 and 7.

Byron Nelson lost the 1939 final to Henry Picard but made amends the following year by defeating Snead 1 up. Nelson made five final appearances in the space of six stagings of the Championships, losing to Vic Ghezzi in the 1941 final, missing out in 1942 when Sam Snead won the first of his three PGAs, losing again in 1944 to Bob Hamilton and winning for a second time in 1945, the year he won 18 tournaments, 11 of them consecutively.

Ben Hogan took his first major title in 1946 with a typical destruction job on Ed Oliver by 6 and 4 and after Jim Ferrier won in 1947, Hogan was just as ruthless in 1948 when he beat Mike Turnesa by 7 and 6. Snead added two more in 1949 and 1951 with Chandler Harper intervening in 1950 but as the big names now ceased to last through to the final, the Championship was poised to change to stroke-play. In 1953, for example, six former champions were beaten in the first two rounds and with Hogan absent through Open Championship duty at Carnoustie, the writing was on the wall.

The switch to stroke-play

Lionel Hebert won the last match-play PGA, defeating Dow Finsterwald in the final, but by a strange quirk of fate Finsterwald came back the next year to win the first PGA at

Right: *Lee Trevino gives the US PGA trophy a kiss in 1984. Trevino had won ten years earlier, but to the man he beat into second place, Gary Player, he was a mere youngster, Player having won over 20 years earlier.*

stroke-play. Victories by Bob Rosburg, Jay Hebert, brother of Lionel, and Jerry Barber followed, and then came the first win by a foreigner, Gary Player in 1962. Jack Nicklaus added his second major title of the year in 1963, having previously won the Masters, but the other member of the Big Three, Arnold Palmer, was to find that the PGA would become that unwanted statistic put against his name as being the best player never to win it. In 1964, Palmer broke 70 in every round at Columbus, Ohio, but still had to give best to Bobby Nichols, whose aggregate of 271 is still the record. Dave Marr had the effrontery to win in Palmer's backyard of Laurel Valley, Pennsylvania, in 1965 and he was followed by Al Geiberger in 1966 and Don January in 1967. At 48, Julius Boros became the oldest winner when he won at Pecan Valley, Texas, in 1968 with Palmer second again and then Ray Floyd won at Dayton, Ohio, from Gary Player in an unpleasant atmosphere marred by anti-apartheid demonstrations against Player. Palmer was second for the third time when Dave Stockton won in 1970 at Southern Hills, this Championship marking a return to US Open courses as venues.

The 1971 Championship was held in February instead of its usual August date and was marked by Jack Nicklaus' second win which gave him a second complete set of the four major championships, his third collection coming after his Open Championship victory at St Andrews in 1978. Gary Player won in 1972 at Oakland Hills, Michigan, another US Open course, and this win was highlighted by a 9-iron shot Player hit over trees and water to the 16th green which finished stone dead. The Nicklaus juggernaut continued to roll over the opposition, and his third PGA title in 1973 enabled him to pass Bobby Jones' record of 13 majors. Nicklaus was second to Lee Trevino in 1974 but was on

Left: Hubert Green at Cherry Hills in 1985 had to withstand a challenge from holder Lee Trevino but held on to win a much-deserved major.

top again in 1975, while Stockton repeated his win of 1970 with another in 1976, this time at Congressional, Washington.

The elegant swing and courageous spirit of Gene Littler, who had fought back from cancer, looked as though it would receive its just reward when he led by five strokes with nine holes to play at Pebble Beach in 1977 but a series of slips allowed Lanny Wadkins to catch him and it was Wadkins who won the play-off. Justice was done in 1978 at Oakmont when John Mahaffey tied with Jerry Pate and Tom Watson. Pate had snatched the US Open from Mahaffey in 1976 but this time it was Pate who could feel aggrieved as he missed a short putt on the 72nd green to fall into the tie and Mahaffey birdied the second extra hole to win.

Nicklaus' long-playing record

Australia's David Graham became the second foreign winner after Player when he beat Ben Crenshaw in a play-off at Oakland Hills in 1979, and then Nicklaus again rewrote the record books. His seven-stroke victory at Oak Hill in 1980 was the largest ever winning margin and he also equalled Hagen's record of five PGA titles.

Larry Nelson won his first major title at the Atlanta Athletic Club, Georgia, in 1981 and Ray Floyd took his second PGA at Southern Hills in 1982, his opening round of 63 tieing the lowest round in Championship history. In only his second year as a professional, Hal Sutton, nicknamed the 'Bear Apparent' because of his blond similarity to Nicklaus, held off Nicklaus himself at Riviera for his first major championship. The evergreen Lee Trevino repelled the challenge of another ageless wonder, Gary Player, in winning at Shoal Creek, Alabama, in 1984, ten years after his first PGA victory, and Trevino challenged again in 1985 at Cherry Hills but had to give best to Hubert Green.

The 1986 Championship found Greg Nor-

Right: A happy family group of Tammie and Bob Tway with the US PGA trophy in 1986. Tway should be extremely happy, as he 'robbed' Greg Norman by holing from a bunker at the last.

Opposite above: Match-play maestro Gary Player offers thanks to the sky after sinking a long putt to win the World Match Play Championship in 1968. Beaten finalist Bob Charles returned to win the following year.

Opposite below: Jack Nicklaus appears none too happy with his lie or the ruling he is receiving from Colonel Duncan, the referee. Nicklaus managed only one World Match Play title, in 1970.

man in his usual place at the head of the field after three rounds, this time four strokes ahead of Bob Tway at Inverness. Norman was still four ahead with nine to play, but Tway drew level and at the final hole dramatically holed out from a greenside bunker for a birdie which Norman couldn't match.

WORLD MATCH PLAY

'Match-play's the thing,' said Freddie Tait, British Amateur champion in 1896 and 1898, 'stroke-play's so much rifle-shooting.' Most amateur golfers will understand Tait's sentiments since match-play is the form of golf which is most popular at their level. On the other hand, professional golfers spend the greatest part of their careers engaged in the rifle-shooting of stroke-play and regard match-play with the highest suspicion. The fact that a player can go round in 68 and lose while another can produce a 75 and win is unacceptable to the modern money-making machines, while the awful finality of defeat leaves no room for excuses.

What makes match-play such a compelling form of golf is that its art lies as much in knowing when to go for the flag as when not to go for it, in being able to strike the telling shot at the right time and being able to cope with the sheer physical presence of an opponent. The issue is further complicated by the fact that as well as being able to see what your opponent is doing, you can also hear what he is saying to you. It is at this point that we enter the darker realms of psychology and its bearing on the outcome of a match. There is no doubt that the mind controls the destiny of a golfer and it is in match-play that this most delicately balanced organism is at its most vulnerable.

Fortunately for golf and the professional game in particular, there is one match-play event which has resisted the stroke-play trend and stands as one of the classic championships of the world. The World Match Play Championship, now under the aegis of Suntory but still often referred to by long-term devotees as the Piccadilly has, since its inception in 1964, created an atmosphere which puts it on the fringe of major championship status. Maybe the taint of commercial sponsorship has prevented it from being acknowledged as the fifth major, but just as April means the Masters and July the Open Championship, so it is that October means the Match Play at Wentworth. The permanency of the venue is an integral part of the tournament's success, but it is the history of blood and guts encounters which have sustained its appeal.

The original concept was to bring together the eight best players of the year and pit them

against one another over 36 holes. The field for that first Championship contained the charismatic figure of Arnold Palmer, the current US Masters champion, Tony Lema, the Open champion, Gary Player, Jack Nicklaus, Ken Venturi, the US Open champion, and Bruce Devlin, with Peter Butler and Neil Coles providing the British interest. The event was given a rousing start when Palmer beat off the stubborn resistance of Coles in the final, eventually holing a birdie putt on the 35th green to win by 2 and 1.

The Player v Lema match

Just as Gene Sarazen launched the US Masters in its second staging with his albatross two on the 15th, so the semi-final match of 1965 between Gary Player and Tony Lema put the Match Play in the forefront of golfing legend. The events of that match have virtually been carved in tablets of stone and it is sufficient to say that there has never been a match like it. Player was the current US Open champion, intense and brooding, a man on a permanent mission to prove that nothing was impossible. Lema was still at the height of the considerable powers that had won the Open the year before, languid, debonair and sophisticated with a Latin air of indolence, a

latter-day Hagen whose liking for the good things in life was exemplified by his nickname 'Champagne Tony'. Certainly the bubbles were getting right up Player's nose in the morning as Lema cruised round in an effortless 67 to lunch six up. He went seven up at the first hole of the afternoon and that, to all intents and purposes, was that. As the crowd drifted away, only one man believed that there was any hope and Gary Player began to put that belief into practice. He was still five down with nine holes left but only three down with seven remaining. He was two down after 13 and then only one down with two to play. Player holed a nasty putt of five feet on the 35th hole to stay in the match and then, on the 36th, after Lema had hooked his second shot to this par five in the classic reflex action of a man in acute distress, Player hit the shot that seemed to be guided by some unseen hand. Launching himself into his second shot with a 4-wood, Player sent the ball perilously close to the trees on the right but it travelled through the branches unscathed and rolled up onto the green to within ten feet of the hole for a winning birdie. Lema was completely shattered and had no answer to Player's solid par four at the 37th. Victory over Peter Thomson in the final was something of an anti-climax but it gave the South African the first of five victories in the event, the last coming in 1973 in another cliff-hanger when he defeated Graham Marsh at the 40th hole of the final.

Player successfully defended the title in 1966, defeating Arnold Palmer in the semi-finals and Jack Nicklaus in the final. This was the match which included the famous signboard incident on the 9th hole when Nicklaus was refused relief from an advertising hoarding on his line by the referee, Tony Duncan. There was no relief for Nicklaus from Player's onslaught as the little man outgunned his opponent by 6 and 4.

It was Palmer's turn again in 1967 when he had the satisfaction of beating Peter Thomson on the final green. The two were not exactly bosom pals, largely due to Thomson's condemnation of the large American ball and all its works, but the final engendered mutual respect between the two with Thomson conceding that he was beaten by a better man.

The Player/Palmer monopoly continued in 1968 with Player gaining his third victory, beating Bob Charles in the final by one hole. Charles was not to be denied in 1969 when, with a magical display of putting, he beat Gene Littler on the 37th hole of the final, having holed from 25 feet on the final green to save the match.

Nicklaus finally captured the title in 1970 after a splendid final with Lee Trevino and then reached the final again in 1971 where he faced his old nemesis, Player. Nicklaus was one up at lunch but there was no holding Player in the afternoon and he romped home by 5 and 4.

Below: Bill Rogers driving off the tee in the 1979 World Match Play. Rogers came to Britain to win the Match Play in 1979 and the Open in 1981, but seemed to lose a little enthusiasm for the game as the 1980s progressed.

Trevino beats Jacklin again

The following year is remembered not so much for Tom Weiskopf's victory over Trevino but more for the magnificent semifinal between Trevino and Tony Jacklin. Having suffered cruelly at the hands of the American in that year's Open Championship at Muirfield, Jacklin was determined not to let Trevino's constant chatter get to him and made his intentions plain by saying he was not going to talk.

'You don't have to talk, Tony,' said Trevino, 'just listen.'

After the morning round Jacklin was listening to a four-hole deficit, but he came out in the afternoon like a lion. He quelled Trevino's ebullience with an outward 29, but still the American kept his nose in front and finally sealed victory with a beautifully fashioned second shot to the final green which made Jacklin's round of 63 a statistical irrelevance.

The events of 1973 have already been touched upon but it is worth mentioning that the Player/Marsh final was not without its moments of needle, particularly when Player accused Marsh of teeing off in front of the markers on the 35th tee. Player's penchant for diverting his opponents' intentions is almost as much a feature of the tournament history as his victories. His behaviour in 1968 in the semi-final against Jacklin when, on the 37th green and with Jacklin facing a testing short putt to stay in the match, he suddenly turned to remonstrate with the crowd, was straight out of Stephen Potter.

Player received his come-uppance in 1974 when he lost his first final at the accomplished hands of Hale Irwin, who proved how tough he was by winning again in 1975 and reaching the final in 1976. This time toughness was no match for the man with a golden putter and David Graham's recovery over the last nine holes left spectators openmouthed in disbelief and, needless to say, Irwin wasn't too impressed either. Putt after putt from Graham dived into the hole, except one on the 35th which just toppled in to keep the Australian in the match, and after that there was no question who would hole on the 37th green for the title.

That was the last year of Piccadilly's sponsorship and the tournament was taken over by the vast Colgate conglomerate with the field being expanded to 16 players and seedings introduced. It was an unhappy transition as the next two years produced little that was memorable in terms of drama but did see Marsh extract some revenge for 1973 with a well-deserved victory in 1977, and Isao Aoki become the first Japanese victor the following year.

The Greg and Seve show

During Suntory's stewardship the Championship has recaptured some of its former glory with the first four Suntory finals going to the 36th hole or beyond. Bill Rogers remains the only American winner in an eightyear spell. With a magnificent pitch to the last green he defeated Aoki in 1979. Since then the title has been the exclusive property of two men, Severiano Ballesteros and Greg Norman.

Norman beat Sandy Lyle in 1980 by one hole: Ballesteros beat Ben Crenshaw in 1981 by one hole and then repeated the trick by holing a monstrous putt across the 37th green to oust the unfortunate Lyle. It was Norman's turn again in 1983 when he beat Nick Faldo in the final by 3 and 2. This was the year of the unfortunate incident when, in an earlier round, Faldo was playing Graham Marsh and struck his second shot through the back of the 16th green. After a lapse of a second or two, the ball reappeared from the crowd onto the green, and since it was ascertained that the ball had not come to rest but had been deflected while still in motion, Faldo was allowed to play it where it finished.

Ballesteros took his total of victories to four in the next two years by beating Bernhard Langer in the finals of 1984 and 1985 and although Lyle made his third appearance in a final in 1986, he succumbed again to Norman.

This Championship marked the return to Wentworth of Jack Nicklaus after a prolonged absence. He dealt with the precocious talents of Jose-Maria Olazabal in his first match but lost an absorbing semi-final to

Below: Sandy Lyle (right) congratulating Greg Norman after the 1980 final, which Norman won by one hole after a terrific struggle had gone to the 36th. Around this time it was unusual for the final to reach the last green.

Above: Greg Norman met one of his heroes, Jack Nicklaus, in the semi-final in 1986, and clearly decided at one stage to lay down and die. However, the Great White Shark eventually got up to beat the Golden Bear by one hole, and he went on to win the final, too.

Greg Norman by one hole. All paled, however, in the light of the second-round match between Lyle and Japan's Tsuneyuki Nakajima in which both players produced rounds of 65-64 to set a new scoring record for the event. It was Lyle who won a match neither really deserved to lose at the 38th.

So the tradition of blood and guts encounters has been maintained with superlative golf from one player sparking off a similar response from his opponent. By comparison, the weekly stroke-play grind is tame stuff. Indeed, match-play's the thing and the World Match Play is the best thing about it.

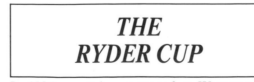

THE RYDER CUP

In 1926 a match was staged at Wentworth, Surrey, between a team of touring American professionals and their British and Irish counterparts. The result was a resounding victory for the home side by 13½ matches to 1½ and it had a profound effect on one man. Samuel Ryder, a St Albans seed merchant, had taken up golf in later life and had even engaged Abe Mitchell, one of the great professional figures of the day, as his private professional. Ryder was so impressed by that victory at Wentworth he decided to present a cup for competition between the professionals of both countries to be played for on a home and away basis every other year. The trophy, when it emerged, was an elegant gold cup with the small figure of a golfer, based on Mitchell himself, adorning the lid.

The first official Ryder Cup match took place in 1927 in Worcester, Massachusetts, and the British had to leave the trophy with their hosts as they went down by 9½ matches to 2½, the match consisting of four foursomes and eight singles, a format which was to remain until 1961.

sent a strong team over to Southport & Ainsdale in 1937 and triumphed there by 8–4, the only home winners in the singles being Cotton and Daì Rees, the latter making an impressive debut by halving his foursome and defeating Byron Nelson in the singles. Cotton took his revenge by winning the Open Championship shortly afterwards with the full American team in the field.

The 1939 match did not take place, and following six years of war with no competitive golf the British were hardly in any condition to provide proper opposition when they travelled to Portland, Oregon, in 1947. The fact they went at all was made possible only by the generosity of Robert Hudson, a Portland businessman who financed the trip. His philanthropy was not matched by the American team who handed out the worst defeat in the history of the Ryder Cup, winning by 11 matches to one with only Sam King of Britain preventing a whitewash by winning his single.

Following that débâcle, the British reassembled at Ganton, Yorkshire, in 1949 with their team in much better order. On the evening before the match began, Ben Hogan, the American captain, created controversy by asking for an inspection of the British players' clubs, and several players had to file the faces of their irons. Whether this was a psychological tactic on the part of Hogan or not, the effect was to stir the British to take a 3–1 lead after the foursomes and Hogan, who was unable to play himself as he was recovering from the road accident earlier in the year which had almost cost him his life, gave his team a severe dressing-down. It obviously worked, for in the singles the Americans mounted a strong counterattack and with some devastating golf won six of them to win by two points.

Below: Most gardeners in Great Britain are familiar with the plant seed catalogue issued every year by the Ryders seed company, but few would associate the seeds with the foremost international golf trophy. But Samuel Ryder was the man responsible for the seeds and the Cup, which was first contested in 1927.

The scores were levelled when the Americans came to Moortown, Leeds, in 1929 and the British won 7–5 with Henry Cotton making his debut and winning both his games. The pattern of home victories was maintained over the next two encounters with the Americans winning at Scioto, Ohio, in 1931 and the British winning at Southport & Ainsdale in 1933. This latter match, however, was a desperately close thing as the outcome depended on the final singles game between Densmore Shute of America and Syd Easterbrook of Britain. Vast crowds swarmed across the course, many people attending in order to catch a glimpse of the Prince of Wales (later Edward VIII) and they all held their breath as Easterbrook holed a nasty, curling short putt on the final green to give Britain victory by 6½–5½.

It was to be the last British win for 24 years as the Americans embarked on a run of successes both home and away. They won at Ridgewood, New Jersey, in 1935 and then

Top: The American Ryder Cup on arrival in Great Britain in April 1929. The famous Walter Hagen is crouching second from the right in the front row. This was the first Ryder Cup contested in Great Britain, and at the time the home country was in the habit of winning.

Above: Tony Lema in blue follows the flight of Neil Coles' drive on the 1965 four-ball foursomes at Royal Birkdale. This was a period of US domination.

Alliss and Hunt slip up at the last

The 1951 match at Pinehurst produced another predictable American victory by the comfortable margin of 9½–2½ and then came the dramatic encounter at Wentworth in 1953. The British lost the foursomes 3–1 but rallied in the singles. Sam Snead was four up on Harry Weetman with six holes to play but then collapsed in a welter of rash strokes to allow Weetman to gain a valuable point for Britain and suddenly all the pressure descended upon the two youngest players in the British side, Peter Alliss and Bernard Hunt, both of whom were making their debut in the match. Alliss was all square with his opponent Jim Turnesa on the last hole but

contrived to take six, having fluffed a chip from the edge of the green and taking three more to get down. That was a point lost and Hunt three-putted the same green to halve his game with Dave Douglas of America. The Americans retained the trophy by 6½–5½.

The British put up a good showing in Palm Springs in 1955, losing by 8–4 and then came the memorable events at Lindrick, near Sheffield, in 1957. British spirits were high but were soon dampened when the Americans took the foursomes by 3–1 but Dai Rees, the British captain, still believed his men could win. In the singles, the British attacked from the start and the American resistance crumbled. In the top game, Eric Brown dealt summarily with Tommy Bolt in an acrimonious encounter and this set the pattern for a string of British victories and a final result of 7½–4½ in favour of the home side.

Following the 1959 match in which the Americans regained the trophy back in Palm Springs the format of the match was changed to two sets of foursomes over 18 holes each on the first day and two sets of 18-hole singles on the second day. This seemed a certain way of ensuring further American victories and so it proved as they won handily at Royal Lytham & St Annes in 1961 by 14½–9½. In 1963 in Atlanta, Georgia, the match was extended to three days and four-balls were introduced to provide a total of 32 points available. The American victory by 23–9 was emphatic and matters did not improve for the British in the next two matches when they

lost by 19½–12½ at Royal Birkdale in 1965 and by 23½–8½ at Houston, Texas in 1967.

Nicklaus' sporting gesture

The events at Royal Birkdale in 1969 produced the most remarkable finish in the entire series. There was never more than a point separating the two sides throughout the three days and 18 of the 32 matches went to the last green. In the end, it all boiled to the last two singles, one between Brian Huggett and Billy Casper and the other between Tony Jacklin and Jack Nicklaus. On the final green Huggett faced a putt of five feet to halve his game with Casper. Just before he putted, a tremendous roar came from behind on the 17th. Huggett, thinking that the noise signified Jacklin winning his match, then holed his putt and collapsed in a wave of emotion. In fact, the roar was for Jacklin holing a long putt on the 17th green to make him level with Nicklaus with one hole to play. With the outcome depending on that last hole, both Jacklin and Nicklaus hit the green in two and Jacklin putted up to around two feet. Nicklaus gave his putt a good run at the hole and it finished three feet away. Nicklaus then holed his putt and immediately conceded Jacklin's putt in a gesture that was symbolic of the occasion, at the same time saying to Jacklin: 'I didn't think you would miss but I didn't want to give you the chance'. At 16 points apiece it was the first, and so far the only tie in the series.

American supremacy was reinstated in 1971 at St Louis, Missouri, by 18½–13½ but there were hopes of a British victory at Muirfield in 1973 when the home side led after the first day. The British couldn't sustain the lead and finally succumbed by 19–13. The match at Laurel Valley, Pennsylvania, in 1975 was pretty disastrous for the British as they lost 21–11, although Brian Barnes did create something of a stir by defeating Jack Nicklaus twice in the same day in the singles.

In order to make the scorelines more respectable another change to the format was introduced at Royal Lytham & St Annes in 1977 with five foursomes on the first day, five four-balls on the second day and ten singles on the last day. It didn't work simply because there was not enough golf being played and the result was still the same with the Americans winning 12½–7½.

Enter the Europeans

By now the contest was in jeopardy since it was clearly no contest with the might of American golf being so much superior than the opposition. Meetings were held between the governing bodies of both countries and it was agreed that since the British were playing many professional tournaments on the Continent, the terms of qualifications should be extended to include Continental European players. The chief factor in this decision was the rise of the Spanish players, particularly Severiano Ballesteros, and it was felt that his inclusion in the side with some of his countrymen would make the difference.

Whether it was still the Ryder Cup in the

Above: Jack Nicklaus putting against Tony Jacklin at Royal Birkdale. The 1969 Ryder Cup match at Birkdale was the only tied match, and Jacklin and Nicklaus featured prominently, halving the last match with Nicklaus not asking Jacklin to hole his final two-footer.

strictest terms of Sam Ryder's original concept of a match between the professionals of Britain and Ireland and America was debatable but the change did at least save the matches for the future.

The first Europe versus the USA Ryder Cup match took place at The Greenbrier, West Virginia, in 1979 and Ballesteros and his countryman, Antonio Garrido, were the only two non-British players in the side. After the first two days the Europeans trailed by just one point but in the 12 singles the Americans came through to win by 17—11 overall. Ballesteros and Garrido contributed only one point between them when they won their first day foursomes.

It was going to take some time for the Continental players to fit in with the team ethos and the fact they were playing for their 'country' rather than themselves and matters did not improve in 1981 at Walton Heath, Surrey. The Americans fielded perhaps the strongest side ever assembled and although the Europeans led after the first day, the second day and the final day singles saw a procession of American victories as they ran out the winners by 18½—9½.

Ballesteros did not play in this match due to some wrangling with the authorities over the question of appearance money but the Continent was represented by Manuel Pinero and Jose-Maria Canizares of Spain and Bernhard Langer of West Germany. Then in 1983, the European team began to gell. Led by Tony Jacklin they took on the Americans, led by Jack Nicklaus, at the PGA National course in Palm Beach and very nearly produced a historic victory. No visiting Ryder Cup team had ever won in America but after the first two days' play the teams were tied, and under Jacklin's inspired leadership victory looked eminently possible.

In the top single, Ballesteros halved with Fuzzy Zoeller by virtue of an incredible 3-wood shot from a bunker on the final hole which nearly reached the green and Nick Faldo and Bernhard Langer put the Europeans ahead. Then Bob Gilder, Ben Crenshaw and Calvin Peete gave America the lead before Paul Way, making his debut at the age of 20, levelled matters by beating Curtis Strange. With only two matches still on the course, the teams were tied. America's Lanny Wadkins earned a half for his side with a marvellous pitch to within feet of the flag at the 18th against Canizares and so the result hung on the match between Tom Watson of America and Bernard Gallacher. Jack Nicklaus, who had no desire to go down in the record books as the first American captain to lose on home soil, was mightily relieved when Watson secured the winning point.

Triumph at The Belfry

The closeness of this result provided a tremendous lift to the Europeans' belief in themselves so that it could be said that when the Americans arrived at The Belfry in 1985, they were probably the underdogs. Bernhard Langer had won the US Masters earlier in the year, Sandy Lyle had won the Open Championship and Ballesteros was generally acknowledged as the best player in the world. The Americans, however, led by Lee Trevino, were still tough as they proved by taking the first day morning foursomes by 3—1. The Europeans came back in the afternoon to cut the deficit to just one point.

In the morning four-balls on the second day occurred the incident which, with hindsight, may have turned the entire match. Europe had won two of the games and lost another but in the final game, the American pairing of Craig Stadler and Curtis Strange were two up with two holes to play against Bernhard Langer and Sandy Lyle. Lyle holed an enormous putt on the 17th to keep the match going but it looked like an American victory when Stadler faced a putt of two feet on the final green to halve the hole and win the match. Incredibly he missed and Europe were still level — but, more importantly, European morale was sky-high while American spirits were at a low ebb. In the afternoon foursomes the Europeans won three of the four games and the Americans found themselves under pressure as they went into the last day singles.

Opposite: European team captain Tony Jacklin and the Ryder Cup with the victorious team after their historic victory at Muirfield Village in 1987.

Below: Two American Ryder Cup stalwarts. Arnold Palmer looks over Jack Nicklaus' head and helps him line up a putt in the 1973 match at Muirfield, which the US won by 19 points to 13.

Above: The Belfry, scene of a famous European victory in 1985. This is the 18th green where Craig Stadler (right) missed a vital short putt in the foursomes match with Langer and Lyle (centre).

Right: Happier days for the USA. The 1983 match at the PGA National course at Florida was desperately close, all relying on the last two matches. Captain Jack Nicklaus, with walkie-talkie, looks happy on the last green with Lanny Wadkins, whose marvellous pitch to close to the flag earned him a decisive half in the penultimate match.

Huge crowds swarmed across the course hoping to witness a historic victory and the European players did not disappoint them, winning seven of the 12 singles. When Sam Torrance holed a curly putt on the final green to defeat America's Andy North the Ryder Cup had returned to its native shores for only the fourth time in the history of the event. The acclaim Tony Jacklin received as an astute captain was thoroughly justified and he was again appointed for the match at Muirfield Village in 1987.

This encounter saw more history made as with a dazzling display of golf the European team established a five point lead after the first two days of foursome and four-ball play. The Americans fought back in the 12 singles but the Europeans' nerve held and they won 15–13 with Severiano Ballesteros clinching the winning point. It was the first time the visitors had won on American soil and also the first time in 60 years of the Ryder Cup that they had retained the trophy.

THE WALKER CUP

The Walker Cup is the biennial encounter between the amateur golfers of the United States of America and those of Great Britain and Ireland. The idea of an international match between amateurs was first mooted in 1920 when a delegation from the United States Golf Association went to St Andrews for a discussion on the Rules with the R & A. The President of the USGA, George Walker, then offered to put up a cup for competiton. In 1921, the USGA sent an invitation to all countries to compete for Walker's cup and none accepted. But in the same year, William

Left: Although Europe's winning margin in 1985 was eventually five points, Sam Torrance had the pleasure of holing the putt which made certain of victory. He didn't have everything his own way though, needing to remove his shoes to play this recovery shot at the 8th.

Fownes, an American who previously organized matches against Canada, assembled another American team to take on the British at Hoylake the day before the British Amateur Championship. The Americans won by nine matches to three. The following year the R & A sent a team to compete for the Walker Cup at George Walker's home club on Long Island, New York, and this was the first official Walker Cup match. The Americans won by 8–4 in a match comprising four foursomes and eight singles. The British captain, Robert Harris, fell ill before the match and his place was taken by Bernard Darwin, who had travelled over with the British side to cover the match for *The Times*. Despite his sudden introduction, he won his match.

At this stage the Walker Cup was held every year alternating between the two countries. Britain came close in 1923 at St

*Walker Cup veterans. **Right:** Francis Ouimet (on the left) played in eight Walker Cup matches for the USA from the very first encounter in 1922 at the National Links, Long Island. Ouimet is with Roger Wethered of Britain during that first match. His record was passed by Joe Carr **(below)** however, the great Irishman playing ten times from 1947 to 1967, without, unfortunately, being on the winning side.*

Andrews, losing 6½–5½. After the 1924 match, which America won easily, it was decided to hold the match alternate years.

The 1920s and 1930s were the golden age of amateur golf and the Walker Cup attracted far more interest than its professional counterpart, the Ryder Cup. Cyril Tolley and Roger Wethered were supreme in Britain while America could call on the incomparable Bobby Jones. Jones played five Walker Cup singles and was victorious each time, winning some of his games by indecent margins. Throughout this period the stream of American victories continued unabated culminating in a slaughter at Pine Valley, New Jersey, in 1936 when Britain failed to score a solitary win and only three halved matches gave the score respectability.

Just as the viability of the Walker Cup was in question the British achieved victory. Under the leadership of John Beck, the 1938 match at St Andrews found all the early attention focused on James Bruen, an Irish prodigy who struck the ball immense distances with a swing which had a closer relationship to shinty than to golf. Bruen regularly went round the Old Course in practice under 70 and this inspired the British to take a 2½–1½ lead in the foursomes. Fortunes fluctuated in the singles but the British tail wagged the stronger and the home side ran out ahead by 7½–4½.

After the war, the matches resumed in odd-numbered years instead of even and the first took place in 1947, again at St Andrews. Unfortunately, there was to be no repeat of 1938 and the Americans assumed their winning ways again. This match saw the first appearance of the Irishman Joe Carr who was to play in or captain the next ten British and Irish sides, a record span which lasted 20 years. The same 1947 match saw the first appearance of Ronnie White, a superb striker of the ball, and he won four of his singles matches in five appearances from 1947 to 1955, defeating some of America's finest players in the process.

The 1953 match at Kittansett, Massachusetts, provided an incident which entirely captured the spirit of the Walker Cup. In a foursomes match, with Gene Littler and James Jackson of America against Roy McGregor and James Wilson, Jackson discovered that he had 16 clubs in his bag instead of the maximum 14 allowed. The penalty at that time was disqualification but the British captain, Tony Duncan, said he had no desire to win points that way and the penalty was modified to the loss of two holes, and the American pair went on to win. The next day a British newspaper carried the headline 'Britannia waives the rules'.

The intrusion of college players

By the late 1950s the basic principles of the Walker Cup were being eroded by the selection of American college players. Certainly they were amateurs in that they did

not play for money, but the sports scholarship system in America meant that they were full-time golfers on campus and therefore practically semi-professional. Players such as Jack Nicklaus, who made his Walker Cup debut at Muirfield in 1959, Deane Beman and Tommy Aaron, all of whom eventually became professionals, were products of the college system. Ranged against the accountants, solicitors and farmers of Britain and Ireland who were pursuing full-time careers in various fields of commerce and industry, it was not surprising that American dominance became more marked.

The result of the 1961 match at Seattle, Washington, when the Americans won 11−1 with only Martin Christmas' victory in the singles preventing whitewash, prompted a change to the format whereby instead of foursomes and singles over 36 holes on each of the two days, the games were 18 holes of foursomes and singles on each day. The first match under this format took place at Turnberry in 1963 and the British attacked with renewed vigour, leading by 6−3 after the first day. A series of tragic errors on the 16th hole on the second day by the British saw their hopes sink in direct relationship to the number of balls they dumped into the burn which runs in front of this green at this otherwise innocuous hole. The Americans turned the tables and won 14−10.

The next match at Five Farms, Maryland,

resulted in the only tie so far in the series. Again the British got off to a good start and at the end of the first day led by 6−3, and after the second day foursomes, by 10−4. They needed three points from the final eight singles to achieve a historic victory on American soil. But they could not get them. Gordon Cosh won his match but the rest of the scoreboard portrayed a string of American victories. In the end it came down to the match between Britain's Clive Clark and America's John Hopkins. Hopkins was one up on the 17th tee and then shanked his tee shot into the woods. From there he hacked out onto the green and holed the putt for a half in par threes. On the final green Clark faced a putt of 30 feet to win the hole, halve his match and tie the Walker Cup. Amazingly he holed it and honours were even.

Britain wins at last

The next two encounters went to the Americans and then in 1971 the match returned to St Andrews for the first time since 1953. This time the British won all the first day foursomes but lost the singles convincingly to trail 5½−6½. They lost the second day foursomes 1½−2½ and went into the final series of singles nursing a two-point deficit overall. Late in the afternoon the match swung imperceptibly towards the British as victory followed upon victory. The deed was finally accomplished when David

Above: The victorious US Walker Cup team at St Andrews in 1975 after their 14−7 triumph. The team contained many players who went on to success in the professional ranks, perhaps the best known being Craig Stadler on the extreme right, still cultivating his walrus moustache, and Jerry Pate, to his right, stooping with one hand holding the Cup.

Marsh struck a wonderful 3-iron onto the green of the notorious 17th, the Road Hole, to ensure that he could not lose against his American opponent. It provided a fitting finale for the British captain, Michael Bonallack, who had made his debut in 1959 and had won just about every honour the amateur game could offer in a long and illustrious career.

Throughout the 1970s the trickle of American college players that had emerged in the 1950s had, by now, become a flood. The 1975 American team at St Andrews was perhaps the strongest in recent times containing such names as Jerry Pate, Craig Stadler, George Burns, Curtis Strange and Jay Haas, all of whom were to go on and carve successful careers in the professional game. Still the British battled gamely on and began to inject some youthful talent of their own. In 1983 at Hoylake, the match was tied going into the final day singles and only American determination won the day. Britain's Andrew Oldcorn, now a professional, set a record by becoming the only British player since the present format was introduced in 1961 to win all his foursomes and singles games. The 1985 match at Pine Valley saw the British put up the best away performance since the tie of 1965. The teams were level after the first day but then Britain lost the second day foursomes 3½–½. The British took the final singles 4½–3½ to lose by just two points.

British and Irish hopes reached a new low in 1987 however, when the match was staged at Sunningdale, the first time it had departed from its traditional links venues. The Americans won the two sets of foursomes by 7–1 and the home side could not hope to make up that defeit from the singles. The final result was a conclusive 16½–7½ victory for the Americans but there is still optimism that the British and Irish will record another victory, perhaps when the contest is staged in Britain again in 1991.

As with the Ryder and Curtis Cups there is now a growing belief among British players that the Walker Cup is no longer the strict preserve of the Americans. It is true that the Americans are more likely to win it than lose it purely because they have a far greater number of good players from which to choose a team and also because of the college system. Many British amateurs are now also taking advantage of golf scholarships at American universities and this can only help the British cause. Perhaps the true amateur spirit of the Walker Cup would be better maintained if selection was restricted to players over the age of 25, thereby eliminating the college influence.

PROFESSIONAL TOURNAMENTS

Such has been the growth of professional golf over the past 25 years that it would be fair to say that in just about every week of the year a professional tournament is taking place in some part of the world, very often two or three! The modern tournament professional is a very different animal from his predecessor of between the wars and, indeed, of just after the Second World War. In those days there was no organized professional circuit and a professional would combine his duties as the professional at a club with the odd foray in tournaments. Furthermore, professionals, particularly in Britain, did not enjoy the exalted status they do today. The professional was expected to be available in his shop from dawn to dusk where he would be called upon to repair equipment, give lessons, sell necessary items such as clubs and balls and even help out with the maintenance of the course. His relationship with the members was very much on a servant–master basis and the professional was not even allowed in the clubhouse.

The first professionals to challenge this feudalism were Walter Hagen and Henry Cotton, both of whom were supreme players and who between them won seven Open Championships. Since they were not allowed in the clubhouses of the various venues which staged the Open, they took to changing in their cars and eating their meals there as well. Hagen, always the showman, performed these functions in the back of a hired Rolls-Royce car, thereby putting up

The United States Walker Cup team enjoying their success at Sunningdale in 1987. The USA have lost only twice and drawn once in the Walker Cup since the first match in 1922.

the metaphorical two fingers to the stuffy administrators within the clubhouse.

The first club to open its doors to professionals in America was Inverness during the 1920 US Open, but progress in Britain was much slower. The story goes that the Prince of Wales (Edward VIII) was playing with a professional at a club in south-east England and after the round invited the professional into the clubhouse. The entry was refused and the heir apparent then declined to give the club the 'Royal' prefix. The story may be apocryphal but it serves to illustrate the attitudes which prevailed.

The Professional Golfers' Association (PGA) of Britain was founded in 1901 under the chairmanship of J.H. Taylor, the five-times Open Champion. Subscriptions were £1 for professionals and ten shillings (50p) for assistant professionals, and membership was initially limited to professionals from London and the south-east but later expanded to include the rest of the country. The Rt Hon Mr A.J. Balfour, later to become Prime Minister, was the Association's first President and to mark the occasion the Association launched its first tournament at Tooting Bec Golf Club with total prize money of £15. The club donated a trophy which is still in existence although it is now awarded to the PGA Member who produces the lowest round in the Open Championship.

The first commercially sponsored event in the PGA's history was in 1903 when the *News of the World* put up £200 of prize-money for the PGA Match Play Championship. Regional qualifying produced 32 finalists for Sunningdale and James Braid won the £100 first prize by defeating Ted Ray in the final. The Match Play Championship continued until 1969. Increasing sponsorship by equipment companies and leading British newspapers were the main features after the First World War with companies such as Dunlop and Penfold leading the way. In 1936, 14 major tournaments were conducted of which seven were national open tournaments and seven sponsored tournaments. In 1937, the Vardon Trophy, named after the six-times Open Champion, was introduced to honour the player with the lowest stroke average throughout the year. The Vardon Trophy is now awarded to the leading money-winner on the PGA European Tour.

At the end of the 1946 season, prize money stood at £25,000, rising to £27,640 in 1949 from a total of 16 events. In 1955, Christy O'Connor won the first £1,000 first prize when he captured the Swallow-Penfold tournament. In the same year the Open Championship also offered a first prize of £1,000, won by Peter Thomson.

The explosion in prize money

By 1960, total prize money had risen to £53,000 from 11 tournaments, and the decade also ushered in sponsorship from tobacco and drinks companies with 1962 finding Neil Coles winning the first £2,000 prize in the Senior Service tournament at Dalmahoy. Prize money topped the £100,000 mark in 1965, but the real explosion was ignited by Tony Jacklin's Open Championship win in 1969. Proof of this was provided by a total of £300,000 prize money in 1970.

By now television was playing an increasing role in the development of the British Tour but it was felt that in order to sustain expansion, the events on the Continent should be co-ordinated into the concept of a European Tour. This was effected by the appointment of John Jacobs, the former Ryder Cup player and respected teacher, as Tournament Director-General in 1971. There were, however, rumblings of discontent from the tournament-playing professionals whose affairs were being governed by a committee dominated by professionals whose livelihood was chiefly obtained from jobs at clubs. The differences between the two elements were resolved in 1975 when the European Tournament Players' Division was formed, later to become the PGA European Tour.

The next catalyst to growth was provided

Below: Doug Sanders of the USA playing in the Benson and Hedges at Fulford in 1978, eight years after Sanders had earned fame by missing a two-foot genuinely 'this-for-the-Open' putt on the last green at St Andrews.

by the emergence of Severiano Ballesteros, who sprang to prominence in the 1976 Open Championship at Royal Birkdale. In 1979, the year Ballesteros won his first Open title, prize money in Europe had risen to £1 million. Since then, with the rise in playing standards and the further emergence of world-class players such as Bernhard Langer and Sandy Lyle, the growth in Europe has been quite phenomenal, prize money rising to £7.5 million in 1987 from 26 tournaments in Britain and Europe. Much of the credit for this is due to Ken Schofield, the Executive Director of the PGA European Tour, who has negotiated shrewdly with sponsors and television to ensure that the present growth is sustained.

Practically each season brings a new record in individual prize money won, and it is significant to note that in 1976, Ballesteros, as leading money winner, banked £39,504 in official prize money. Ten years later, he again topped the money list with £259,275.

The prize money in Europe, and also that in Japan, Australia and the Far East, pales by comparison with that available in America. The American PGA Tour is the richest in the world, currently offering close on $30 million from 46 tournaments. The American PGA was founded in 1916 and was modelled on the British PGA. It was basically created to serve the interests of professionals employed at clubs but in the 1920s a forerunner of the Tour developed when, in the winter months, tournaments were held on the West Coast,

Texas and Florida and then, in the spring, players migrated north up the East Coast. Resorts and hotels realized the publicity they could attract by staging a tournament, and players such as Walter Hagen, Gene Sarazen and later, Sam Snead, helped pull in the crowds. During the 1930s the Tour grew into a regular rotation of events throughout the country, and despite the Depression the leadership of Tournament Directors Bob Harlow and Fred Corcoran kept the money coming in.

Following the Second World War, players such as Ben Hogan and Byron Nelson emerged, but it wasn't until the late 1950s and early 1960s that the Tour really exploded. Two factors were responsible for this, one human and one mechanical. The human factor was Arnold Palmer, whose dashing style of play and remarkable powers of recovery turned golf into a form of unarmed combat. The mechanical factor was television, which was able to project Palmer's flamboyant approach into millions of homes. Palmer and television made golf a boom sport in America and tournament purses started to rocket.

As was to be the case in Britain, the tournament side of the game was still controlled by the US PGA which was mainly made up of club professionals, and in the late 1960s a severe breach between the two parties developed. In 1968 these differences were resolved with the formation of the Tournament Players' Division, now the PGA Tour. Apart from the US Masters, the US Open and the US PGA Championship, the PGA Tour is responsible for running the weekly events which make up the annual schedule.

The Palmer and Nicklaus era

The Palmer era, which began in 1958 when he was leading money winner with $42,607, continued until the mid-1960s when his supremacy was assumed by Jack Nicklaus. Palmer had been the first player to win more than $100,000 in a season (1963) and also the first to pass the $1 million mark in career earnings (1968), but Nicklaus then took a grip on the game, and having been leading money winner in 1964, was leader seven more times over the next 12 years. Nicklaus was also the first man to pass $2 million in career earnings and he has now won over $5 million since he turned professional in 1962. He has 71 PGA Tour victories to his name, 13 less than Sam Snead who was in his prime when tournament purses were much lower.

In 1975 total prize money stood at $6 million but the Nicklaus domination was about to end as he cut down on his playing schedule and the figure of Tom Watson emerged. Watson was leading money winner four years in a row from 1977 to 1980, the last year seeing him become the first man to win over $500,000 in a single season. Watson was again top in 1984, but in 1986 Greg Norman set a new money-winning record

Below: Tall, elegant, seemingly imperturbable Tom Weiskopf in the Benson and Hedges at Fulford in 1981, eight years after his Open success.

with $653,296. This is unlikely to last very long, particularly as there are now at least three tournaments offering prize money of $1 million with first place cheques of over $200,000.

In recent years the Tour has also masterminded the development of the PGA Senior Tour for professionals over the age of 50. This began in 1980 with just two events but has now mushroomed to 36 events and over $10 million in total prize money. The spark for this was again Palmer, who turned 50 in 1979. He himself wasn't too keen on being used as the 'front' man for such a project, believing he could still compete with the youngsters on the main Tour. Since its inception, however, the Senior Tour has

become a lucrative area for many players, with veterans like Don January, Miller Barber and Australia's Peter Thomson quickly reaching the $1 million mark in winnings from the Senior Tour.

The age of supersonic travel means that the touring professional can ply his trade round the world for 12 months of the year. The tournament circuits of Japan, Australia and South Africa beckon during the winter months and even the Americans, who are usually content to remain in their own country, recognize the importance of being acknowledged in global terms. The idea of a world circuit, first mooted by Peter Thomson some 20 years ago, is almost a co-ordinated reality for the travelling professional.

Above: Miller Barber taking the winner's cheque after a Seniors tournament at Canterbury in 1983. Nowadays the Seniors Tour is the biggest growth area in the game, and Barber's cheque was a big one in more ways than one.

The Great Players

From Aaron to Zoeller, from Alliss to Zaharias, the great players have enriched the game with their achievements. The argument as to who was the greatest player of all time can never be satisfactorily settled since all a player can do is beat those who are around at the same time. Therefore the discussion as to whether Bobby Jones was, in his prime, a better player than Jack Nicklaus in his prime will have to remain unresolved. Every player listed in this chapter has, in some way, contributed to the history of the game while a few of them have stamped their character on an era. There is no question that the early years of the Open Championship were dominated by Old and Young Tom Morris, followed by the 'Great Triumvirate' of Vardon, Taylor and Braid. The 1920s were the preserve of Jones and Hagen, to be succeeded by Cotton. Following the Second World War it was Hogan, Locke and Thomson, and then came the next triumvirate of Palmer, Player and Nicklaus, overlapping into the present day of Ballesteros, Norman and Watson.

Left: Without doubt the greatest golfer to emerge from Europe, Seve Ballesteros' pleasant manner has made him one of the sport's most popular heroes.

Right: Tommy Aaron is less famous for the Masters that he won than for the Masters when he marked down a wrong score on Roberto de Vicenzo's card and prevented him from winning.

Tommy AARON

b 1937

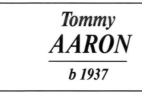

Aaron is probably better known for a mistake than for what he accomplished on the golf course. This stems from the 1968 US Masters, when Aaron credited Roberto de Vicenzo with a par four instead of a birdie three at the 71st hole. De Vicenzo didn't notice the mistake until it was too late and signed for a 66 instead of a 65. It cost him victory as Bob Goalby won by a single shot.

Five years later Aaron enjoyed a much happier Masters, winning by a single shot from J.C. Snead. By then he had earned the nickname 'The Bridesmaid' after persistently finishing second in tournaments. After turning professional in 1960 he chalked up 14 runner-up spots, eventually breaking through to win the 1969 Canadian Open. He also earned Walker and Ryder Cup honours.

Percy ALLISS

b 1897 – d 1975

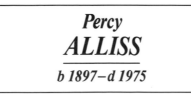

Father of the most famous voice in British golf, Peter Alliss, Percy Alliss was himself a fine player, who competed successfully throughout the 1920s and 1930s against some of the legends of the game. A regular Ryder Cup player, he represented Great Britain and Ireland in 1929, 1933, 1935 and 1937, and during this time he also won the British Professional Match Play Championship twice, in 1933 and 1937, his biggest successes.

Percy Alliss was recognized as a fine swinger of the club and an outstanding long-iron player whose putting sometimes let him down and almost certainly cost him an Open Championship title.

He came closest to capturing the game's greatest trophy in 1931 at Carnoustie, in Scotland, when he looked odds-on to win. However, he faltered in the closing stages to finish in third place behind the 'Silver Scot', Tommy Armour, and Jose Jurado, who claimed the runner-up place.

He was a man who liked to travel and after starting his career as the professional at Royal Porthcawl, in Wales, he moved to Germany and the Wannsee Club in Berlin where his son Peter was born and where Percy remained the professional for eight years.

The Alliss family returned to Britain in 1936 and moved to Temple Newsham, Leeds. Then in 1939 Percy Alliss moved once more, this time to Ferndown in Dorset, where he remained as the club professional until his retirement.

Peter ALLISS

b 1931

Born in Berlin during his father Percy's spell as club professional at the fashionable Wannsee Club, young Peter Alliss inherited his father's talent for the game of golf and during his career was considered to be one of the finest players Great Britain has ever produced.

Peter Alliss joined the professional ranks in 1946 after gaining international honours as an amateur. When playing in his first Open Championship the following year at the tender age of 16, his talent was spotted by the legendary *Daily Telegraph* Golf Correspondent Leonard Crawley, who recommended that Peter be selected for the Ryder Cup team by virtue of his being the best young player in the country at the time.

National Service in the RAF put a temporary brake on Peter's progress and it was 1951 before he once again played in the Open. However, he was soon back in the limelight with a victory in the 1952 British Assistants Championship and claimed his first major title two years later by winning the Daks tournament, the first of over 20 professional tournament wins in a distinguished career.

Peter Alliss was a fine long-iron player who had superb poise and balance, combined with natural flair and power. A prolific winner, he captured five national titles and during one inspired spell was the holder of the Italian, Spanish and Portuguese Championships at the same time.

His talent was further emphasized by the fact that he won the Vardon Trophy on two occasions, in 1964 and 1966.

When it came to the Open Championship, Peter Alliss, like his father before him, was let down by indifferent putting. Nevertheless, he finished eighth on three occasions and but for that single flaw in an otherwise flawless game could well have won the coveted Open 'Jug' on several occasions in the 1950s and early 1960s.

His outstanding play during this era also earned him Ryder Cup honours and he had a fine record, collecting several famous American scalps, among them that of Arnold Palmer when the great man was at the very height of his powers.

After the 1969 Ryder Cup Peter Alliss decided to retire from the professional game and today his fine knowledge of the intricacies of the game, coupled with a wry sense of humour, has made him much in demand as a TV commentator both at home and abroad.

Willie ANDERSON

b 1878 – d 1910

After emigrating from North Berwick as a teenager just before the turn of the century, Anderson established a US Open record that has never been bettered. He won it four times, 1901, 1903, 1904 and 1905 (a feat later equalled by Bobby Jones, Ben Hogan and Jack Nicklaus) and was also second once, third once, fourth twice and fifth three times. He also established some scoring records: 288 for a standard golf course in winning the Western Open in 1908 (one of his four victories in the event) and in the US Open a one-round record of 73 in 1904, which he lowered to 72 the following year. Considering the courses and the equipment in those days, it was some achievement. His premature death at the age of 32 robbed the Scot of many more victories.

Above: Peter Alliss is known to many golf followers today as a TV pundit, but during the 1950s and 1960s he was a leading player whose comparative weakness at putting prevented him from gaining the major prizes.

Below: Isao Aoki chips from a bunker. His putting, accomplished with the toe of the club pointing upwards, is a distinguishing feature of his game.

Isao AOKI

b 1942

Renowned for his highly individual putting style, Isao Aoki has been one of the leading Japanese golfers for many years, although he did not become a top-class player until he was 30 years old. He made the leading four in Japan in 1973, and has maintained his position, as well as becoming an international golfer.

Aoki's toe up, heel down putting action works extremely well and is coupled with a superb short game. It's not surprising that Isao is the joint record-holder of the lowest

single-round score in the British Open by virtue of a 63 at Muirfield in 1980.

Aoki has not confined his low-scoring feats to Britain and his homeland, where he has won over 40 tournaments. He is also a regular competitor on the US Tour where he has won once, claiming the 1983 Hawaiian Open, but in the 1980 US Open he came within two shots of beating Jack Nicklaus.

His most notable achievements in Britain have been winning the 1978 World Match Play Championship and the 1983 European Open.

Tommy
ARMOUR
b 1895 – d 1968

One of the few golfers to become a legend in his own lifetime, the 'Silver Scot', as he was known, achieved his greatest successes after going to live in America in the early 1920s. He also achieved a unique record. He played *against* the US in 1921, staying in America to play in the first official Walker Cup match the following year. Then in 1926, as a professional, Armour played *for* the USA at Wentworth in the last pre-Ryder Cup encounter. He went on to win the US Open in 1927 and the US PGA in 1930, then returned to Carnoustie a year later to take the Open Championship. In later years he earned a glowing reputation in America as a teacher although he was plagued with putting problems, inventing the term 'the yips'. He was the author of two highly successful instructional books.

Left: An outstanding player who dominated the British Amateur Championship from its inception in 1887 until the First World War, John Ball also won the Open in 1890, the first amateur to do so.

John
BALL
b 1861 – d 1940

The only man other than Bobby Jones to win the British Amateur Championship and the British Open in the same year, John Ball was one of the game's finest early players.

The British Amateur Championship did not begin until John Ball was a well established player and he quickly became a dominant figure in the event, with wins in 1888, 1890 (when he also won the Open), 1892, 1894, 1899, 1907, 1910 and 1912: a span of over two decades between his first and last victories.

John Ball continued to compete in the Amateur Championship until 1921, by which time he was 60 years old. Yet he still reached the sixth round of the Championship.

Considered to be the equal in his day to Bobby Jones and Harry Vardon, John Ball was a first-class shot-maker and a master craftsman with the whippy, hickory-shafted clubs of the day.

One of his finest wins came in the 1912 Amateur when he found himself five down with only seven holes to play but fought back and went on to win the Championship for the last time in his distinguished career.

Left: Tommy Armour was known as the 'Silver Scot', one of the first players to acquire a nickname. After a brilliant playing career he became a famous teacher in America.

Seve
BALLESTEROS

b 1957

Unquestionably the finest natural talent to appear on the golf scene in the past 20 years, Seve Ballesteros has already secured a place among the greats of the game.

Born in a small fishing village in the north of Spain, he is the youngest of four brothers, all of whom are golfers. By the time he was eight years old he had made his own golf club, using an old iron head and a stick cut to length for the shaft. It was with this crude implement that he was to develop the touch and skill that has become the hallmark of his game.

Below: Seve and silver go together naturally, especially the silver of the World Match Play Championship, which Ballesteros has won four times in the 1980s. By the mid-1980s he was generally acknowledged as the world's finest player.

Ballesteros first came to prominence during the 1976 British Open at Birkdale when his cavalier style of play produced some of the most exciting golf ever seen in the long history of the Championship. It also took the 19-year-old Spaniard into a tie for second place with Jack Nicklaus, behind the actual winner Johnny Miller. Ballesteros continued to improve at a rapid rate with several top-ten finishes in Tour events throughout Europe. His first win came at Zandvoort in the 1976 Dutch Open, where he became the youngest player ever to win a European Tour event.

Over the next three seasons he began to dominate the game in Europe, and in 1979 at Royal Lytham he realized one of the major goals of his career by capturing his first British Open title, a win he was to repeat at St Andrews in 1984.

After his Lytham victory, he set his sights on America and in 1980 confirmed his status as an emerging superstar by winning the US Masters for the first time. Ballesteros was to capture the Masters title again in 1983. However, he was, and still is, reluctant to commit himself to playing full-time on the US Tour, preferring instead to travel the world and compete in Japan, Australia, Europe and America.

Seve Ballesteros excels in both strokeplay and matchplay formats, as his record in the World Match Play Championship at Wentworth, with four victories since his first win in 1981, clearly shows. In the Ryder Cup he has been an inspiration to the European team and played a vital role in their historic win at The Belfry in 1985.

In 1986 Ballesteros once again topped the European Order of Merit, thanks mainly to a devastating spell when he captured five consecutive tournaments, finishing the season with over £200,000 in prize money and a stroke average of 68.95.

Pam
BARTON

b 1917–d 1943

Pam Barton was one of Britain's most talented lady amateur golfers but sadly she was never fully to realize her talent before she was killed when the aeroplane in which she was flying crashed on take-off from RAF Manston during the Second World War.

A natural left-hander, who was persuaded to play right-handed, Pam, along with Dorothy Campbell and Catherine Lacoste, had the rare distinction of holding both the British and American titles in the same year.

Pam's first major breakthrough came in 1934, when as a 17-year-old, she won the French Championship, an event in which she was to finish runner-up on three more occasions in her all-too-short career.

In 1934 and 1935 she also reached the semi-final stages of the British Ladies' Amateur but failed to make the final on either occasion. However, the following year was to prove third time lucky for Pam when she won the title for the first time. She was to win the Ladies' Amateur title once more, in 1939, before her untimely death in 1943.

Patty
BERG
b 1918

Patty was one of the three founder members of what is now the American Women's Professional Tour back in 1948, the others being Babe Zaharias and Betty Jameson. One of the greatest women players of all time, she won an estimated 83 pro tournaments, half of which were official events, and became the first woman to top $100,000 in winnings.

In her amateur career Patty won 40 tournaments, including the US Women's Amateur in 1938 after twice being a beaten finalist. She turned pro in 1940, winning the Western Open the following year and a first prize of $100. However, a smashed knee in 1942 needed several operations and it wasn't until 1943 that she returned to winning ways. On the pro tour Patty was leading money winner in 1954, 1955 and 1957, won the World Championship four times (1953, 1954, 1955 and 1957) and was a consistent winner until 1959. She underwent a cancer operation in 1971 but remained on the Tour for ten more years.

Tommy
BOLT
b 1918

A fiery, uncompromising character whose low boiling point was in direct contrast to his golfing ability, 'Thunderbolt' often took his temper out on his clubs when things went wrong, although many stories have become more than a little coloured over the years. But he was certainly an abrasive character who believed passionately in his own qualities, which were soon evident after he turned pro in 1950 aged 32. He was in the top 60 every year until 1967, with two exceptions. But he won only one major championship, the US Open in 1958 with a four-shot advantage over Gary Player.

He came close to winning the Masters in 1952 and the US PGA in 1971 at the age of 53. However, since joining the senior ranks he has run up another string of victories, both home and overseas. He played in two Ryder Cups and his only defeat was by 4 and 3 by Eric Brown in 1957 at Lindrick.

Michael
BONALLACK, OBE
b 1934

Arguably the finest amateur golfer that Great Britain has produced in the modern era, Michael Bonallack has won almost every honour the game has to offer. Throughout the 1960s and 1970s, despite a rather ungainly swing, he was virtually unbeatable, thanks to a deadly short game and a superb putting touch.

Like Ted Dexter, another fine amateur golfer from the same generation, the young Bonallack had a flair for cricket. But unlike Dexter, who went on to captain England in the bat and ball game, Michael decided that golf was the game for him.

His first major success came in 1952 when he won the Boys' Championship. Walker Cup selection followed at the age of 22 and he was to become a regular member of the team over the next 20 years.

Despite a fine individual performance in the amateur game, Bonallack did not have an outstanding record in Walker Cup matches, with only three singles victories to his credit. But when you consider that he inevitably found himself playing at number one in the

Left: Perhaps the greatest British amateur of recent times, Michael Bonallack played in the Walker Cup for 20 years, and won the British Amateur Championship five times. He is now Secretary of the R & A.

team and facing the best of the Americans, it was hardly surprising.

His record in the major British amateur championships in modern times is unsurpassed. Five British Amateur titles, three in succession from 1968 to 1970, another five wins in the English Amateur and a further four English Stroke-Play titles, all bear witness to his golfing prowess.

Perhaps the highlight of Michael Bonallack's distinguished career came in 1971 when he captained the Walker Cup team to a dramatic victory over the Americans at St Andrews. In the same year he was awarded the OBE for his services to golf but by then increasing business commitments were beginning to curtail his golfing activities. It was then that he decided to concentrate his efforts on the administration of the game; a decision which eventually led to the coveted position Michael Bonallack holds today as Secretary of the Royal and Ancient Golf Club of St Andrews.

Below: Julius Boros was the oldest player to win the US open and the oldest to win a major — not bad for a player whose health forced him to take it easy.

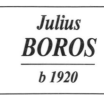

Julius BOROS

b 1920

Boros could be described as a late developer but he lost no time once he got started. After turning professional in 1950 at the age of 30 and joining the US Tour, he completed a magnificent hat-trick in 1952, winning the US Open, and becoming Player of the Year and leading money-winner. He also won the US Open title in 1963 when he was 43, the second oldest to land the crown. When the US PGA title came his way in 1968 it made him the oldest player to win a major. He was one of the most consistent players on the US Tour, passing a million dollars in winnings in 1977. Strangely he achieved this record with the minimum of practice, not wishing to subject himself to extra strain because of numerous ailments. Of Hungarian extraction, Boros was four times a Ryder Cup player and won the US PGA Seniors in 1971.

Harry BRADSHAW

b 1913

One of a crop of fine Irish golfers who emerged on the scene in the early 1940s, Harry Bradshaw is best remembered for his famous shot played from the broken beer bottle, during the 1949 Open at Royal St George's. Golfing legend recalls that during the second round of the Championship Harry found his ball had come to rest inside the remains of a broken beer bottle which had been left in the rough at the 5th hole. Although he was almost certain that he was entitled to a free drop, Harry decided to play the ball as it lay. The subsequent shot travelled only a few yards and he finished up by scoring a two-over-par six. Rounds of 68, 77, 68 and 70 left Harry in a tie for the title with Bobby Locke, but he was well beaten by the South African in the ensuing 36-hole play-off for the Championship.

Harry Bradshaw was a fine golfer, who won the Irish Professional title on no less than ten occasions. He also campaigned successfully on the mainland, winning the Dunlop Masters twice, in 1953 and 1955.

James BRAID

b 1870–d 1950

One of golf's 'Great Triumvirate', along with J.H. Taylor and Harry Vardon, James Braid was a Scot, born in a small village on the

Championship in 1903, Braid went on to win the event on three more occasions before 1907. He won the Championship once more in 1911 and even in his late 50s he was still a force to be reckoned with, reaching the final in 1927 when he lost to Archie Compston.

James Braid's first Open triumph came in 1901 after several near misses. But once he had made the breakthrough he was to dominate the Championship to the same extent as his illustrious contemporaries, Taylor and Vardon. His affinity with the Open was reflected by his outstanding win at Prestwick, venue for the first ever Championship. Opening rounds of 70 and 72 put him some 15 shots ahead of Harry Vardon, and although he faltered slightly in the third round he was soon back on form with a closing 72 to take the title with a comfortable eight-shot margin.

A powerful swing and a calm temperament were James Braid's greatest assets, and regardless of the excitement around him, he always appeared calm and unperturbed. One of his few disappointments was, when partnered by Sandy Herd, he lost a series of four matches for prize money of £400 to the combination of Vardon and Taylor.

Age it seems was no barrier to Braid and he regularly beat his age around the course. On one occasion he returned a 74 on his 78th birthday. Problems with his sight led to his gradual decline from the pinnacle of the game and although he continued to play well after the First World War he was never again to be the dominant figure in the game he once was. He died in London in 1950 and will always be remembered as a great player and a modest and kind man.

Gay
BREWER
b 1932

For someone so consistent on the US Tour, Brewer's record in the majors is somewhat frugal. He joined the Tour in 1956 and finished in the top 100 every year for the next 22 years. Not only that, he was only out of the top 60 once up to 1973, was in the top 25 three times and his highest place was fifth in 1966. But as far as the majors were concerned, Brewer made an impression only in the Masters. In 1966 he had the chance to win but three-putted the last green to tie with Jack Nicklaus and Tommy Jacobs. He shot 78 in the play-off to Nicklaus' 70 and Jacobs' 72. But that was forgotten a year later when Brewer single-putted ten greens in a final-round 67 to win by one, his only major victory. Also in 1967 he won the Alcan Golfer of the Year at St Andrews, retaining the title at Birkdale a year later. He also played in the 1967 and 1971 Ryder Cups and enjoyed several overseas successes.

Left: James Braid comes out of the sand. One of the all-time greats, Braid's career at the top stretched from the 1890s, when he became one of the Great Triumvirate, till the 1920s, when he was good enough in 1927 to reach the PGA Match Play Championship final.

shores of the Firth of Forth. He is best remembered for his outstanding performances in the Open. He won the Championship five times and finished fifth or better on no fewer than 15 occasions in his remarkable career.

As an amateur Braid worked as a club-maker in London but was catapulted to fame in 1895 when he held the Open Champion of the time, J.H. Taylor, to a halved match. He joined the professional ranks shortly afterwards and got a job as club professional at Romford Golf Club in Essex. In 1904 he moved to Walton Heath, which he also helped design, and he stayed at the beautiful Surrey course for the next 40 years.

Winner of the inaugural PGA Match Play

Right: Eric Brown (on the right) had a very successful Ryder Cup career, winning all his four singles matches from 1953 to 1959. He became the non-playing captain and is seen exchanging cards with American captain Sam Snead in 1969, when the match was tied.

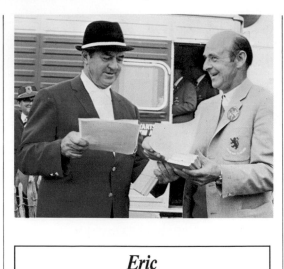

Eric
BROWN
b 1925–d 1986

Eric Chalmers Brown, who died suddenly after a short illness in 1986, was one of Britain's finest exponents of match-play golf. He was a man who relished the cut and thrust of man-to-man encounters, and this was reflected in his distinguished Ryder Cup record, both as a player and as non-playing captain.

A fine amateur career culminated in his winning the 1946 Scottish Amateur Championship, after which he turned professional. His breakthrough in the paid ranks came in 1951 when he won the Swiss Open. He then went on to collect four more international titles along with seven major tournament victories, including the 1957 Dunlop Masters. That same year also saw him enjoy one of his finest Ryder Cup triumphs with an emphatic win over American tough guy Tommy Bolt. It was felt that Brown's win that day inspired the rest of the team and the result was a rare triumph for Great Britain and Ireland.

Eric Brown went on to captain the Ryder Cup team twice in a non-playing capacity, in 1959 at Royal Birkdale and again in 1971 when the venue was St Louis, in America. The sometimes fiery Scot's fighting spirit and leadership qualities were instrumental in holding the Americans to a drawn match at Birkdale.

James
BRUEN
b 1920–d 1972

It's unlikely that Jimmy Bruen would have won many awards for style and poise when it came to swinging a golf club. But although the likeable Irishman may have used a unique and unorthodox method, he was nevertheless an outstanding golfer, renowned for his long hitting.

Jimmy Bruen won the Boys' Champion-

ship in 1936 and the following year captured the Irish Close Championship, a feat he was to repeat in 1938 when he also captured the Irish Open Championship. He made his Walker Cup debut in the same year and although Jimmy lost his singles match to Charlie Yates, his form during the practice rounds was so good that it's said he inspired his fellow team members. The result was a rare home victory.

Jimmy Bruen's long-hitting strength which made light of the heaviest rough, coupled with a fine putting touch, were ideally suited to demands of links courses and this was confirmed in the 1946 Amateur at Royal Birkdale, which he won.

Jimmy Bruen returned to Walker Cup duty after the Second World War, playing in 1949 and 1951, but his forceful style of play began to take its toll physically and a wrist injury, which also caused him to withdraw from the 1960 Amateur Championship, was the main reason behind his gradual decline from the international scene.

Jack
BURKE
b 1923

Until America's defeat in the 1985 match, Jack Burke held the unenviable title of the only losing US Ryder Cup captain since the Second World War. He now shares that honour with Lee Trevino. Burke's setback came at Lindrick in 1957 and it was during that contest that he suffered his only personal defeat in five Ryder Cups from 1951 to 1959. He went down 5 and 3 to Peter Mills. He was captain again in 1973 when he had better luck.

Burke's pro career began in 1940 and he joined the Tour 10 years later. In 1952 he won the Vardon Trophy and was runner-up to Sam Snead in the US Masters. He went one better in 1956, winning the coveted green jacket despite being eight shots behind with a round to go, and he took the US PGA the same year. Injury cut short his career but he later linked with Jimmy Demaret to build the Champions Club, near Houston.

JoAnne
CARNER
b 1939

One of the greats of women's golf, JoAnne Carner enjoyed a brilliant career both as an amateur and a professional. She compiled one of the finest amateur records ever, capturing five US Amateur titles (1957, 1960, 1962, 1966 and 1968), the US Girls Junior in 1956 and playing in four Curtis Cup matches.

Left: Irishman Joe Carr was an outstanding amateur player for 30 years, during which time he averaged a major win each year, including three Amateur Championships. He was good enough to compete in professional events, finishing eighth in the Centenary Open.

She went from strength to strength after turning pro in 1970 at the age of 30, and to the end of the 1986 season had captured 42 tournament victories. She has twice won the US Open, in 1971 and 1976, which gave her the unique record of being the only woman to have won USGA Junior, US Amateur and US Women's Open titles. She was the leading money-winner three times on the Tour, was three times Player of the Year and five times winner of the Vare Trophy for the lowest scoring average. Carner became the LPGA Tour's second player to top $2 million in winnings and was elected to the Hall of Fame in 1982 following her 35th tournament win.

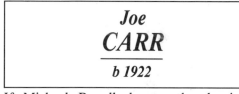

Joe
CARR
b 1922

If Michael Bonallack was the dominant figure in amateur golf during the late 1960s and early 1970s then Joseph Benedict Carr was the man who held sway over the preceding decade. His first victory came in 1941 in the East of Ireland Amateur Championship, and thereafter he was never far from contention in almost every major amateur event over the next 30 years.

In his prime, Joe Carr had a typical Irish swing: full-blooded, free and seldom executed at less than full throttle. It was exciting to watch but also took him to some of the more uncharted regions of the course. However, he was also blessed with excellent powers of recovery which often allowed him to turn what seemed like a certain bogey into a miracle birdie.

Joe Carr won more than 30 major amateur titles during his distinguished career, including three British Amateur titles in 1953, 1958 and 1960. He was also a semi-finalist on three occasions and a beaten finalist in 1968 at the age of 48.

All-conquering in his native Ireland, he was Irish Open Champion four times in a ten-year period between 1946 and 1956. An automatic choice for the Walker Cup team between 1947 and 1965, he holds the record for the most number of appearances for a player from either country, and although he made only a few visits to America, outside of Walker Cup duty, he did reach the semi-final of the US Amateur Championship in 1961.

Despite being an amateur, Carr often competed in professional events and produced several outstanding performances; the

best being in the 1960 Centenary Open at St Andrews when he finished in eighth place behind the winner, Kel Nagle of Australia.

In Ireland, where he is treated as a living legend, Carr came close to winning the Dunlop Masters at Portmarnock in 1959 when it took a blistering finish from Christy O'Connor to pip him for the title.

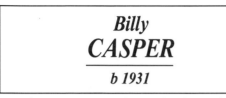

Billy
CASPER
b 1931

Consistency was perhaps the best club in Casper's bag. He was never out of the top 60 on the US Tour from 1955 to 1976 and his winnings reflected that status as he was the second man after Arnold Palmer to top $1 million on the Tour.

Not a colourful player, he was one of the greatest putters ever. He is considered among the best half-dozen of modern times, a fact underlined by his needing just 112 putts to win the 1959 US Open, one of three major championship victories. It is argued that he didn't do himself justice in the majors despite his other successes. He was second three times in the US PGA, while his highest finish in the Open Championship was fourth. The US Masters course at Augusta didn't really suit his game with its fast undulating greens, but he did win there in 1970 after a play-off with Gene Littler. However, his best win was in the 1966 US Open in San Francisco against the formidable Palmer. With nine holes left Casper trailed by seven shots and was just looking for second spot. But Palmer shedded strokes like confetti and they eventually tied. In the play-off Palmer led by four after nine only to fade again as Casper took his second title.

Casper's total of 51 Tour victories leaves him sixth behind Snead, Nicklaus, Hogan, Palmer and Nelson, while he has also triumphed overseas, winning the Brazilian, Lancome, Italian and Mexican titles. He has played in a record eight Ryder Cups from 1961 to 1975, then was the non-playing US captain in 1979. He is now active on the US Seniors Tour.

Bob
CHARLES, OBE
b 1936

The greatest left-handed player the game has ever produced, Bob Charles can also claim the distinction of being one of golf's finest putters.

The lanky New Zealander's first major victory was in his native Open in 1954, which he won while still an amateur. His first

appearance in Britain was in 1961 and his greatest successes in Europe were back-to-back victories in the John Player Classic and the Dunlop Masters in 1972.

The only 'lefty' to win the Open, his victory at Royal Lytham in 1963 came almost a year after he left the European scene to concentrate on playing in America, where he won five tournaments between 1963 and 1974.

The 1969 World Match Play Championship was to provide the stage for one of the most devastating demonstrations of his putting prowess. With only ten holes to play in the final against American Gene Littler, Charles was trailing by several holes. Then the New Zealander holed putts of 45, 25 and 50 feet to pull back to one down with one to play. At the 36th hole he struck again, this time holing from all of 25 feet to force a play-off which he won at the first extra ball.

The elegant left-hander's only other opportunity to win the British Open came earlier that same year, again at Royal Lytham. However, on this occasion he had to be content with second place behind Tony Jacklin.

During the last few years Charles has competed successfully on the US Seniors Tour and his sole 1986 victory, partnering US woman professional Amy Alcott, brought him a staggering $250,000 in prize money.

Billy Casper (opposite) should have been one of the most discussed and colourful players in the game: his Mormon religion, food allergies and 11 children frequently featured in the news stories. But as a golfer his game was subdued — consistency and brilliant putting kept him at the top. Bob Charles (above) was the greatest of all left-handed golfers, the only one to win the Open. He began to wear spectacles later in his career, when he became a leading player on the Seniors Tour.

Neil COLES, MBE

b 1934

If there is one swing in European professional golf which has stood the test of time, it is that of Neil Coles. He turned professional at the age of 16 with a handicap of 14 but over the years he has developed a highly successful swing and his smooth, rhythmic style has become an outstanding feature of the tournament scene and the envy of many of his fellow professionals.

Coles' first victory as a professional came in 1955, and within six years he had established himself as a prominent money-winner on the Tour. Over the next two decades he was never out of the top 20. He was the first man to take his career earnings through the £200,000 barrier. In the light of today's huge prize funds this may not seem a great achievement, but one has to remember that when Coles was in his prime the first prize was equivalent to ninth or even 19th place in the present Tour.

In all, Coles amassed some 27 major tournament wins, a remarkable achievement by any standards and one which the leading players of today will be hard pressed to surpass.

In his youth, Coles was reputed to have a fiery temper which many observers felt held him back. As he matured and gained confidence, he mastered that problem and became outwardly calm and unflappable, at least on the golf course. But the relaxed style disguised a fiercely competitive nature and this, allied to a superb short game, made him a consistently low scorer, a fact confirmed by his winning the Tooting Bec Cup (awarded to the home player who returns the lowest round in the Open Championship) on three occasions. Among many victories were three PGA Match-Play Championships, in 1964, 1965 and 1973.

An unhappy experience on a flight between Edinburgh and London left Coles with an aversion to flying, and although he played most of the Continental events on the tour by driving by car to and from the tournaments, his unwillingness to fly prevented him from exploiting fully his talents in the international stage.

An outstanding Ryder Cup record of 40 matches played over a period of 16 years bears testament to the staying power of one of Britain's outstanding professionals.

Henry COTTON, MBE

b 1907

It is said that every tournament professional should pay a percentage of everything he earns to Henry Cotton, for he was the man who did more than any other to upgrade the status of the golf professional from that of lowly employee, who was not permitted to enter the clubhouse, to the superstar level enjoyed by many of them today.

Educated at a public school in Dulwich, Henry Cotton broke the mould for professional golfers, who previously had come into the game either as former caddies or as the son of existing golf professionals.

He made his breakthrough in 1926 when he won the Kent Open for the first time. He

Left: Henry Cotton in elder statesman guise. The only Briton of recent years to win three Open Championships, he became the most influential of players, helping to raise the status of the professional from employee to superstardom.

quickly moved on to greater things and by 1929 he had been selected for the Ryder Cup team. The following year saw Cotton confirm his position as one of Britain's leading professionals and he finished runner-up in the PGA Matchplay Championship. In 1931 he won the Dunlop Southport event, a victory he was to repeat the following year.

In 1934, despite poor form in practice, Cotton captured the first of his three Open titles. The foundations for his Sandwich win were laid with two magnificent opening rounds of 67 and 65 (the latter giving the name to the famous Dunlop 65 golf ball), which gave Cotton a nine-stroke lead and although he faltered in the final round he recovered to win by five strokes.

At Carnoustie in 1937 he faced the whole of the American Ryder Cup team, who were in Britain for the Cup matches, and despite foul weather during the final two rounds Cotton's straight hitting and fine long-iron play stood him in good stead and provided the platform for an outstanding victory.

Cotton's final Open triumph at Muirfield in 1948 heralded his swansong in major events. Although he won the 1954 Penfold tournament at the age of 47, he had by then become an infrequent competitor on the circuit.

Right: Ben Crenshaw plays out of a bunker to where he will be able to use his greatest asset — his putting skill. His US Masters win in 1984 came at a time when it seemed the popular Ben might miss out on the majors.

Ben CRENSHAW

b 1952

As someone who is judged one of the finest putters in professional golf, Crenshaw should have a string of victories to his name. In fact the little Texan, once rated as a challenger to Jack Nicklaus' crown, has fallen short of what was expected of him after a glittering amateur career.

That trend wasn't apparent when he turned pro in 1973. He won his first event, the Texas Open, with rounds of 65, 72, 66, 67 and by the end of nine events had amassed over $76,000 for 34th place on the Tour. Since then his winnings have topped $2 million but his victories total just 13. It was a similar story in major championships until 1984, when he won the US Masters just when it seemed a big title would elude his grasp. What made it all the more sweet was his last-round 68 which left him two shots ahead of Tom Watson. His record in the Open Championship has followed a similar path, with several high finishes to his credit. He is an avid golf historian and a collector of golf memorabilia. His collection of golfing artefacts is said to be worth over $500,000.

Fred DALY

b 1911

Fred Daly's rise to fame was temporarily halted after he won the 1940 Irish Professional Championship by the Second World War. Some might have been bitter at losing those vital years between 1939 and 1946 but Daly promptly took up where he had left off in 1940 by winning the Irish Professional Championship again in 1946, and then going on to take the Irish Open title in the same year.

This double victory quickly established Fred Daly on the British tournament scene and he further enhanced his reputation by finishing eighth in the Open that same year.

Daly's liking for the Open Championship

was soon to become even more apparent for the following year at Hoylake he went on to win the title with rounds of 73, 70, 78 and 72. The weather, which had been unpredictable throughout the Championship, deteriorated just as Daly completed his final round and none of the others in contention were able to match his total of 293, which gave him victory by a single shot from Reg Horne and the great American amateur, Frank Stranahan.

In 1948 Daly finished in second place behind Henry Cotton at Muirfield and at Troon the following year he retained his reputation as a gritty Open contender with a third place behind South Africa's Bobby Locke. For the next few years he continued to strive for his second Open title but was never able quite to achieve that goal.

Daly played in the Ryder Cup team on four occasions between 1947 and 1953 with a fair amount of success but by the early 1950s he had begun to suffer from ill health and over the next few years his tournament appearances became fewer and fewer.

Fred Daly was a small man but he made up for any disadvantages by using a very heavy driver and developing a full, supple swing that produced long straight shots. His other great asset was a superb judgement of pace, something which always stood him in good stead on the big links greens of the Open Championship venues.

Jimmy DEMARET
b 1910 – d 1983

Although he failed to win either the US Open or US PGA Championships, Demaret stamped his mark on the US Masters, winning it three times. In 1940 he won by four shots, then a record, from Lloyd Mangrum and was first again in 1947 ahead of Byron Nelson and Frank Stranahan. When he won again in 1950 he became the first three-time winner. His US Open record shows he came close, being runner-up to Ben Hogan in 1948, then finishing one shot out of the 1957 play-off between Mayer and Middlecoff.

Demaret joined the US Tour in 1938 after lifting the Texas PGA Championship five times consecutively from 1934, and in his first year on tour he won the Los Angeles Open. In 1940 he won six events apart from the Masters and he claimed another half-dozen in 1947 when he was leading money-winner and won the Vardon Trophy for the lowest stroke average. He played in three Ryder Cups between 1947 and 1951 with an unbeaten record and also represented the US in the 1961 World Cup. He has 44 tournament wins and was elected to the PGA Hall of Fame in 1960.

Left: The first Irishman to win the British Open, Fred Daly drives off. His 1947 win was followed by a string of good performances which just failed to win him a second title.

Below: Roberto de Vicenzo might have looked like this when missing out on the Masters through a technicality, but this look of anguish was due only to a missed putt. The popular Argentinian's Open win made up for years of near misses.

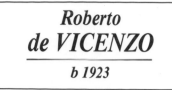

Roberto
de VICENZO

b 1923

Roberto de Vicenzo has the unique distinction of being more famous for a tournament he lost, rather than one he won. In 1968 he stormed through the field in the final round of the US Masters with a brilliant closing score, seemingly to force a play-off with American Bob Goalby. Unfortunately it was then discovered that he had signed his card for a 66 when in fact he had scored a 65. Sadly the score he had signed for had to stand and the South American lost his chance of a play-off with Goalby.

One of the game's most popular players, Roberto de Vicenzo is the finest golfer South America has ever produced and his driving ambition was to win the British Open. Year after year, he made the pilgrimage to Britain in search of his personal 'Holy Grail' and although he came close on several occasions, as the years passed, it seemed his chance was gone. But he refused to give up and in 1967 at Hoylake, aged 44, he finally became Open champion.

Despite his pre-occupation with the British Open, de Vicenzo still found time to win the Argentine Open nine times and collected more than 200 tournament victories worldwide throughout his long and distinguished career. Seldom has there been a more popular golfer and Roberto de Vicenzo still attracts a host of admirers when he appears on the Seniors Circuit.

Below: Roberto de Vicenzo might have looked like this when missing out on the Masters through a technicality, but this look of anguish was due only to a missed putt. The popular Argentinian's Open win made up for years of near misses.

Nick
FALDO

b 1957

Nick Faldo is a natural athlete who before he took up golf was a keen cyclist and swimmer. He first became interested in golf when he saw the Open Championship on TV, and with a superb natural rhythm and the help of teaching professional Ian Connelly he made rapid progress in learning to play the game. By 1974 he had won Youth International honours and over the next few years swept all before him on the amateur circuit, winning such prestigious events as the Berkshire Trophy, the County Champion of Champions and the English Amateur Championship at the record age of 18 years and 8 days.

Faldo joined the professional ranks in April 1976 and the following season he won his first tournament, the Skol Lager Individual. He continued to improve rapidly and 1978 saw him win the first of his three PGA Championships, his other two victories coming back-to-back in 1980 and 1981. That same year Faldo also finished third in the Order of Merit and established himself as an outstanding prospect for the future.

In 1983 he won five times in Europe to top the money list and the following year broke through in America by winning the Heritage Classic. At this stage in his career, Faldo decided to make major changes to his swing under the guidance of David Leadbetter, a Zimbabwe professional resident in Florida. It was an arduous process and Faldo spent two

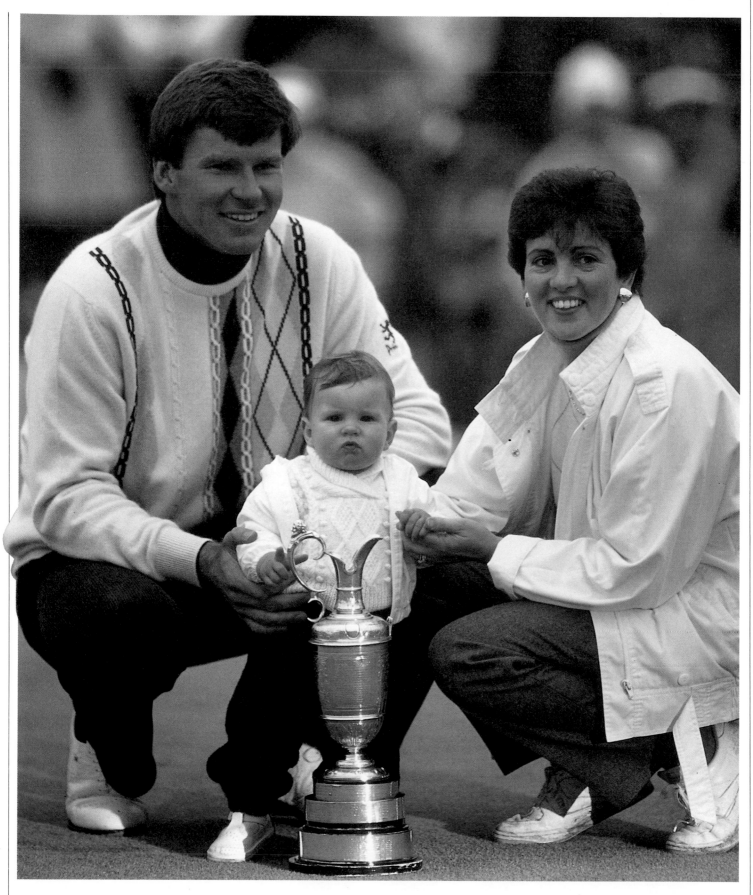

years struggling with his game before any improvement emerged.

His determination was justified when he recorded his first victory for three years by taking the 1987 Spanish Open over the difficult Las Brisas course and then, at a wet and windy Muirfield for the 1987 Open Championship, he reached a new pinnacle. Lying one stroke behind the leader after three rounds, Faldo played superbly in the final round and, under mounting pressure, completed the last 18 holes with par figures on every hole. His round of 71 was good enough to give him the Open title by one stroke.

Above: Nick Faldo and his family pose with the Open Championship trophy of 1987, when he became the second Briton in three years to win. His final winning round was an oddity: par for every hole.

Max
FAULKNER
b 1916

One of the game's true eccentrics, Max Faulkner's exceptional talent more than compensated for constant changes in the way he played and the different types of clubs he tried. He was constantly changing his clubs and experimenting with new theories and at one time was reputed to have owned over 300 putters and used every one of them!

There was nothing strange about his Open Championship victory at Portrush in 1951, except the fact that he was signing autographs: 'Max Faulkner, Open Champion' when there were still two rounds to play. However, his confidence was fully vindicated as he went on to take the title, finishing two shots ahead of Antonio Cerda.

Although considered a little eccentric in his attitude to golf, he was nevertheless a player who was renowned for his straight driving and excellent long-iron play. During his career on the professional circuit, he won eight major tournaments, three Spanish Open titles and, at the age of 52, the Portuguese title.

Faulkner played in the Ryder Cup matches five times but unfortunately never won a singles match. His colourful character was matched by his taste in golf attire and he loved to wear outlandish colours and fashions. There was no way you could mistake Max Faulkner as he strode the fairways.

Ray
FLOYD
b 1942

If there is one man who can never be written off whenever a major championship comes around then it is Raymond Floyd. Twice a winner of the US PGA (1969, 1982) and once the US Masters (1976), he collected his first US Open title in 1986 and now only needs an Open Championship to complete his set.

This sort of record contrasts with his playboy image during the early years of his pro career, when a colourful night-life held more sway than the fairways. However, when he put his mind to golf he proved a fierce competitor who has only been out of the top 60 in the Tour money list three times since he joined in 1963. His career earnings are now approaching $3 million which proves he can never be discounted. He shares with Jack Nicklaus the Masters low aggregate record of 271, including 21 birdies and an eagle. Veteran of six Ryder Cup matches and a regular away from America with wins in Brazil, Canada and Costa Rica, he went to

Far left: Max Faulkner was a flamboyant golfer who dressed and played with a flourish, especially in 1951 when he won the Open in style.

Left: Ray Floyd is another colourful golfer who early in his career managed what was thought to be the first topless band, 'The Ladybirds'. He plays best when it matters most, winning three of the four majors and the Sun City $1 million Challenge.

South Africa and won the Sun City $1 million Challenge in 1982.

Al
GEIBERGER
b 1937

If he never hits another ball, Al Geiberger will always be remembered as the first player to break 60 for a round in an official Tour event. It came during the second round of the Memphis Classic at the Colonial Country Club on 10 June 1977, when he shot a 59 including 11 birdies and an eagle, which earned him the nickname 'Mr 59'. And he had to sink an eight-foot birdie putt on the final hole to seal it. His only other real claim to fame was victory in the 1966 US PGA Championship, his only major win, but he has twice been second in the US Open.

Geiberger joined the Tour in 1960 with reasonable success and has been five times in the top ten and on the money list. He played in the 1967 and 1975 Ryder Cups but ill-health has dogged him since the 1970s, necessitating several operations. He had surgery for an intestinal disorder in 1978, a knee operation in 1979 and had his colon removed a year later. There have been other operations since and he now plays infrequently on the Tour.

David
GRAHAM
b 1946

Although a native of Australia, David Graham has played the majority of his golf in America. Among his many achievements since joining the US Tour is the unique distinction of being the only non-American to win both the US Open and PGA titles.

In the 1979 US PGA he won a dramatic play-off against Ben Crenshaw, holing two monster putts for halves on the first two extra holes and then making a birdie three at the next hole for victory.

David Graham's final round of 67 in the 1981 US Open at Merion was considered by many to be one of the finest demonstrations of accuracy ever witnessed in a major championship. He had started the day three shots behind the leader George Burns II, but Graham's closing 67 swept him to a three-stroke victory.

In 1976 he captured the World Match Play title at Wentworth, thanks to some remarkable putting that left American Hale Irwin dazed and defeated.

Sometimes described as rather a hard-nosed character, Graham has a machine-like swing that works very well for him and since joining the US Tour in the early 1970s, he has won eight tournaments and finished in the top ten on numerous occasions. In recent years he has also become involved in designing golf clubs for a leading American manufacturer.

Below: David Graham urges in a putt. An Australian, Graham has played most of his professional golf on the US Tour where he has produced some brilliant golf.

Left: Walter Hagen drives at Muirfield's 14th in 1929 on his way to his fourth and final Open Championship. Hagen did not like the 'toffee-nosed' attitude of the British golf establishment and mocked it, helping to force a change in attitudes.

Hubert GREEN
b 1946

Green possesses a deep Southern brogue and one of the most unorthodox swings in golf. Despite the swing Green is a talented player and always one to be watched. He joined the US Tour in 1971 and except for a couple of occasions has always collected one tournament each year. His best year so far was 1974 when he finished third on the money list after four wins. In 1976 he joined the elite by winning three events in a row, the Doral Eastern Open, Greater Jacksonville Open and the Sea Pines Heritage Classic. The first of his two majors came with the 1977 US Open at Southern Hills, the second when he took the US PGA at Cherry Hills in 1985.

Green looked set to take the 1978 US Masters when he went into the final round with a three-shot lead. But Gary Player shot 64 and Green missed a 30-inch putt on the final hole to tie and instead finished runner-up with Tom Watson and Rod Funseth. He has finished third and fourth in the Open Championship but can claim victories in Ireland and Japan. He has played in three Ryder Cups, in 1977, 1979 and 1985.

Walter HAGEN
b 1892 – d 1969

Flamboyant, brash, colourful, controversial — these are all adjectives used to describe Hagen, the former caddie who strode golf like a giant before and after the First World War. He was certainly a pioneer, lifting the game out of its dull jacket and breeches era into the age of colourful clothes and brash showmanship. He also broke down the social barriers between the pro and amateur. Altogether he won 11 major championships, a record exceeded only by Jack Nicklaus and Bobby Jones. He was extremely popular with crowds and always happy to chat to fans between shots.

Hagen began competitive golf in 1912 and two years later took his first US Open. He did it again in 1919 although it needed a play-off, but his greatest achievements came in the US PGA when it was a match-play event. From 1921 to 1927 he won the Championship five times, four in a row from 1924, was runner-up once and didn't enter on the other occasion. He also had a glowing record in the British Open, winning in 1922 at Sandwich, in 1924 at Hoylake, 1928 at Sandwich again, and 1929 at Muirfield and he was runner-up to Arthur Havers at Troon in 1923. Hagen was also third once, and all this from 10 entries.

Despite his 1922 victory, he wasn't keen on conditions in Britain as professionals were not allowed to change or eat in the clubhouse at Royal St George's. Hagen countered by hiring a limousine in which to change his shoes and eat, and he parked it in front of the clubhouse. Then, on seeing the size of his prize he handed it to his caddie.

A year later, on finishing second to Havers, Hagen refused to attend the presentation in the Troon clubhouse, preferring to invite the crowd for a drink at a local pub instead. He did not win another major victory after 1929, although he remained a threat. He was eclipsed by Jones, who clinched his Grand Slam in 1930.

Harold
HENNING
b 1934

A regular visitor to Europe between 1961 and 1979, the Johannesburg-born Harold Henning, or 'Horse' as he was nicknamed by his fellow professionals, is one of the top South African golfers to emerge on the scene over the past 30 years.

Renowned for his superb putting touch, Henning was never out of the top 50 in seven out of the eight years he competed full-time in Europe, winning 13 tournaments, with five victories in Britain and eight on the Continent. His biggest payday in Britain, by a long way, was the £10,000 he collected for a hole-in-one when winning the Esso Golden Tournament at Moor Park in 1963 — an enormous sum of money in those days.

Henning, who amassed 54 tournament wins worldwide during his career, also partnered his fellow South African, Gary Player in several World Cup campaigns, winning it in 1965.

His British Open record is impressive, and although he has never won the Championship he was twice third, in 1960 at St Andrews and at the same venue again, this time in 1970. He also has two wins in America to his credit and has captured the South African PGA title four times, the last time being in 1972.

Still playing in the late 1980s Harold Henning competes regularly on the Seniors Tour in America.

Right: Harold Hilton was an amateur who twice won the Open Championship, one of only three amateurs to do so. He also has the distinction of winning the British and American Amateur titles in the same year.

Below: South African Harold Henning was one of the most consistent golfers in Europe during the 1960s and 1970s without quite winning the major events. He now plays on the Seniors Tour in the USA.

Far right: Not only one of golf's greatest players, but the hero of one of sport's greatest stories, Ben Hogan came back after an accident which all but killed him to win major championships in inspiring fashion.

Harold
HILTON
b 1869–d 1942

With four British Amateur titles, two Open victories and one US Amateur Championship to his credit, Britain's quirky, cap-wearing Harold Hilton certainly deserves his place among the greats of the game. His career spanned almost 25 years and he was a consistent winner from the 1890s until the First World War.

Short in stature, Hilton was a ferocious hitter with an all-out attacking style, which at times almost led to him swinging himself off his feet, yet he was remarkably accurate, especially with his woods.

One of only three amateurs to win the Open Championship (John Ball and Bobby Jones are the others), Hilton's victory has historical significance, as it was the first time the Championship had been played over four rounds.

Hilton's first Open victory came at Muirfield in 1892. His second title came five years later at Hoylake when he won by a single shot from James Braid and by six strokes from Harry Vardon, winner of the Championship the previous year.

Hilton won the British Amateur title for the fourth time in 1913 but instead of resting on his laurels, he crossed the Atlantic and claimed the US Amateur Championship in the same year.

As well as designing numerous golf courses, Harold Hilton also found time to become the editor of *Golf Monthly* and *Golf Illustrated*.

Ben
HOGAN
b 1912

It was no exaggeration when the mantle 'a legend in his own lifetime' was bestowed on Hogan. He did, after all, win the Masters, US Open and British Open in the same year, 1953, on his way to nine major championships. And it is argued that he only failed to win the US PGA that year because he was unable to get back from Carnoustie in time for it!

But although Hogan achieved much on the course, it was his bravery off it that bolstered his appeal to golf fans everywhere. On a foggy morning in February 1949 his car collided head on with a bus on a road in Texas and Hogan was left for dead, his legs mangled in the wreckage. He was eventually taken to hospital, but many doubted if he would ever walk again, let alone play golf. But Hogan is made of stern stuff. He not only recovered but was back playing the following January to tie with Sam Snead in the Los Angeles Open only to lose the play-off.

However, in that year he won the US Open in five rounds after another tie, retained it in 1951 and triumphed again in 1953. As he had registered his first victory in 1948, that was his fourth Open success. He had won the US PGA twice before his accident, in 1946 and 1948 while the US Masters also fell to him in 1951 and 1953.

Hogan's success in winning all four majors is matched only by Gene Sarazen, Jack Nicklaus and Gary Player. He was a late developer. A professional from the age of 17, he trod a long, hard road to the top. By constant practice he acquired what many feel was the perfect swing, but he didn't win his first tournament until he was 25 and it was another eight years before he took his first major.

By the end of his career he had won 62 tournaments on the US Tour, and was a member of four Ryder Cup teams, twice as US captain. He was elected to the PGA Hall of Fame in 1953 and is generally acknowledged as one of the three greatest players in the history of golf, along with Jack Nicklaus and Bobby Jones.

Brian
HUGGETT, MBE
b 1936

Nicknamed the 'Welsh Bulldog' for his fighting qualities, Brian Huggett is generally accepted as the best golfer Wales has produced since Dai Rees.

Huggett joined the professional ranks in 1961 and finished a highly creditable 22nd on the Order of Merit in his first year. He went on to establish himself quickly as one of Britain's top professionals.

Huggett topped the money list only once in his career, in 1968, but finished in third spot on no less than four occasions, 1963, 1969, 1970 and 1972. Three may have been his lucky number, because he was placed in the top ten a further three times. He also won three tournaments in a single season three times in his career: 1967, 1968 and 1970.

His most prestigious wins in Britain came in 1968 in the PGA Match Play Championship, and in 1970 when he won the Dunlop Masters event at Royal Lytham with a superb final round of 65. He was also a consistent winner in Europe with a number of resounding victories in the German, Dutch and Portuguese Opens.

Perhaps Brian Huggett is best remembered for his Ryder Cup performances, especially that dramatic finish to his singles match against Billy Casper in 1969 when he bravely holed a six-foot downhill putt for the half which he believed had won the Ryder Cup for the home team. The match, in fact, ended in a draw but few people who witnessed the match will ever forget the little Welshman's gutsy performance.

The same fighting qualities also served Huggett well in the Open Championship and he came close to winning the title in 1965 when he was joint runner-up to Peter Thomson.

On his retirement from the Tour, Huggett spent a brief spell as club professional at St Pierre Golf and Country Club.

Bernard
HUNT, MBE
b 1930

One of the finest medium- and short-iron players of the 1950s and 1960s Bernard Hunt became successful only when he shortened his long flowing action to a three-quarter swing. His misfortune was that his successful period came before the explosion in prize money.

Right: Welshman Brian Huggett remembers one Ryder Cup match particularly — that of 1969 when he thought his six-foot putt had won the Cup and reacted accordingly, only to learn shortly afterwards that the match had been tied.

Left: Hale Irwin is one of those successful and consistent players who has not quite entered the consciousness of the public at large, perhaps because his 20 tournament wins and $2 million in prize money have come from solid consistency rather than extravagant flair.

Tall and slim, Hunt adapted his game so successfully that he became a consistent money winner and in 1953, one of his best years, he collected no fewer than six titles. He was a spectacular scorer, and produced some remarkable low rounds which included playing the first nine holes in the 1953 Spalding tournament in 28 strokes. Among his other low scoring achievements was a run of seven straight birdies and four rounds of 66, 63, 66 and 67 in the 1966 Piccadilly World Match Play event held over the East course at Wentworth.

In all, he collected 37 victories in his professional career and he also put together an outstanding series of Open Championship finishes with four top ten places. A regular Ryder Cup player between 1953 and 1969, Hunt had the unfortunate distinction of three-putting the final green in his debut match when two putts would have secured a tie. Thereafter he won four and halved three of his ten singles, beating such players as Doug Ford, Jerry Barber, Dow Finsterwald and Gene Littler.

After a fine start to the 1970 season which saw him win the first three events, he began to compete less on the Tour, but he was still figuring in the top 50 on the Order of Merit in 1975. Today, he is the club professional at Foxhills Golf and Country Club, near Weybridge in Surrey.

Hale IRWIN
b 1945

Solidly competitive, Irwin has won over 20 tournaments since turning professional in 1968 and has topped $2 million in earnings.

Irwin's first big success was the 1971 Heritage Classic and his second came in the same tournament two years later. In 1974 he sprang something of a surprise by winning his first major, the US Open at Winged Foot, by two shots. His only other major success came in the 1979 US Open at Inverness when he beat Gary Player and Jerry Pate into second spot, despite a final round of 75. That year he also led the Open Championship going into the final round at Royal Lytham, but he fell away as Seve Ballesteros took his first major victory. Irwin's best Open finish is joint second with Andy Bean behind Tom Watson in the 1983 event at Birkdale.

Irwin's biggest successes in Britain came in the World Match Play at Wentworth. In 1974, the same year as his US Open success, he took the title and retained it a year later. He was deprived of a hat-trick when David Graham beat him at the 38th hole in 1976. Irwin has also played in four Ryder Cup teams.

Above: The career of Tony Jacklin is one of the most interesting in golf. For a short period he was arguably the best player in the world, but he subsided from this pinnacle after a string of bad luck in a couple of Opens.

Tony JACKLIN, OBE

b 1944

For twelve glorious months beginning in July 1969, Tony Jacklin performed at a level of golfing excellence seldom achieved by even the greatest names the game has known. His dramatic victory at Royal Lytham and St Annes in the Open Championship, when he became the first British golfer since Max Faulkner to win the title, heralded not only the emergence of Jacklin as a truly world-class player, it also served to signal the revival of the belief that Britain could still produce players to challenge and beat the best in the world. In the same year he played a vital role in the Ryder Cup, earning a halved match against the mighty Jack Nicklaus.

In June the following year, at Hazeltine National course in Minnesota, Tony Jacklin confirmed his world-class status when he became only the second British golfer after Ted Ray in 1920 to capture the US Open.

But sadly, just as the British Open had provided the stage for Jacklin's greatest achievement, it was also to be the setting for what many believe to be the beginning of his fall from grace.

The year after his triumph at Royal Lytham he began the defence of his title at The Old Course in St Andrews in spectacular fashion, racing to the turn in an amazing 29 strokes. A birdie at the 10th provided the perfect start for his homeward run but then the heavens opened and play had to be abandoned for the day. The following morning the midas touch had deserted Jacklin and although he went on to finish the championship in a very creditable fifth place behind

Jack Nicklaus, he must have felt that a golden opportunity had passed him by.

It happened again in 1972 at Muirfield, but on this occasion he was the victim of cruel luck and an inspired Lee Trevino.

Although Jacklin went on to win many more tournaments including a dramatic play-off win over Bernhard Langer in the 1982 PGA Championship his putting touch had begun to deteriorate along with his appetite for the tough grind of the professional circuit.

He retired from the tournament scene in the mid-1980s but was soon back in the spot-light again, this time as the non-playing captain of the victorious European Ryder Cup team which he inspired to a historic win at The Belfry in 1985, at which time he was promptly given the job of skippering the team again for the 1987 Ryder Cup matches in America.

Bobby JONES
b 1902 – d 1971

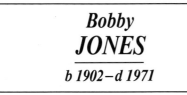

The greatest amateur of all time, Jones reached the climax of his comparatively short yet highly successful career in 1930 when he completed the Grand Slam. Jones won the British Open and Amateur titles, then returned to America for a ticker-tape reception before going on to win both the US Open and Amateur Championships. It is safe to say that the feat will never be repeated.

Jones was virtually invincible during the period 1923–1930, during which he won 13 of what were then regarded as the major championships. This, of course, was before the Masters and US PGA replaced the Amateur Championships of Britain and America as Grand Slam events. He took the US Amateur five times in seven years from 1924 and the US Open in 1923, 1926, 1929 and 1930. In addition he became a firm favourite in Britain by winning the Open three times, in 1926, 1927 and 1930. His 1927 Open win and his British Amateur success came at St Andrews where, on his first visit in 1921, he had torn up his card in frustration. When he returned there in 1958 as captain of the American team for the inaugural World Amateur Team Championship he was given the freedom of the borough.

Incredibly, after his 1930 Grand Slam success, Jones retired at the tender age of 28. He wrote articles on golf and made instruc-tional films, then was responsible for helping design the course at Augusta National and for instituting the US Masters. He played in the first Masters in 1934, and continued until 1947, when he was forced to retire with shoulder pains after two rounds. Towards the end of his life he was crippled by a muscular disease.

Tom KITE
b 1949

If ever a golfer qualified for the title 'The Nearly Man' then it must be Kite. The be-spectacled Texan has been close to winning more tournaments than he cares to remember yet somehow they always seem to slip from his grasp. He is certainly one of the most consistent golfers anywhere, having collected over $2½ million in winnings since he joined the US Tour in 1972. Yet in all that time he has won only ten tournaments. He was lead-ing money winner in 1981 and apart from his first two years on the circuit he has never been out of the top 30. His record in the majors is almost parallel. He has yet to win a title but he has been in the top five in the Masters four times including second spot in 1983 and 1986 and was joint runner-up to Jack Nicklaus in the 1978 Open Champion-ship at St Andrews. His only overseas success came in the 1980 European Open at Walton Heath while in four Ryder Cup appearances Kite has taken 9½ points out of 15.

Left: Bobby Jones has a unique position in golf. An amateur who was almost unbeatable in the late 1920s, his career was climaxed by the unique feat in 1930 of achieving golf's only 'Grand Slam'.

Bernhard LANGER
b 1957

Bernhard Langer's greatest claim to fame could well be the fact that he is one of the few professional golfers to have successfully overcome the dreaded putting 'yips'. A superb striker of the ball, Langer had never been an outstanding putter but when the yips struck, early in his career, he found it almost impossible to get the ball into the hole, especially from inside six feet. However, to the young German's credit, he persevered when lesser men might have given up and his salvation came in the shape of an old 'Bull's Eye' putter which he found in the professional shop at Sunningdale in 1980. Suddenly, his confidence returned, his stroke became smoother and putts began to drop. The following week at Moortown in the Car Care tournament, he finished with rounds of 64 and 65 to take fifth place. Then a few weeks later he became the first German to win a European Tour event when he claimed the Dunlop Masters title with rounds of 70, 65, 67 and 68, leading from start to finish and averaging only 27.5 putts per round. His putting yips now under control, if not fully cured, Langer went from strength to strength and soon established himself as a major force in European golf.

Langer made his first strong bid for a major title in 1981, finishing second in the British Open to America's Bill Rogers at Royal St George's. A few weeks later, he was runner-up again, this time behind Tom Weiskopf in the Benson and Hedges International at Fulford. He then went on to win the Bob Hope Classic at Moor Park the following week. Altogether in 1981 he won twice, was six times runner-up, and was out of the top ten on only three occasions in 17 European tournaments. With £95,990 in prize money he was £40,000 ahead of Nick Faldo in second place. He also made his US debut at the World Series at Firestone, finishing sixth.

He was by now gaining recognition as a great golfer, a reputation finally confirmed on the international stage in 1985 when he won the US Masters at Augusta. Now a regular competitor on the US Tour, Langer's precision play is ideally suited to the tight American courses, and along with his first US Tour victory at the Sea Pines Heritage Classic, he has also been a top ten finisher.

Langer made his Ryder Cup debut at Walton Heath in 1981 and has played in both the matches since then, including the great win at The Belfry in 1985 where he was one of the mainstays of the European team.

Langer was born in Bavaria, and one of his proudest moments came in 1981 when he won his native German Open, a victory he repeated in 1985 and 1986.

Tony LEMA
b 1934 – d 1966

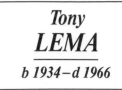

Potentially Lema possessed all the qualities to become one of golf's greatest players but tragically his death in an air crash at the age of 32 leaves only question marks. At the time of his death he was one of the top four players in the world and only two years before he had landed his only major championship, the Open at St Andrews. It was his first golf tournament in Europe and therefore the first time he had set eyes on the Old Course.

Lema earned the nickname 'Champagne Tony' after fulfilling a promise to the press on winning a tournament in America, but his early years on the US Tour were far from champagne stuff. He turned pro in 1955 and although he won his first event two years later he didn't hit the high spots until 1962. He won three events that year, then finished fourth in the money list in 1963 including second place behind Jack Nicklaus in the Masters and equal fifth in the US Open. He had an impeccable Ryder Cup record. In two matches he scored 9 points out of 11. He also reached the semi-finals of the World Match Play in 1965, losing to Gary Player at the 37th.

Lawson LITTLE
b 1910 – d 1968

Little by name but big by reputation, Lawson was the scourge of amateur golf between the wars.

When he reached the semi-finals of the US Amateur in 1933 it earned him a Walker Cup spot the following year, when he paid scant regard to the reputation of Britain's top players. With Johnny Goodman, Little thrashed Britain's best, Wethered and Tolley, 8 and 6, then Little slammed Tolley 7 and 5 in the singles. He was equally ruthless a matter of days later when he reached the Amateur Championship final at Prestwick, beating J. Wallace 14 and 13. Little shot 66 in the morning and had scored 82 for 23 holes when the match finished. Back in America, he took the US Amateur by 8 and 7. In 1935 Little was back in the British Amateur final at Royal Lytham but Dr William Tweddell held him to a one-hole margin. He again took the US Amateur title that year and was sixth in the Masters. He turned pro in 1936, and soon registered the first of his seven wins. However, although he won the US Open in 1940, beating Sarazen in a play-off, Little never did become the top pro many thought he would.

Gene
LITTLER
b 1930

A fine player who could have joined the greats if he had possessed a little more determination and the will-to-win, Littler was casual by nature, content to make a good living off the US Tour while spending as much time as possible with his family and his collection of vintage cars. Nevertheless he managed to win 29 tour events and top $1½ million in winnings since turning pro in 1954. This followed his victory in the 1953 US Amateur and his winning the 1954 San Diego Open as an amateur, which prompted him to join the paid ranks with justified success. However, his record in majors is meagre. His only title came in the 1961 US Open, while he was second in 1954. He tied with Billy Casper for the 1970 US Masters but lost the play-off, while he should have won the 1977 US PGA but jettisoned a lead, allowing Lanny Wadkins to catch him and win the play-off. He is now active on the US Seniors Tour where he collects regular cheques and the odd title.

Right: Bobby Locke of South Africa won four Open Championships between 1949 and 1957, by which time he was a stately figure in plus-fours on the fairways. His main strength was an exceptional touch on the greens.

Bobby
LOCKE
b 1917 – d 1987

One of the true stars of the game, Arthur D'Arcy Locke, along with Australian Peter Thomson, dominated the golfing world during the post-war era. Winner of the British Open on four occasions between 1949 and 1957, Locke's career spanned some 50 years during which time he won 28 professional and amateur events in his native South Africa, 18 tournaments in Great Britain, 15 in America and another 5 overseas.

Always immaculately dressed in plus fours, white shirt, tie, white cap and white shoes Bobby Locke was as meticulous about his play as he was about his appearance, never being rushed into an error.

When it came to technique Locke was the master of the draw, hitting every shot to the right and then curving the ball back onto the target with radar-like accuracy. He had not started out playing this way. It was a technique he adopted when he first came to Britain to enable him to hit the ball further without hitting any harder.

Perhaps the most famous of Bobby Locke's Open wins was at St Andrews in 1957 when the Championship was televised for the first time. On the final green Locke marked his ball to allow a fellow competitor to putt out. However, he inadvertently misplaced the ball before, in front of the TV audience and the thousands of spectators crowded round the final green, he putted out to win. It was

not until later that Locke's error was noticed on a news film, but it was decided that as he had gained no benefit from the situation his victory would stand.

Locke made his first appearance in America in 1947 when he finished 14th in the Masters. Shortly afterwards he won his first US tournament, the Houston Invitational, then went on to become a consistent winner there during the next three years.

Bobby Locke died in 1987 after a short illness at his home in South Africa.

Nancy
LOPEZ
b 1957

When she won the New Mexico Amateur at the age of 12 it was obvious that Nancy Lopez was a champion in the making. From that small beginning she has become one of the greatest women players of recent times. A bubbling, extrovert personality, she has been the dominant figure on the US LPGA Tour since she won five tournaments in a row, nine in all, in 1978, her first full season. She finished number one that year, repeated the feat in 1979 and 1985 and has only been out of the top 10 in 1983 and 1986, the two years when her daughters were born.

Nancy represented America in the Curtis

Cup before turning professional in 1977 and in her first tournament she was second in the Colgate European Open at Sunningdale, which she returned to win in 1978 and 1979.

At the start of the 1987 season she recorded her 35th victory on the LPGA Tour which earned her a place in the LPGA Hall of Fame. She is fourth on the all-time money list with $1¾ million.

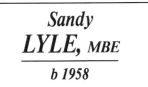

Sandy
LYLE, MBE
b 1958

With only nine holes left to play in the 1985 Open Championship at Royal St George's, Sandy Lyle was battling to get on terms with the leaders. Then birdies on the 14th and 15th swept him into the lead. A dropped shot at the final hole meant a nerve-racking wait to see if anyone could catch him, but when Bernhard Langer's birdie attempt slipped by the 72nd hole, Lyle became the first British winner of the Championship since Tony Jacklin in 1969.

Lyle has the perfect pedigree for a professional golfer. The son of club professional Alex Lyle, he was swinging a golf club around Hawkstone Park almost as soon as he could walk, and as he progressed through the amateur ranks it became apparent he had the potential to go right to the top. He began his career as a professional by winning the 1977 Tour Qualifying School and his first victory came the following year when he won the Nigerian Open. It was the forcrunner of many victories and he soon began to dominate European golf, finishing top of the PGA European Tour money list in 1979, 1980 and 1985.

Lyle made the breakthrough in America when he won the 1986 Greater Greensboro Open and then in 1987 took the US Tour's most important title when he captured the Tournament Players' Championship.

A former Walker Cup player as an amateur, Lyle made his Ryder Cup debut in 1979 and has been a regular in the European team ever since.

John
MAHAFFEY
b 1948

By no means a prolific winner, Mahaffey has nevertheless earned close to $2 million on the US Tour and it might have been more but for injury. After finishing low amateur in the 1970 US Open, he turned pro in 1971 with reasonable success. His first pro victory came in the 1973 Sahara Invitational at Las Vegas but his second win was a 'big one', the US

PGA in 1978. At Oakmont he tied with Tom Watson and Jerry Pate but won the play-off at the second extra hole. This has been his only major success to date but he twice came close to winning the US Open. In 1975 he tied with Lou Graham but lost an 18-hole play-off by two shots then the following year he led eventual winner Pate by two shots going into the final round only to slip away and finish joint third. After his PGA triumph in 1978, he returned the lowest individual score in the World Cup in Hawaii. The following year he was a member of the US Ryder Cup team.

Above: A good-natured kiss of the Open Championship trophy for the photographers from Sandy Lyle, whose 1985 victory ended a 16-year drought for Britons. The long-hitting Lyle went on to success in America.

Lloyd MANGRUM
b 1914–d 1973

Until 1986, Mangrum shared the record for the lowest round in the US Masters. In fact he set it at 64 in finishing runner-up in the 1940 event to Jimmy Demaret. The mark was equalled by several players before South Africa's Nick Price shot 63 to set a new record in 1986. Having been pipped for that 1940 major, Mangrum had to wait until 1946 before taking his only US Open, winning after one of the few 36-hole play-offs in US Open history.

After a distinguished war record, when he won two purple hearts and was twice wounded, he rejoined the US Tour in 1946, and for the next nine years was never out of the top ten money winners. In 1950 he tied for the US Open but lost the play-off and was in the top four on three other occasions. He rarely played in the British Open but competed in the Ryder Cup from 1949 to 1953, losing just two of eight matches and being US captain on the last occasion. All told, he won 46 tournaments including 34 tour events.

Graham MARSH, MBE
b 1944

Formerly a maths teacher, Graham Marsh was runner-up in the 1967 Australian Amateur Championship and winner of the West Australian title before he turned professional in 1968. Since then, 'Swampy', as he is known to his fellow pros, has become one of the most successful international players in the game, winning tournaments in all the major golfing countries around the world. He is the brother of Australian wicket keeper Rodney Marsh.

In 1979, his first year on the European Tour, Marsh finished in 88th place in the Order of Merit, due mainly to the fact that he played only a few tournaments, preferring instead to concentrate on the more lucrative Asian and Far East circuits where he had been the top money winner in 1972 and 1973. Marsh won his first Japanese tournament in 1972, the first of 21 victories he was to achieve there over the next ten years.

Graham's only win in America was the 1977 Heritage Classic, and although finishing 22nd in the money list that year, he rarely appears on the US Tour, preferring now to play in Europe where his most important victories have been the 1977 World Match Play title and the 1981 European Open.

Despite his success around the world, Marsh had to wait until 1982 for his first major victories in his home country. In that year he captured the Western Australia Open and then the Australian Masters.

Graham Marsh has a simple, no-nonsense swing that has to date brought him over 40 victories worldwide, and although he is reducing the number of tournaments he plays in each year, there seems little doubt he will continue to add to that total.

Arnaud MASSY
b 1877–d 1958

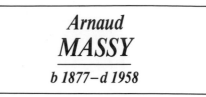

Arnaud Massy became the first non-Briton to win the British Open Championship when he held off the challenge of J.H. Taylor at Hoylake in 1907. He also had the distinction of being the only Continental golfer to win the Open until Seve Ballesteros came on the scene at Royal Lytham in 1979.

A consistent performer in the Open, Massy, who had been fifth in 1905 at St Andrews and sixth at Muirfield in 1906, made a strong challenge to capture the title for a second time at Sandwich in 1911 when he tied with Harry Vardon, but lost the subsequent 36-hole play-off. Back on home ground Massy was an even more formidable opponent, winning the French Open three times and beating Ted Ray and Harry Vardon in the process.

Massy's successes in Europe were considerable and included the French closed title in 1925 and 1926, the Belgium Open in 1910 and the Spanish on three occasions: 1911, 1927 and 1928.

From the Basque region, Massy was probably the finest golfer that France has ever produced. A soldier in the First World War, he was wounded in action at Verdun.

Cary MIDDLECOFF
b 1921

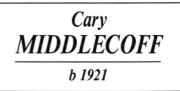

A qualified dentist who went under the nickname 'Doc', Middlecoff also knew how to extract tournament victories. In a professional career lasting from 1947 to the 1960s he secured 37 Tour wins which leaves him in seventh place in the all-time list. After turning pro, he won a tournament in his first season and did so every year until 1961. In 1949 he won the first of two US Opens, winning by one from Clayton Haefner and Sam Snead. He won the Championship again in 1956 by one from Julius Boros and Ben Hogan. Middlecoff was labelled a slow player but it didn't stop him winning the 1955 Masters which he dominated, finishing seven shots ahead of Hogan, then a record margin. He was also runner-up in the 1948 Masters to

Claude Harmon and in the 1955 US PGA to Doug Ford.

Middlecoff took part in the longest play-off in US Tour history, 11 holes being completed in the 1949 Motor City Open when darkness enforced an agreed halt with Lloyd Mangrum. Middlecoff played in the 1953, 1955 and 1959 Ryder Cups.

Johnny
MILLER
b 1947

There was a time in the mid-1970s when Miller almost made the bogey obsolete. From the 1973 US Open at Oakmont, which he won with a final round 63, to his triumph in the 1976 British Open at Royal Birkdale, he strode the world of professional golf like a colossus. The Oakmont performance put him on the map, then in 1974 he won the first three US tournaments on his way to eight victories that year and first place in the money list. At one stage Miller produced 23 rounds of par or better and even though he took two months off, he returned with a similar set of performances. Four more wins came in 1975 during which he carded two rounds of 61. At Birkdale Miller trailed a young Seve Ballesteros going into the final round of the Open but shot 66 to win.

Having scaled the peaks and earned a fortune, Miller fell from grace while also curtailing his number of tournaments. In 1979 he won the Lancome in Paris but during the 1980s victories have been few and far between. He has 23 US Tour victories since turning professional in 1969 and was twice a member of America's Ryder Cup teams.

Above: Like Billy Casper, whose career he followed, Johnny Miller is a Mormon. From 1974 to 1976, when he won the British Open, he was just about the most successful golfer in the world, but then for some reason he slid rapidly down the money list.

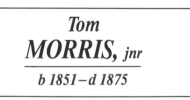

Right: Old Tom Morris, who won the Open four times, despite being 39 when it was inaugurated. He was the most famous player of his day.

Abe
MITCHELL
b 1887–d 1947

Described by J.H. Taylor as the finest player never to win the British Open Championship, Abe Mitchell was one of Britain's best golfers during the 1920s. Mitchell first made his reputation as an amateur, getting to the semi-final of the 1910 Amateur Championship then reaching the final in 1912 where he lost a close encounter to John Ball on the 38th hole at Westward Ho!

Although Abe Mitchell struggled to find his best form in stroke-play events, he suffered no such inhibitions when it came to head-to-head encounters. He won the Match Play Championship on three occasions, in 1919, 1920 and 1929 and also had an excellent record against the United States, halving his singles match with the great Walter Hagen in 1921 and trouncing Jim Barnes 8 and 7 in 1926.

In his first Open Championship after joining the professional ranks, Mitchell finished a highly creditable fourth which, ironically, was his highest finish ever in the Championship. He was in the top six on five occasions and many believe his best opportunity to clinch the title came in the first Championship to take place after the First World War. Mitchell led the eventual winner, George Duncan, by no fewer than 13 shots after 36 holes, only to fall away over the final two rounds and let a golden opportunity slip through his fingers.

Tom
MORRIS, *snr*
b 1821–d 1908

One of the most famous names in golf, Tom Morris (or Old Tom as he came to be known) began his career as an apprentice golf-ball maker, employed by the famous Allan Robertson, who at that time was the premier manufacturer of the 'feathery' golf ball.

Although he was 39 years of age before the first British Open Championship was actually played, Old Tom won the title four times, his final victory coming when he was 46 years old. In fact, Tom Morris snr played in every Open Championship between 1860 and 1869 and his final appearance was at the age of 75.

Morris left his native St Andrews after a dispute with his employer, Allan Robertson, because he preferred to play the new gutta-percha ball in preference to the feathery. He moved to Prestwick on the west coast of Scotland and it was here that he narrowly missed becoming the first-ever winner of the British Open Championship in 1860 when he finished runner-up to Willie Park.

Old Tom returned to St Andrews in 1864 to become the town's first golf professional and greenkeeper, a post he held for many years.

Sadly, Tom Morris died in a tragic accident in 1908 when he fell down a flight of stairs in his home.

Tom
MORRIS, *jnr*
b 1851–d 1875

Tom Morris jnr was perhaps the finest natural talent the game of golf has ever produced. Despite a tragically short career, Tom Morris set playing and scoring records that are remarkable, even by today's standards.

Son of Old Tom Morris, young Tom was a golfing prodigy who by the time he reached the age of 13 had already beaten many leading professionals in a local tournament. And just to prove his victory was no flash in the pan he then went on to win another tournament at Carnoustie after a play-off against Willie Park and Bob Anderson, two of the leading players of the day.

At the age of 17 Tom Morris jnr won his

first British Open, taking the title at Prestwick in 1868, a feat he was to repeat the following year when his father, Old Tom, finished runner-up.

Young Tom went on to demonstrate his remarkable talent and also his domination of the Open Championship by taking the title for the third successive year and thus winning the Championship belt outright. There was no Championship the following year, but in 1872 when the familiar claret jug was introduced as the new Open trophy, Tom Morris jnr was the first name to be engraved on it.

Declining health meant that Young Tom's best finish over the next three years was a solitary second place and when his wife died in childbirth in 1875 it was felt that he lost heart. And in truth he was never again to be a dominant force in the game. He began to suffer from bouts of depression and to drink heavily, all of which contributed to his premature death at the age of 24. Some say his death was the result of a lung complaint, while others claim the cause was a broken heart.

But one fact remains undisputed, and that is that as a golfer he stood head and shoulders above his contemporaries in a manner not to be seen again until the arrival of the 'Great Triumvirate' many years later.

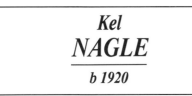

Kel
NAGLE
b 1920

Winner of the 1960 Centenary Open at St Andrews, Kel Nagle was 29 before he won his first important event, the 1949 Australian PGA, his success coming after three years as a professional. Known early in his career as a long hitter but a poor putter, Nagle made little impact over the next few seasons but gradually he improved his putting until he became one of Australia's most consistent players, winning the New Zealand Open on seven occasions between 1957 and 1969.

Kel Nagle first came to Britain in the early 1950s without much success but he did achieve international acclaim partnering his fellow countryman, Peter Thomson, to victory in the World Cup on two occasions: in 1954 and 1959.

Nagle's Open victory at the age of 40 was hard won with two world-class players, Arnold Palmer and Roberto de Vicenzo hard on his heels throughout the final day's play. It was no flash in the pan, for over the next few years he was never far from contention in the Championship, finishing fifth the following year and second at Troon in 1962 behind Arnold Palmer.

Kel Nagle won the Canadian Open in 1964 and then tied with Gary Player in the 1965 US Open before losing the subsequent play-off, and from being a man who did not like to travel too far from home he eventually became a fine international golfer, adding ten wins in Europe between 1960 and 1971 to his victory in Canada, not to mention his Australian tally of 21 events.

Tsuneyuki
NAKAJIMA
b 1955

Because TV commentators in America and Europe found his first name almost impossible to pronounce, the talented Nakajima was christened 'Tommy' and the name has stuck with him since.

The youngest player, at 18, to win the Japanese Amateur title, Nakajima joined the professional ranks in 1976 and shot into the top three on the Japanese Order of Merit thanks to three victories. The following season he claimed his first big title, winning the Japanese PGA Championship.

Despite becoming well known in his own country Nakajima was a comparative unknown in Europe and America but two disastrous holes in separate major championships soon changed that. The first embarrassing moment came at Augusta National when he ran up a 13 at the par three 12th, and the second followed a few months later when he found himself trapped in the famous Road Hole bunker at the 17th hole on the Old Course, St Andrews, and finished with a 9.

However, Tommy Nakajima has put both incidents well behind him and gone on to become a world-class player and a serious contender for major international honours.

Below: Australian Kel Nagle occupies a special place in golf history as the winner of the Centenary Open at St Andrews in 1960.

Byron NELSON
b 1912

Truly a legend in his own lifetime, Byron Nelson's name is spoken in awe and reverence in the same way as are those of Nicklaus and Palmer. His fame stemmed from an astonishing record prior to and during the Second World War. In 1944 Nelson won 13 of 23 tournaments but the following year he demolished all American records by winning 18 events including 11 in succession stretching from 11 March to 4 August. This record stands today, but some are disparaging it because many other top players were away on war service. Nelson, as a haemophiliac, was exempt from military duties. Yet he still carded 19 consecutive sub-70 rounds and a season's stroke average of 68.33. He also won five major championships, beginning with the Masters twice, in 1937 when he came from four behind Ralph Guldahl to win by two shots, and again in 1942, beating Ben Hogan in a play-off. His US Open win came in 1939 at Philadelphia after a three-way tie with Craig Wood and Densmore Shute. Nelson and Wood tied with 68s as Shute was eliminated then in a second 18-hole play-off Nelson won by three after holing a full one-iron for an eagle at the fourth. In the US PGA, he reached the final five times in seven years including three consecutively from 1939. He beat Sam Snead in 1940 and Sam Byrd in 1945 but lost the other three. He only made two British Open appearances, finishing fifth behind Henry Cotton in 1937 at Muirfield, then gracing the 1955 event at St Andrews when Peter Thomson triumphed. But he did win the French Open that year at the age of 43. A former caddie, he has been an influential teacher and the mentor of Tom Watson. He was also non-playing captain of the successful US Ryder Cup team at Birkdale in 1965.

Jack NICKLAUS
b 1940

Without doubt Jack Nicklaus is the greatest golfer of the modern game with 18 major championship victories — 20 if you include two US Amateur titles. He has won the Masters six times, the US PGA five times, the US Open four times and the British Open three times. It is a record unsurpassed. It has eclipsed those of such former greats as Ben Hogan, Walter Hagen, Bobby Jones and Sam Snead and is one which is unlikely to be equalled. His amateur crowns came in 1959 and 1961 but he underlined his potential in 1960 when finishing second to Arnold Palmer in the US Open, while still an amateur.

After turning pro in late 1961, it took Nicklaus only a matter of months before he had the US Open title under his belt, this time beating Palmer, then the great American hero, in a play-off. Since then Nicklaus has stamped his seal on the major championships, so much so that he has completed the 'set' of four on three occasions. Only three other golfers, Hogan, Gene Sarazen and Gary Player, have completed 'sets', then only one each. To the end of 1986, Nicklaus had 71 US Tour victories to his credit, second only to Snead's 84, but his career earnings of almost $5 million are way out in front. Eight times he finished top of the money list and on only two occasions, 1962 and 1979, has he failed to earn less than $100,000 in a year.

Nicklaus has also been a prolific winner outside America with 18 titles, including the World Match Play in 1970 and six Australian Open titles. He has played in six Ryder Cup matches and has twice been non-playing captain, 1983 and 1987. Throughout his career he has acquired nicknames, such as 'Ohio Fats', given him when he was a raw, chunky youngster with a crew cut. But now he is affectionately known as the 'Golden Bear'. Nicklaus has trimmed his tournament appearances in recent years to concentrate on his businesses, which include golf course construction in at least a dozen countries.

Greg NORMAN
b 1955

Greg Norman did not become interested in playing golf until he was 17 years of age, preferring instead to caddy for his mother, who was a keen player. However, once he was bitten by the golfing bug he became a scratch player in just two years. Norman was a natural golfer and success was to come quickly to the big blond Australian, now known throughout the golfing world as the 'Great White Shark'.

Norman joined the professional ranks in 1976 and it took him only four events to land his first win, the West Lake Classic. After just six professional appearances, he was chosen to represent Australia in the World Cup.

In 1977 Norman appeared on the European scene with a reputation for big hitting and an aggressive style of play. Unfortunately, his chipping and putting left a lot to be desired. This is something that he has worked hard on over the past few years and his current high standing in the game today is the direct result of a great improvement in his short game.

That first season in Europe saw Norman win the Martini tournament and finish 20th on the Order of Merit. Over the next few years he began to assert himself as a major

Opposite: The Golden Bear living up to his name with his sweater, hair and even background reflecting the golden theme. Nicklaus' feats mark him out as the greatest of modern golfers, his total of 20 majors being unsurpassed.

Above: Greg Norman's early impact as a big hitter but an erratic player around the greens was changed with a vengeance in the mid-1980s, when he developed a touch which made him a contender in every major tournament he entered. He is pictured with his 1986 Open trophy.

force not only in Europe but also the Far East and in his native Australia.

It was a natural progression for Norman, who along with Seve Ballesteros was the top attraction on the European Tour, to test his mettle in America. With his big hitting and positive style of play, Greg was an instant hit with the American golf fans and in 1983 he became a regular member of the US Tour. That year he finished in seventh position and since then he has climbed to the very top, finishing the 1986 season with $653,296 in prize money and top of the money list. He also played himself into a strong position to win each of the game's four major championships. He missed out at Augusta to Jack Nicklaus, led the US Open going into the final round, and had victory in the US PGA snatched from his grasp when Bob Tway holed out from a greenside bunker at the 72nd hole. However, he did manage to capture his first major that year when he won the Open Championship at Turnberry in Scotland in convincing style.

Norman also excels in match-play golf as his record of three wins in the World Match Play Championship confirms. Now accepted as one of the top three players in the game today, Norman's aim is to capture those other major championships that eluded him in 1986.

Known affectionately to every golfer in his native Ireland as simply 'Himself', Christy O'Connor snr has developed a swing that has withstood the test of time.

While many of his contemporaries have long since given up competitive golf, it appears that O'Connor, like vintage wine, improves with age, a point he demonstrated admirably in 1982 when, aged 57, he won the Seniors Championship for a record fifth time. Perhaps the secret of his staying power can be found in that swing; smooth and unhurried with much of the power provided by his strong hand action and superb timing.

O'Connor made his debut in Great Britain in 1954 when he took Henry Cotton to the 23rd hole in the semi-final of the Penfold event.

Two years later he claimed the first of his numerous tournament victories when he won the Swallow Penfold.

He was the first golfer to win a cheque for £1,000 in a British tournament but his biggest pay day by far was the record £25,000 first prize in the 1970 John Player Classic at Hollinwell.

Although strongly tipped as a potential Open champion, he was never quite able to make the breakthrough, his best finish being in 1958 when he took third place at Royal Lytham.

A Ryder Cup regular, O'Connor compiled an excellent record, playing in every match between 1955 and 1973. In all, he won 24 European events in his career before joining the Seniors Tour.

Peter OOSTERHUIS

b 1948

After an outstanding amateur career which included successes in the Berkshire Trophy and the British Youths as well as winning Walker Cup selection, Peter Oosterhuis turned professional in 1968. Two years later he won his first professional event, the Young Professionals' Championship and, going from strength to strength, climbed to seventh place in the 1970 Order of Merit table.

Oosterhuis went on to dominate the British golf scene in the early 1970s, leading the Merit Table and winning the Vardon Trophy for the lowest stroke average for four consecutive seasons. He ousted Tony Jacklin as Britain's most successful player. In 1972 he finished in the top ten on no less than 17 occasions in 19 tournaments.

After conquering Europe, Oosterhuis set

Left: Christy O'Connor Snr is now a Senior in golfing terms, and continues to mop up Seniors titles as throughout his career he won tournaments in Britain and Ireland. Christy can thank his perfect swing for his successes.

his sights on America and in 1973 came close to winning the US Masters at Augusta, when he found himself leading the field by three shots going into the final round. Unfortunately, a closing 74 dropped him back into third place but nevertheless his overall performance persuaded him to compete regularly on the US Tour and in 1975 he left Britain to live and play in America.

Over the years Oosterhuis has returned to Britain mainly for the Open Championships and when selected for Ryder Cup duty, but in the main he has competed on the demanding US Tour where his one major victory came in the 1981 Canadian Open.

Alf
PADGHAM

b 1906 – d 1966

With a swing described by the great Harry Vardon as 'perfect', it's hardly surprising that Alf Padgham emerged as a leading player of his era. A consistent challenger for the British Open title, Padgham finished in the top six each year between 1933 and 1937, and a sequence of third in 1934 and second in 1935 culminated in his only victory the following year at Hoylake. Padgham's win that year was not without drama, for just as he was about to set out at 8 am on the final two rounds, he discovered that his clubs were still locked away in the professional's shop. With no sign of the pro, and due to tee off in a few minutes time, Alf was forced to smash a window in the shop to redeem his clubs. The episode obviously did not upset him for he returned two 71s to take the title by a stroke from Jimmy Adams.

In normal tournament play Alf Padgham put his name into the record books with four consecutive victories from 1935 to 1936, and he also won the Irish, German and Dutch Opens. He played in three Ryder Cup matches in this period, but without winning a match.

After the Second World War he faded from the tournament scene but his deceptively slow and gentle action and smooth, powerful striking will long be remembered as parts of one of the finest swings of his era.

Arnold PALMER

b 1929

Jack Nicklaus may have won more titles, but Arnold Palmer is the golfer who commands most respect among the game's followers. He is generally credited with doing most to revive American interest in the British Open and setting it on to the road to its present status. His first Open appearance was in the centenary event at St Andrews in 1960, when he finished second behind Australia's Kel Nagle. Palmer won the following year at Royal Birkdale and again in 1962 at Troon: a second and two firsts in three years. In all he has won seven major championships plus one US Amateur, and but for the arrival of Nicklaus on the scene in the early 1960s he would probably have won many more. Ironically his only US Open success came in 1960 when he pipped Nicklaus, then an amateur, by a shot at Cherry Hills. This win followed weeks after his second Masters triumph and established Palmer as a golfing great.

In the 1960 Palmer drew vast crowds whenever he played and these became known as 'Arnie's Army'. However, they couldn't inspire him to a US PGA victory, the only major to elude his grasp, although he finished second three times. Today Palmer still commands a vast following wherever he goes, although he spends most of his playing days on the US Seniors Tour.

Palmer was four times the leading money winner on the US Tour and was the first player, in 1968, to pass $1 million in career earnings. His 61 US victories leaves him fourth on the all-time list, while he also won 19 times overseas including two World Match Play titles, one British PGA, one Australian Open and one Spanish Open. He played in six US Ryder Cup teams and was non-playing captain in 1975. He was elected to the World Golf Hall of Fame in 1974 and the PGA Hall of Fame in 1980, a year after being awarded honorary membership of the Royal and Ancient.

Below: The most charismatic of modern golfers, Arnold Palmer inspired his own 'Army' to follow him through a successful career which brought new enthusiasts to golf and over $1 million to Arnie, the first golfer to win this sum.

Jerry PATE

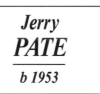

b 1953

For someone who enjoyed a glowing amateur career and a magical start in the professional ranks, Pate could have expected to have amassed more tournament victories than eight on the US Tour plus one in Japan. But he has earned $1½ million despite a severe neck muscle injury and subsequent torn shoulder cartilage which required surgery, curtailing his play.

Pate's brilliant amateur career was highlighted by victory in the 1974 US Amateur Championship, equal first place in the individual in the World Amateur Team Championship and a Walker Cup place in 1975. His first year as a professional, 1976, was full of glittering prizes, none more so than the US Open at Atlanta when he beat Tom Weiskopf and Al Geiberger by two shots. He followed up with the Canadian Open on his way to finishing 10th in the money list. But he came to grief at Royal Birkdale in the British Open, slumping to an 87 in the third round.

Only once since 1976 has Pate come close to winning another major, three-putting the final green in the 1978 US PGA to tie with Tom Watson and John Mahaffey then losing the play-off. Between 1978 and 1982 he was never out of the top 11 in the money list, becoming, at 27, the youngest player to reach one million dollars in winnings. But since 1982 he has struggled to recapture that earlier form.

Gary
PLAYER
b 1935

Pound for pound, Gary Player is the finest golfer of the modern era. Standing only 5 ft 7 in tall and weighing 150 lb, his greatest assets over a long and distinguished career have been his excellent physical condition and sheer determination to succeed.

He first visited Britain in 1955 and was criticized by many of his fellow professionals for having a bad grip, faulty stance and numerous other technical deficiencies. These criticisms served only to harden Player's resolve to succeed and he won his first title that same year, defeating fellow South African Harold Henning in the final of the Egyptian Match Play Championship.

It may not have been the biggest event in golf, but Player's win in Egypt was the vital breakthrough he needed and laid the foundation on which he has built a record of international victories second to none.

The first of his three Open wins came in 1959 at Muirfield when he stormed through the field with a final round of 68. Before that Muirfield win, Player had already made his presence felt in America where he won the Kentucky Derby Open and he was well on his way to becoming the third member of the 'Big Three' along with Arnold Palmer and Jack Nicklaus.

Season 1961 saw Player top the US money list, winning $64,540. That same year he also won the US Masters in a dramatic struggle with Arnold Palmer. The following year Player won his third major title, the US PGA, becoming the first overseas player to win it. Then, in 1965, he joined an elite band of golfers, Jack Nicklaus, Gene Sarazen and Ben Hogan, when he captured the US Open and went into the record books as winning all four of the game's major titles.

Player kept up his globe-trotting schedule, jetting between the golfing capitals of the world without any noticeable effect on his health or form. He is renowned for his determination, and this facet of his character has served him well, especially in match-play situations. Five times a winner of the World Match Play Championship, his most famous win was against the tall Tony Lema in 1965, when he fought back from a seemingly hopeless position of seven down with only 17 holes to play, to triumph.

Player's list of achievements compares favourably with any of the game's legends and he most certainly made his mark in the major championships with three British Opens, three US Masters, one US Open and two US PGA titles to his credit.

Described as the finest bunker player in the game, he is quoted as saying after holing a sand shot: 'The more I practise, the luckier I get'.

A fitness fanatic, Player has won more than 120 tournaments around the world and since joining the Seniors Tour, he has steadily added to his haul.

Above: Gary Player in unusual light garb. He preferred black because he thought it absorbed the sun's rays.

Above: Allan Robertson (third from right), the best player of his day, whose superiority was acknowledged even before there was an Open Championship to prove it. Second left is Old Tom Morris, his successor as the best.

Ted RAY

b 1877 – d 1943

With Harry Vardon and Tony Jacklin, Ted Ray is one of only three British golfers to have won both the US and British Open Championships.

A tall, powerfully-built man, Ray hit the ball huge distances with a violent action that almost swung him off his feet — yet he never lost his grip on the pipe he kept firmly clenched between his teeth while playing.

Ray first came to prominence in 1903 in the final of the Match Play Championship, when he finished runner-up to James Braid, and by 1907 he was also becoming a serious challenger for the Open title which he eventually won in 1912 after a series of high finishes over the previous six years.

Ted Ray's US Open victory came in 1920 at the Inverness Club, Ohio. As the championship neared its climax, it appeared that Vardon was heading for a comfortable win but Ted Ray finished strongly to snatch the title by a single shot from Harry Vardon, Jack Burke, Leo Diegel and Jock Hutchison.

Ray's win signalled the end of British domination of the American championships.

Dai REES, CBE

b 1913 – d 1983

Standing only 5 ft 7 in in height, Dai Rees may have been considered on the short side for a top-class golfer, but whatever he may have lacked in inches, the little Welshman more than made up for in fighting qualities and skill. And the 21 tournament wins he recorded in his career confirm his position among the great British players.

It was in the PGA Match Play Championship that Rees first made the headlines when, after being five down with only 12 holes to play against Ernest Whitcombe, he fought back to win.

In all Dai Rees won four match-play titles and reached the final on another three occasions in 1953, 1967 and 1969.

Along with Abe Mitchell, Rees was probably the best British golfer not to win the Open Championship. On several occasions he seemed to have the title within his grasp, only to see his chance slip away in the final round.

He came closest to winning the Championship in 1954 at Birkdale when he came to the final hole requiring a par to tie. He hit a good approach shot which ran just through the green, but Rees failed to get down in two more shots and finished in second place behind Peter Thomson of Australia.

Rees was a Ryder Cup regular throughout his career and he captained the team as a player in the four matches between 1955 and 1961, and was also a non-playing captain in 1967. A victory for Great Britain and Ireland in 1957, the first British win since the Second World War, was a highlight of his career.

Age proved no barrier to success as he proved in 1973 when, aged 60, he tied for second place in the Martini Tournament.

Rees had a full-flowing swing and throughout his career used a double-handed or hammer grip, which was unique among the top professionals of his day.

Allan ROBERTSON

b 1815 – d 1858

It is difficult to assess fully the talents of Allan Robertson, for he never had the opportunity to compete in the Open Championship, which was first played at Prestwick in 1860, two years after his death.

However, from the records which are available Robertson was undoubtedly the outstanding player of his time. It has been suggested that the Open was instigated after his death to find the best golfer; for while he was alive there had not been any doubt about who held that position.

There was known to be a great rivalry between Allan Robertson and Tom Morris snr, both on and off the course. Morris, who was an apprentice 'feathery' maker working for Robertson, left to manufacture the new gutta-percha ball in competition to his former employer, something which Robertson saw as a threat to his livelihood.

Before their disagreement Robertson and

Morris had often partnered each other in many matches against other top names of the day.

Allan Robertson was the first man to break 80 around the famous Old Course at St Andrews and when he eventually conceded that gutta-percha golf balls had come to stay, he was among the first to investigate the difference they would make to the game when allied to the introduction of iron clubs for playing approach shots to the greens.

Bill ROGERS

b 1951

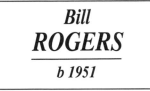

When Bill Rogers won the Open Championship at Sandwich in 1981 it was by a somewhat bizarre route. First he was persuaded to enter by a close friend, Ben Crenshaw, then he was lucky not to be disqualified before hitting a ball. He misread the starting sheet and only the intervention of a pressman got him to the first tee in time. He wasn't the most fancied champion as he began with 72 but a second round 66 put him one ahead before a 67, 71 finish saw him join the exclusive club. That year he went on to take the World Series, the Suntory and Texas Opens, reach the semi-finals of the World Match Play, then venture 'down under' to win the Australian and New South Wales Opens: five wins in six outings.

Rogers was a superstar but his early pro career, which started in 1974, took some time to get off the ground. His first win came in the Bob Hope Classic in 1978. Then he came to Britain to take the 1979 World Match Play Championship, beating Isao Aoki in the final. In recent years he has lost much of his enthusiasm for the game and successes have been few and far between.

Doug SANDERS

b 1933

Doug Sanders is probably best known for the most famous putt of the modern game and it cost him dearly. It was in the 1970 Open Championship at St Andrews and, having had to pre-qualify because of an indifferent US Tour record, he looked to have the title won when he splashed out of the notorious Road Hole bunker to earn his par. All he needed was another par at the comparatively easy 18th and he was champion ahead of Jack Nicklaus. A good drive was followed by an indifferent chip to the back of the green. The long putt finished three feet away but one more stroke would still give him the title. He missed, which proved a shattering experience

as Nicklaus went on to win the following day's play-off by a stroke, Sanders, ironically, birdieing the 18th. He also finished a shot behind Nicklaus in the 1966 Open and was fourth in 1972, both at Muirfield. Sanders suffered similar fates in other majors, finishing joint second in the 1961 US Open and the 1959 US PGA. Sanders was a US Tour player from 1957, winning 20 events and over $¾ million. These days he plays on the Seniors Tour and promotes junior golf.

Gene SARAZEN

b 1902

A dapper little man in plus fours, Sarazen was born Eugene Saraceni but changed his name because he felt it sounded as if he should be playing a violin. His golfing career has spanned half a century, from Vardon to Nicklaus, but despite all his success it was one shot that put him on the map as far as British golf fans are concerned. It came when he accepted an invitation, as a former champion, to play in the 1973 Open at Troon. Sarazen was then aged 71 but the Champion-

Below: Gene Sarazen teeing off in the 1970 Masters, when he was 68 years old. He had won the US Open as far back as 1922. In 1973 he played in the British Open at Troon to celebrate the 50th anniversary of his first Open appearance, and holed in one.

ship marked the 50th anniversary of his first appearance in the Open at the same venue when, as the latest star of the American scene, he failed to qualify. This time, playing with two other ex-champions, Fred Daly and Max Faulkner, he holed his tee shot at the Postage Stamp eighth and the TV cameras were there to record it.

A natural golfer, Sarazen won the first of his two US Open titles in 1922 at the age of 20 and a couple of months later added the US PGA crown. He retained it the following year, inflicting on Walter Hagen his only defeat in five successive finals. A barren spell followed but in 1932 Sarazen returned to Britain to win his Open Championship on the only occasion it has been held at Prince's, Sandwich. He also won the US Open that year, then in 1933 he triumphed in the US PGA for the third time.

Sarazen's only Masters crown came in 1935 when an albatross two, sinking his 4-wood over water at the long 15th, enabled him to catch Craig Wood and win the play-off. Sarazen's Masters victory also made him the first man to complete a 'set' of major titles.

He played in six successive Ryder Cups from 1927, losing only once in the singles, then met with more success in the Seniors competitions. He is generally credited with inventing the sand wedge.

Below: Sam Snead won more events on the US Tour than anybody before or since, an amazing 84 victories spread over nearly 40 years. His failure to win the US Open is the only blot on a career which otherwise carried all before it.

Horton SMITH

b 1908 – d 1963

In the winter of 1928/9 Horton Smith burst on to the US tournament scene with a vengeance. He won eight of the nine events, a record which earned him a place in Walter Hagen's American Ryder Cup team, but although he won his singles it wasn't enough to prevent Britain winning 7–5. However, he maintained an unbeaten record through two more Ryder Cups, 1933 and 1935, and was chosen again in 1939 and 1941 only for the Second World War to prevent either match being played.

After his 1928/9 performances, Smith was a regular winner over the following ten years and is remembered as being the first winner of the US Masters in 1934. In 1936 he won again, making up seven shots on Harry Cooper to win by one. He was third in the 1930 US Open behind Bobby Jones and Macdonald Smith, joint third the same year in the Open Championship at Hoylake and third again in the 1940 US Open.

Macdonald SMITH

b 1890 – d 1949

Macdonald Smith was arguably the best of the three Carnoustie-born golfing brothers of whom Alex and Willie were the others. But Macdonald never managed to win a major championship despite coming close on a string of occasions. He tied for the US Open in 1910 but lost the play-off with Johnny McDermott and his own brother Alex, who became champion. He was second again in 1930 to Bobby Jones and in the top six four more times. In the British Open his record was even more incredible. He was second in 1930 — to Jones again — and 1932, third in 1923 and 1924, fourth in 1925 and 1934 and fifth in 1931. He should have won in 1925 when he had a five-shot lead going into the final round at Prestwick, but he shot an 82. However, in a career that spanned over a quarter of a century, Smith enjoyed a successful tournament record.

Sam SNEAD

b 1912

Sam Snead is one of a small band of famous players whose illustrious careers contain one flaw: they missed out on one of the major championships. With Arnold Palmer it was the US PGA. With Lee Trevino it was the US Masters and with Snead it was the US Open. But he came incredibly close, finishing second on four occasions, sometimes when he could have expected to have won. In 1939 at Philadelphia he took eight at the final hole when five would have been good enough; in 1947 he missed a comparatively short putt on the final hole of the play-off after a tie with Lew Worsham.

Despite these slips, Snead won the Masters and the US PGA three times and the British Open once, in 1946 at St Andrews when the Championship resumed after the Second World War. Perhaps the stage for Snead's greatest achievements was Augusta where, with Ben Hogan, he helped establish the Masters as a prestige event. Between 1949 and 1954 Snead won three times and Hogan twice. Snead's US PGA hat-trick victories in 1942, 1949 and 1951 were all in match-play, a side of golf that seemed tailor-made for him. This was fully illustrated in the Ryder Cup where, in seven matches between 1937 and 1959 he was beaten only once, by Harry Weetman at Wentworth in 1953.

Snead was back on the Ryder Cup scene in 1969 as the American non-playing captain at Royal Birkdale for that famous tied match. However, he is believed not to have been best pleased with Jack Nicklaus' generosity in conceding a missable putt to Tony Jacklin for a half on the last green of their encounter: a gesture which is now famous as one of the most sporting in the game.

Snead's playing record is second to none. On the US Tour he amassed 84 victories, substantially more than anyone else, and 13 more than Nicklaus. His success was based on a beautiful swing — 'Swinging Sam Snead' became a newspaper description — which helped him remain a great player well into middle age.

Hal
SUTTON
b 1958

Following such a distinguished amateur career, it was felt that Sutton would be a natural winner when he turned professional late in 1981. Those predictions came true in 1982 as the former Walker Cup man made an instant impression on his way to finishing 11th in the money list. He had eight top ten finishes including two seconds and a third place but had to wait until the final event of the season, the Walt Disney Classic, before claiming his first victory. The following year Sutton won the TPC then the US PGA at the Riviera County Club, California, pushing Jack Nicklaus into second spot. He finished leading money winner that year and despite not claiming a victory in 1984, bounced back with two wins in each of the following two

years. In his amateur days he won Walker Cup honours in 1979 and 1981 and was top amateur in the Open Championship at Sandwich in the latter year.

J.H.
TAYLOR
b 1871 – d 1963

In 1894 John Henry Taylor became the first English professional to win the Open, on the first occasion that the Championship was held outside Scotland, at Sandwich in Kent.

Taylor, a member of the 'Great Triumvirate', along with Harry Vardon and James Braid, began his life as a golf professional at Burnham in Somerset. He was already by 1894 an excellent player and proved it the following year when he defeated Andrew Kirkcaldy in a match, shortly thereafter following the Scot as professional at Winchester.

The 1895 Open was played at St Andrews, where Taylor retained the trophy and was heralded as the finest player in Britain. A year later J.H. Taylor and Harry Vardon first met in a head-to-head match, played at Ganton where Vardon was the professional. Taylor suffered a heavy defeat going down 8 and 7. A month later they were battling against each other once again but on this occasion it was in a play-off for the Open Championship at Muirfield. Vardon was the victor once again.

St Andrews was to provide the venue again for Taylor's victory in the Open, and this time his victory was an emphatic one; beating his main rival Harry Vardon by seven shots and becoming only the third man to break 80 in every round. Third place on that occasion went to James Braid, the third member of the Triumvirate.

Over the next few years it was Braid who captured most of the major honours, although J.H. Taylor demonstrated remarkable consistency, finishing second in the Open Championship on four consecutive occasions between 1904 and 1907. Taylor was rewarded for his consistency with his fourth Open title at Deal in 1909, when he returned rounds of 74, 73, 74 and 74 to win by four shots from Braid. His final victory came at Hoylake in 1913 after he had to hole a six-footer to qualify for the championship proper.

After his fifth Open win J.H. Taylor began to decline as a major figure in the game, although he was still good enough to play in the first America v Great Britain match in 1921. He was also victorious as winning Ryder Cup captain in 1933.

As a founder member of the PGA in 1901 Taylor served as both chairman and captain. He finally returned to his native Northam in 1957 when he was 86 years of age.

Right: *Sam Torrance munches an apple between shots. His most famous shot was his birdie putt at the 18th in the 1985 Ryder Cup match which won the point which took the European side past the winning post.*

Peter
THOMSON, CBE
b 1929

By far the best Australian golfer until Greg Norman arrived on the scene in the early 1980s, Peter Thomson can claim more British Open victories than any other golfer since Harry Vardon. Thomson's five Open titles came in 1954, 1955, 1956, 1958 and 1965, the three successive wins from 1954 equalling the record set by Tom Morris jnr.

Not renowned as a long hitter, Peter Thomson's strengths were his chipping and putting, allied to good long-iron play. His first tournament victory came in 1950 when he won the New Zealand Open, a feat he was to repeat a further seven times.

Thomson's first visit to Britain was in 1951 when he finished a creditable sixth in the Open. He improved on that position the following year when he was second behind South African Bobby Locke, with whom he was to dominate the Championship throughout the 1950s.

Thomson was encouraged to compete in America, which he did successfully, winning the 1956 Texas Open, but the Australian never seemed comfortable playing there, some say because he preferred to play the small ball as opposed to the larger 1.68 ball used on the US Tour. However, in the same year as his win in Texas, he also finished only four strokes behind Cary Middlecoff in the US Open and the following year was fifth in the US Masters.

Apart from his five Open Championship titles, Peter Thomson won 20 other events, including the PGA Match Play on four occasions, the Dunlop Masters twice and the Alcan Golfer of the Year.

Throughout his career Thomson has been a strong advocate of a 'World Tour' which would allow the top players in the game to compete freely in all the major golfing countries without being restricted by their own National Tours.

Thomson's success as a player stemmed from his simple basic swing and, in particular, his meticulous preparation in setting-up before playing a shot.

He announced his retirement from tournament golf in 1979 and since then he has been involved in broadcasting and writing for an Australian national newspaper. However, he recently returned to play on the Seniors Tour with great success, ironically in America.

Sam
TORRANCE
b 1953

If one man captured the golfing public's imagination during those dramatic and exciting final holes in the 1985 Ryder Cup matches at The Belfry, it was Scotsman Sam Torrance. It was he who delivered the *coup de grace* to America's evaporating Ryder Cup hopes with a marvellous birdie at the 18th hole to beat Andy North.

Torrance turned professional in 1972 and the same year won the Under-25 Match Play Championship. He went on to be voted Rookie of the Year and ended his first full season on the Tour in 37th place on the Order of Merit. Son of club professional Bob Torrance, he has an unquenchable appetite for the game and rarely misses an event during the course of the season.

Torrance has continued to make impressive progress on the European Tour and when on top form he is an exciting player to watch, with the talent to produce some spectacular low-scoring rounds. His best finish in the

Open Championship was in 1981 at Sandwich when he holed in one at the 16th in the final round and looked odds-on to finish top home player. Unfortunately, a 6 at the last spoiled his round and dropped him back to fifth place.

Torrance is blessed with an excellent temperament, allied to a smooth yet powerful swing and despite a slight lapse in form during the 1986 season he has all the necessary qualities to climb right to the very top.

Walter TRAVIS
b 1862–d 1927

Despite being a late starter in golf — he only took the game up in his mid-30s — Travis was soon a champion. He won the US Amateur three times in four years, 1900, 1901 and 1903, then the following year he came to Britain to take the Amateur Championship at Sandwich. Although outdriven by Edward Blackwell in the final, Travis, a demon putter, won 4 and 3 to become the first overseas player to take the title. In the Championship, Travis used a centre-shafted putter, the Schenectady, and his victory was not a popular one. Shortly afterwards the R & A banned such putters, much to Travis' annoyance. In 1905 he founded *The American Golfer* magazine which he edited for many years while still playing tournaments. He also took up course designing and soon found himself at the centre of controversy again when he was deemed to have forfeited his amateur status through his off-course activities. He was later reinstated.

Lee TREVINO
b 1939

One of the characters of the game, Trevino is a bubbling extrovert who mixes sparkling golf with constant chatter interspersed with a good line in jokes. Some say his banter and nonstop quips contain a generous slice of gamesmanship which has been known to distract many an opponent. But more often Trevino's clowning is all part of the professional scene.

Trevino was born on the wrong side of the tracks and learned the game the hard way, hustling for dollars in money matches. After four years in the Marines, he worked as an assistant in El Paso and managed to develop his game despite working mainly in the pro shop, polishing shoes and fitting grips. He joined the US Tour in 1967 and just a year later won the US Open as a virtual unknown, having finished 54th and sixth the previous

two years. He won again in 1971, beating Jack Nicklaus in a play-off at Merion.

By now Trevino had arrived and weeks later at Royal Birkdale he collected the Open Championship, becoming only the fourth player to have won both titles in the same year. When he arrived at Muirfield a year later to defend the crown many felt that Tony Jacklin was in line for his second Open triumph. They were at the front of the field in the last round and things looked bright for Jacklin until Trevino holed three chips and a bunker shot to destroy the Englishman's hopes. Supermex, as he had become known, retained the title with Nicklaus again in second spot.

Trevino has never won the Masters — in fact he has felt that his game wasn't suited to the Augusta course — but he has collected two US PGA Championships, first in 1974 and again ten years later, at the age of 44. In all he has won 27 US Tour tournaments and many more worldwide, and all this despite suffering frequent back trouble after being struck by lightning during the 1975 Western Open. He underwent surgery, yet continues to be among the best players in the world. He is a frequent visitor to Britain, and has played in six Ryder Cup matches. He was non-playing captain in 1985 at The Belfry when he had the dubious distinction of seeing America lose their grip on the trophy after a spell of 28 years.

Below: Joker Lee Trevino appears to be shooting at somebody. Trevino is one of the most entertaining players in the world, as his chatter and antics keep all amused, not to mention the extraordinary shots he has the habit of producing at critical moments.

Flory van DONCK
b 1912

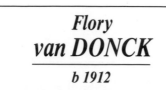

Possibly the best European professional of his day, Belgium's Flory van Donck was a major force in the game in the late 1940s and early 1950s. In eleven years between 1949 and 1960 Flory finished in the top ten of the British Open on nine occasions and in 1956 finished runner-up to Australian Peter Thomson. He repeated that performance in 1959, this time finishing just two shots behind South African Gary Player at Muirfield.

Flory van Donck was also runner-up twice in the PGA Match Play Championship, losing in the final on both occasions to Fred Daly, in 1947 and 1952. His best year was probably 1953 when he won the Vardon Trophy for the lowest stroke average.

In all, van Donck won a total of 31 events in Europe including 26 national open titles. He captured five tournaments in Britain and also won the Dutch Open on five occasions. His last major appearance was in 1979 when at the age of 67 he played in the World Cup.

Harry VARDON
b 1870 – d 1937

By the time he was 20 years old, Harry Vardon had played golf only on a couple of dozen occasions but when he saw that his brother Tom was making money at the game, he decided to follow suit.

Vardon's childhood had been spent on Jersey, where there was little opportunity for him to play golf. But inspired by his brother's success, he was to become one of the legends of the game and win its highest award, the Open Championship, no fewer than six times: in 1896, 1898, 1899, 1903, 1911 and 1914.

Harry Vardon's first position as a club professional was at a nine-hole course at Ripon in Yorkshire. He quickly moved to Bury St Edmunds and then on to Ganton.

Vardon's first Open appearance was in 1893, when he made little impression, but he improved dramatically the following year to finish in fifth place. Then a month before the 1896 Open at Muirfield, the Ganton members raised the money for a challenge match between Vardon and the current Open champion, J.H. Taylor. Vardon won 8 and 7 and then went on to win his first Open title, again defeating Taylor in the process.

Vardon had a major influence on the technical aspects of golf, especially the method of gripping the club. He developed a way to compensate for the slimmer handles that became a feature of the hickory-shafted clubs which superseded the thicker, more cumbersome implements used previously. This method of gripping the club became known as the 'Vardon grip' and it is still favoured by most of the top modern players. Once he became established as a member of the 'Great Triumvirate', many keen young golfers followed Vardon's lead in both his grip and more upright swing.

Harry Vardon's victory in the US Open in 1900 was the climax of a year-long tour of exhibition matches in America, but while competing in the 1903 British Open Vardon was taken ill and was forced to spend some time in a sanatorium. As he grew older he was to spend more time under treatment. It is generally accepted that Vardon was at his peak between 1896 and 1903, thereafter his form declined due, it is believed, to tuberculosis.

Harry Vardon's great strength was his accuracy, especially with fairway woods. It was said that he had problems when playing a course twice in the same day, because he always hit his ball into the divot holes from his own shots in the previous round! That story is fiction, but it is in recognition of Vardon's accuracy that the award, presented each year to the player with the lowest stroke average, the Vardon Trophy, was named after the great man.

Ken VENTURI
b 1931

When Ken Venturi commentates on the US Masters for one of America's main TV networks he probably reflects on some bitter memories of Augusta. In 1956, when still an amateur, he shot 66, 69 to lead and despite a 75 was still well placed going into the final round. With two holes left he still led, but a bogey at the 17th proved his undoing as Jack Burke grabbed a birdie to win by one shot with a 71 to Venturi's 80.

Four years later, and now a seasoned pro, Venturi suffered again. After three rounds he trailed Arnold Palmer by one stroke but with two holes left he had turned that into a one-shot lead. But again it was not to be as Palmer birdied two of the last three holes to restore his one stroke advantage and take the title. However, Venturi did secure one major title, the US Open in 1964, despite trailing by six at half-way. A third round 66 put him four ahead of Palmer, and in the final round — 36 holes were then played on the final day — despite heat problems, he held on to win.

In the early part of his professional career, Venturi was a frequent winner on tour, being a noted iron player, but he lost consistency and his health began to suffer. This forced a premature end to his career in 1967 after 14 tour wins.

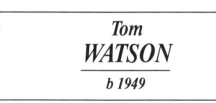

Lanny
WADKINS
b 1949

Like many of today's top American tour players, Lanny Wadkins enjoyed a highly successful amateur career. He was only 16 when he finished high up the order in the US Amateur and he reached that particular pinnacle in 1970 when he won the American title as well as two other championships. He played in the 1969 and 1971 Walker Cup matches, finishing on the losing side in the latter. Soon after he turned pro but not before taking the runner-up spot in the 1970 Heritage Classic. In 1972, his first full year on tour, he won the Sahara Invitational and that year ended 10th on the money list. It won him the Rookie of the Year award but his career has seen many peaks and troughs.

Arguably Wadkins' best year was 1977 when he won his only major, the US PGA at Pebble Beach, beating Gene Littler in a play-off at the third extra hole. He has also been runner-up twice, in 1982 and 1984, while he also filled second place in the 1986 US Open behind Ray Floyd. Outside America he has been successful in Japan and Australia as well as playing in four Ryder Cup and three World Cup teams.

Tom
WATSON
b 1949

In nine years from 1975 to 1983 Tom Watson stamped his presence on the major championships as well as dominating the game in America. He was just another young tour player when he arrived at Carnoustie in 1975 for the Open Championship, but a few days later his name was to become emblazoned across the world wherever golf is played. It was his first Open but he tied with Australia's Jack Newton, then in the 18-hole play-off he won by one shot to take his first major.

Since then Watson has chalked up four more British Opens, 1977, 1980, 1982 and 1983, two US Masters, 1977 and 1981 and one US Open in 1982. Several of those victories have been real thrillers, none more so than the 1977 Open at Turnberry, when he survived a last round shoot-out with Jack Nicklaus which reached a fitting climax on the final green. Nicklaus slotted in a long putt for a birdie which looked like securing a play-off until Watson followed him in to take the title with a 65 to Nicklaus' 66. It was a similar story in the 1982 US Open at Pebble Beach when Watson birdied the final two holes to pip Nicklaus again, the crunch coming when he chipped in at the short 17th after looking set to take four. Watson again had Nicklaus

as his victim in the 1977 Masters when, despite a typical final round of 66 from the Golden Bear, Watson shot 67 to win by two shots.

Having won the Open again in 1982 at Troon and the following year at Birkdale, Watson went to St Andrews in 1984 seeking a hat-trick. And he was tied with Seve Ballesteros when he reached the Road Hole 17th in the final round, but he overclubbed with his second, left the ball almost against the retaining wall and could only make bogey. That left him a shot behind and when Ballesteros birdied 18 the Spaniard had the title.

So far the only major that has eluded Watson is the US PGA for which he was pipped in a play-off by John Mahaffey in 1978. He has topped the US money list five times, including four years running from 1977, and has played in three Ryder Cups. With eight majors to his credit, Watson can be called one of golf's greats.

Below: Tom Watson is the most recent golfer to challenge Harry Vardon's record of six Open wins. In 1983 he registered his fifth, and was in contention up to the 71st in 1984. Watson has won eight majors.

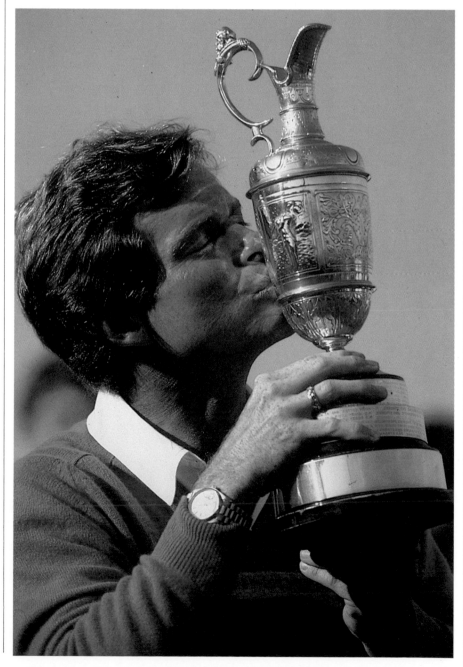

Tom
WEISKOPF
b 1942

The pursuit of perfection is something many choose but few attain. Tom Weiskopf was a perfectionist at golf and it was probably his undoing. He acquired the nickname 'Towering Inferno', not only because of his stature, being 6 ft 3 in tall, but also his tendency to produce fits of anger when he failed to reach the peaks of perfection he set himself.

After turning pro in 1964 Weiskopf played the circuit for 20 years during which he won over 20 tournaments worldwide and over $2½ million. He possessed a majestic swing and when he was in the mood he was almost unbeatable. One such time was in 1973 when in the space of eight weeks he won five tournaments, finishing with the British Open at Troon when he led from start to finish. It was his only major victory although he was second in the US Open in 1976 and runner-up in the Masters four times between 1969 and 1975. In 1972 he was at Wentworth, winning the World Match Play with a 4 and 3 success over Lee Trevino in the final. He played in two Ryder Cup matches but he gradually lost his motivation, spending more time away from the golf course. He has moved into course designing while making the occasional tournament appearance and commentating on TV.

Joyce
WETHERED
b 1901

Joyce Wethered took up golf at the age of 17 during a family holiday in Scotland encouraged by her brother Roger, one of the outstanding amateur players of that era.

In 1920, aged 19, Joyce entered the English Championship at Sheringham just, so she said, to keep a friend company. However, she did much more than that, reaching the final where she caused a major upset by defeating Cecil Leitch, the finest lady golfer in the country at that time.

It soon became apparent that a major new talent had arrived on the scene and so it proved to be, as she went on to dominate the women's game. Over the next four years she was virtually unbeatable; playing 33 matches and winning them all. And although she lost the 1921 British Amateur to Cecil Leitch, thereafter, Joyce held the upper hand in their other encounters.

Joyce Wethered retired from championship golf in 1925 but returned to compete at St Andrews in 1929, and in one of her finest performances beat the top American Glenna Collett by 3 and 1. This crowned a fabulous career and with nothing left to conquer or prove, Joyce Wethered, like her male counterpart Bobby Jones, finally retired at the very height of her powers.

Over the years, there has been speculation about who was the best woman golfer, but whenever the subject is discussed the name of Joyce Wethered is always among the leading contenders.

Kathy
WHITWORTH
b 1939

In terms of tournament wins and money earned, Kathy Whitworth is the most successful woman golfer of all time. At the end of the 1986 season she had won 88 tournaments, more than anyone else in the history of women's golf, six more than the legendary Mickey Wright. Kathy still plays the LPGA tour and although she had cut back her schedule in recent years she is still a formidable opponent capable of even more wins. Some measure of her ability and her impressive record can be gauged by her 11 holes-in-one, while she has won more accolades than any other player. She was leading LPGA money winner eight times, Player of the Year seven times, and Vare Trophy winner on seven occasions.

Kathy's victory march began in her fourth year on tour, 1962, and 20 years later she caught Mickey Wright's record when she won her 82nd victory, taking the record four weeks later. Kathy was also the first woman player to reach $1 million in career earnings when she earned her cheque for third place at the 1981 US Women's Open. She was elected to the LPGA Hall of Fame in 1975 and is also a member of three other American Halls of Fame. When asked what she felt was the secret of her success, Kathy replied: 'Keeping the ball in play'. She might also have mentioned that she is one of the best putters in the game.

Craig
WOOD
b 1901 – d 1968

Few players can have suffered more disappointments in major championships than Craig Wood. A formidable player in the 1930s and early 1940s, he was nearly always the bridesmaid in the big events. His chapter of woe began in 1933 when he was third in the US Open, then he lost a play-off for the British Open to Densmore Shute at St Andrews. The following year he finished a shot behind Horton Smith in the US Masters, then lost in the final of the US PGA to Paul

Opposite: The tall and elegant Tom Weiskopf. He won the British Open and the World Match Play Championship on British courses, but strangely in America his record in the majors was one of many second places. He now commentates on the game on American TV.

Runyan. In 1935 he led the Masters by three shots going into the final round and despite faltering, played the last eight holes four under par to look the likely winner. The cheque was being prepared for him when Gene Sarazen had an albatross two at the 15th. Wood was so shattered he lost the play-off over 36 holes by five shots. Still the fates hadn't finished. In the 1939 US Open, Wood tied with Byron Nelson and Shute to force an 18-hole play-off. Shute was eliminated as Wood and Nelson each shot 68. Out they went again only for Wood to be pipped again as Nelson sank a full one-iron. Wood's luck was to change in the 1941 Masters when he took revenge on Nelson to win his first major by three shots. That gave him a boost and he went on to take the US Open that year. He was also a Ryder Cup player from 1931 to 1935.

Mickey
WRIGHT
b 1935

One of the greatest women golfers of all time with four US Women's Opens and four LPGA titles to her credit, Mickey Wright turned pro in 1954 after a distinguished amateur career then set about creating records galore. Long and powerful, she gained five tour wins in 1958 including the first US Open and US LPGA. Between 1959 and 1968 she won 79 of her 82 career wins averaging almost eight wins per year in that period. In 1961 she won three of the four LPGA majors, a feat which hasn't been matched, and twice she has won four consecutive LPGA events. Her 13 victories in 1962, out of a total of 32, is a record that will never be matched, while her round of 62 in the 1964 Midland, Texas, tournament also still stands as a record.

Wright was leading money winner four times, leading tournament winner on six occasions, and Vare Trophy winner for the lowest stroke average on five occasions. Her 14-year win streak, 1956 to 1969, is bettered only by Kathy Whitworth's 17-year record, while her 82 tournament wins is also second to Whitworth's 88.

Babe
ZAHARIAS
b 1914 – d 1956

Probably one of the greatest sportswomen of all time, Babe Zaharias was far more than a great golfer. Born Mildred Didrikson, she became the 'Babe' when she won six of seven track and field events that preceded the 1932 Olympics. In the Games themselves she won

the hurdles, javelin and high jump, but was later deprived of the high jump gold medal because her method of clearing the bar head first was declared illegal.

Didrikson progressed to golf around the mid-1930s just as easily and with her remarkable power, was soon a winner. But after taking the Texas Open in 1935 she was declared a professional because she earned from her other sports. Three years later she married wrestler George Zaharias and in 1940 won both the Western and Texas Opens but refused the prize money. In 1943 she was reinstated an amateur, then in 1946 and 1947 she won 17 events in a row including the US Amateur and the British Ladies' title at Gullane, accounting for Frances Stephens and Jean Donald on the way to a 5 and 4 victory against Jacqueline Gordon in the final. In 1948 Zaharias turned professional of her own accord, was a founder member of the ladies pro tour and won the US Open at Atlantic City, one of her three victories from eight events. She won the Open again in 1950 and the following year claimed seven wins as the tour expanded to 14 events.

In 1953 the Babe underwent an operation for cancer but she was soon back on tour, winning five events the following year including the Open by 12 strokes. She won twice more in 1955 but further operations followed, and she lost her battle against the disease in 1956. In all she claimed 31 tournament wins.

Fuzzy
ZOELLER
b 1951

Frank Urban Zoeller, nicknamed 'Fuzzy' because of his initials, is one of the game's blithe spirits, believing that playing golf certainly beats working. He turned professional in 1974 but had to wait until 1979 for his first victory on the US Tour when he captured the San Diego Open. Two months later he found himself tied with Ed Sneed and Tom Watson in the first sudden-death play-off in the history of the US Masters. Zoeller took the title at his first attempt when he holed a birdie putt on the second extra hole.

From then on Zoeller became a regular winner, and then in 1984 elevated himself still further when he captured the US Open after a play-off with Greg Norman. His towel-waving gesture on the 72nd hole of Winged Foot in that Championship won him the hearts of millions.

Troubled by a back injury sustained during a basketball game at school, Zoeller underwent surgery in late 1984 but has won four more titles since. His best year on the US Tour came in 1986 when he won over $350,000 and his career earnings now stand at over $2 million.

Left: Last in the alphabet but not on the course, Fuzzy Zoeller explodes from the sand in the US Open in 1986, which was his most successful year. His US Open victory, however, came two years earlier in 1984.

Women in Golf

History reveals that the first woman golfer of note was Mary, Queen of Scots, who paid the ultimate penalty for lifting her head by having it removed. Three centuries later, lady golfers began to make their first tentative swings at a ball, although these attempts were mocked by their male counterparts. The emergence of Cecil Leitch and Joyce Wethered in the 1920s gave the women's game the impetus that has now made ladies' golf one of the fastest growth areas in the sport. Dollar millionairesses now abound on the US LPGA Tour and the women's professional game is developing quickly in Britain and Europe. Players such as Nancy Lopez have demonstrated that great skill is not merely confined to male players, while the glamour and fashion of women's golf has been emphasized by the attractions of Laura Baugh and Jan Stephenson.

Left: The Great Britain and Ireland Curtis Cup team of 1986 made history by becoming the first visiting team to win on American soil.

The role of women in golf has always been an emotive subject. Although the female of the species has played the game almost as long as the male, her presence on and around the golf course has been viewed with much scepticism if not sheer hostility. To say that men didn't approve of women playing golf is an understatement of enormous proportions. The ladies had to battle hard and long for some small recognition. It was a fight akin to the Suffragette movement but, unlike the 'votes for women' cause, the tussle for equality in golf is still being fought in many parts of Britain.

In the old days women were barred from certain courses, were allowed only to indulge in putting at others while their presence within the portals of many clubhouses was regarded by most of the male membership as equal to an act of indecency. These were the stumbling blocks that women had to endure and even now, in these days of equal opportunity and women's rights, opposition still lurks in certain bastions of the game. In some places women still cannot enter the clubhouse or, if they can, are confronted with a men-only bar and they are also prohibited from using the course at certain times. Some claim that the introduction of ladies-only bars has gone some way to redressing the balance but is it just fobbing off the issue?

Despite all the opposition, the brickbats and sheer hostility it has had to face, women's golf is flourishing and will continue to do so because it is part and parcel of the whole golfing scene. And the ladies can point to an early niche in golfing history because one of the first references to women and golf came with Mary, Queen of Scots. In her trial she was accused of playing golf in Seton Fields on the day after the death of the Earl of Darnley. Whether the accusation was true or not, it didn't do her a lot of good — she wasn't the first to lose her head over this fascinating yet often infuriating game.

Further references to women and golf are few and far between but there are records dating back to the late 18th century of the fisherwives of Musselburgh playing the game. Golf was an important leisure activity in the Scottish town and it was noted that as the women's work and strength was equal to the men, then their amusements were also of a masculine kind. So the women took their places on the links and to quote words chronicled in the history of the old town, 'were a special and admired feature, a loving invasion dear to the youthful gentlemen of the green. Daintily attired, perchance in a becoming "Tam o' Shanter" bonnet while beneath beams the sweet youthful countenace glowing with health.' It is also written that as early as 1810, the ladies of Musselburgh played in a competition, the prizes for which were a new Barcelona handkerchief and a new fish creel and shawl.

However, Musselburgh apart, there seems to have been little other women's golf documented from that early period until 1867 when a Ladies' Golf Club was formed at St Andrews. The club leased a portion of Pilmour Links, north-west of the Swilcan Burn, and play was mainly on the putting green, although there were competitions over a short course. The popularity of the club can be gauged by the number of members, which reached 1,312 by 1893. At that time the entrance fee was seven shillings and sixpence

Right: Mary, Queen of Scots is depicted playing golf at St Andrews in 1563. Her liking for golf was brought up against her in her trial. She played in France, where she called the students who carried her clubs 'cadets', the word from which 'caddie' is derived.

(37½p) and annual subscription two shillings and sixpence (12½p).

Another significant development occurred in 1868 when ladies' golf spread south with the formation of the Ladies Club at Westward Ho! Its official title was the Westward Ho! and North Devon Ladies' Club which had its own nine-hole course on Northam Burrows, adjacent to the men's course. The total length was 1,895 yards with the longest hole 380 and the shortest 120 yards. According to records, the greens were splendid but the hazards numerous. This first club had 47 full members, all ladies, and 23 associate members, all men, plus its own professional, the brother of the steward at Royal North Devon. He, and he alone, was allowed to teach the ladies, his opposite number at the men's club being forbidden to take on the role. At the start, play was also different to that of today, being restricted to alternate Saturdays from May to October, while the only club permitted was a putter. Needless to say, play was somewhat genteel on two counts. Firstly vigorous exercise and the display of a shapely ankle was not the done thing, and secondly the bulky fashions of the day clearly made a full swing of the club a physical impossibility.

Despite all this, the ladies of Westward Ho! took their golf seriously and from September 1868 they played for a Challenge Medal donated by J. Benet of Royal Blackheath Golf Club. When the club was reconstituted in 1893 the number of members had increased to 132, including 60 honorary, while the annual subscription was ten shillings and sixpence (52½p). The club rules at that time also state that 'any lady member or honorary member may introduce a lady to play on the links for three consecutive days without payment and friends staying in members' houses may be introduced to play on the links for one week without payment, after which period a payment of three shillings and sixpence a week in advance shall be made, the introducing members being responsible for the payment, such privilege of free play to be enjoyed only once a year'.

Ladies' Golf Union

So it was that ladies' golf was gaining a foothold in Britain and it wasn't long before more clubs were springing up. The London

Above: Two ladies indulging in a genteel but serious game of golf at Westward Ho! in 1873, five years after the formation there of the first English Ladies' club. Clothing inhibited stroke-making, but there was a Challenge Medal from earliest days, so it was taken seriously.

Scottish Ladies was formed in 1872, playing on Wimbledon Common, and here the golf was played in a more familiar fashion, more in the Musselburgh style than that of Westward Ho! In 1890 the club was reformed as the Wimbledon Ladies' Club and it was through this cradle of women's competitive golf that a watershed occurred in 1893 with the formation of the Ladies' Golf Union. Invitations were sent out by the Wimbledon committee inviting representatives from various clubs to a meeting in London which took place on 19 April 1893. Among those who attended were clubs from St Andrews, Barnes, Eastbourne, Blackheath, Minchinhampton, Holywood, Southdown and Brighton, Ashdown Forest, Wimbledon and Lytham St Annes. This group agreed on the formation of the LGU after the advantages were outlined by the acting chairman, Laidlaw Purves. The first honorary secretary was Issette Pearson, one of the best players of the day, and she was also mainly responsible for the Union system of universal handicapping.

Miss Pearson was no mean competitor on the course and when the British Ladies' Championship was played over nine holes for the first time at Lytham St Annes in 1893 she reached the final, only to be beaten 7 and 5 by perhaps the outstanding lady player of the day, Lady Margaret Scott. The two met again in the 1894 final at Littlestone with the same outcome although the match was closer, Lady Margaret winning 3 and 2. She completed a hat-trick in 1895 at Portrush with a 5 and 4 success over Elizabeth Lythgoe, but then dropped out of major competitive golf. The Championship itself was extended to 18 holes then 36 after 1912, with an ever-growing roll of honour which contains many of the great players of their respective eras. But more of that later.

Throughout the concluding years of the 19th century women golfers were fighting prejudice and barriers despite their growing numbers and were often restricted to putting, the only concession being granted at certain masculine strongholds. It was also written that 'constitutionally and physically women are unfitted for golf. The first women's championship will be the last. They are bound to quarrel and fall out on the slightest, or no, provocation.' How wrong, patronizing and shortsighted can you be?

It couldn't have been much fun as a woman golfer in those early days, having to battle against chauvinistic attitudes. All credit must be given to those early pioneers. A measure of their determination can be gauged from the writings of Amy Pascoe, who added her name to the English Ladies' Championship as the winner in 1896 at Hoylake. In 1899 she wrote that there were 128 ladies' clubs in Britain at that time and nearly all had been constituted since 1880. Of course, with the growing number of women golfers, there was an equally increasing demand for equipment so the clubmakers and ballmakers of the day were in ever-pressing demand.

Another significant first occurred in 1897 with the opening of the Jubilee Course at St Andrews. This was a boon for women who were tired of the restrictions of glorified putting greens but the breakthrough at the home of golf came a year later with the formation of the St Rule's Ladies' Golf Club. It is generally understood that it was the members of this club who instituted the first Ladies' Golf Championship of Scotland back in 1903, staged on the Old Course, with the winner being Alice Glover who beat Margaret Graham by one hole.

Just before the turn of the century women's competitive golf threw down roots in the United States. In 1895 came the inaugural US Women's Amateur Championship whose early years were dominated by Beatrix Hoyt. She won it three times in a row from 1896 and was only 16 when she won for the first time. It seems that golf was attract-ing the young because when the British Championship was decided over the New-castle, County Down, links in 1899, the winner, May Hezlet, was only 17. The ladies may have been a curiosity on the golf course but they still attracted their followers, even among royalty. It is documented that Prince Leopold, a young son of Queen Victoria, and himself a golfer, took the opportunity in 1876 when driving himself in as Captain of the Royal & Ancient Club at St Andrews, to watch the ladies in action and that he later sent a special prize to the winner. It is uncertain what that prize was but down the years royalty has maintained a certain link in this respect. There was almost a carbon copy of that earlier event in 1922 when the then Prince of Wales, later to become the Duke of Windsor, was also installed as Captain of the R & A. He had afternoon tea in the Ladies' Club and presented silver cups to the winner and the runner-up, Mrs Benson and Mrs MacAllen, of a women's competition held that same day.

Far left: A more streamlined style of dress gave the lady golfer greater ease of movement in 1890. Not every club, however, allowed the ladies a full swing — at many they were restricted to putting.

***Below:** Two ladies putt on the well-kept greens of Portrush in County Antrim. Women's golf was still in its infancy in 1897, but the large attendance of spectators shows that this is an important match, as does their indifference to the rain.*

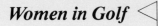

Left: *The rich and famous practise their swing at the fashionable golf club at Cannes. Despite claims to being among the pioneers of the game, the French have produced few great golfers, although among the women Catherine Lacoste was outstanding.*

Eight years later the then Duke of York, later King George VI, continued the tradition while our present Queen Elizabeth II is patron of the Royal & Ancient, although few of the current royal family are golf conscious.

Cecil Leitch and Joyce Wethered

As the 20th century reached its first decade, women's golf was growing more firmly rooted and many more ladies were taking up the game. Soon champions of a marked stature were emerging, perhaps the forerunner being Cecilia (Cecil) Leitch. Born in 1891, she made a somewhat quiet, almost unnoticed, arrival in the Ladies' Open at St Andrews in 1908 as a 17-year-old. She began with a 9 and 8 victory over an American, then battled through to the semi-finals only to go down on the 18th to the eventual winner, Maud Titterton. Clearly Cecil was one to watch. Possessing strong hands and arms, she was an attacking player with something of a male approach to the game. This was

borne out in 1910 when she played 72 holes against the legendary Harold Hilton and, given a stroke on alternate holes, Cecil was the winner. She repeated the feat against another male champion, John Ball.

In 1912 Cecil won the French title for the first time then two years later, prior to the outbreak of the First World War, she won the British, French and English Championships, repeating the trick the next time each event was held after the cessation of hostilities. In 1920 at Sheringham she was a strong favourite to win the English crown again but after reaching the final she was beaten by a then unknown Joyce Wethered. This was the first of a series of battles between these two fine players as they reigned supreme over British women's golf in the early 1920s. Wethered was generally regarded as the better player but in the 1921 British and French finals Leitch triumphed again, although that was the last time she was to do so. Cecil ran up her fourth British title victory in 1926 when Wethered was not playing and that completed a remarkable record. In the period from 1912 to 1926 Cecil won 12 national titles. Her biggest triumph came in the final of the Canadian Championship in 1921 against Mollie McBride. Cecil was 14 up at lunch and needed only three holes in the afternoon, winning them all, to complete a 17 and 15 victory. For the stark statistics of the 21 holes played, Cecil won 18, lost one and two were halved.

While Cecil Leitch's record was remarkable, Joyce Wethered, later Lady Heathcoat-Amery, could be described as the greatest player in the history of British women's golf. She was head and shoulders above her contemporaries and it could be argued that she didn't receive the acclaim her exploits deserved. Fluent and with magical timing, she frequently outdistanced her opponents and regularly shot rounds of 72 and 73, no doubt benefiting in her early years from playing with her brother, Roger. She was taught the game by him from the age of 17 during family holidays at Royal Dornoch and, as he was one of the top amateurs of his

Below: A young Joyce Wethered holds the Ladies' Open Championship cup, which she won four times in the 1920s.

Below right: Now Lady Heathcoat-Amery, Joyce tees off at the Worplesdon foursomes in 1938. She won this event eight times altogether, with seven different partners.

day, she couldn't have had a better schooling. It also gave her a hard, competitive edge which stood her in good stead throughout her career and none more so than in her first English Championship, the aforementioned clash at Sheringham in 1920.

She entered for a bit of fun and to keep a friend company, hoping to gain a little experience. But she reeled out a string of victories until she came up against Cecil Leitch in the final. There was a stark contrast between the two rivals. Cecil, at the age of 29, was at the peak of her prowess with a string of titles to her name. Joyce was ten years her junior and a championship novice. At lunch Cecil was four up and this was extended to six after the first two holes of the afternoon. But then the battle began to change. Wethered produced a run of threes, gradually chipping away at Cecil's lead until she went ahead with four holes to play. It was decisive as the youngster went on to win 2 and 1, an upset of some magnitude at the time.

Wethered won the title in the following four years, making five in a row, and apart from the Leitch final, her lowest winning margin was 7 and 6 and the highest 12 and 11. In those five years from 1920 to 1924, Joyce played 33 matches in the English Championship and won them all. The British Championship proved a little more difficult although her record was just as impressive. After losing to Leitch in the 1921 final, she reversed the order the following year, winning 9 and 7, lost in the semi-finals a year later, then won again in 1923 and 1925. In the latter she again beat her old rival Leitch in their closest final, the match going to the 37th.

After that Joyce retired from top line golf but was back in 1929 when the British Championship returned to St Andrews. Again she reached the final where she met the best player of the time from America, Glenna Collett, in what many felt was an unofficial world championship.

It proved a magnificent match with the American going five up at the turn with a score of 34. However, her lead had been trimmed to two at lunch after which Joyce Wethered proceeded to turn on some of her greatest golf. She was soon all square then romped four ahead. Collett came back as the see-saw continued to reduce the deficit to two holes but in the end Wethered prevailed 3 and 1. It was to be her swansong and she departed the Championship with a record of just two defeats in 38 matches.

She was never again seen in a championship although she did play against France in 1931 and in the Curtis Cup the following year. But by then she had little to prove and preferred instead to play for fun with none of the strain of top-flight competition. She maintained her competitive interest in the Worplesdon Mixed Foursomes for many years, winning the event eight times between 1922 and 1936 with seven different partners.

Left: Babe Zaharias, US champion, could hit the ball great distances. Her free swing and uninhibited manner fully expressed the emancipation of women golfers.

She even partnered her husband to the final in 1948.

In 1935 she embarked on a series of exhibition matches in America, a move which saw her lose her amateur status. Her opponents were usually Horton Smith, Gene Sarazen and Babe Didrikson, later Babe Zaharias. She was immediately compared with the great American but is said to have outscored her by several shots a round. She more than proved her prowess by breaking 18 course records in 52 matches. Such was Joyce's expertise with golf clubs that both Bobby Jones and Henry Cotton rated her among the best players of all time, male or female. Cotton went so far as to examine her game so thoroughly that he concluded that her driving was comparable to a scratch male, her fairway woods were as straight as the short irons of most professionals and her chipping and putting were second to none. He added that she compared with Harry Vardon for straightness while Jones said that after a round with Joyce he had never felt so outclassed.

Madame and Mademoiselle Lacoste

When the domination of Leitch and Wethered ended in the middle 1920s the British Championship title went abroad for the first time in 1927 won by the capable skills of Frenchwoman Simone de la Chaume, later

Madame Rene Lacoste. She had been beaten in the semi-finals the previous year by Cecil Leitch but went one better in 1927 at Newcastle, County Down. It was a notable double because three years earlier she had been the first overseas player to win the girls' title. She was clearly the best French player of her time, winning the closed title in 1929 and 1930 and again from 1936 to 1938, while she won her national Open title six times, beating Cecil Leitch in 1926.

She married Rene Lacoste, the French tennis champion, and their daughter Catherine took to golf like a natural. She proved even better than her illustrious mother, making her mark in the late 1960s

Amateur in both 1965 and 1966, losing on both occasions, 4 and 3 and then at the 39th. The two also clashed in the 1966 French Closed and again Mademoiselle Varangot prevailed 6 and 5. However, the turning point was just around the corner and when they faced each other a fourth time in the 1967 French Open Catherine had her revenge by 8 and 6.

Lacoste also made a name for herself abroad by finishing tied for first place in the individual event in the Women's World Amateur Team Championship in 1967. Then America beckoned and Catherine was to make a major splash in the US Women's Open in that year. At Hot Springs, Virginia,

Above: Babe Zaharias (left) discusses the merits of an American putter in 1951. A fine all-round sportswoman, she followed a brilliant athletics career with an equally successful golfing one.

and early 1970s, both in France and overseas. Although France is not known as a power in golf, the country has produced a string of top women players and Catherine was pitched into a tough school. There was the Vicomtesse de Saint Sauveur, who although in the twilight of a distinguished career, was nevertheless still a formidable opponent, Claudine Cros and Brigitte Varangot. Catherine met the latter in the final of the French Open

she reached the half-way stage with a five-stoke lead. This she increased to seven and despite faltering towards the end she still won by two shots with a four-round tally of 294. At just a few days beyond her 22nd birthday, she was not only the youngest player to win the title but also the first amateur to achieve such a feat, a magnificent achievement by any standards.

She again won the French Closed

Championship in 1968, beating Brigitte Varangot, and this time took the individual title in the World Championship. Yet her greatest year was still to come. In 1969 she again beat her old rival, Mlle Varangot, in the French Closed, collected the French Open for the second time by beating Britain's Elizabeth Bradshaw 12 and 11 in the final, then turned her attention to the British crown at Portrush. It was a closely fought final against Ann Irvin but the darling of the French got home by one hole. Still Catherine wasn't finished. Back in the United States she claimed a fourth title, winning the US Amateur by beating Shelley Hamlin 3 and 2 in the final. In doing so she became one of only three women to win the British and American titles in the same year. On her marriage, Catherine retired from international competition, and although she returned she was not the same dominant force. She added two more French Open titles to her record in 1970 and 1972 and also captured further titles in Spain, America and Britain.

Enid Wilson takes the stage

After the successive reigns of Cecil Leitch, Joyce Wethered and Madame Lacoste, the next dominant British woman golfer was Enid Wilson, whose achievements were confined to the late 1920s and early 1930s. Her first success was winning the British Girls' Championship at Stoke Poges in 1925 then two years later she was pipped at the post for the English Ladies' crown, losing by one hole in the final at Pannal. It was a different story a year later at Walton Heath when Enid reached the final again and made no mistake, claiming her first national title by an emphatic 9 and 8 against Dorothy Pearson. The English Championship certainly had the appeal for Enid and when she reached the final again at Aldeburgh in 1930 she ran up her best-ever result, a 12 and 11 victory. The British Ladies' title also came under Enid's spell and she had quite a record in the seven years from 1927. That year she reached the semi-finals. A repeat performance the following year and again in 1930 would have been enough to convince most players that the Indian sign was on them. But not Enid. She went back in 1931 at Portmarnock and won, did it again in 1932 at Saunton then completed a hat-trick the following year at Gleneagles and each time her margin of victory was clearcut, twice by 7 and 6 and once by 5 and 4. She also joined Lady Margaret Scott and Cecil Leitch as the only three players to win the title three times in a row.

Enid also tried her luck in America with the US Championship but although she reached the semi-finals in 1931 and 1933, being qualifying medallist with 76, then a record, in the latter, she couldn't quite pull it off. Later Enid made her mark reporting golf for the *Daily Telegraph*.

Double Champion Pam Barton

The year after Enid Wilson completed her hat-trick of Ladies' Championships, the spotlight fell on a 17-year-old of supreme talent. Pam Barton, a Londoner, took the French Championship in 1934 and also reached the final of the British Ladies' that year only to be beaten 6 and 5 by Helen Holm. She repeated the performance the following year only to suffer defeat again, losing 3 and 2 at Newcastle, County Down, to Wanda Morgan. But it was third time lucky in 1936 at Southport and Ainsdale when she was still only 19 years old. That same year Pam also won the US Amateur title, joining Dorothy Campbell and Catherine Lacoste as

Below: Catherine Lacoste of France won almost every honour in the amateur game during the 1960s. Her mother, Simone de la Chaune, who married the tennis champion Renee Lacoste, was also a champion golfer.

the only players to have won both titles in the same year.

That year Pam just failed to make it a hat-trick when she was runner-up for the French Championships and she was the beaten finalist again in 1938. Pam Barton was a natural left-hander who was persuaded to switch to right hand, a move vindicated by her tremendous run of successes. Sturdily built, she possessed a fine swing and was a good striker of the ball. When she won the British title for the second time in 1939 at Portrush, it seemed that she was destined for a long reign at the top. But, joining the WAAF as a Flight-Officer in the Second World War, she was tragically killed in an air-crash at Manston RAF Station in Kent in 1943 at the age of 26. Who knows to what heights she might have reached? She is still regarded as one of the finest British women golfers of all time. She was an England international from 1935 to 1939 and played in two Curtis Cup matches against the United States. When she made her debut at the Chevy Chase club Pam was the youngest competitor to gain that honour, but the 17-year-old was given a tough baptism, losing 7 and 5 in the most one-sided match of the contest as the Americans won 6½–2½.

The all-round Babe

Before the outbreak of the Second World War, one of the most remarkable sports-women of this century burst on to the golfing scene. Mildred 'Babe' Didrikson was a natural at most sports and she made a name for herself well before she took up golf. Born in 1914 in Port Arthur, Texas, Mildred acquired the nickname 'Babe' from the legendary baseball player Babe Ruth when she made a habit of hitting home runs during her schooldays. Yet it was basketball at which she first excelled nationally, earning All-American honours from 1930 to 1932. Then she took up athletics and within a year had set US records for the javelin and won national titles in the long jump and hurdles. In the 1932 US AAU Championships 'Babe' raised many eyebrows by competing in eight events and winning six. In the process she broke four world records. The Los Angeles Olympics followed the same year and she won the javelin and 80-metres hurdles, setting records in both, but in the high jump she was disqualified for adopting the Western Roll technique.

Although she was persuaded to try her luck at golf — and she soon impressed people with her big hitting — Babe did not take it seriously for several years. Instead she concentrated on baseball and basketball, playing both as a professional, taking golf lessons whenever the opportunity permitted. It is believed that she played her first golf competition in 1934 and such was her progress that she won the Texas Amateur title the following year. It was her remarkable hitting that caught the eye and none other than Byron Nelson believed that there were only around half a dozen men who were longer off the tee. However, this statement is greeted with some scepticism in certain quarters.

Nonetheless she could certainly drive the ball over 250 yards and occasionally around 300, and this was a great drawing card with spectators. However, Babe was banned from being an amateur by the USGA in 1935 because, although she was not a professional at golf, she certainly was at other sports. It was ironic that in the same year Joyce Wethered, having also lost her amateur status, albeit temporarily, for working in a sports shop, toured America and played two matches against Didrikson. The British player won both decisively for although she was frequently outdriven, Joyce had the sharper short game while the American's was somewhat undeveloped.

However, in 1938 Babe married wrestler George Zaharias, known as the Weeping Greek from Cripple Creek, and went off at a tangent, trying her talent at tennis. But again she was banned from amateur competition, this time by the US LTA. After this she applied for reinstatement as an amateur golfer. While awaiting a decision she won two professional events, the Western and Texas Opens, but refused the prize money on both occasions. By 1943 she was an amateur again, which led to her running up a remarkable record. Between the summers of 1946 and 1947 Babe is claimed to have won 17

Below: Pam Barton was a golfing prodigy. She made her debut in championship golf at 17 and became the youngest player ever to represent Britain in the Curtis Cup. Her life was tragically cut short by the Second World War, when she promised to become an outstanding champion.

consecutive tournaments. In that tally is her victory in the 1946 US Amateur in Tulsa which she dominated, winning the final 11 and 9. She came to Britain in 1947 with her sights set on the British title which had never been won by an American. The Championship was held at Gullane in Scotland and a measure of her strength can be judged by her performance on a par-five hole of 540 yards which she covered with a wood and a 4-iron. With such power, she soon dismissed such fine players as Frances Stephens and Jean Donald. In six matches on her way to the final, she lost just four holes. In the final against Jacqueline Gordon, Babe faced stern opposition, and Miss Gordon led by two holes after 11. But she was pegged back to all square at lunch, and on the resumption Babe drew away to win 5 and 4.

Soon after that she turned professional again and after taking part in an exhibition tour, Babe joined Patty Berg to reorganize what was the embryo American Women's Professional Tour. In 1948 Babe won three of

the eight events including the US Women's Open, then claimed two victories from the seven events in 1949. Six from nine was her tally in 1950, again including the US Open, then in 1951, when the Tour expanded to 14 events, Babe won seven times. In each of the four years she was the leading money winner although it was small beer compared to today's rich pickings. She was the biggest draw while only five other players, Berg, Betsy Rawl, Betty Jameson, Louise Suggs and Beverly Hanson, won events.

In 1952 she was not so dominant, winning four times to six each by Suggs and Rawls, while in 1953 she underwent a major operation for cancer. However, she was soon back on the fairways and a year later claimed five events including her third US Open by a staggering 12 strokes. It was her last appearance in the Open and although she won two more events in 1955, the cancer returned and she was hospitalized for further operations. In the end the illness claimed her life on 17 September 1956 at the age of 42. There is

Above: Six of the greatest women players in British golf. (1) Francis 'Bunty' Stephens, one of the leading Curtis Cup players. (2) Marley Spearman, one-time West End dancer. (3) Diana Fishwick, who won the Opens of Holland, Germany and Belgium. (4) Jessie Valentine, veteran of seven Curtis Cup matches, was awarded the MBE in 1959. (5) Joyce Wethered, perhaps the greatest of all. (6) Ireland's Philomena Garvey, 15 times Irish champion between 1946 and 1963.

little doubt that Babe Zaharias had a major influence on women's golf for she proved that women can hit golf balls as far as men.

Scotland's Jessie Valentine

Another great player whose career spanned the Second World War was Jessie Valentine. Her winning ways began with the British Girls' title in 1933 and her name was at the top of British women's golf for over 30 years. As Miss Jessie Anderson she made the first of a record seven Curtis Cup appearances in 1936 at Gleneagles and she was the heroine of the first draw between Great Britain and Ireland and the United States. With one match left to be completed, Great Britain and Ireland were one down and the outcome rested on the clash of Miss Anderson and Mrs L.D. Cheney. After 17 holes they were level but the brave Scot rolled in a putt of some 20 feet to win her match and square the overall tussle. At the after-match presentations the Americans asked the British side to accept the trophy but the non-playing captain, Doris Chambers, graciously declined so the Americans were allowed to keep possession of the trophy which they didn't relinquish until 1952, when Jessie Valentine was among the victorious British and Irish line-up.

A year after her Curtis Cup debut, Jessie won her first major title when she took the British Ladies'. Then in 1950 she reached the final again only to lose to the Vicomtesse de Saint-Sauveur. But the title was back in her grasp in 1955 after beating Barbara Romack 7 and 6. Two years later she tasted defeat again, losing to Philomena Garvey 4 and 3 in the final at Gleneagles, but in 1958 at the age of 43 she marked her fifth final appearance by winning the trophy for the third time, beating Elizabeth Price by one hole at Hun-

stanton. It made her the oldest winner, but that record has since been beaten by another Scot, Belle Robertson.

If Jessie was prominent in British and international golf, she was dominant on the domestic scene in Scotland. She took the Scottish Ladies' Championship for the first of six times in 1938 and the last in 1956 while she also won national titles in New Zealand and France. Her international career spanned 24 years, from 1934 to 1958, and was only ended when she turned professional in 1959, one of the first British women to take the step into the paid ranks.

The Curtis Cup

Turning to the subject of the Curtis Cup, it is worth recalling its inception and the aims behind the biennial match between the amateur women of Great Britain and Ireland on the one hand and the United States on the other. The instigators were the American sisters Margaret and Harriot Curtis from Boston, Massachussetts. Both were fine golfers, winning the United States Championship several times between them in the early years of this century. Margaret was the younger by two years but she was the more successful, being the beaten finalist in the US Ladies' in 1900 and 1905 then winning it two years later at the expense of her sister by 7 and 6 in the final. Margaret was also cham-pion in 1911 and 1912 while Harriot's only success in the Championship was in 1906 while she also reached the semi-finals in 1913. But these milestones are little recalled against their achievement of setting up the major international competition in women's amateur golf.

Its beginnings were in 1905 when Margaret and Harriot came to Britain and

Right: Angela Bonallack chips from the edge of the 9th green at Lindrick, where she partnered Elizabeth Price to accomplish Britain's only win in the 1960 Curtis Cup foursomes.

played in the British Championship at Cromer. They failed to reach the final but they took part in an unofficial international match between the ladies of Britain and America. Whether that stirred the Curtis sisters is unknown but when another unofficial encounter took place at Sunningdale in 1930 it created such interest that the sisters donated a trophy to be competed for regularly. The inaugural match occurred at Wentworth in 1932 and although the British fielded a strong side including such gifted players as Joyce Wethered, Enid Wilson, Molly Gourlay and Wanda Morgan, the Americans won by five matches to three. That was the first sign of the American domination of the matches with the trophy only leaving their possession three times, the last being the most recent and magnificent British victory at Prairie Dunes in Kansas, the first time Britain has won on American soil.

In the early days it was stated that the competition be set up 'in the hope that other countries will join at some future date'. But it has been a strictly Anglo-American confrontation to this day. The first contest in America resulted in another comprehensive defeat for the British and Irish but the third meeting, at Gleneagles in 1936, saw the first draw when Jessie Anderson (Valentine) sank that memorable long putt.

After that, America returned to their winning ways in 1938 and again in the first two contests after the Second World War. In fact, in the 1950 match at Buffalo, the British suffered their heaviest defeat to that date when they won only one match out of nine with one more halved. It was Frances Stephens, a key British player between 1950 and 1960, who was the only British player to avoid defeat, gaining the only win with Elizabeth Price in the foursomes then halving her singles. For the rest there were some heavy defeats, with Jessie Valentine losing 7 and 6, Jean Donald 6 and 5, and Elizabeth Price 5 and 4.

But what a contrast in the 1952 match. At Muirfield, Great Britain achieved their breakthrough with virtually the same line-up that had been crushed two years earlier. Britain and Ireland led 2–1 after the foursomes but then drew the singles 3–3 to take the Cup for the first time 5–4. It was a cliffhanging encounter that was decided when Miss Price took the 16th hole of the final singles to win 3 and 2, the rest of the side being Jean Donald, Jessie Valentine, Frances Stephens, Moira Peterson, Philomena Garvey and Jeanne Bisgood.

America won the Cup back two years later at Merion, taking swift revenge 6–3, building the foundation for their victory with a whitewash of the foursomes. But at Prince's, Sandwich, two years on, the see-saw continued with the British again achieving a 5–4 triumph despite this time losing the foursomes 1–2. Again the outcome was

settled in the final match, and this time the heroine was Frances Stephens, later Mrs Frances Smith, who got home on the last green. Paired with American Cup veteran Polly Riley, the British player found herself all square with one to play and the match tied at 4–4. But Miss Riley took six while Miss Stephens got home in five to set the Union Jacks flying.

In 1958 came the second tied encounter, at the Brae Burn club in Massachussetts, and again the outcome hinged on a clash between Frances Smith and Polly Riley, this time Mrs Smith winning by two holes. As Great Britain had won two years earlier, they thus retained the trophy, which marked the only occasion that the Cup remained in Britain for four consecutive years. The 1958 match also marked the last Curtis Cup appearance of Jessie Valentine, 22 years after she made her debut.

The run of Mrs Bonallack

One player who would have equalled Mrs Valentine's record and possibly overtaken it was Mrs Angela Bonallack. She began her Curtis Cup run in the 1956 match as Miss Angela Ward but by 1958 had married top men's amateur Michael Bonallack. The start of her link with the Curtis Cup is remarkable as she began with the 1956 victory at Sandwich then played in the 1958 tie, a record few British amateurs can claim. She then competed in successive Cup matches until 1966,

Above: Peggy Conley is 'chaired' by her teammates and supporters after her victory had clinched the 1964 Curtis Cup for America.

Above: Scotland's Belle Robertson enjoyed a spectacular career both at home and abroad. In 1981 she became the oldest winner of the British Amateur Championship, having first played in the final in 1959.

Opposite: Laura Baugh was only 16 when picked for the American team in the 1972 Curtis Cup. She was later voted Most Beautiful Golfer of the Year by Golf Digest, a title which allowed her to earn over $300,000 in 1975 alone from endorsement. This should not disguise her ability, which made her the youngest winner of the US Amateur title in 1971 at less than 16¼ years old.

her sixth appearance, and would have made it seven in 1974, when although selected she wasn't available for the whole tour and thus declined.

The Kent-born Miss Ward had captured the British Girls', along with the Kent, Swedish and German Ladies' titles before becoming a Curtis Cup choice. And in 1956 she took the Scandinavian crown while launching the England international career that was to stretch 17 years to 1972.

The first of her two English Ladies' titles came in 1958 when she beat Bridget Jackson 3 and 2 in the final at Formby and the second in 1963 at Liphook with a 7 and 6 success over Elizabeth Chadwick. In between she was twice runner-up, then was beaten in the final again in 1972 at Woodhall Spa by Mary Everard. Mrs Bonallack also made her mark in the British Ladies', although it was one title that eluded her grasp. She was twice runner-up, in 1962 to Marley Spearman by

one hole at Royal Birkdale and in 1974 by 2 and 1 to the American Carole Semple at Royal Porthcawl. Understandably she was hugely successful on the county scene, winning the Kent title three times, then the Essex Championship on six occasions after her marriage and subsequent move north of the Thames.

Her Curtis Cup performances were no mean affairs either, although her record shows she was more successful in the four-somes than the singles. She was in a losing pair only once in five matches but her singles record might have been a great deal better had she not been drawn so often to play the crack American JoAnne Gunderson, now the highly successful professional JoAnne Carner.

In 1960 the Curtis Cup match moved to Lindrick and Angela Bonallack and Elizabeth Price gave the home team a great start by winning the opening foursomes. But from then on the progress was strictly downhill with only Ruth Porter's win and a half from Miss Price giving Britain and Ireland 2½ points to America's 6½. So the Cup went back across the Atlantic for the first of 13 consecutive victories, ended only in 1986 with Mrs Diane Bailey's magnificent side ending the sequence at Prairie Dunes.

A long period of US supremacy

The 1960 match brought the Cup debut of Marley Spearman although she had been an England international since 1955. No doubt her early career as a stage dancer, with appearances at several of London's top theatres, developed the balance and timing which made her such a successful golfer. Her rise was meteoric, and she was a trend-setter with regard to the stylish dress for women golfers. On the course she won the British Ladies' title twice, in 1961 by beating Diane Robb 7 and 6 at Carnoustie and the following year at Royal Birkdale overcoming Angela Bonallack. It was the first time since Enid Wilson's three-in-a-row victories in the early 1930s that anyone had won the title in consecutive years. She also won the New Zealand Championship in 1963 and the English Ladies' the following year but she didn't have the pleasure of playing on a winning Curtis Cup side. After the 1960 defeat, Marley was a member of the 1962 side that was thrashed 8−1 at Colorado Springs with Diane Robb, then Mrs Frearson, gaining the only victory.

Although only 18 years old, Mrs Frearson clinched a memorable victory with an 8 and 7 margin over Judy Bell who, ironically, was to captain the Americans in 1986 when their 26-year supremacy ended.

Mrs Frearson won the Girls' title in 1959 and 1961, was a girl international from 1957 to 1961 and a full England international in 1961, 1962 and 1971, while she also played in the 1968 World Team Championship. But her two Curtis Cup appearances were separated

Right: Gillian Stewart was one of three British players to win a singles match in the 1980 Curtis Cup encounter at St Pierre, Chepstow, but it was the usual story so far as the overall result was concerned: a 13–5 victory for the USA.

by ten years, the second coming in 1972.

Until 1964, the Curtis Cup had been decided over three 36-hole foursomes and six 36-hole singles. But that year the format changed to three 18-hole foursomes and six 18-hole singles on each of the two days of the contest which meant there were 18 points at stake instead of nine. The first time this format was used was at Royal Porthcawl and it proved a much closer affair before the Americans got home 10½–7½. In those days it was becoming a trend for the more ambitious American amateurs to cut their teeth on the Curtis Cup before moving on to the professional game which by now was flourishing in the USA. In 1964 the American team contained three newcomers who between them clinched their side's victory by winning their singles on the second day. Among them was Peggy Conley, who as a 17-year-old was the Americans' youngest member — but that didn't stop her from accounting for Bridget Jackson by one hole. Miss Conley later joined the American professional ranks and now plays on the Women's tour in Europe. That year's contest was also the fourth and final appearance of JoAnne Gunderson before she turned professional.

America clinched another easy victory in 1966 at Hot Springs, Virginia, after racing to a 7–2 first day lead. They extended this to 13–5 by the finish, with Miss Ita Burke and Angela Bonallack gaining a singles victory each for Great Britain with a lone foursomes success by Miss Burke and Elizabeth Chadwick. But when the contest returned to Ireland in 1968 and the magnificent links at Newcastle, County Down, the home side had high hopes of bringing the trophy back especially after ending the first day with a slim 5–4 lead. But those hopes died on the following morning when the Americans won two foursomes and halved the third, and then reduced the British to just one singles success in a 10½–7½ defeat. By now the home team had gained an infusion of new talent such as Mrs Belle Robertson, Vivien Saunders, Pamela Tredinnick and Diane Oxley but it still didn't lead to a change in fortunes.

Belle Robertson and Vivien Saunders

Mrs Robertson was to enjoy a spectacular career at home and abroad although she didn't enjoy the thrill of a Curtis Cup triumph until she had celebrated her 50th birthday by announcing her impending retirement from international competition. Nevertheless the resilient Scot reached the final of the British Ladies' as long ago as 1959 as Isabella McCorkindale, losing to Elizabeth Price at the 37th hole at Ascot. Six years later, after her marriage, she reached the final again but with the same outcome, as Brigitte Varangot took her second title with a 4 and 3 scoreline at St Andrews. She was on the losing end of a final for a third time in 1970 at Gullane when there was just one hole

Left: Mary McKenna was another British golfer who fought hard to stem the American tide in the 1970s and 1980s. She won singles matches in 1974 and 1980 and with Belle Robertson a foursomes in 1982, but they were isolated wins in a wave of defeats.

separating her from Curtis Cup colleague Diane Oxley.

Fortunately there was a happy ending as Belle at last won the title in 1981 when she beat Wilma Aitken, who was born in 1959, the year Belle reached the final for the first time. But it wasn't easy for the veteran Scot. She was five up with five to play at Conway only to see that lead evaporate. But she eventually came through on the 20th to become the oldest winner of the trophy at the age of 45. It may have taken her some time to achieve that success but it was a different story in her native Scotland where Belle was a more frequent finalist. She won the title seven times — in 1965, 1966, 1971, 1972, 1978, 1980 and 1986 — and was runner-up in 1959, 1963 and 1970. Down the years she has also had her name inscribed on many more championships such as the British Ladies' Open Stroke-play, the Sunningdale Foursomes, the Avia Foursomes, the Helen Holm Trophy and the Roehampton Gold Cup.

Vivien Saunders was a girl international from 1964 to 1967, while in 1966 she reached the final of the British Ladies' at Ganton only to lose 3 and 2 to Elizabeth Chadwick. Two years later came her only Curtis Cup appearance in that tussle at Newcastle. She might have made more but in 1969 she turned professional and became the first European to qualify for the American Tour. She made excursions to other distant parts, winning twice in Australia. Back home in 1977 she took the British Open after a tie with Mary Everard. Her name also appeared on certain makes of clubs while she was a founder member of the Women's Professional Golf Association in 1978, becoming its chairman that year and in 1979. These days she is a successful golf writer, a coach to international sides and now a golf club owner.

The British hit rock bottom

The 1970 Curtis Cup threw up another who was to write her name in honour across women's golf in Britain and her native Ireland. Mary McKenna made a great start to her Cup career, winning her opening foursomes with Diane Oxley at Brae Burn then taking another point in her first singles. But it wasn't enough to prevent another American victory, this time by 11½ – 6½.

In 1972 at Western Gailes the home team again made a bright start, winning the opening foursomes 2 – 1. But as was to become the custom over the next five matches, the singles were to prove the Achilles heel. The Americans soon edged ahead and were able to keep that lead to win again, 10 – 8. They also made history by clinching their first win in Scotland, having drawn at Gleneagles and lost at Muirfield. The visitors also paraded their youngest ever player in Laura Baugh, just a few days beyond her 17th birthday — she had been under 17 when named in the side. She

Below: Michelle Walker, known as Mickey, was a strength in British golf from 1971, when she won her first British Ladies' title. She was one of the few to beat an American in a singles match in the Curtis Cup in the 1970s.

was also voted the Most Beautiful Golfer of the Year and was to later turn professional with increasing success. Youth was certainly the Americans' theme as they also included 18-year-old Hollis Stacy, another who has starred on the pro tour.

San Francisco was the venue for the 1974 Cup match but it was a similar story. Although the British tied the opening foursomes, the singles again proved a disaster with only Mickey Walker winning, following her foursomes success with Mary Everard. At the end of the first day America led 6 – 3 which they extended to 13 – 5, surrendering only two matches on the second day, to Julie Greenhalgh and Tegwen Perkins in the foursomes and to Mary McKenna in the singles.

So to Lytham St Annes in 1976 but with the visitors fielding such future champions as Nancy Lopez, Beth Daniel and Debbie Massey, the outcome was almost inevitable. The British trailed 2½ – 6½ after the first day and their only consolation was halving the second day's singles to go down 6½ – 11½.

At Apawamis, New York, in 1978, the British again were quick off the mark, dropping only half a point in the foursomes, a style of golf that doesn't figure too promi-

Left: One of the greatest of all women golfers, Nancy Lopez was a sensation in her first full season, 1978, when she won five consecutive events and finished top of the money list with a record total of $189,813. Only the birth of her children has seriously interrupted her progress since.

nently on the Americans' calendar. But it was a false sense of security. By the end of the day the home side led 5–4 and when they whitewashed the opposition in the second day foursomes, having now got the hang of it, they were on their way to a 12–6 success and their 10th successive victory.

The 1980 match at St Pierre, Chepstow, failed to break the sequence with the British team again outclassed in every department. They lost each series apart from the final singles which were tied 3–3, thanks to Mary McKenna, Gillian Stewart and Linda Moore. But they were the only winners, the other two points in a 13–5 defeat coming from two halved matches.

If that result was regarded as another disaster, the 1982 encounter at Denver hit rock bottom. Again only three victories were achieved, by Janet Soulsby and Belle Robertson in the singles and Mary McKenna and Belle Robertson in the foursomes. Otherwise the Americans made a clean sweep to hand Britain and Ireland their heaviest defeat in the 50-year history of the Cup, completing a 14½–3½ success.

By this time it seemed that the British and Irish players were never going to get within striking distance of their trans-Atlantic rivals. Although the Americans changed their line-ups almost every year they were still streets ahead in class and skill. But in 1984 with the match returning to Muirfield, the Americans must have wondered if the Muirfield hoodoo might strike again. The opening foursomes were drawn, while America just edged the singles to end the first day only one point ahead, 5–4. It was still the same after the second series of foursomes and the home side felt they could clinch a famous victory. But it wasn't to be and the visitors held on in the closing singles to retain their slim advantage, winning 9½–8½.

Glory at Prairie Dunes

Half of that British team were assigned for the 1986 battle which took place at Prairie Dunes, Kansas, and together with four newcomers they were not only to upset the form book but put an end to the Americans' domination, in their own backyard to boot. Led by a splendid captain in Diane Bailey, the British and Irish team completely whitewashed the opening foursomes but we had seen something like this before. When the first series of singles added to the lead, there was a hint of an upset of gigantic proportions in the offing.

Pat Johnson, Lillian Behan and Jill Thornhill had collected two wins apiece and the visitors went into the second day with a healthy 6½–2½ lead. Only three points were needed and when the morning foursomes went 2½–½ in Britain's favour, the Cup was almost on its way back across the Atlantic. It was left to Patricia Johnson, one of the babes of the side and the star with four wins, to secure the victory as Britain and Ireland romped to a 13–5 triumph. Not only had they ended the Americans' stranglehold on the match but the victory was a vindication of Mrs Bailey's detailed planning of acclimatization to American conditions and the extreme heat. In the end the heat was on the United States while most agreed that a British victory was long overdue and a marvellous boost for the event as a whole.

Of the triumphant side, Mrs Robertson, who at 50 had at least tasted a Curtis Cup victory, retired, while Miss Johnson and Ireland's Miss Behan switched to the professional ranks like so many before them.

Below: The star of the magnificent and long overdue British triumph in the Curtis Cup at Prairie Dunes in 1986 was Pat Johnson, one of the younger wave, who registered four wins in the 13–5 victory.

The Ladies' Professional Golf Association

Women professional golfers existed before the Second World War but the Women's Professional Golfers' Association was formed in the United States in 1946. The story began two years earlier when three relatively unknown women golfers — Hope Seignious, Betty Hicks and Ellen Griffin — took steps to get a women's pro tour off the ground. The US Women's Open was first staged in 1946 and was won by Patty Berg, who had been Amateur Champion in 1938. But the tour didn't prosper long and by 1947 it was on fragile ground. The end soon came but a rescue act was staged by the Wilson Sporting Goods company in 1948 under a new label, the Ladies' Professional Golf Association, and with marketing director Fred Corcoran, Babe Zaharias' personal manager, at the helm. Fred, a former executive director of the men's pro tour, saw distinct possibilities for a women's tour and, as the old saying goes, from little acorns, great oaks grow.

The new association was officially chartered in 1950 and soon had solid support from sponsors and the public. In the first year the total prize money was $45,000 for nine tournaments which pales into insignificance against today's figures. Nevertheless it was a good start, even if most of the prize money went into the pockets of Berg and Zaharias. In fact they won 19 of the 23 tournaments in the first two years. By 1952 the total number of tournaments had reached 21, but the influx of players was slow while the idea of women professionals was not greeted enthusiastically in many areas. This can be measured by the fact that the LPGA was restricted to playing only public courses in certain locations. Yet progress was made and sponsorship increased. Much of the success was down to the players of the era. Zaharias, Louise Suggs, Marilyn Smith, Betsy Rawls and Peggy Kirk all helped boost the tour's appeal and reputation while their skills on the course drew greater numbers of spectators. By 1959 there were 26 tournaments while prize money had risen from $50,000 to $200,000.

Mickey Wright's influence

From 1961 to 1964 it was Mickey Wright who dominated the tour. As Mary Kathryn Wright, she reached the final of the US Junior Championship in 1950. Two years later she won it and was off on a career that was to make her one of the greatest women golfers of all time. In 1954 she won the World and All-American Amateur titles, reached the final of the US Amateur and was fourth and leading amateur in the US Open. She turned professional that same year but had to wait until 1956 for her first pro victory. Three more wins followed in 1957 and by then she had joined Berg, Rawls and Suggs as the big names of the US tour.

Left: *Laura Davies emerged as one of the most exciting players in the 1980s, winning the US Open in 1987, the first British woman to achieve this feat. At the time she was also British champion. While striking the ball immense distances, she nevertheless has a delicate touch around the greens.*

A year later she was the undisputed number one as she won five events including her first US Open and US LPGA. The US Open was retained in 1959 and she won three more events, but she became the supreme champion between 1961 and 1964, winning 45 tournaments to take her tally to 63 including four US Opens and four US LPGAs. It was this sort of form that drew the attention of the media and from then on the Tour prospered. In 1963 the Tour was first televised, albeit only the final round of the US Open. However, it proved a success and that was the start of a long-term association between TV and the Tour. The projection of women's golf on the small screen brought greater public awareness of the Tour and much of this credit is attributed to Mickey Wright. Today's players still owe a major debt to the player who, in direct contrast to the razzmatazz of the Tour, was shy and retiring and withdrew as much as possible from the spotlight and public gaze. As Judy Rankin, who joined the Tour at the height of Wright's supremacy, said: 'Mickey got the outside world to take a second look at women golfers and when they looked, they discovered the rest of us.'

Reorganization of the Association

With the TV coverage, sponsorship accelerated and by the end of the decade prize money had reached $600,000 with the schedule extended to 34 events. Wright dropped out of the scene in 1965 to concentrate on her studies — she was also having trouble with an arthritic wrist. But she was soon back playing full time and still winning, though not so consistently. At the start of the 1970s the LPGA Tour seemed to be hail and hearty with prize money still escalating and more players of quality joining the ever-increasing membership. In 1973 the players were playing for $1.5 million and the prospects continued to look rosy. But storm clouds were gathering and the Association found it could not keep pace with its rapid expansion. Bankruptcy beckoned and another rescue act was needed. It came from Ray Volpe, a former Vice-President of Marketing for the National Hockey League, who took over as the Tour's first Commissioner.

Right: JoAnne Carner was a brilliant amateur (originally as JoAnne Gunderson) and then a prolific winner in the professional ranks. She won at all levels from the US Junior amateur title in 1956 to the first of her US Opens in 1971, when she became the first woman to take the US Junior, Amateur and Open titles.

He moved the Tour's headquarters from Atlanta to New York and expanded his staff to deal more efficiently with the administration. Volpe also formed a Board of Directors and appointed a Player Council to improve the link between the players and staff. Volpe stayed in charge for seven years during which time the prize money rose to $6.4 million, while the average field for each tournament doubled from around 60 to 120 players. Television coverage increased while other benefits came to the players including a home course and headquarters at Sweetwater County Club in Texas. Volpe handed the reins to John Laupheimer in 1982 and the expansion has continued under his control.

Kathy Whitworth's records

Such has been the success that the LPGA is now one of the largest organizations in women's professional sport. In 1987 the prize money stood at $10.65 million while the Tour now lasts almost the whole year. Its membership contains 14 millionaires. Although Mickey Wright won her last tournament in 1973 and retired from the tour in 1980, her total of 82 wins has been beaten only by Kathy Whitworth, who at the start of the 1987 season had 88 wins to her credit. In almost 30 years on tour she has compiled a glittering array of statistics: leading money winner eight times, Player of the Year seven times and Vare Trophy winner (for the lowest stroke average) also seven times.

Kathy's performance along with that of several other leading players has underlined the enormous improvement in the standard of women's golf in America. In the same category is JoAnne Carner who at the start of 1987 was sixth in the list of career wins with 42, level with Sandra Haynie but behind Rawls with 55 and Suggs with 50. Carner, the last amateur to win an LPGA event, has won over $2 million, been Player of the Year three times, leading money winner three times and five times Vare Trophy winner. She has twice won the US Open and is the only woman to have won the USGA Junior, US Amateur and US Women's Open titles.

The rapid rise of Nancy Lopez

Perhaps the brightest rising star on the American tour is Nancy Lopez. A bubbling, outgoing personality, she has stamped her character and outstanding skills on the tour in less than 10 years and such has been her success that she has already won almost $1¾ million. To the start of 1987 the 30-year-old had amassed 34 victories, including two US LPGA titles, three Player of the Year awards and three Vare Trophy successes. All this against the background of two marriages and two children. There is little doubt that after Babe Zaharias and Mickey Wright, Nancy Lopez has the ability to stir the passions for fans of women's professional golf. Before joining the pro ranks Nancy represented the US in the Curtis Cup and the World Team

Championship and after turning professional in 1977 her first event was the Colgate European Open at Sunningdale in which she was second. That, together with winning over $20,000 in America was a sign of things to come. In 1978 she won nine events, including a return to England to take the European Open and another win in Japan. But what was remarkable was that five of her US wins were consecutive.

She won the European Open again in 1979 among a tally of eight wins, was Player of the Year and her stroke average of 71.20 stood as an all-time LPGA record until she beat it in 1985 with 70.73. A long-hitter and bold putter, Nancy is a major draw on the US Tour. It has often been suggested that someone of the style and calibre of Nancy Lopez is needed to boost the fortunes of the WPGA tour in Europe.

Women's pro golf in Europe

Certainly the women's professional circuit in Britain and Europe has had a chequered career not too dissimilar to that in America albeit of a somewhat shorter duration. The tour was founded in 1979 and faced a tough struggle during its formative years. At times some must have wondered if there was a place for a women's pro tour in this part of the world. In those early days sponsorship was comparatively small as were the numbers of spectators and the players involved. But, as on the other side of the Atlantic, gradually numbers grew in each category but still the tour lacked that spark to ignite the fire. Unfortunately things got worse before they got better and in 1983 the tour was on the point of collapse. However, it was rescued by the Professional Golfers' Association and came under the umbrella of the men's organization at The Belfry in Sutton Coldfield.

Gradually more sponsors and prize money were found, more tournaments were arranged, especially on the continent of Europe, while more players took the plunge from the amateur ranks with the prospect of building themselves a solid career. The tour organization has grown in both strength and efficiency until in 1987 it is ticking along like a well-oiled machine. In 1987 prize money broke through the £1 million barrier and many more fans are attending tournaments to see a gallery of highly skilled players. There are now almost 150 members of the WPGA and it is a highly international 'family' with members from America, Australia, New Zealand, Zimbabwe, Sri Lanka and Colombia as well as most countries in Europe.

And perhaps the Tour has found a player or two of the quality of a Nancy Lopez. In Laura Davies, who topped the Order of Merit in 1985 and 1986, the Tour has someone of unquestionable quality, a striker of unrivalled length and deftness of touch while Sweden will claim that in Liselotte Neumann they also have a personality of some note.

Famous Courses and Holes

The overwhelming desire to hit a ball with a stick has been with man for centuries. Designing an area to fulfil that desire has been a more recent discovery and has its roots on the coasts of Scotland where the area between the land and the sea was found to be ideal. Thus the great links courses led the way in the development of golf courses throughout the world. Of these, St Andrews stands as the original blueprint; fashioned by nature with little influence by man.

Inland courses owe their existence to man's ingenuity in being able to visualize a golf course on sometimes unpromising landscapes and since the turn of the century the golf course architects have enriched the game with their grand designs.

Among the courses under discussion here are those which have witnessed some of the great deeds in the game by virtue of the many championships and tournaments which have been played upon them. All of them, however, provide a challenge to golfers of any standard for the hallmark of a great course is one which gives equal enjoyment to every player.

Left: *Bernhard Langer on the 9th tee at Turnberry in the 1986 Open Championship. The drive has to be struck over the sea which intrudes into the course by means of an inlet between tee and green.*

There are thousands of golf courses throughout the world, some still in the early stages of construction, others which have been in existence for centuries. All of them provide, or will provide, a degree of pleasure to those people who set foot on them whether it be for the challenge they present or simply as a place for fresh air and exercise. There are courses set on parkland, on meadowland, on mountains and beside the sea; some have even been constructed in deserts. There are courses awash with water hazards, others swarming with bunkers, some with tree-lined fairways, others with hardly a tree in sight, some are inordinately long, others extremely short. Each will be different from the other so that a golfer could spend a lifetime travelling the world and still find something fresh and stimulating.

Of course, there are degrees of stimulation and this is where the golfer has to make a judgement as to what constitutes a great course, a good course or an indifferent one. This judgement should not be based on how a golfer fares through the round — a bad score doesn't necessarily mean a bad course. There are more objective ways of assessing a golf course. For example, does the course provide equal enjoyment to all golfers, no matter what their standard? Could the golfer, at the end of the round, sit down and have instant recall of every hole? Does the course draw upon the full repertoire of strokes from controlled drives to delicate pitches? Do the holes require the golfer to think and assess before hitting each shot? And finally, and perhaps most importantly from the average golfer's point of view, is it a course where he or she could happily play for the rest of their days without staleness ever dulling its edge?

These are the criteria for a memorable course and the game has been fortunate that there have been course architects who have tackled these fundamentals with a creative instinct which elevates their designs a shade above the rest. Their courses stand as memorials to their talents and have assumed the mantle of greatness.

GREAT BRITAIN

Practically all of the courses which have achieved fame or notoriety owe their standing to a strip of land hard by the coast near a small Fifeshire fishing town.

St Andrews

St Andrews stands as the original masterpiece fashioned by nature, with a few additions by man and beast. Some people say that God was so preoccupied with the business of Creation that He devised the Old Course as a sort of practice ground for the real thing, but leaving aside any fanciful explanations, the truth is the Old Course simply emerged and

evolved. Its basic design has not changed over the centuries and the problems it presents to the golfer are still severe, despite the modernization of equipment and the improved physical prowess of the current top players.

Many golfers start off by believing that the Old Course is a pushover if they hook the ball around it since most of the trouble, particularly the out-of-bounds, is on the right. Any golfer who follows this route will find a veritable Pandora's Box of trouble and quickly re-assess that game plan. Indeed, the first hole provides an excellent example of how the Old Course can sucker-punch the golfer from the start. Possessing the widest fairway in golf, the player is naturally lured to the left by the out-of-bounds on the right but the further left the tee shot travels, the harder the second shot over the snaking Swilcan Burn becomes. The optical illusion created by the flatness of the fairway leads the player to believe the green is nearer than it is. Even Jack Nicklaus, who has won two Opens at St Andrews, fell victim to this illusion when, after his opening drive in the 1984

Open, he struck what he described afterwards as a perfect pitch, perfectly into the muddy waters of the Swilcan.

In exactly the reverse direction, the 18th poses the same problem. Again the out-of-bounds fence on the right forces the golfer to drive to the left. From here, the deep hollow in front of the green, the Valley of Sin, presents the golfer with the dilemma of whether to pitch the ball all the way to the flag or run it up through that deep depression. Such a dilemma faced Doug Sanders in the 1970 Open when he needed a four at the last to win. An accomplished manufacturer of shots, Sanders elected to pitch the ball all the way and in making sure he cleared the hollow he put the ball some 30 feet above the hole. The putt looks more downhill than it is and Sanders left it three feet short and then perpetrated probably the most famous miss in the history of the Championship to fall back into a tie with Nicklaus. Curiously enough, in the play-off the following day, Sanders played a perfect pitch and run on the same hole to secure a birdie which left him only one stroke behind Nicklaus who

had matched that birdie three.

The legacy that the Old Course has left to golf is probably encapsulated in three holes, the 11th, the 14th and 17th. The 11th, or High hole, is a short hole of 172 yards and stands as one of the most copied holes in the game. Played out towards the Eden estuary which lies over the back of the green, the hole is guarded by two deep bunkers, the Strath on the front, right-hand side and the Hill on the left. The pin is invariably tucked in behind the Strath but if the golfer is overstrong with the tee shot, a putt of daunting proportions has to be faced down a precipitous slope and the ball can easily finish up in the very bunker that dictated the terms from the tee. It was here that Bobby Jones, playing in his first Open at St Andrews in 1921, took six and then tore up his card, vowing never to return. Fortunately he did, and he triumphed there in 1927. In the 1933 Open, Gene Sarazen finished one stroke out of the play-off between Densmore Shute and Craig Wood having taken three strokes to emerge from the Strath bunker, a cavern so deep that it is alleged that Sarazen was invisible.

Above: One of the huge double greens at St Andrews. The 4th and 14th in play during the 1984 Open Championship. The 14th is the longest hole on the Old Course and cost Bill Rogers, a recent champion, an 11 in the 1984 Championship.

St Andrews

Royal and Ancient Golf Club of St Andrews, Fife, Scotland

Old course

Out	3,528 yards	36
In	3,432 yards	36
Total	6,960 yards	par 72

Card of the course

No.			
1	Burn	370 yards	par 4
2	Dyke	411 yards	par 4
3	Cartgate (out)	398 yards	par 4
4	Ginger Beer	463 yards	par 4
5	Hole o'Cross (out)	564 yards	par 5
6	Heathery (out)	416 yards	par 4
7	High (out)	372 yards	par 4
8	Short	178 yards	par 3
9	End	356 yards	par 4
10	Bobby Jones	342 yards	par 4
11	High (in)	172 yards	par 3
12	Heathery (in)	316 yards	par 4

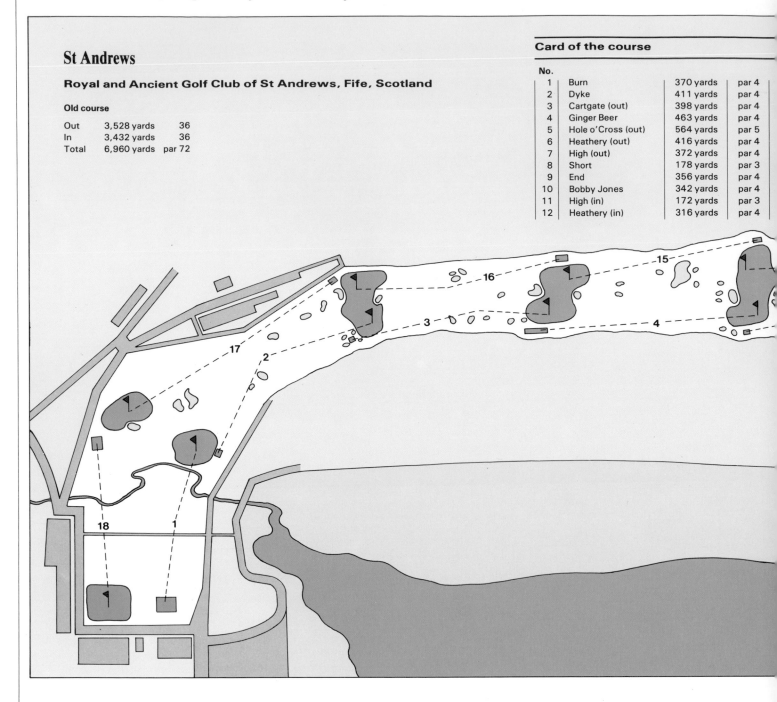

The 14th, or Long hole, is 567 yards long and strewn with disaster. From the tee, the out-of-bounds wall creeps insidiously into the fairway from the right, automatically pushing the player's aim towards the grasping set of five bunkers on the left, known as the Beardies. If the fairway, named the Elysian Fields after the Greek abode of the dead, is found, the decision has to be made whether to carry the enormous Hell bunker with the second or play to the left or right of it. Either route leaves a perilous approach over a steeply sloping bank to the green. In the 1939 Open Bobby Locke came to the 14th standing at five under par and then hooked his tee shot in a strong wind into the Beardies. His attempted recovery was too ambitious and he left the ball in the sand. His fourth shot found Hell and he finished with an eight. The aforementioned Sarazen also took eight there in 1933 following a clash with Hell

bunker and even Peter Thomson's serene progress to the second of his three consecutive Open titles in 1955 was shaken when he tangled with the Beardies to take seven. In the 1984 Open, with the full might of modern technology at his command, American Bill Rogers, who had won the Open in fine style at Royal St George's three years earlier, contrived to put three tee shots over the wall and walked off with an 11.

And so to the 17th. Ever since David Ayton took 11 here to lose the 1885 Open by two strokes, the Road Hole has been assured of its place in Open tragedy. It is 461 yards long and a par four but that figure is irrelevant to even the greatest exponents, most of whom would take a five and walk gladly to the 18th tee.

The hole is a marvellous example of the use of angles to confuse and frustrate. From the tee, the presence of the out-of-bounds on

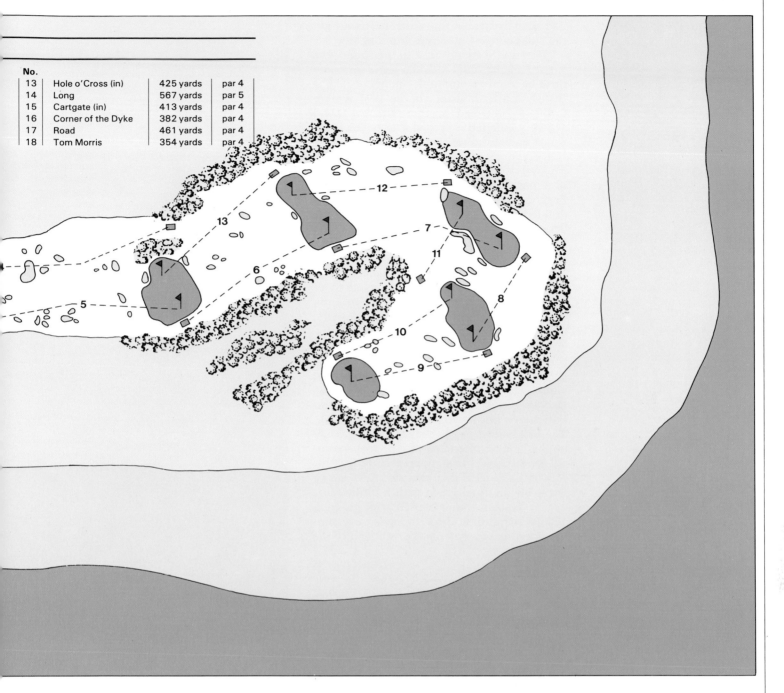

No.			
13	Hole o'Cross (in)	425 yards	par 4
14	Long	567 yards	par 5
15	Cartgate (in)	413 yards	par 4
16	Corner of the Dyke	382 yards	par 4
17	Road	461 yards	par 4
18	Tom Morris	354 yards	par 4

the right instinctively draws the aim away to the left. But the further left the tee shot, the more imperceptible becomes the target of the green. And what a target. The front of the green rises alarmingly to a narrow shelf and again, the angle of the green in relation to the approach, means that any shot slightly over-hit will skitter through onto the dreaded road. That really should be enough but nature has conjured up one more impossible trick in the shape of the Road bunker on the left of the green, a bubbling pot of perdition which gnaws into the putting surface.

The Road Hole played its part in Bobby Jones' Grand Slam triumph in 1930 when, while engaged in a ferocious semi-final match with Cyril Tolley in the British Amateur of that year, his second shot is alleged to have struck a spectator standing on the back of the green. Jones went on to halve the hole and win the match on the 19th but the question

remains as to whether the ball was stopped or would have stayed up anyway. Nowadays, no spectators are allowed in this area and are kept behind the wall beyond the road.

Thirty years later the Road Hole proved the stumbling block in Arnold Palmer's quest for the Centenary Open. He played the hole in four strokes more than the eventual winner, Kel Nagle. Palmer did not learn by experience for 18 years later in the 1978 Open he was still trying to bludgeon it into sub-mission. Tied for the second round lead, he drove hugely out-of-bounds to take seven. The next day he repeated the process for another seven. This was also the year when Japan's Tsuneyuki 'Tommy' Nakajima wrote his name in the record books. On the front of the green in two shots, Nakajima putted up the slope only to watch in disbelief as his ball curved gently left and plopped into the Road bunker. The sands of Nakajima had been excavated four times before he got the ball out to eventually hole out in nine.

Because of its position in the round, the Road Hole has also been the scene for many thrilling and memorable moments. The British and Irish victory in the 1971 Walker Cup was clinched at the 17th by David Marsh's superlative second shot to the green which ended the resistance of his opponent, Bill Hyndman of America. In 1978, Jack Nicklaus secured his third Open title by virtue of a magnificent long putt from the front of the green, while six years later the Road Hole decided the outcome of the enthralling battle between Severiano Ballesteros and Tom Watson. Ballesteros came to the 17th tied with Watson who was playing behind him. The Spaniard had failed to make four in each of his three previous attempts and had vowed that he would do so or come back on the Monday, presumably for the play-off, and have another go. His drive finished in the left rough, hardly the best place to exert enough control on the ball to stop it on the green. The stroke, with a 6-iron, appeared almost lackadaisical compared with the lashing impact one usually associates with Ballesteros but its result was no less telling. The ball landed just to the right of the Road bunker and bounced up onto the green, coming to rest 30 feet from the pin. With his four secure, Ballesteros then executed the *coup de grace* on the final green with a birdie putt, just as Watson found himself with his back against the wall on the 17th having overshot his target massively from the right half of the fairway.

Carnoustie

From St Andrews it is but a short journey across the Tay to another links course which has played a major role in the outcome of Championships. While the Old Course may be regarded as the epitome of strategic design in that it provides the player with a number of routes on each hole and it is up to the golfer to choose which one suits his ability, Carnoustie is ruggedly and brutally penal. From the start, Carnoustie requires golf of an impeccable order if a score is to be built, and even a sound foundation can be mercilessly ripped out by the severity of the final three holes.

The Open was first staged there in 1931 and last held in 1975. That first Carnoustie Open resulted in victory for the native born Tommy Armour who had emigrated to America after the First World War. Armour won by one stroke from Argentina's Jose Jurado, who wrote the first chapter in the book of Carnoustie's finishing holes by taking six on the 17th in the final round. The 17th, 454 yards long, is intersected twice by the Barry Burn, requiring the golfer to carry at least one strip of water with the tee shot. This Jurado did but then lifted his Latin head on the second and topped the ball into the second strip of the burn. The 18th also has

two sections of the burn crossing it, with the second part lying just in front of the green and Jurado, unaware of his position in the field, played it safely in five only to discover that his earlier six meant he had needed a four to tie.

For the 1975 Open, the 18th was shortened from a par five to a par four of 448 yards. Tom Watson birdied the hole on the final afternoon with a drive and short iron to ten feet. This put him in a tie with Australia's Jack Newton and in the weather conditions of the play-off the following day, Watson needed a 2-iron to the heart of the 18th green to take the title by a single stroke.

Completing this trilogy of terror is the 16th, quite possibly the toughest par three in the world. The hole is 235 yards long with two fronting bunkers and a green shaped like an upturned saucer. The tee shot must be long and straight if the ball is not to fall away off the green leaving a chip of infinitely delicate proportions. In his valiant but

Left: *The 18th green at Carnoustie, the scene of an Open-winning shot in 1975, when Tom Watson dropped his second ten feet from the pin and sank the birdie putt for a play-off on his way to the first of five Opens.*

eventually futile chase of Gary Player in the 1968 Open, Jack Nicklaus struck a full-blooded drive into the teeth of the wind to put the ball 20 feet from the pin, a stroke of staggering quality. Alas, he missed the birdie and Player went on to win by two strokes.

In most people's minds, Carnoustie inspires visions of Ben Hogan and his incomparable victory in the 1953 Open but it also has equal associations with Henry Cotton who took his second Open title there in 1937 against the full might of the recently victorious American Ryder Cup team. The final round was played in continuous torrential rain and Cotton's round of 71 could be regarded as perhaps his finest. Cotton and Hogan both displayed a chilling detachment in their striking of a golf ball; their methods brooked no argument and the ball had no choice but to follow the path they intended. It is indicative that Carnoustie demands nothing less from those who wish to conquer it.

Prestwick

Throughout the history of the Open Championship it is the Scottish courses which have played the dominant role. Prestwick, where the first Open was held in 1860, Royal Troon and Turnberry make an impressive west coast trio. Although Prestwick hasn't been used for an Open since 1925, holes such as the 3rd, with its huge sleepered Cardinal cross-bunker, the 5th with its blind tee shot over a dune and the 17th, with its blind approach over the Alps dunes, must have presented a daunting prospect in the days of the gutty ball.

Troon

Troon is still on the Open rota and will stage the Championship in 1989. Its most famous hole is the 126-yard 8th, known universally as the Postage Stamp because of the small green, which is heavily guarded by deep bunkers. The hole was the scene of the second highest score in the Championship's history

when, in 1950, a German amateur, Hermann Tissies, took 15 strokes to hole out after ping-ponging his ball across the green from one bunker to another. One player who did lick the Postage Stamp was Gene Sarazen, who holed in one there in the 1973 Open. Troon provides a rugged test, particularly over the inward half where the wind invariably quarters over the left shoulder. The 11th, known as the Fox, requires much guile and cunning if a par five is to be obtained as the drive has to carry a wilderness of gorse and scrub and be kept away from the out-of-bounds wall on the right. To reach the green in two needs a shot of extreme accuracy since the green is tucked in close to the wall. The hole claimed a notable victim in the 1962 Open when Jack Nicklaus, making his debut in the Championship, completed it in 10. The winner of that Open, Arnold Palmer, was not out-foxed by the 11th — his four rounds included an eagle, two birdies and a par.

Turnberry

The majestic cliff-top setting of Turnberry had been the venue for many tournaments and championships but never the Open. Its scenic qualities could not be ignored however, and in 1977 the R & A took the Open there for the first time. The result was the lowest 72-hole aggregate in the history of the event but, to be fair, there was little wind that week and the course was bathed in sunshine. Four years earlier, Turnberry had wreaked havoc among the competitors in the John Player Classic when gale-force winds swept across the course, and it was also no pushover when the Open returned there in 1986 and nobody finished under the stiff par of 280 after 72 holes. The most compelling hole visually is undoubtedly the 9th with the tee built on a rocky promontory of the cliff edge requiring the drive to be struck over a foaming inlet below. The tee itself is a little

fraudulent since it is not the work of nature but was built from the torn up runways that infected the course when it was used as an airfield during both World Wars. No one would deny that the tee does not provide the death-or-glory challenge so relished by golfers, even though the carry itself is not enormous.

Water of a less turbulent nature plays its part on Turnberry's 16th, a par four of 415 yards with the green perched on a knoll, beneath which trickle the innocuous waters of the Wee Burn. Generations of golfers have watched in anguish as their second shot has landed on the front banking of the green and rolled back into the water. None was more anguished than the members of the 1963 British and Irish Walker Cup team who threw away the chance of victory against the Americans by constantly failing to take enough club on this treacherous hole.

Royal Dornoch

To omit Royal Dornoch from any list of great Scottish courses would be an unforgivable oversight. Because of its northerly location and inaccessibility it has not staged many championships but it was given its due recognition when the 1985 British Amateur was held there, resulting in a win for Ulster's Garth McGimpsey. Curving along the shores of Embo Bay at the mouth of the Dornoch Firth, the course is true linksland, wandering through banks of whin bushes. Near the turn of the century, Old Tom Morris was commissioned to lay out a further nine holes to the nine which already existed but the land needed little interpretation by man to become a classic course.

The chief feature of Dornoch is its raised greens which place a high premium on chipping for those players who fail to find them with the approach. This is exemplified by the 459-yard 14th, which contains no bunkers

Opposite: The dramatic sky can now be enjoyed by the golfers who have safely found themselves on the 8th green at Troon. Called the Postage Stamp because of its small size, it was the scene of Gene Sarazen's famous hole-in-one in 1973.

Left: Spectators surround a green at Turnberry during the 1986 Open in a period of calm. The course for much of the Championship was the victim of wind and rain, and not even Greg Norman, the winner, could beat par for the four rounds.

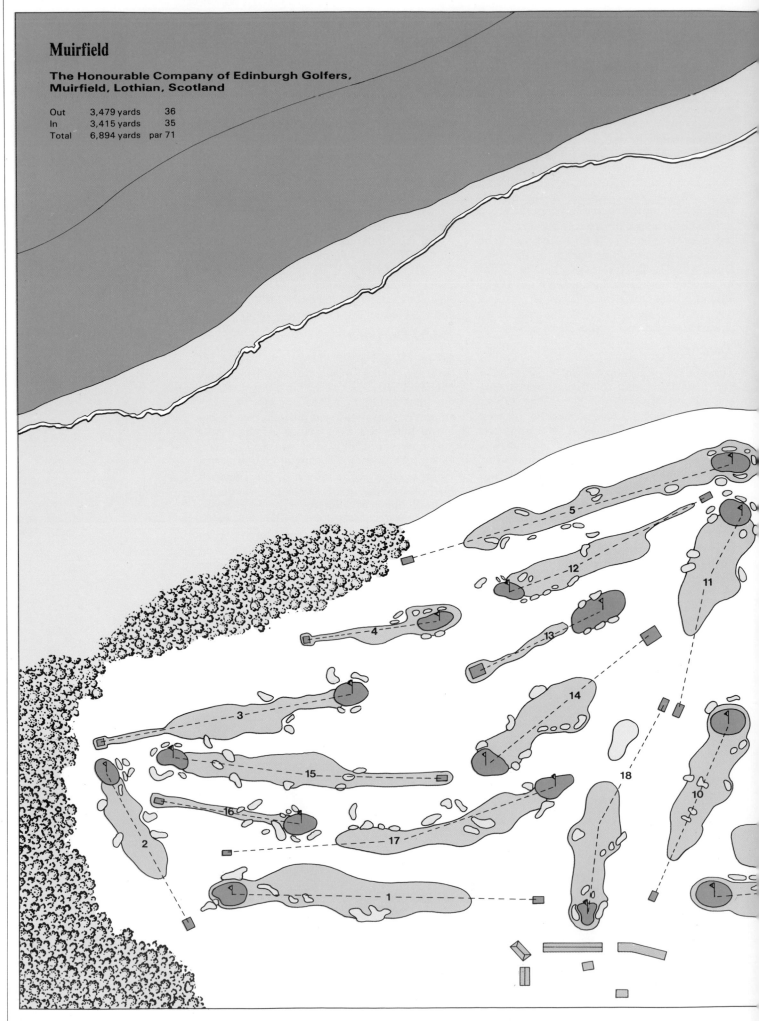

Muirfield

**The Honourable Company of Edinburgh Golfers,
Muirfield, Lothian, Scotland**

Out	3,479 yards	36
In	3,415 yards	35
Total	6,894 yards	par 71

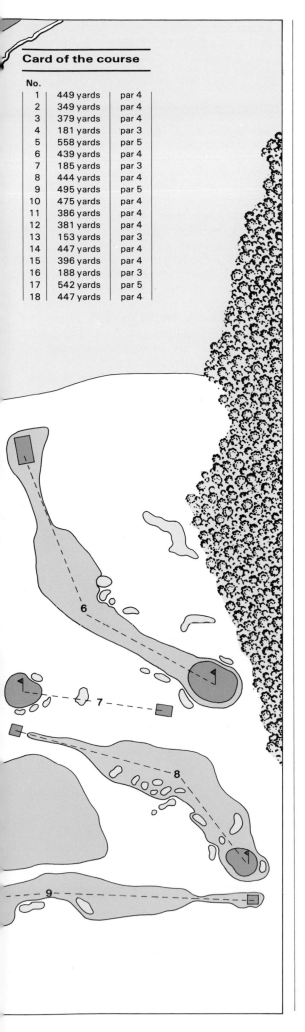

Card of the course

No.		
1	449 yards	par 4
2	349 yards	par 4
3	379 yards	par 4
4	181 yards	par 3
5	558 yards	par 5
6	439 yards	par 4
7	185 yards	par 3
8	444 yards	par 4
9	495 yards	par 5
10	475 yards	par 4
11	386 yards	par 4
12	381 yards	par 4
13	153 yards	par 3
14	447 yards	par 4
15	396 yards	par 4
16	188 yards	par 3
17	542 yards	par 5
18	447 yards	par 4

but needs two outstanding shots for its green to be reached. Those who come up short, and there are many, face the choice of pitching over the slope to the green or running the ball up the bank.

The influence of Dornoch on American course architecture must also be recognised. This was spread by Donald Ross, the club's professional for four years, who emigrated to America at the turn of the century and designed over 500 courses in that country. His most eloquent monument, the No. 2 course at Pinehurst, North Carolina, features the basic character of Dornoch's raised greens which create delicate chipping situations. In addition, Ross also was responsible for Seminole in Florida, a course much respected by Ben Hogan, Oak Hill in New York, Inverness in Toledo, Ohio, and Scioto in Columbus, Ohio, the course where Jack Nicklaus grew up.

Muirfield

The finest of Scottish links courses has been saved until last. Muirfield, home of the Honourable Company of Edinburgh Golfers, stands supreme as the fairest test of all the seaside courses. Lying on the southern shores of the Forth, the course is bounded by a grey wall on three sides with the northern side protected by buckthorn-covered dunes. These boundaries create the privacy for which Muirfield is famous, a privacy which is jealously guarded by the membership. Muirfield is totally open and honest — there is only one blind tee shot on the course, so the player can see exactly what has to be done on all but one hole. It is a course which places great premium on accurate driving, for any visits to the thick, tangly rough means the loss of at least a stroke.

There are 18 superb holes waiting to draw upon every stroke in the golfer's repertoire and perhaps it is invidious to select any of them as having particular merit over the others. Tom Watson, however, had no difficulty in making a choice following his victory in the 1980 Open there. His selection was the 153-yard 13th, played to a tightly bunkered, raised green set amid the dunes, a hole that Watson said he would like to package up and ship back to America. It was on the 13th in the 1972 Open that Tony Jacklin took six during the third round but still finished with a 67.

The climax to that Championship came at the 17th on the final day when Lee Trevino perpetrated his outrageous chip-in to deliver the final body blow to Jacklin's hopes. The 17th is a par five of 542 yards which dog-legs gently to the left. At the corner of the curve, a seething nest of bunkers waits to catch the drive which has attempted to bite off too much from the corner. Further up the fairway lie a group of cavernous cross-bunkers waiting to catch the timid second shot while the green is protected by two fronting bunkers and a large mound on the right.

It was here in 1966 that Jack Nicklaus clinched the first of his three Open titles when, with a following wind and using the small ball, he struck a 3-iron from the tee and a 5-iron into the heart of the green to secure the vital birdie he needed. For very good reason Nicklaus named his own American creation Muirfield Village.

Above all, Muirfield is a great watching course with its inner and outer runs of nine holes which mean that no hole is more than a few minutes walk from the clubhouse. This design ensures that the wind is hardly ever in the same direction on consecutive holes and the golfer has to remain aware of the changing problems it presents. The greatness of Muirfield is apparent to all who appreciate that bold, accurate golf should receive its just reward.

Hoylake

The north-west coastline of England provides a positive plethora of championship links from a cluster of courses in Southport, to Royal Lytham & St Annes in Blackpool, to Hoylake on the Wirral Peninsula. Of them all, the Royal Liverpool Club at Hoylake has the longest pedigree, indeed after Westward Ho! in Devon, it is the second oldest seaside course in the country. Hoylake's traditions are rooted firmly in amateur golf as the club was responsible for starting the Amateur Championship in 1885 and it also staged the first international of all, the England versus Scotland encounter in 1902. Hoylake also inaugurated the first international match between Britain and America in 1921 — the forerunner of the Walker Cup. Its most famous son was John Ball, eight times winner of the Amateur Championship and, in 1890, the first amateur and the first Englishman to win the Open. He was closely followed by Harold Hilton, another son of Hoylake, who won the Amateur four times, the US Amateur once and the Open Championship twice, the first time at Muirfield in 1892 when the Championship changed from 36 to 72 holes.

Hoylake is unique among championship courses in that it is possible to be out-of-bounds within the confines of the course. The large practice ground to the right of the first hole is bounded by a turf wall, or 'cop' and over this wall is out of play. This feature comes into play for both the drive and second shot to the first, and then returns again to haunt the golfer on the 15th and 16th. The last five holes in fact represent one of the most gruelling finishes to be found anywhere, totalling 2,318 yards in length and with out-of-bounds threatening on three of them. The second shot to the 17th, 418 yards, can be most taxing, and a shot struck with the merest trace of slice can slide away on the wind to roll underneath the boundary fence to the right of the green. Great champions abound at Hoylake from Ball and Hilton to Bobby Jones, who won the second leg of his

Grand Slam there in 1930 despite taking seven at the 8th in the final round, and on to Peter Thomson and Roberto de Vicenzo, who won the last Open to be played at Hoylake in 1967.

Royal Lytham & St Annes

Royal Lytham & St Annes does not appear to be a seaside course since the sea cannot be seen from any hole and the course is bounded by the red brick of well-to-do suburbia. It is an honest test with few weaknesses and possesses a finish which has seen many potential champions see their chances slip away. A score must be built over the first nine holes at Lytham in order to leave some strokes in reserve for the long haul home. Therefore, most of Lytham's great moments have been condensed into the final three holes and of these, Bobby Jones' second shot from the scrubland to the left of the 17th fairway is certainly the most famous. Locked in deadly combat with his playing companion Al Watrous for the 1926 Open title, Jones hooked into this wilderness while Watrous

Right: Seve Ballesteros' progress to the 72nd hole of the 1979 Open at Royal Lytham & St Annes was famous for the places he visited that few champions had ever been before, such as the car park (at least few had been there to play a shot). Seve nevertheless won, and the spectators round the final green cheer his victory.

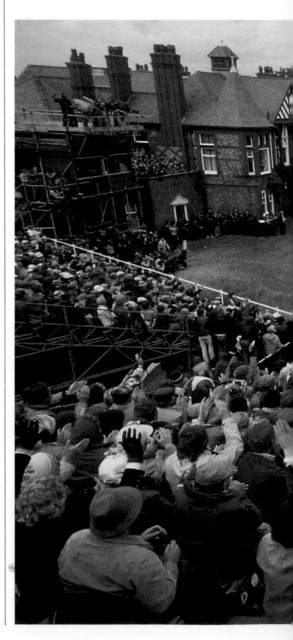

was down the middle and on the green in two. Jones found his ball lying on sandy wasteland but managed to get enough club to it to send it soaring over the trouble onto the green to finish inside Watrous' ball. 'There goes 100,000 bucks' is the remark Watrous is alleged to have made as he saw that stroke and three putts later he was right.

Lytham holds a special place in the hearts of British golf followers for it was here that Tony Jacklin ended an 18-year victory drought for Britain when he captured the 1969 Open. The climax to that unforgettable day came at the final hole when Jacklin lay two strokes ahead of his nearest challenger, Bob Charles, the New Zealander who himself had won the Open at Lytham six years earlier. The 18th at Lytham provides the most demanding final tee shot of any British links. The hole is only 386 yards long but running into the fairway from the left are a group of seven bunkers lined up to catch any stroke with the hint of pull about it while on the right lies a formidable spinney of bushes. Threading the eye of this particular needle

was beyond the capabilities of Eric Brown, Christy O'Connor and Argentina's Leopoldo Ruiz in the 1958 Open who all bunkered their tee shots when a straight drive may have given them glory, and Jack Nicklaus' hopes were also destroyed in similar fashion in 1963.

Jacklin, however, rose to the occasion magnificently and with a smooth, unhurried swing rifled the ball unerringly down the fairway to make the Championship his. Severiano Ballesteros' victory in the 1979 Open was notable for the lack of time he spent on the fairway, highlighted by his famous 'parking lot' drive on the 16th in the final round. This stroke into the right hand rough was deliberate for it meant that Ballesteros was then pitching into the wind to find the green, rather than with the wind if he had been in the fairway. The tactical sense of this approach was confirmed when he birdied the hole virtually to sew up the title and maintain Lytham's curious record of never to date providing an Open to an American professional.

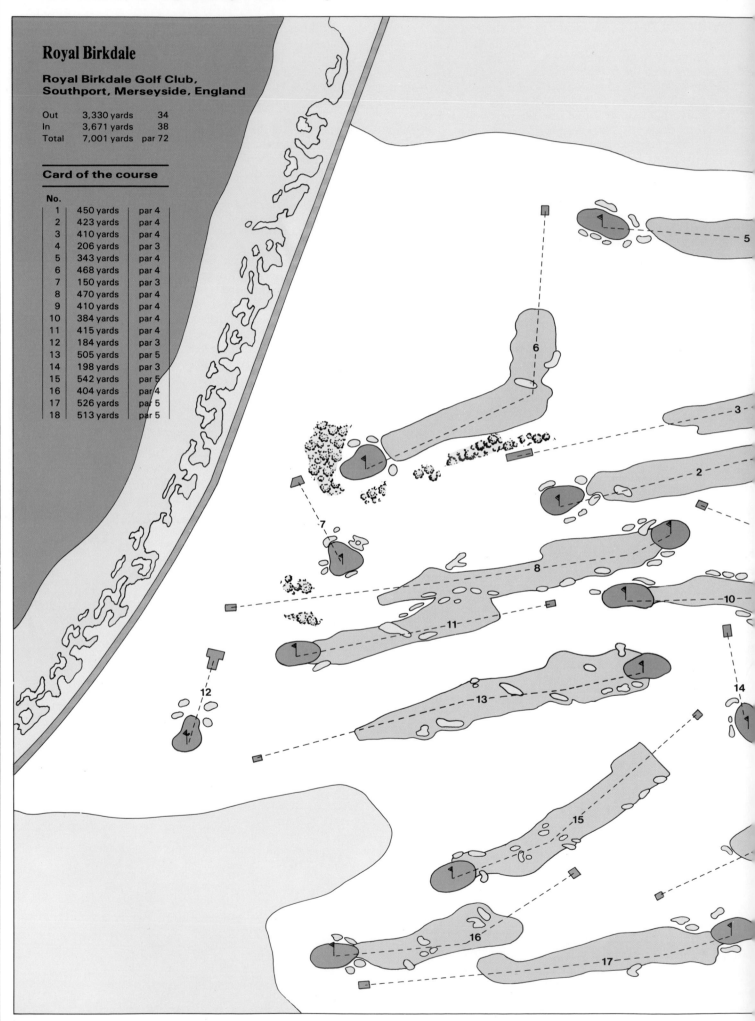

Royal Birkdale

**Royal Birkdale Golf Club,
Southport, Merseyside, England**

Out	3,330 yards	34
In	3,671 yards	38
Total	7,001 yards	par 72

Card of the course

No.		
1	450 yards	par 4
2	423 yards	par 4
3	410 yards	par 4
4	206 yards	par 3
5	343 yards	par 4
6	468 yards	par 4
7	150 yards	par 3
8	470 yards	par 4
9	410 yards	par 4
10	384 yards	par 4
11	415 yards	par 4
12	184 yards	par 3
13	505 yards	par 5
14	198 yards	par 3
15	542 yards	par 5
16	404 yards	par 4
17	526 yards	par 5
18	513 yards	par 5

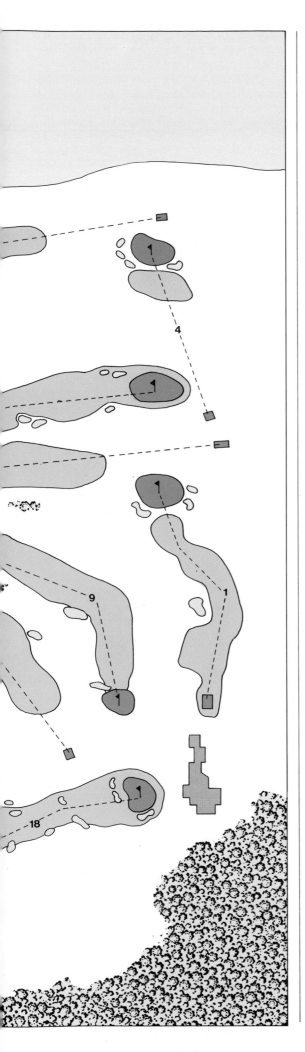

Royal Birkdale

Of that cluster of courses in the Southport area, Royal Birkdale is the one which stands supreme. It is not a seaside course of traditional design, for although the dunes reach stunning height, the fairways do not go over them but run between in a series of green ribbons. This creates a feeling of solitude rarely found on such exposed landscapes, a solitude that can be rudely interrupted by the anguished cries of golfers trying to extract their ball from the cloying willow-scrub rough. Birkdale is no place for wayward drivers. Straightness is the watchword as is shown by the fact that Peter Thomson, a master of accurate wooden club play, won two of his five Open titles there in 1954 and 1965. That 1954 Open was Birkdale's first but it had also staged the 1946 Amateur, won by James Bruen, he of the legendary looping swing, and since the Second World War championships and international matches have flocked to its gates.

The climax to Tony Jacklin's golden year of 1969 occurred at Birkdale when he and Jack Nicklaus fought out their epic halved match in the Ryder Cup to bring about the first tie between Britain and Ireland and America. Two years later Jacklin was involved in the battle for the Open title, eventually won by Lee Trevino by one stroke from Taiwan's Lu Liang Huan, affectionately known as 'Mr Lu'. Trevino's victory margin would have been greater if he had not drifted off the straight and narrow on the 71st hole by hooking into the huge sand dune which guards the entrance to the 17th fairway, an error which cost him a seven. Tom Watson also visited the same spot on his way to victory in the 1983 Open but he escaped with a five and then sealed his win with a magnificent 2-iron second to the 18th green.

Arnold Palmer's first Open title in 1961 is commemorated by a plaque on the 16th from where the great man ripped out a 6-iron shot from the rough onto the green on his way to a one-stroke margin over Dai Rees. The hole was the 15th in those days. Johnny Miller in 1976 completes the list of Open winners at Birkdale, a Championship which first saw the emergence of a young Spaniard named Ballesteros. Clearly, Birkdale is no place for mugs.

Ganton

By tradition, the Open is always played on seaside courses which owe little or nothing to man's intervention. Inland, man's role as a golf course architect finds its fulfilment in many splendid examples. Ganton in the Eastern flank of Yorkshire is a particularly fine test laid out by Harry Vardon, who was professional there, and Tom Dunn with additions by Harry Colt. Set in the Vale of Pickering a few miles from Scarborough, Ganton is a heathland course featuring large, deep bunkers amid banks of gorse. The 18th, a left-hand dog-leg of nearly 400 yards, is a testing finishing hole which has often resolved the outcome of the many Amateur Championships and professional tournaments which have been held there.

Vardon also had a hand in another superb inland test, that of Woodhall Spa in Lincolnshire. The present course was reconstructed after the Second World War by the Hotchkin family which owned the land, and fully utilizes the heather, broom and silver birch topography.

Sunningdale

This heather and broom type of land has been bounteous to golf, and nowhere has the harvest been more richly reaped than in a stretch of country to the West of London. In this area of pine, birch, heather and firm, sandy subsoil are a multitude of truly outstanding courses. Sunningdale, Wentworth, Walton Heath and The Berkshire are the names which readily spring to mind, with Sunningdale being the one course where most golfers would happily spend the rest of their days.

The Old Course at Sunningdale was laid out at the turn of the century by Willie Park jnr, twice Open Champion, who was paid the princely sum of £3,800 for the commission. He created an enchanting work, featuring a number of short par four holes, the finest of which is the 325-yard 11th. This hole is reachable from the tee for the siege-gun driver, but what menace awaits the stroke which veers off line. Running along the right-hand edge of the fairway up to the green is a tall stand of pines while a deep bunker and more trees lie in wait for the hook. From the fairway a pitch of exacting requirement is faced, for the green possesses a slight crown in the middle, beyond which the pin is invariably placed. Judging the weight of the approach is the key, something that American Donna Young did to the ultimate degree in the 1975 Colgate Ladies' tournament when

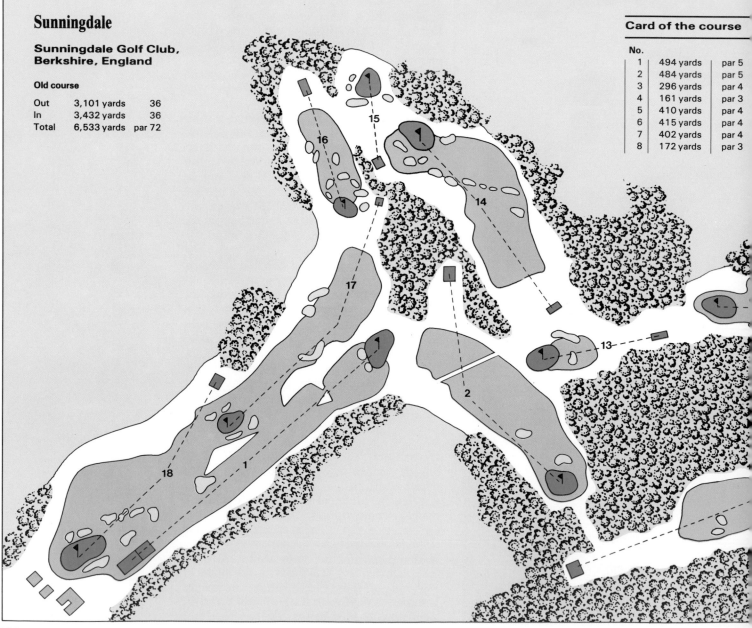

Sunningdale

**Sunningdale Golf Club,
Berkshire, England**

Old course

Out	3,101 yards	36
In	3,432 yards	36
Total	6,533 yards	par 72

Card of the course

No.		
1	494 yards	par 5
2	484 yards	par 5
3	296 yards	par 4
4	161 yards	par 3
5	410 yards	par 4
6	415 yards	par 4
7	402 yards	par 4
8	172 yards	par 3

Left: The Old Course at Sunningdale is typical of the birch, heather and sandy courses around West London. The Colgate Ladies tournament was held here in the 1970s.

No.		
9	267 yards	par 4
10	478 yards	par 5
11	325 yards	par 4
12	451 yards	par 4
13	185 yards	par 3
14	509 yards	par 5
15	226 yards	par 3
16	423 yards	par 4
17	421 yards	par 4
18	414 yards	par 4

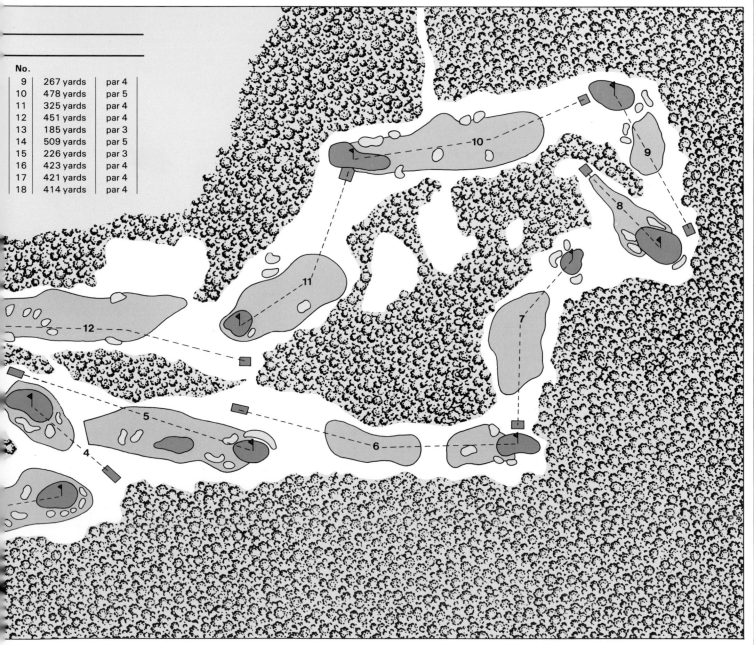

she holed out for a two in her last-round progress to victory.

The Old Course witnessed what is often quoted as the perfect round of golf when Bobby Jones holed it in 66 strokes in qualifying for the 1926 Open, which he went on to win. The round contained 33 putts and 33 other shots, with every hole completed in three or four. As many will testify, Sunningdale is the sort of course which inspires such perfection.

Wentworth

Just down the road from Sunningdale, Wentworth has gained great exposure through the televising of the World Match Play Championship held there every autumn. It is a long course, maybe too long for the average player, requiring strong accurate driving and quality iron play. Its most famous hole is the 17th, a curving par five containing only one bunker and dominated by an out-of-bounds running the entire left-hand side. The drive is quite terrifying as the out-of-bounds creeps in from the left, forcing the ball to be kept to the right. The fairway slopes sharply to the right towards a clump of trees. From the fairway, the second shot is played over the brow of a hill which drops down to flat, unencumbered green which requires great judgement of depth perception for the pitch. The hole has been, and will continue to be, the graveyard of many hopes.

A similar rugged test exists at Walton Heath where the 16th on the Old Course, a long two-shotter to a raised green, stands out as a great hole by anybody's standards while The Berkshire provides an enjoyable game of golf in tranquil natural surroundings of great beauty over two courses, the Red and the Blue.

Royal St George's

Our journey South should cause us to stop off in Sussex and exmine Rye, Crowborough Beacon and Pulborough or the cornucopia of courses in the Bournemouth area, such as Parkstone, Broadstone and Ferndown but our final English destination has to be the last of the great British links, Royal St George's at Sandwich, Kent.

St George's history is long and glorious. Founded in 1887, the club staged the first Open to be held outside Scotland when J.H. Taylor won in 1894, and the course quickly established itself as a severe examination of skill. Its holes progress through a desolate expanse of dunes and its fairways dip and rise in switchback fashion to greens that are heavily guarded. Walter Hagen, Henry Cotton and Bobby Locke are numbered among the champions who won there. After Locke's victory in 1949, the Championship which contained the infamous broken bottle incident which affected Harry Bradshaw's run for the title, the Open did not return there until 1981, having stayed away because of poor road access. The course has staged the

Amateur Championship on many occasions and also hosted numerous professional tournaments.

The short 16th witnessed the first televised hole-in-one during the 1967 Dunlop Masters tournament when Tony Jacklin, on his way to a winning final round of 64, achieved this feat. Following the resurrection of the course as a modern Open venue in 1981, the Championship quickly returned there, and in 1985 Sandy Lyle became the first British winner since Jacklin in 1969. Lyle suffered agonies on the final hole, a stiff par four of 442 yards made by a solitary bunker on the right of the green. In steering clear of

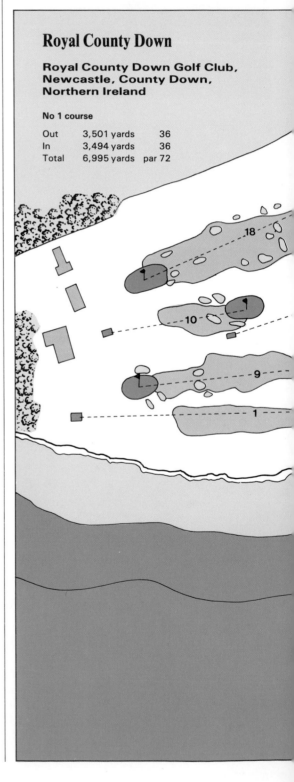

Royal County Down

Royal County Down Golf Club, Newcastle, County Down, Northern Ireland

No 1 course

Out	3,501 yards	36
In	3,494 yards	36
Total	6,995 yards	par 72

this hazard, Lyle's second shot saw his ball trickle off the green into thick rough below a steep bank. This area is known as 'Duncan's Hollow' after George Duncan, the British professional who needed to get down in two from this spot to catch Hagen in the 1922 Open. He failed in his attempt and Lyle very nearly didn't get down in three as his chip up the hill was not quite strong enough and the ball ran back to his feet. Courageously, he got down in two more to write yet another stirring page in the history of British championship golf, and its long association with those superb but unpredictable courses which nature gave to man.

IRELAND

Few countries in the world possess such an abundance of courses as Ireland. Here lies such a wealth of magnificent courses that one is put in mind of the visitor to Ireland who, on seeking guidance from a local, was informed: 'If I were you I wouldn't start from here.'

From Royal County Down and Royal Portrush in the North to Ballybunion and Lahinch in the South, Ireland is one long strip of beautiful green fairway.

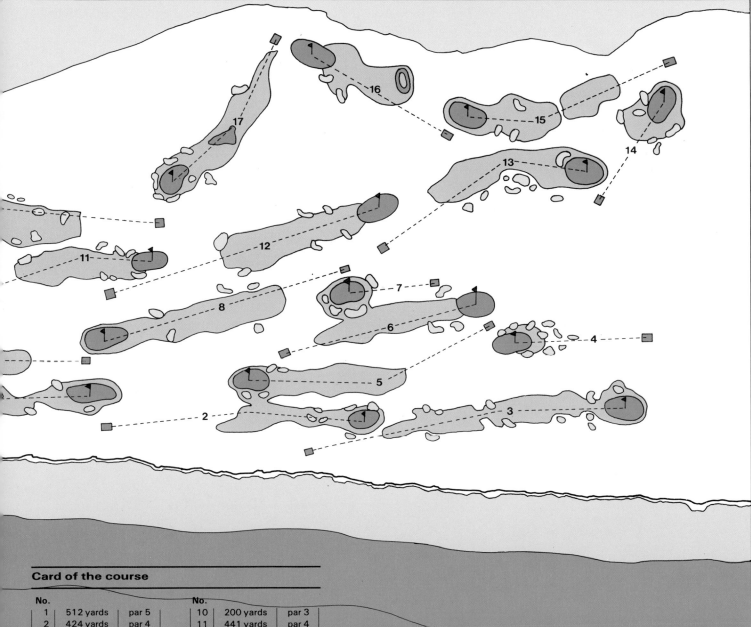

Card of the course

No.			No.		
1	512 yards	par 5	10	200 yards	par 3
2	424 yards	par 4	11	441 yards	par 4
3	468 yards	par 4	12	503 yards	par 5
4	211 yards	par 3	13	445 yards	par 4
5	440 yards	par 4	14	216 yards	par 3
6	394 yards	par 4	15	454 yards	par 4
7	137 yards	par 3	16	267 yards	par 4
8	427 yards	par 4	17	420 yards	par 4
9	488 yards	par 5	18	548 yards	par 5

Royal Portrush

Royal Portrush stands as the only Irish course to have staged the Open Championship. Max Faulkner won there in 1951 in conditions which saw only two players break 70 during the course of the event. Set amid tumbling dunes, the main course at Portrush is called Dunluce after the ancestral home of the Lords of Antrim. Its layout is the work of many men, primarily Harry Colt who improved it to modern standards with a great premium placed on driving. Only the first and last holes run straight; the rest curve and it is this aspect, rather than the hazards of bunkers and rough, which make it so challenging.

Its most famous hole, some would say the most famous in Ireland, is the 211-yard 14th, aptly named Calamity Corner, which invariably requires a wooden club shot into the wind to a green set on top of a hill, below which the ground falls away alarmingly to the right into a gaping chasm full of rough and misery.

Royal County Down

For sheer breathtaking beauty, few courses are the equal of Royal County Down just outside Newcastle (NI). Here the Mountains of Mourne sweep down to the sea and provide a compelling vista for golfers who may find these distractions alleviate or perhaps exacerbate the problems of keeping their shots out of the banks of flowering gorse which abound. Purists may baulk at the number of blind shots the course possesses but no golfer could be blind to the stunning scenery of the place.

Below: The Royal County Down course near Newcastle, Northern Ireland, is one of those beautiful Irish golf courses where it is almost a pleasure to make a treble bogey, or to have to search for the ball in those masses of yellow gorse.

Portmarnock

Links golf of an honest, straightforward nature is to be found at Portmarnock on a fine strip of coastland on the northern side of Dublin Bay. Portmarnock's challenge lies in the wind and with the holes laid out on inner and outer runs, the direction of the wind is constantly varied. Many championships and tournaments have been held at Portmarnock. It is a regular venue for the Irish Open, and was also the venue for the 1960 Canada Cup, now World Cup, when Arnold Palmer was first sighted on the British side of the Atlantic.

Ballybunion

Any golfing pilgrimage to Ireland must be made with the ultimate destination in mind, that of Ballybunion at the mouth of the River Shannon in Co Kerry. *En route*, the pilgrim may pause at Killarney, whose 18th hole along the shores of Lough Leane prompted Henry Longhurst to comment: 'What a lovely place to die', or Ireland's most westerly links, Waterville, or travel north up the coast into Co Clare where the goats of Lahinch act as clerks of the weather at the course known as the St Andrews of Ireland. These, however, are simply appetizers for the links which are universally regarded as the finest in the world, moving Tom Watson to say that Ballybunion is a course where golf course architects should live and play before building golf courses. Swooping down among the sandhills with the Atlantic rollers surging in beneath, Ballybunion is majestic. The club is doubly fortunate in that it now has another course, the New, which is equally splendid, laid out by Robert Trent Jones, the indefatigable American course architect, upon whose creations the sun never sets.

Discovering the charm of Irish golf is an experience to be savoured, preferably in a leisurely fashion and in the company of two or three friends. The local hospitality is notorious for its generosity and a strong constitution is a vital extra club in the bag.

Above: Arnold Palmer played his first competitive round on the British side of the Atlantic in the 1960 Canada Cup, held at Portmarnock, and would have experienced the challenge of the wind which comes off the sea in Dublin Bay.

AMERICA

Without doubt the greatest influence on American golf course architecture is to be found at the Augusta National Golf Club in Georgia, home of the annual Masters tournament. For millions of golfers throughout the world who watch the Masters every year on television, the course is almost as familiar to them as the one they play every weekend and the beauty of its setting loses nothing through its constant exposure.

Augusta

Augusta is the shrine of American golf, the place where the faithful come to worship the legend of Bobby Jones, the only man to have won the Open and Amateur titles of both Britain and America in a single year (1930). Following that tumultuous year, Jones retired from competitive golf, although aged only 28, but retained the desire to found a private club on a course which he himself would design.

Luckily for golf he found the perfect site — 365 acres of rolling land in the small winter resort of Augusta. The land had been developed as a nursery by a Belgian baron and abounded with azaleas, dogwoods, magnolias and redbuds and the setting was completed by an antebellum mansion overlooking it. Because of his peerless record as a player, any course which Jones put his name to was bound to be influential, but in creating his dream course he showed a wisdom beyond his years by combining his knowledge of shot-making requirements with the architectural genius of Alister Mackenzie. Mackenzie was a Scottish doctor who had emigrated to America and given up medicine in order to concentrate on golf. He had already shown his flair for design in creating Cypress Point in California and thus had the right credentials for building courses in areas of great natural beauty.

At first sight, Augusta National does not look difficult. Its fairways are generously wide, there is hardly any rough and very few bunkers. The stately Georgian pines separate the holes to create a cathedral-like atmosphere of peace and the flowering shrubs provide a colourful framework which lead the golfer to believe that this truly is paradise on earth. It is only when the course is played that the greatness of its challenge becomes apparent.

Jones wanted a course that would provide equal enjoyment to both professionals and amateurs. If a player is content to go round in one over par on every hole, then the course will not tax that requirement. If, however, a player is looking for pars and birdies then Augusta will stretch his shot-making abilities to the limit. It is a course where planning must start on the tee of each hole for the placement of the drive will dictate

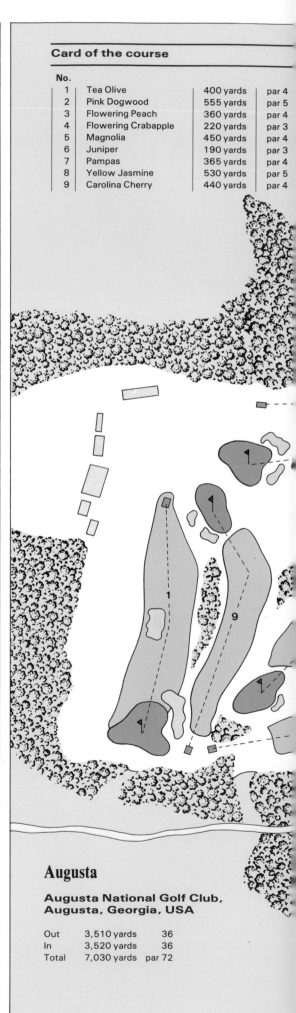

Card of the course

No.			
1	Tea Olive	400 yards	par 4
2	Pink Dogwood	555 yards	par 5
3	Flowering Peach	360 yards	par 4
4	Flowering Crabapple	220 yards	par 3
5	Magnolia	450 yards	par 4
6	Juniper	190 yards	par 3
7	Pampas	365 yards	par 4
8	Yellow Jasmine	530 yards	par 5
9	Carolina Cherry	440 yards	par 4

Augusta

Augusta National Golf Club, Augusta, Georgia, USA

Out	3,510 yards	36
In	3,520 yards	36
Total	7,030 yards	par 72

No.			
10	Camellia	485 yards	par 4
11	White Dogwood	445 yards	par 4
12	Golden Bell	155 yards	par 3
13	Azalea	485 yards	par 5
14	Chinese Fir	420 yards	par 4
15	Fire Thorn	520 yards	par 5
16	Red Bud	190 yards	par 3
17	Nandina	400 yards	par 4
18	Holly	420 yards	par 4

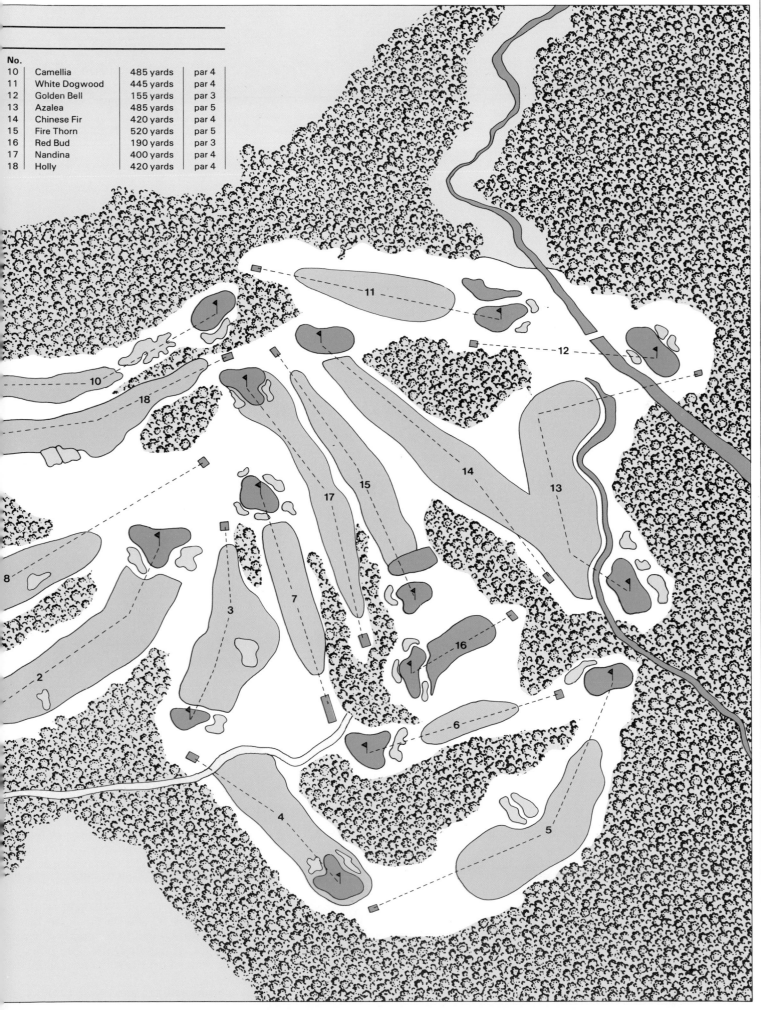

Above: The 13th hole at Augusta, one of the 'Amen Corner' holes where water comes into play. There are some rather pretty little bunkers too. Many a would-be Master has come to grief here.

the approach to the green and the position of the flag will dictate which part of the green the ball should finish. It could be said that it is the greens which set the entire strategy of the course. Huge, slick and undulating, Augusta's greens show the influence of St Andrews on Jones and his respect for the traditions of the game is captured in their topography.

The course was completed in 1933 and the following year Jones invited his friends, amateur and professional, down for his first tournament get-together. The press also turned up and before the event, won by Horton Smith, was over they had given it the tag 'The Masters'. A year later came the shot that was heard round the world and set the pattern for a host of spectacular strokes in its wake.

The closing stages of the 1935 Masters found Gene Sarazen standing in the middle of the 15th fairway needing three birdies to catch Craig Wood, who had already finished. Sarazen faced a shot of some 220 yards carry over the lake in front of the green, and since

he was in a do-or-die situation, he elected to go for it with a 4-wood. The ball flew unerringly over the water, landed on the green and ran straight into the hole for an albatross. With that one stroke, Sarazen had tied with Wood and when he won the play-off the next day, the Augusta legend had its first foundation stone.

Since then, full approach shots have fallen into the hole with almost monotonous regularity. Indeed, only three holes on the course have not been the scene of this unexpected bonus with nobody, as yet, having holed his second shot to the par five second, holed-in-one at the short fourth, a hole which captures the spirit of the 11th at St Andrews, or holed his second to the par five 13th. Even the eighth, the longest hole on the course, succumbed to the onslaught when in 1967 Australian Bruce Devlin holed his second shot during the first round. Such liberties do not go unpunished as two holes later Devlin walked off the 10th green with a seven.

The margin between success and failure

more famous for its victimization of players. Most notable of these is Tom Weiskopf who, during the first round of the 1980 Masters, put five balls into the creek and eventually walked off with a 13.

The 13th is an absolutely gorgeous hole of 485 yards, dog-legging gently to the left. The creek weaves its insidious path along the left side of the fairway before crossing directly in front of an enormous green which slopes down towards the creek. Every stroke on this hole must be carefully pondered. If the drive is long and drawn round the corner of the dog-leg then the green can be reached with a long iron: if the drive is out to the right then the decision has to be made as to whether to go for the carry over the creek or lay up and hope to get down in a pitch and a putt. Many a Masters challenger has seen his hopes plunge into the water through making an incorrect decision when faced with this dilemma. In the 1985 Masters, Curtis Strange looked set to perpetrate the greatest recovery in the history of the event when he opened with an 80 and then followed that with rounds of 65 and 68. Leading in the final round, he put his second to the 13th in the creek and repeated the error on the 15th for a couple of sixes which allowed Bernhard Langer to come through and win. Back in 1937, Ralph Guldahl was leading Byron Nelson by two strokes but splashed his way through the 12th and 13th in 5 and 6 while Nelson played them in 2 and 3 to overhaul him for victory. In 1978 Tsuneyuki Nakajima made it a very unlucky 13th for himself when he completed the hole in 13 strokes, five of which were penalty strokes, two being incurred when he tried to play the ball out of the creek and the ball bounced off the bank and hit him.

Thus the legend of Augusta has been built. In the 50 plus years of Masters history, the course has inspired and rewarded the brave, regularly served up the unexpected and treated the world to some of the most spectacular moments in the game. From Sarazen's albatross in 1935 to Jack Nicklaus' unprecedented sixth victory in 1986, from Sam Snead and Ben Hogan to Gary Player and Arnold Palmer, from Tom Watson to Severiano Ballesteros, the list of winners at Augusta includes the greatest names of the era. The present course record stands at 63, set by Nick Price in 1986 but that particularly low score does not detract from Augusta's challenge, for it shows that the man who thinks his way round will have fulfilled all the requirements of Bobby Jones' design.

Pebble Beach

While America contains a vast number of courses in a variety of landscapes, the country does not possess any traditional linksland as is found in Britain. But for golf by the sea America is amply compensated by two magnificent courses on the Monterey Peninsula on the west coast of California.

has always been extremely fine at Augusta simply because the course constantly tempts the player to bite off a little more than can safely be chewed. Nowhere is this more evident than on the last nine holes, five of which contain water, thereby making them the Venice of championship golf. Three of the water holes are in succession and because of their placing in the round and the psychological pressures they exert, the 11th, 12th and 13th have been dubbed 'Amen Corner' presumably because if a player gets through them without mishap he gives a prayer of thanks. Of these the 12th, at 155 yards the shortest hole on the course, is, in the words of Jack Nicklaus, 'the most psychologically demanding hole in championship golf'. Fronted by Rae's Creek, the green is less than 30 feet in depth with two sloping bunkers at the back and another bunker in the centre-front. Set in a pocket of tall trees, the hole is subject to capricious wind changes which can swirl the ball into the water or into the back bunkers. The 12th has been aced but in the pressured atmosphere of the Masters it is

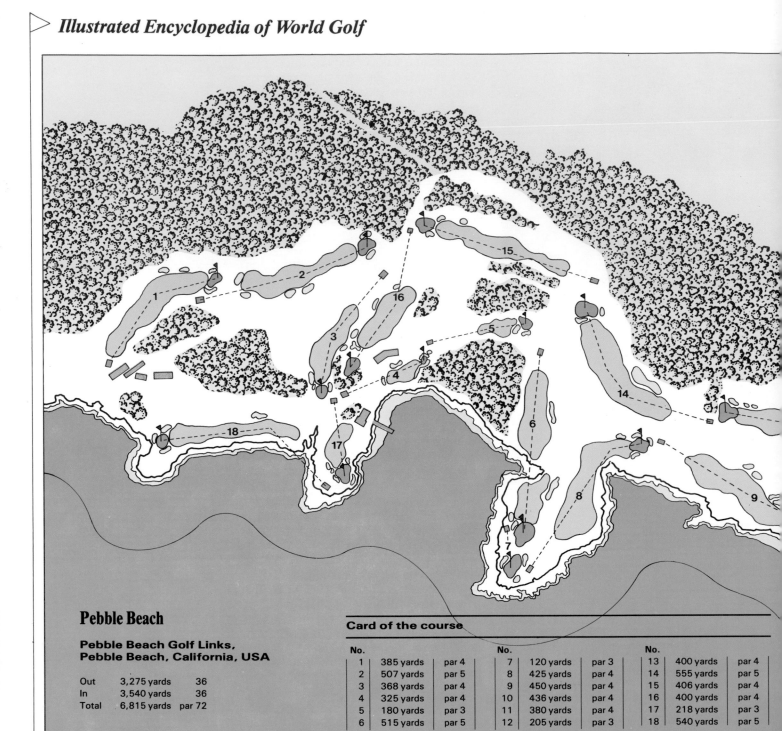

Pebble Beach

**Pebble Beach Golf Links,
Pebble Beach, California, USA**

Out	3,275 yards	36
In	3,540 yards	36
Total	6,815 yards	par 72

Card of the course

No.			No.			No.		
1	385 yards	par 4	7	120 yards	par 3	13	400 yards	par 4
2	507 yards	par 5	8	425 yards	par 4	14	555 yards	par 5
3	368 yards	par 4	9	450 yards	par 4	15	406 yards	par 4
4	325 yards	par 4	10	436 yards	par 4	16	400 yards	par 4
5	180 yards	par 3	11	380 yards	par 4	17	218 yards	par 3
6	515 yards	par 5	12	205 yards	par 3	18	540 yards	par 5

Pebble Beach and Cypress Point are enshrined in American golfing folklore as courses where that harmony between nature and man is pitched in exactly the right key.

Faced with such a compelling vista of cliff-top land with the Pacific rolling in beneath, the architects of both courses could have easily gone overboard in their designs. Instead they showed admirable restraint and stuck to the principle that the best courses are built into the land that is available and the less nature is tampered with the better.

Pebble Beach has seven holes running along the edge of the cliffs and each of them provides at least one death-or-glory flirtation with the foaming ocean. The first glimpse of sea occurs at the fourth but it is at the short seventh that the golfer first finds the senses stirred. This short hole of 120 yards is played directly towards the crashing breakers with the green entirely surrounded by bunkers and angled on line with the tee so that the target is only eight yards wide. On a still day it is no more than a wedge, but with the wind whipping in a punched medium iron may well be necessary to keep the ball on line.

The eighth, ninth and tenth are a trio of gruelling par fours where drives and second shots are fully exposed to the elements of wind and water. The merest hint of a slice can mean either a visit to the beach or a rinse in the world's largest bath. From the 10th the course turns inland and does not return to the cliffs until the 17th and 18th and it is here that the denouements of many tournaments and championships have taken place.

the ball close, but with one of the most memorable strokes in recent times he lobbed the ball gently onto the green and danced in delight as it trickled into the hole. Disaster could still have overtaken Watson on the 18th as the full length of its 540 yards is flanked on the left by the sea. Many professionals have seen their hopes dashed on the rocks by going flat out for the green in two shots but Watson played it cannily to be on the green in three and the birdie putt he did hole was merely icing on the cake.

Cypress Point

The remarkable thing about Pebble Beach is that it was laid out by two amateur architects, Jack Neville and Douglas Grant, neither of whom did much work elsewhere yet their instinct for the land cannot be faulted. At Cypress Point however, just a mile away from Pebble Beach, pure genius has been at work. Designed by Alister Mackenzie of Augusta National and Royal Melbourne fame, Cypress Point is regarded by many people as the loveliest golf course in the world. It is only 6,500 yards long and there are just three holes which run along the cliff-tops while the remainder wend their way through sandy dunes and woodland. No major championships have been held there but it is the venue for the annual Bing Crosby National Pro-Am, now called the AT & T, and every player in the field is aware that the first 15 holes are merely a prelude for the symphony of design that is the 16th.

This hole is preceded by the exquisite minor movement of the short 15th, only 139 yards long across the rocky inlet and then the golfer is faced with what is certainly the most photographed hole in golf. Measuring 233 yards, the 16th is played across the ocean to a green where the presence of a group of bunkers could be regarded as relief when compared to the perdition that awaits in the rocks and ice-plant below. No golfer worth his salt could resist the temptation to make at least one attempt to carry the ball all the way to the green, although there is an area of fairway short and to the left for the less brave, or perhaps the less foolhardy. The record highest score for the hole is 19, set in 1959 by a professional named Hans Merrell who clambered down the cliffs to his ball and spent some considerable time among the ice-plant before finally emerging. Appropriately, Bing Crosby himself stands as only one of two golfers, Jerry Pate is the other, to have holed-in-one at the 16th.

Olympic

Further north on the west coast lies a course of an entirely different nature to the seaside spectaculars of Moneterey. This is the Lakeside course of the Olympic Club Country Club in San Francisco, a cumbersome title that is usually shortened to plain Olympic. Golf here is of a far more penal type than is generally the case for

In the two US Opens that have been staged at Pebble, 1972 and 1982, the 17th was the scene of the decisive strokes. This 218-yard par three is played directly towards the sea with the cliffs falling away on the left. The green is long from side to side but narrow back to front and protected by a large fronting bunker. In 1972, Jack Nicklaus assured his third US Open title when he struck a 1-iron witheringly through the wind almost into the hole. Nicklaus was also involved in the finish to the 1982 Open when he set the target only Tom Watson could beat. Watson needed two pars to tie but his hopes looked slim when his tee shot to the 17th landed in thick rough to the left of the green. With the pin set on the left side of the green, he had hardly any room to manoeuvre

courses built before 1930, an era when architects followed the creed that golf should temper the spirit with excessive hardship.

Olympic was constructed in 1922 on sloping land to the west of the city and the holes having been laid out, the Club then planted hundreds of pine, eucalyptus and cypress trees. Some 25 years later the trees had reached full maturity and created an arboreal nightmare in which golfers were constantly playing through a funnel of trees whose very branches appeared to be reaching out to grab the ball. Add to this a number of dog-leg holes where the land slopes in the opposite direction to the flow of the dog-leg and it can be understood why Olympic is a fearsome test, even for the mighty.

Of the three US Opens staged at Olympic, in 1955, 1966 and 1987, the first two provided major upsets. In 1955, Ben Hogan was safely in the clubhouse on the brink of an unprecedented fifth US Open title. Out on the course, only one man could catch him, an obscure professional from Iowa called Jack Fleck. Fleck eventually came to 338-yard 18th needing a birdie three to tie and stunned the golfing world by holing a putt of seven feet to achieve it. In the play-off, Fleck stood one stroke ahead on the 18th tee and Hogan, in attempting to combat the left to right camber of the fairway, hooked violently into the left-hand rough from where he needed three strokes to recover, and that was that.

Eleven years later, Arnold Palmer had taken the Championship by the scruff of the

Right: *Arnold Palmer in the 1983 US Open at Oakmont gets the ball out from what are called the Church Pews, a picturesque part of the course for the spectator but one where the players might feel they should kneel down and pray.*

neck and with nine holes to play was seven strokes clear of his closest challenger, Billy Casper, with whom he was also playing. With four holes left to play, Casper still trailed by five shots but by virtue of some brilliant play coupled with Palmer's errors, had drawn level by the 18th, and that is how it remained. Palmer's crisis occurred on the monster 604-yard 16th, when he strove for distance from the tee and hooked into the rough, finally taking six to Casper's immaculate birdie four. The play-off saw Casper again come from behind to win and demonstrate that Olympic is a course where any attacking instincts of the kind upon which Palmer built his career must be suppressed.

Oakmont

While Olympic uses trees to intimidate the golfer, across the country in Pennsylvania stands the Grand Vizier of penal design. Split in two by the Pennsylvania Turnpike on the outskirts of Pittsburgh, Oakmont Country Club has the reputation of being the toughest golf course in America. It is a reputation founded on severe bunkering (more than 200 bunkers) and greens whose swiftness has passed into legend. The course was laid out by steel magnate Henry Fownes in 1904 and his dream of creating a murderous course has been substantiated by a series of high winning

scores in the six US Opens that have been held there. The lowest 72-hole aggregate for the US Open at Oakmont is the five under par 279 set by Johnny Miller in 1973 which contained a final round of 63, a record round still matched only by Jack Nicklaus and Tom Weiskopf in the 1980 US Open at Baltusrol. Miller's round was certainly helped by the fact that during the previous night heavy rain was accompanied by someone inadvertently leaving the sprinkler system running which turned the greens into dartboards and greatly reduced their terrors.

Prior to Miller's astonishing surge, Bobby Jones, Ben Hogan and Jack Nicklaus had all added to Oakmont's history: Jones through his victory in the 1925 US Amateur when he was never taken beyond the 14th in any of his matches, Hogan for his awesome last round mastery of the final four holes which he played in a total of 13 strokes on his way to a five-stroke victory in the 1953 US Open, and Nicklaus breaking through for his first professional victory in the 1962 US Open after a play-off with Arnold Palmer.

From its furrowed bunkers, which used to be raked two inches deep and two inches apart using a special rake, to its lightning fast greens, Oakmont is the kind of course which simply does not tolerate inadequacy in any department.

Above: Plenty of sand and foliage guard the 12th green at Pine Valley, a course described as a bunker with trees. Unfortunately there is no room for spectators, or perhaps the golfers think this is fortunate.

Pine Valley

Pine Valley Golf Club, Clementon, New Jersey, USA

Out 3,401 yards 35
In 3,364 yards 35
Total 6,765 yards par 70

Card of the course

No.			No.		
1	427 yards	par 4	10	145 yards	par 3
2	367 yards	par 4	11	399 yards	par 4
3	185 yards	par 3	12	382 yards	par 4
4	461 yards	par 4	13	446 yards	par 4
5	226 yards	par 3	14	185 yards	par 3
6	391 yards	par 4	15	603 yards	par 5
7	585 yards	par 5	16	436 yards	par 4
8	327 yards	par 4	17	344 yards	par 4
9	432 yards	par 4	18	424 yards	par 4

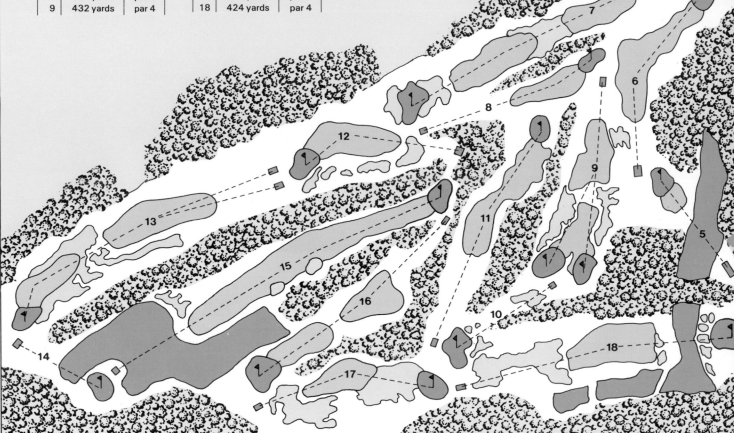

Pine Valley

Cast in a different, rougher mould is Pine Valley, quite possibly the most terrifying course in the golfing universe. The brainchild of George Crump, a Philadelphia hotelier, Pine Valley, on the New Jersey side of that city, took seven years to complete and was opened in 1919. The trees which separate each hole are the least of the golfer's problems, for the entire course is laid out on one huge 184-acre bunker with trees, fairways and greens forming havens of refuge amid the sandy wasteland. The psychological pressures of having to hit from one green island to another with absolutely no room for error is too much for most players and there is a standing bet that nobody will break 80 at the first attempt. Such a bet was irresistible to

Arnold Palmer back in 1954 when he was US Amateur champion and desperate for some money prior to his elopement and marriage. He collected all the bets he could find, knowing that he couldn't afford to pay them if he lost, and went round in 68. Few golfers are as gifted as Palmer, however, and for many 68 would be a reasonable score for the first nine holes.

Pine Valley has never staged the US Open, as its layout would not accommodate the crowds, but it has been the venue of two Walker Cup matches, 1936 and 1985. The most famous story concerning the terrors of Pine Valley and the mental strain it creates involves one Woody Platt, a gifted Philadelphia amateur. Platt set off on a round as follows: three (birdie), two (eagle), one (ace),

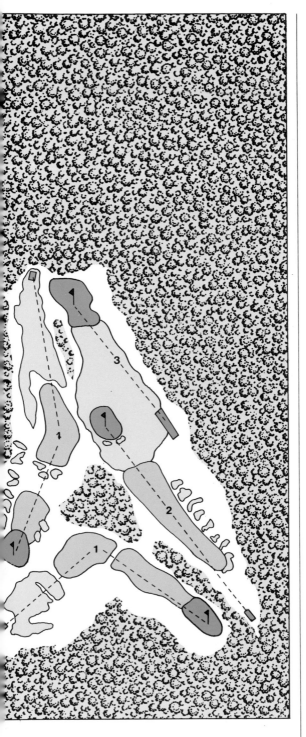

which rewards accurate, attacking golf, it has few equals. The essence of Merion is contained in its greens, which are extremely fast, and its greenside bunkering which make the player think carefully of the best line of approach to the target. Merion is ony just over 6,500 yards long and possesses 120 bunkers but each one has been placcd in precisely the right position by the architect, Hugh Wilson, who completed his work in 1912.

Great moments at Merion read like a potted history of American golf and it is appropriate that its most famous hole, the 11th, was the scene of the final act in Bobby Jones' Grand Slam year of 1930 when he won the US Amateur by closing out his opponent in the final by 8 and 7. This hole, known as the Baffling Brook, entirely captures the spirit of Merion. Only 370 yards long, it dog-legs gently to the left. After intersecting the fairway, the brook runs past the right edge of the green which is also protected by a left-hand bunker. For the accomplished player, the hole is no more than a drive and a short iron, but the approach is most exacting as it has to flirt with that ribbon of water.

The 18th at Merion is built on a more heroic scale; 458-yards long, the drive is played through a funnel of trees to a fairway which runs downhill in the landing area. It was here in the 1950 US Open that Ben Hogan, still hardly recovered from his horrific road accident a year earlier, began his come-back by striking a magnificent 2-iron shot into the heart of the green to tie for the title. In 1971, Jack Nicklaus repeated that stroke with a 4-iron to tie with Lee

Below: The 11th hole at Merion, the Baffling Brook, famous for being the hole at which Bobby Jones won his Grand Slam in 1930 with an 8 and 7 win in the US Amateur Championship.

three (birdie). Thus he had played the first four holes in six under par. These first four holes make a full circle back to the clubhouse and Platt decided to retire inside for a restorative glass of something to brace himself for what lay ahead. Possibly he over-celebrated his hole-in-one for he never emerged to complete the round.

Merion

The West course at Merion on the other side of Philadelphia from Pine Valley is not blessed with any of the naturally rugged terrain of that 184-acre sand trap. Indeed, Merion's 18 holes are squeezed into a compressed 110 acres, barely enough to accommodate some of the more modern courses' parking lots. Yet, for subtlety of design

Trevino for the US Open. Ten years later, again in the US Open, Merion was the site of what is generally regarded as the closest to a perfect final round ever played in a major championship, a 67 from Australia's David Graham, who plotted his way to victory by not missing a fairway or green in regulation figures over the entire 18 holes.

Baltusrol

The legacy of a murdered farmer provides the setting for another US Open course, that of Baltusrol in Springfield, New Jersey. In 1825, Mr Baltus Roll was found murdered and the land on which he farmed eventually became a golf course for rich New Yorkers. In the 1920s, the club was expanded to two courses and it is the Lower course which has staged the US Open and other national tournaments. Baltusrol is a tree-lined parkland course which stretches over 7,000 yards. The contoured greens and variety of bunkering are the hallmarks of the original architect A.W. Tillinghast.

Baltusrol first staged the US Open in 1936 when the surprise winner was Tony Manero. The US Open did not return there until 1954 and on this occasion Ed Furgol emerged victorious. The last two holes are both par fives, the 17th measuring a monstrous 623 yards and the 18th a more reasonable 542 yards. On the final hole in 1954 Furgol hit a wild hook from the tee and then played his second through the trees onto a fairway on the adjacent Upper course, from where he played back onto the correct green to win.

The last two US Opens at Baltusrol, in 1967 and 1980, both resulted in victories for Jack Nicklaus. In 1967 he finished with a final round of 65 to defeat Arnold Palmer by four strokes and in 1980 he simply rewrote the record books. He opened with a record-equalling 63 and went on to set a new US Open record score of 272 as he captured his fourth US Open title 18 years after his first.

The most controversial hole at Baltusrol is the 194-yard par three 4th. Played across water to a narrow green with bunkers at the

Below: Few murder victims can be so strangely remembered as Mr Baltus Roll, the owner of the land on which the Baltusrol golf course was built. This flag is the 17th, to reach which the golfer must cover 623 yards.

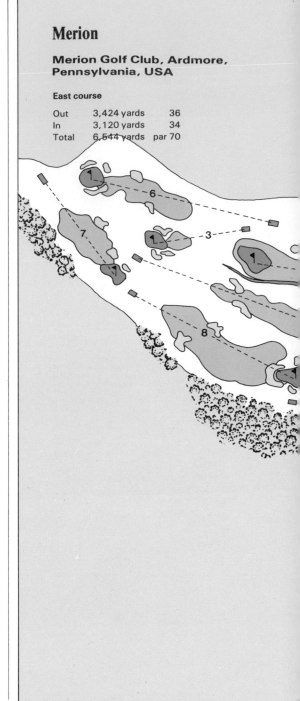

Merion

Merion Golf Club, Ardmore, Pennsylvania, USA

East course

Out	3,424 yards	36
In	3,120 yards	34
Total	6,544 yards	par 70

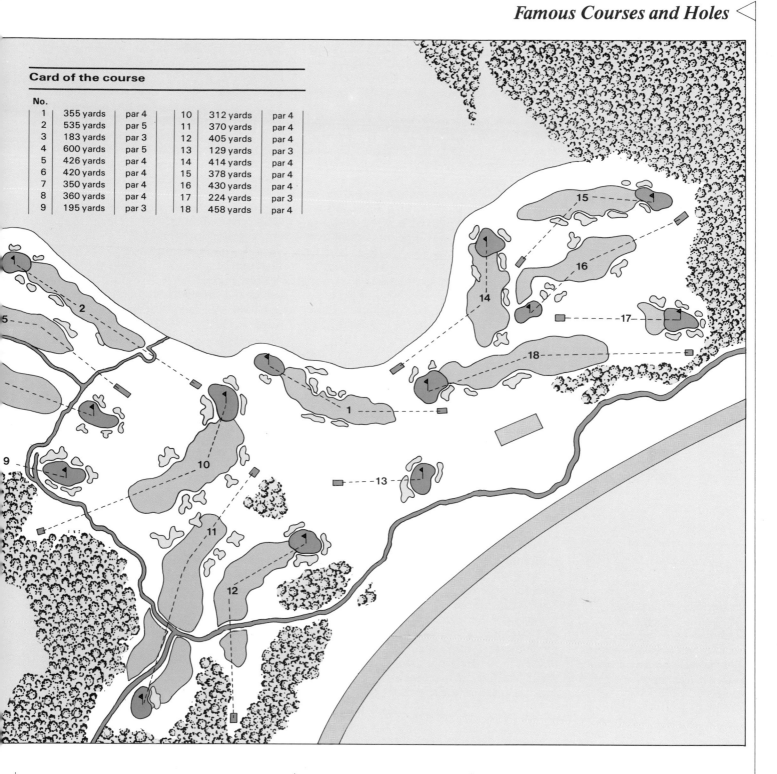

Card of the course

No.					
1	355 yards	par 4	10	312 yards	par 4
2	535 yards	par 5	11	370 yards	par 4
3	183 yards	par 3	12	405 yards	par 4
4	600 yards	par 5	13	129 yards	par 3
5	426 yards	par 4	14	414 yards	par 4
6	420 yards	par 4	15	378 yards	par 4
7	350 yards	par 4	16	430 yards	par 4
8	360 yards	par 4	17	224 yards	par 3
9	195 yards	par 3	18	458 yards	par 4

back, the hole, in its present form, was considered too tough when it was redesigned by architect Robert Trent Jones prior to the 1954 US Open. Jones disagreed with the committee that the hole was too difficult and so everyone assembled on the tee to try it out. After the committee members had all played, Jones then teed up his ball and hit it straight into the hole for a hole-in-one, 'As you can see, gentlemen,' said Jones, 'this hole is not too tough.'

Winged Foot

Further north in the rich suburbia of Westchester County outside New York lies another Tillinghast creation, Winged Foot. The name was taken from the emblem of the New York Athletic Club whose members got together to form a golf club in 1923. They called in Tillinghast and he finally presented them with two courses, the East and the West, and it is the West which has staged the US Open and other championships.

Winged Foot is a gruelling test featuring many long par four holes which require a long accurate drive and a controlled second shot, very often with a long iron. The bunkering round the greens is deep and the greens themselves are fiercely contoured and contain many subtle burrows. The last five holes are par fours all measuring over 420 yards, thereby representing one of the most taxing finishes in championship golf. It is therefore not surprising that of the four US Opens held there, only one has resulted in a winning score under the par of 280 for the 72 holes. Bobby Jones won in 1929 with a score of 294 after a play-off with Al Espinosa and 30 years elapsed before Billy Casper took the honours in 1959 with a score of 283. In 1974 Hale Irwin won with 287 and then came the memorable tie between Fuzzy Zoeller and Greg Norman on a four under par score of 276. Over the last four holes, Norman executed some astonishing recoveries and on the final green had holed from fully 30 feet for a par four. Zoeller, waiting behind on the 18th fairway, thought Norman's putt was for a birdie and then waved a white towel in mock surrender. It was a gesture which won him the hearts of millions. Moments later he holed out to tie the Australian and then Zoeller won the play-off handily. For most ordinary mortals however, Winged Foot is a course where throwing in the towel is no disgrace.

The Country Club

There are thousands of country clubs throughout America but only one of them is entitled to call itself *The* Country Club. The Country Club of Brookline, Boston, is the correct title of the country's first club of this type and to call it anything else is sacrilege. The Country Club was founded in 1860 but it wasn't until 30 years later that the land, originally purchased for horse-riding, was devoted to golf, and even then there were only six holes. In 1910 these were extended to 18 and three years later the course provided the setting for the birth of American golfing supremacy.

In 1913, the US Open appeared to be a question of which of two British professionals, Harry Vardon and Ted Ray, would take the title, as they had tied at the end of 72 holes. Then, from out of nowhere, an unknown local amateur, Francis Ouimet, birdied the 17th to join them in the play-off. Since Vardon, at the time, was considered practically invincible, Ouimet's achievement,

Below: The 16th green at Shinnecock Hills, one of America's oldest courses, recently restored to Open duty. It is the nearest championship course to a links course in the States.

if put in a modern context, was like a county amateur tieing Jack Nicklaus for the Open. In the play-off, Ray was out of the running and Ouimet stood one stroke ahead of Vardon as they arrived at the 365-yard 17th. The hole dog-legs to the left with a small, deep bunker set at the corner of the dog-leg. Vardon drove into that bunker and took five and with Ouimet duplicating his birdie three of the day before, American golf had a hero.

It was another 50 years before the narrow fairways and small greens of The Country Club hosted the US Open but the examination it set in 1963 resulted in the highest winning score since 1935. Again the 17th played a decisive role in the outcome. Arnold Palmer took five on it in the final round and finished in a tie, Tony Lema took five and finished one behind and Jackie Cupitt took a six to tie with Palmer and the eventual winner, Julius Boros.

The Country Club's small greens place a great premium on chipping for it is inevitable that approach shots will fall away from the putting surfaces, particularly in the kind of windy conditions which prevailed in 1963. The 1988 US Open will provide the opportunity for The Country Club to test and frustrate yet another generation of golfers.

Shinnecock Hills

While The Country Club had to wait 50 years between US Opens, another course on the Eastern seaboard of the United States had a gap of 90. Shinnecock Hills in the summer resort of Southampton at the eastern end of Long Island, New York, lays claim to being the oldest golf club with a real course in America. The course was constructed in 1891 on a piece of land which did bear some resemblance to a traditional British links in that it was sandy-based and rolling. There were no dunes however, and the main terror was, and still is, the thick, reedy grasses which edge the fairways. A rasping wind from the Atlantic completes the feeling that this is as close to a links course as can be found in America.

From an original 12 holes laid out by Scotsman Willie Dunn in 1891, the course was extended to the full 18 the following year, and five years later it hosted the US Open, won by Jim Foulis. His rounds of 78 and 74 were considered low for the era and as the course measured less than 5,000 yards it was considered too short for championship standards. In 1931, architect Dick Wilson restructured the course and gave it some more teeth in terms of length and bunkering. Good driving is essential at Shinnecock and the course is laid out in such a way that the wind is never in the same direction for more than two consecutive holes.

Shinnecock is a rugged test and was no more so than on the first day of the 1986 US Open when the championship returned there after that 90-year gap. The best score on a stormy day was a level par 70 and even the

Left: The 10th hole at Winged Foot may look quite harmless, but it forms part of a course that is well known for being a gruelling test of golf.

eventual winner, Ray Floyd, was content with his opening 75. Floyd conceived a game plan for the course and stuck to it rigidly throughout the four rounds, finishing with a final flourish of 66 to become the only player to break the par of 280.

Other American Courses

Such is the vastness of America that it is impossible to cover all the notable courses in the space available. Therefore, apologies must be made for omitting such classics as Pinehurst, Medinah, Harbour Town, Southern Hills, Cherry Hills, Oakland Hills, Oak Hill, The National, Inverness and of the modern era, Muirfield Village (the course that Jack Nicklaus built), the Tournament Players' Club and PGA West. They, and

many other superb examples of the architect's craft, would take several other books to examine.

Unlike the great links courses of Britain and Ireland, which evolved naturally, course architecture in America is largely a triumph of man's perception coupled with the mechanical grab. Such machinery can be used to dramatic effect as in the case of the island 17th green at the aforementioned Tournament Players' Club in Florida, a product of Pete Dye, probably the most creative of modern designers and certainly the most controversial.

New courses in America are now emerging almost daily and many former tournament players such as Arnold Palmer, Gary Player and Tom Weiskopf have, along

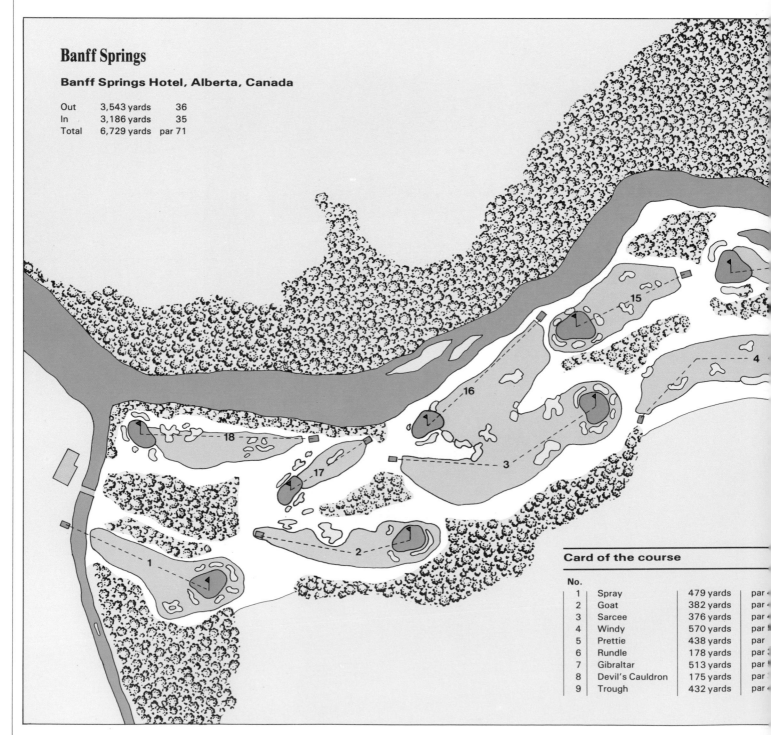

Banff Springs

Banff Springs Hotel, Alberta, Canada

Out	3,543 yards	36
In	3,186 yards	35
Total	6,729 yards	par 71

Card of the course

No.			
1	Spray	479 yards	par
2	Goat	382 yards	par
3	Sarcee	376 yards	par
4	Windy	570 yards	par
5	Prettie	438 yards	par
6	Rundle	178 yards	par
7	Gibraltar	513 yards	par
8	Devil's Cauldron	175 yards	par
9	Trough	432 yards	par

with Nicklaus, plunged wholeheartedly into course architecture. Their desire to create a lasting masterpiece is no less compelling than their predecessors and their works will add to the enjoyment of the most populous golfing nation on earth.

CANADA

Not surprisingly it was the Scots who first introduced Canada to golf, probably via the fur trappers of the Hudson's Bay Company, many of whom were of Celtic descent. In the middle of the 19th century, Montreal had a curling club and it was therefore appropriate

that the city should be host to the first golf club. The club was founded in 1873, thereby making it the oldest golf club on the North American Continent, 15 years ahead of the USA's first club, which played on rough ground at Yonkers, New York. The club became Royal Montreal in 1884 and was joined by other pioneering clubs in Quebec, Ontario and Toronto and in 1896 the Royal Canadian Golf Association was formed.

In the more northerly areas of the country, where weather conditions can be quite savage, play is limited to only two months in the year, although golf can be played the year round in British Columbia. Generally the Canadian season runs from March into November when the first snows arrive.

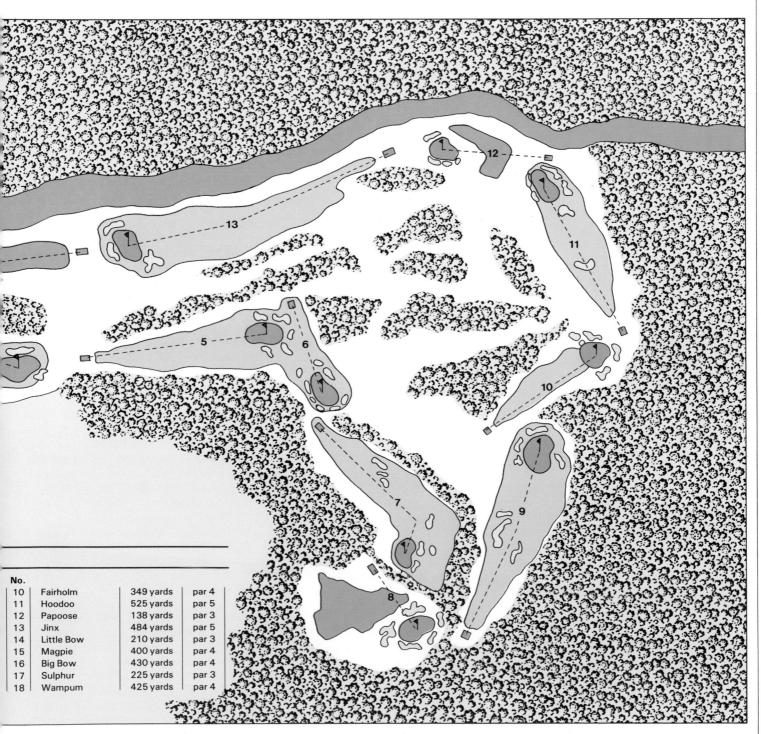

No.			
10	Fairholm	349 yards	par 4
11	Hoodoo	525 yards	par 5
12	Papoose	138 yards	par 3
13	Jinx	484 yards	par 5
14	Little Bow	210 yards	par 3
15	Magpie	400 yards	par 4
16	Big Bow	430 yards	par 4
17	Sulphur	225 yards	par 3
18	Wampum	425 yards	par 4

Banff Springs

Such is the vastness of Canada that golf of practically all varieties is available, with the exception of the traditional seaside links type. Certainly the most spectacular course is that of Banff Springs, set high in the Rockies 80 miles west of Calgary and originally constructed in 1911 by the Canadian Pacific Railway, which also built the Banff Springs Hotel, a Gothic edifice whose baroque towers are entirely in keeping with the Alpine atmosphere. The present course was created in 1927 by Stanley Thompson, a Canadian architect who also designed Jasper Park, Capilano and Cape Breton Highlands.

Wherever he could, Thompson left nature well alone at Banff and allowed the 6,729-yard course to wander its way through tunnels of pine trees while, at the same time, he cunningly brought into play the Spray and Bow Rivers to make the last six holes a rugged test of the golfer's nerve. Thompson's forte, however, lay in creating exciting par three holes and nowhere is this better exemplified than at Banff's 8th hole. Known as the Devil's Cauldron, this 175-yard short hole is recognized as one of the outstanding holes in golf. From a high tee, the ball is played to a green set beneath the sheer rise of Mount Rundle. In between the tee and the green lies a glacial lake which has to be carried. The high tee and the presence of the lake naturally force the golfer into the mistake of taking too much club with the result that many balls fly into the trees behind the green or hit the bank at the back and bounce back into the water. A shot of the utmost precision is required if a par is to be secured. On the homeward run, the par three 14th at 210 yards requires another exacting tee shot across water and no respite is given on the 16th, a par four of 430 yards which is rated the hardest hole on the course. Before the sanctuary of the hotel is reached, the 425-yard 18th must be navigated with caution since the hole contains no less than 28 of Banff's 144 bunkers. All in all, Banff Springs is a golfing experience not to be missed.

Capilano

Capilano on the outskirts of Vancouver is another fine example of Stanley Thompson's instinct for golf over rugged terrain. Backed by the coastal mountains, Capilano was built in 1937 on land which slopes steeply away from the clubhouse, dropping some 300 feet at its lowest point. The course was hewn from a forest of Douglas firs and conifers and although the fall of the land is steep, Thompson's skill ensured that the golfer is not aware of the gradient, particularly when returning up the hill back to the clubhouse. Although the firs line every hole, they do not encroach and the fairways are generously wide. The greens are extremely large and place great emphasis on accurately judged approach shots.

As with Banff Springs, the short holes are outstanding, in particular the 4th and 11th. Both are played across water to heavily bunkered greens with the 11th, at 155 yards, requiring a medium-iron shot to an undulating green set among the pines. The last four holes provide a stern conclusion to the round with the 15th at 420 yards, the 16th at 254 yards, the 17th at 415 yards and the 18th an uphill climb of 575 yards, which is rarely reached in two shots. Capilano is kept wonderfully green all year round by the rains off the mountains or by the sea mists which sweep in from Vancouver Island. Wet or dry, most golfers will relish the challenge of Capilano.

Royal Montreal

While the founding of Royal Montreal makes it the oldest club in North America, its present site is far removed from the original. In fact, the club has had three courses in its 115-year history. The first was at Fletcher's Field, a public park within the city, but after 23 years the growth of Montreal caused the club to up sticks and move ten miles west to an area called Dixie. The Dixie course became the venue for many national championships, including the Canadian Open. The club also staged the world's first international club match when, in 1901, it took on the The Country Club of Brookline, Mass.

By the late 1950s, further urban development caused the club to move once again and a site on Ile Bizard in the Lake of Two Mountains was found and the American architect, Dick Wilson, was called in. Wilson left the membership with a total of 45 holes. The Blue course is the one which is used for championship play and features huge greens which are severely bunkered. The last four holes on the Blue course are interwoven with a large lake which feeds the watering system on the course. The result of many a tournament has been decided over this watery stretch, none perhaps more emphatically than the 1975 Canadian Open which found Jack Nicklaus and Tom Weiskopf battling for the title. Nicklaus hooked into the water on the 18th in the final round to fall back into a tie with Weiskopf and on the first extra hole of the play-off, the 15th, Weiskopf hit a 7-iron across the water to within two feet of the hole to win.

The Canadian Open remains one of the few titles Nicklaus has never won in his illustrious career, even though it is now played on a course he himself designed, Glen Abbey in Ontario. The 16th at Royal Montreal is an intimidating par four of 430 yards where the drive and second shot have to be played across the lake. In that same 1975 Canadian Open, a little known US Tour player, Pat Fitzsimons, hooked his drive and saw his ball heading for the water. But luck was with him for the ball landed on a small island whereupon Fitzsimons waded out with a 4-iron and then hit the ball cleanly onto the

green for a very unlikely par four. The island is now named after him.

Other Canadian Courses

Other fine courses in Quebec include Royal Quebec, Le Club Laval sur-le-lac, Pinegrove, Carling Lake, Manoir Richelieu and Le Chateau Montebello, many of which reflect the French influence in their names.

The Atlantic Provinces of Nova Scotia, New Brunswick and Prince Edward Island offer a variety of scenic and challenging layouts with Stanley Thompson making another vibrant contribution at Cape Breton Highlands near Ingonish Beach, Nova Scotia, a course which wends its way through a combination of mountain, valley and seaside terrain. Also worth visiting are The Pines Hotel Golf Course at Digby, Oakfield Country Club and Ashburn near Halifax, the latter a Geoffrey Cornish design of 7,121 yards carved from woodland around the Kinsac and Spruce Lakes.

Of the 1,000 plus courses in Canada, one seems to capture the essence of golf in that beautifully harsh landscape. This is the Yellowknife Golf Club, a nine-hole layout in the Northwest Territory. Every year the club stages its Midnight Tournament when play commences at one minute past midnight and, thanks to the midnight sun, continues uninterrupted for the next two days.

AUSTRALIA

As with most countries within the Commonwealth, Australia was provided with its first taste of golf by a Scot; in this case the Hon James Graham who struck the first shot in 1847 somewhere around Melbourne. The subsequent discovery of gold temporarily diverted everyone's attentions away from the game and although a number of clubs were formed they either disbanded or simply disappeared. Royal Melbourne, founded in 1891, therefore lays claim to being the oldest established club on the Continent followed by Royal Sydney and the revived Royal Adelaide in 1893, Royal Perth in 1895 and

Above: The oldest club in Australia is the Royal Melbourne, founded in 1891. The Royal Melbourne courses, East and West, were created in the 1920s, and the two are combined for championship play.

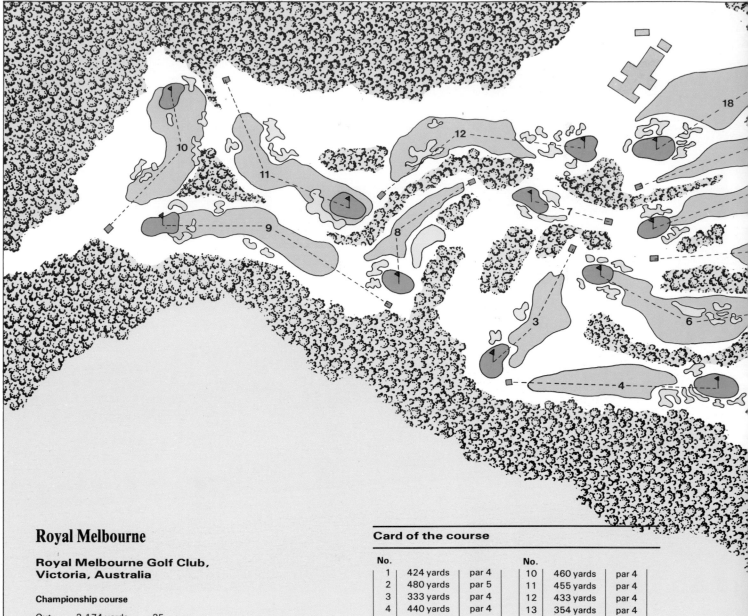

Royal Melbourne

**Royal Melbourne Golf Club,
Victoria, Australia**

Championship course

Out	3,174 yards	35
In	3,772 yards	36
Total	6,946 yards	par 71

Card of the course

No.			No.		
1	424 yards	par 4	10	460 yards	par 4
2	480 yards	par 5	11	455 yards	par 4
3	333 yards	par 4	12	433 yards	par 4
4	440 yards	par 4	13	354 yards	par 4
5	176 yards	par 3	14	470 yards	par 4
6	428 yards	par 4	15	383 yards	par 4
7	148 yards	par 3	16	210 yards	par 3
8	305 yards	par 4	17	575 yards	par 5
9	440 yards	par 4	18	432 yards	par 4

Newlands in Tasmania in 1896. In 1908 the Australian Golf Union was founded but it wasn't until after the Second World War that the Australian golf rush began and the country started producing players of the calibre of Norman von Nida, Peter Thomson, Kel Nagle and, latterly, Graham Marsh, David Graham and Greg Norman.

Now there are some 1,500 courses on which to play, most of which are concentrated upon the major cities. Of these cities, the one most blessed with natural golfing terrain is Melbourne whose southern confines contain a 25 square mile area known as the Sand Belt. This rolling countryside, covered with fine grasses and many indigenous trees was just waiting for the golf course architect to make his mark.

Royal Melbourne

It is at Royal Melbourne that this mark has been most elegantly registered with the creation of the East and West courses. These were designed by Alister Mackenzie in tandem with Alex Russell, the 1924 Australian Open champion, and the work began in 1926. Mackenzie, who was to go on to design Augusta National plus a host of other celebrated courses, made full use of the splendid golfing land at his disposal. Clever bunkering and subtle shaping of the holes are features of Royal Melbourne but the real terror is to be found on the greens, which are huge and frighteningly fast. For championship purposes, six holes of the East course, Russell's creation, are incorporated with 12 of Mackenzie's West, thereby producing a

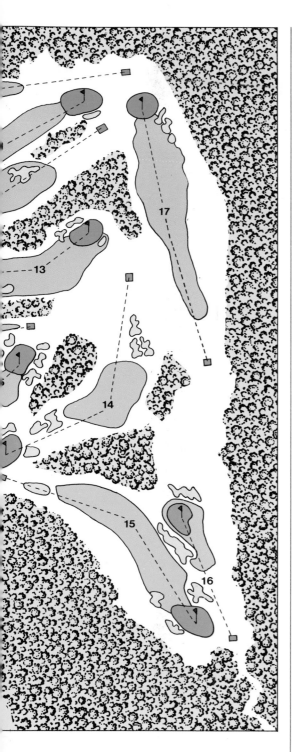

cluster of daunting bunkers has to be carried and if the golfer plays to the left of them, the hole becomes nearly 500 yards long. The fairway over the bunkers slopes downhill, thus making the stance for the second shot uneven. More bunkering round the green leaves little margin for error and most golfers should be content to play the hole as a par five. Both the 8th and the 14th are classic holes on a classic course.

Other courses in the Sand Belt area include the Metropolitan Golf Club which features strategic fairway bunkering and large, undulating greens, Kingston Heath, another course to fall under the Mackenzie influence, Commonwealth Golf Club, possessing narrow fairways with out-of-bounds threatening on six holes, Victoria Golf Club, where five times Open Champion Peter Thomson was called in to redesign the original layout and Huntingdale, built in 1941 by Charles Alison, and where 7,000 yards and glassy greens now accommodate

Below: Adelaide is one of Australia's most beautiful cities, and the Royal Adelaide course, designed by Alistair Mackenzie, appropriately resembles Scottish links courses.

course of nearly 7,000 yards in length with a stiff par of 71. Two holes in particular encapsulate Mackenzie's philosophy of design, the 8th and the 14th.

The 8th is a mere 305 yards long, almost driveable for today's long hitters, but the temptation to go for the green from the tee must take into account the large bunker set in a gentle hill in a direct line from the tee. Failure to make the carry can result in disaster but the golfer is presented with an alternative route to the right of the trap from where the hole turns half left to a small green which requires an accurate approach.

The 14th is much more taxing in terms of length, being 470 yards and needing two big hits to find the green which lies at the end of the right-hand dog-leg. From the tee, a

the Australian Masters tournament, the richest in the country.

Royal Adelaide

Mackenzie's sojourn in Australia during the mid-1920s also saw him at work on Royal Adelaide, the nearest thing to a genuine links course as can be found in the country. Much of the Scottish influence is evident here and although there are far more trees than would be seen on a links course, the flow of the land is evocative of links golf. This is exemplified by the 11th, a par four of nearly 400 yards where Mackenzie designed the hole around a large depression full of scrub and tangly grasses. The drive must carry a hill and once reached the true merits of the hole are revealed as the golfer has to carry this scrubland and also has to hit a sure shot to find a green that is guarded by bunkers on either side and surrounded by trees.

Royal Sydney

Royal Sydney is another Australian course which has a links feel to it although it lies a few miles from the heart of the city. Narrow fairways, numerous bunkers, fierce rough and strong coastal breezes provide a tough challenge. Set in a narrow strip of land the course has rather too many parallel holes which can make handling the wind somewhat tedious but it has been a regular venue for the Australian Open.

The Australian Golf Club and the New South Wales Golf Club are other notable tests in the State with the latter overlooking

Botany Bay and subject to a constant harassment by the wind. Across the continent lies Perth, regarded by the locals as the second windiest city in the world. This is the home of Lake Karrinyup, another Mackenzie/Russell creation, which runs around the lake of its name.

NEW ZEALAND

The origins of golf in New Zealand date from 1871 when a Scot, Charles Howden, helped found the Dunedin club, later called the Otago. However, the business of colonising the country took precedence over any leisure

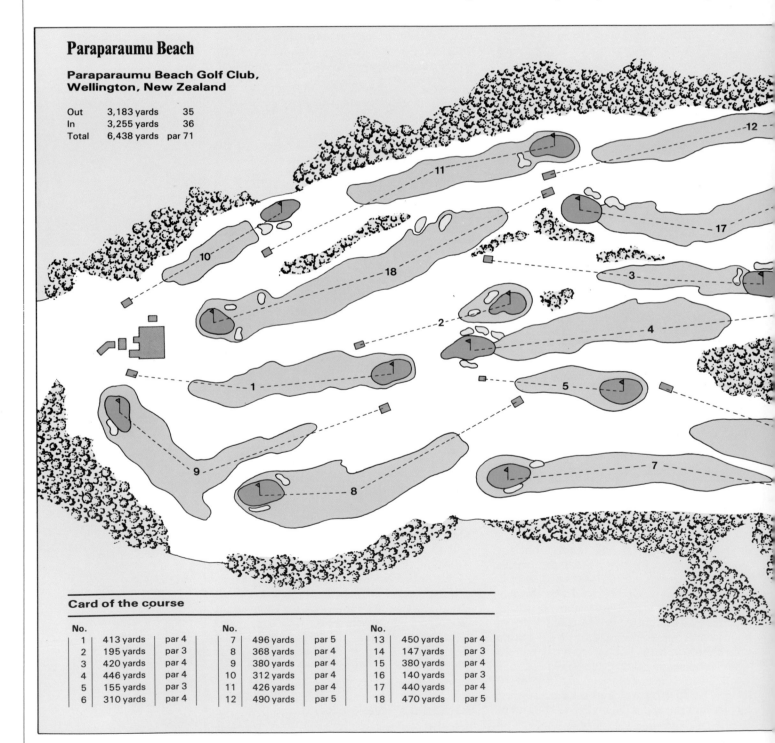

Paraparaumu Beach

**Paraparaumu Beach Golf Club,
Wellington, New Zealand**

Out	3,183 yards	35
In	3,255 yards	36
Total	6,438 yards	par 71

Card of the course

No.			No.			No.		
1	413 yards	par 4	7	496 yards	par 5	13	450 yards	par 4
2	195 yards	par 3	8	368 yards	par 4	14	147 yards	par 3
3	420 yards	par 4	9	380 yards	par 4	15	380 yards	par 4
4	446 yards	par 4	10	312 yards	par 4	16	140 yards	par 3
5	155 yards	par 3	11	426 yards	par 4	17	440 yards	par 4
6	310 yards	par 4	12	490 yards	par 5	18	470 yards	par 5

activities and 20 years elapsed before the city of Christchurch led a golfing revival which spread throughout the two islands and saw the formation of clubs in Auckland, Wanganui, Timaru, Poverty Bay, Manawatu, Napier and Wellington. The New Zealand Golf Association was founded in 1910. New Zealand's most famous golfing son is undoubtedly Bob Charles, who in 1963 became the only left-hander and the only New Zealander to win the Open Championship.

Paraparaumu

Paraparaumu, north of Wellington in the North Island, is a rarity in the Antipodes in that it is a real seaside links. It was constructed in 1930 by Alex Russell, who had

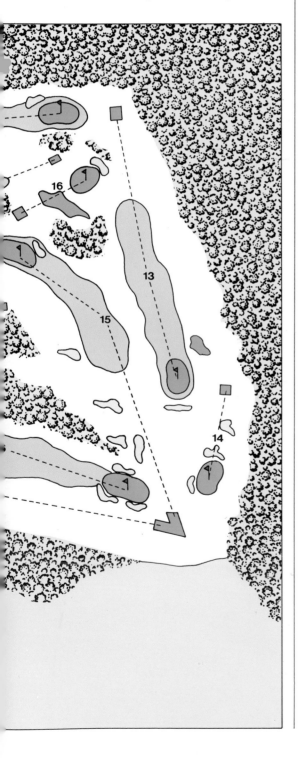

collaborated with Alister Mackenzie at Royal Melbourne, and he carefully designed a course which has all the feel and aspect of a Scottish links. Russell did not go overboard on the bunkering, preferring to make them small and let the dunes and undulating land provide the drops around the greens. This approach is highlighted by the 155-yard 5th hole which ranks alongside such classic short holes as the 11th at St Andrews or the 8th at Troon. The hole has no bunkers but the green sits atop a shaved-off dune with a fearsome drop all round. The golfer who misses the putting surface could spend a long time trying to get the ball back. Good holes abound at Paraparaumu and for the golfer who loves the challenge of links golf, the course will constantly beckon.

Wairakei

Further north on the North Island lies Wairakei which was built in the mid-1950s by the British architect, the late John Harris. This is golf among the geysers as the course itself is built on pumice and is in sight of the Karapiti and Rogue geysers whose steam and spray rise hundreds of feet into the air. The Rogue has given its name to Wairakei's 14th hole, a 608-yard monster played towards the geyser through a narrow valley to a horseshoe-shaped green. Following two good blows, the third shot is crucial as a single pine tree can block the approach while the green itself is heavily bunkered.

From the back tees, Wairakei is 6,903 yards long with a stiff par of 72. It is not a golf club in the strictest sense, having been built as a tourist facility and any visitor can play on the presentation of a few dollars.

The South Island

Although the courses on the North Island are more famous, there is plenty of good golf on the South Island, particularly at Christchurch and Otago. Christchurch is the longest course in the country at 7,000 yards and is a mix of linksland and parkland. It has staged several New Zealand Open Championships. Otago in Dunedin is a hilly course and contains a challenging hole in the 350-yard 11th. The hole has a steep slope on the right-hand side and out-of-bounds and water on the left. The hole presented a challenge to Arnold Palmer which he could not resist and he overcame all the trouble by driving the green.

JAPAN

No other country in the world has experienced such an explosion of interest in golf as Japan. Although the first course was built in 1901 near Kobe, it was not until 1957 that the spark was ignited. This was when the Canada Cup, now the World Cup, was staged at the Kasumigaseki Club in Tokyo and resulted in a home victory by the team of Torakichi Nakamura and Koichi Ono. At that time there were 79 courses in Japan: today there are over 1,000, and this number is still not enough to cope with a fanatical playing population of well over 10 million, many of whom never actually play on a proper course but fulfil their desires in one of the many driving ranges which have been built with two or three tiers.

Golf club membership in Japan is stratospherically expensive, $250,000 a year being commonplace, and in fact memberships are bought and traded as a commodity and a prime investment. The proliferation of courses on such small, densely populated islands has resulted in *gorufu kogai* (golf pollution) and land in urban areas is no longer available. Consequently, courses have been forced higher up into the mountainous regions where the game is played at a permanent awkward angle, but this does not seem to matter to the Japanese, for it is real golf played in the open and that is what really counts.

Yet for all the recent development, the two most famous courses in Japan were both built prior to the Second World War. Hirono near Kobe (see the plan of the course, *below*) and Kasumigaseki were both designed by English architectural artist, Charles Alison, although the latter was first laid out by a local player, Kinya Fujita, before Alison was called in to make a number of ingenious refinements.

Hirono

Hirono Golf Club, Kobe, Japan

Out	3,410 yards	36
In	3,540 yards	36
Total	6,950 yards	par 72

Card of the course

No.		
1	500 yards	par 5
2	430 yards	par 4
3	440 yards	par 4
4	400 yards	par 4
5	150 yards	par 3
6	430 yards	par 4
7	200 yards	par 3
8	350 yards	par 4
9	510 yards	par 5
10	360 yards	par 4
11	445 yards	par 4
12	550 yards	par 5
13	180 yards	par 3
14	380 yards	par 4
15	555 yards	par 5
16	380 yards	par 4
17	230 yards	par 3
18	460 yards	par 4

Hirono

Hirono was built in 1932 on land which closely resembled that of the Surrey heather and pine belt upon which Alison, an Englishman, had worked. He created a course of 6,950 yards containing a great variety of holes set amid great natural beauty.

Alison's lasting legacy to Japanese golf came in the form of his bunkers at Hirono. Deep and penal they have passed into Japanese folklore to the extent that bunkers of a similar type are called 'Alison'. Water comes into play on six holes and is particularly menacing at the 5th, 13th and 17th holes, all par threes requiring a carry across the water to tightly bunkered greens.

The 12th and 15th are both classic dog-leg par fives requiring the golfer to use brain as well as brawn but perhaps the outstanding hole at Kirono is the short 7th. This par three of 200 yards has no water hazards but is played across a deep shelving ravine to a green surrounded by pine trees and the shot is invariably into the wind.

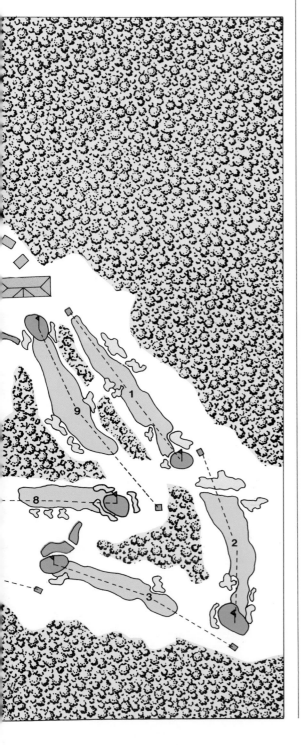

Kasumigaseki

Golf at Kasumigaseki is played in a Japanese garden. Immaculately maintained, there is hardly a leaf out of place and the more exposed trees are wrapped in hessian to protect them against the ravages of winter. The original layout by Fujita was marvellously varied considering he was a rank amateur in course design. There are two courses, the East and the West, and it is the East which is used for championships and tournaments and where Alison laid his imprint in the bunkering and the guidance of the player through the wood-lined fairways. Again, it is with a short hole, the 180-yard 10th, that he showed his skill by forming a small green with deep bunkers all round so that the penalties for missing the target were obvious. That the hole is also played across water adds to its terrors and its beauty. The same lake also lies in wait for the severely hooked second shot to the 475-yard 18th but again it is the greenside bunkering which makes any attempt to reach the green in two shots a hazardous affair.

Fujioka

At Nagoya lies another excellent course which was built in the early 1970s. Fujioka is set among pines with a number of lakes creating an atmosphere not unlike that of Augusta National. The course contains a number of holes which are unusual in their design, particularly the 12th and the 17th. The 12th is a gentle left-hand dog-leg of 440 yards but there are two greens, one which is straight ahead and the other further left and hard by a lake: either green can be used depending upon the whim of the committee on the day. The 17th also offers a choice but this lies in the approach to a solitary green which is divided into two areas by a central ridge. The position of the flag thus dictates the line from the tee which is over a lake and between the pines. The last three holes at Fujioka have all been built around water, with the 608-yard 16th requiring a strong nerve for the third shot with water threatening the left-hand side, while the 18th, at 430 yards, has a ditch running in front of the green and a lake edging in towards the green on the left.

Perhaps the most impressive example of Japan's almost religious fervour for the game is to be found at the Karuizawa 72 complex, 125 miles north of Tokyo. Here is a modern development of four 18-hole courses, hence the 72 in the title: 36 holes designed by Robert Trent Jones and 36 holes by his son, Bob jnr. Starting times have to be booked as much as six months in advance!

EUROPE

The great land mass which stretches from Scandinavia in the north to Portugal in the south offers a variety of golf courses which is hardly matched anywhere else in the world. While all the countries involved are not strictly European in terms of the EEC Community, in golfing terms they are all aligned under the European banner and practically all of them stage a national Open Championship under the aegis of the PGA European Tour.

The greatest growth in European golf facilities has taken place in Spain and Portugal where golf tourism has expanded at a frenetic rate. Spain's Costa del Sol and Portugal's Algarve are the places the inhabitants of the colder northern climes flock to in winter for a golfing break in the sunshine, and, as the traffic has increased, so has the number of courses.

Spain

The blueprint for all this activity is Sotogrande, 20 miles from Gibraltar on the Costa del Sol. It was built in 1965 and designed by Robert Trent Jones, his first venture into Europe. The American influence is prevalent at Sotogrande with the Jones' hallmark of long tees and large greens with the punishing aspect of water being brought into play at several holes. Threading its way through the groves of cork trees, Sotogrande

Sotogrande

Club de Golf Sotogrande, Cadiz, Spain

Old course

Out	3,357 yards	36
In	3,553 yards	36
Total	6,910 yards	par 72

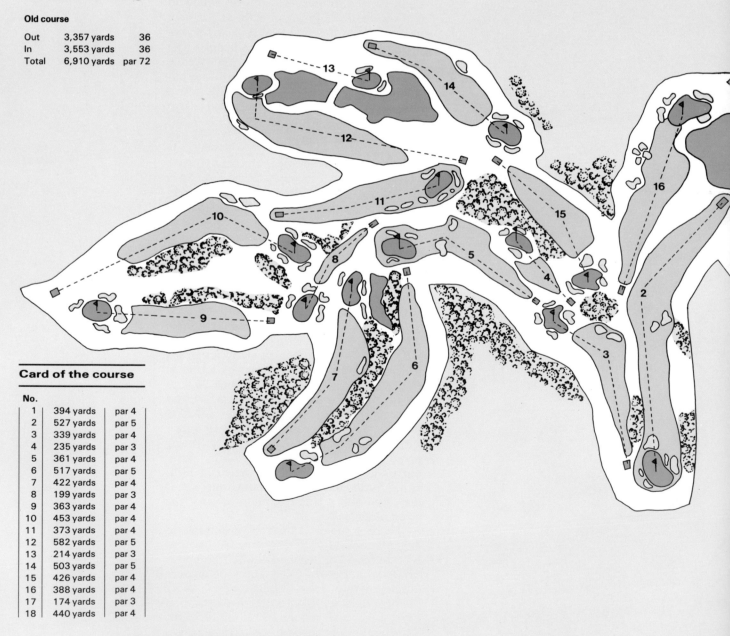

Card of the course

No.		
1	394 yards	par 4
2	527 yards	par 5
3	339 yards	par 4
4	235 yards	par 3
5	361 yards	par 4
6	517 yards	par 5
7	422 yards	par 4
8	199 yards	par 3
9	363 yards	par 4
10	453 yards	par 4
11	373 yards	par 4
12	582 yards	par 5
13	214 yards	par 3
14	503 yards	par 5
15	426 yards	par 4
16	388 yards	par 4
17	174 yards	par 3
18	440 yards	par 4

is too tough to be considered a holiday course and it was not intended to be such. Probably the most spectacular hole on the course, and certainly the most photographed, is the 7th, a par four of 422 yards. From the tee, the hole turns to the left but it is the second shot which poses severe problems as the land surrounding the green falls away to the right into a lake which invariably catches the stroke that is not quite strong enough. Water also comes into the play on the 12th, 13th and 14th, two par five holes each side of a par three, and again at the 16th and 17th and it is a very good player, or a very lucky one, who does not consign at least one golf ball to the *agua* during a round.

More brutality can be found at Las Brisas, formerly Nueva Andalucia, near

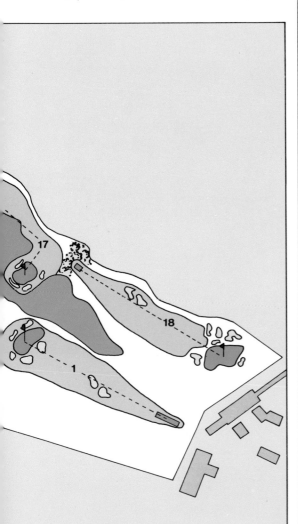

Marbella, another Trent Jones creation where water dominates. Site of the 1973 World Cup, when America's Johnny Miller set a record 65, the course provides a number of death-or-glory challenges, most notably the 520-yard 12th. Water runs along the left-hand side of the fairway and then crosses in front of the green. Two solid strokes and a pitch is the sensible way to play the hole but for the long hitter there is the temptation to go for the green in two shots. Confrontations such as these provide the elements for a great and demanding course.

Not all golf in Spain is confined to the Costa del Sol. There are a number of good courses in Madrid, including Puerta de Hierro, a regular site for the Madrid Open, and the Club de Campo, while Barcelona boasts a fine test in El Prat set amid the umbrella pines near the airport. Recently La Manga, on the Costa Blanca, has sprung into prominence as a golfing resort which has everything. While golf tourism in Spain is a boom industry, the greatest spin-off from this has been the emergence of Spanish players from caddie ranks who have gone on to become household names, with Severiano Ballesteros now ranked as the outstanding player in the world.

Portugal

For many years, golf in Portugal centred upon the coastal playground of Estoril, which possessed a sporty test which really wasn't long enough for championship standard. The development of the Algarve gave birth to several courses which combined holiday golf with a stern examination of skill. Chief among them is Penina, laid out by the three-times Open Champion, Henry Cotton, over 340 acres of boggy land. Cotton planted over 350,000 trees on the site, firstly to break up the flatness of the terrain and secondly to absorb the moisture from the soil. The course

Below: Puerta de Hierro near Madrid, where the Madrid Open is frequently played. Tourism, Spain's biggest 'import', is responsible for a golfing boom in the sunshine, although nearer the coast than the heights of Madrid.

Chantilly

Chantilly Golf Club, Oise, France

Out	3,498 yards	36
In	3,631 yards	35
Total	7,129 yards	par 71

Card of the course

No.					
1	454 yards	par 4	10	465 yards	par 4
2	394 yards	par 4	11	427 yards	par 4
3	153 yards	par 3	12	402 yards	par 4
4	375 yards	par 4	13	457 yards	par 4
5	410 yards	par 4	14	219 yards	par 3
6	217 yards	par 3	15	417 yards	par 4
7	439 yards	par 4	16	219 yards	par 3
8	480 yards	par 5	17	429 yards	par 5
9	576 yards	par 5	18	596 yards	par 5

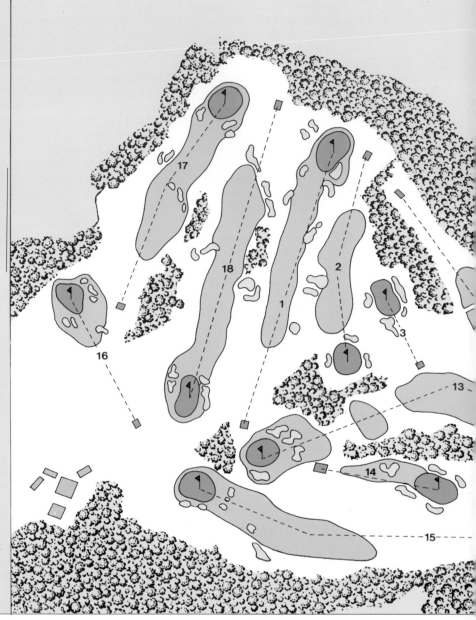

Right: *La Manga is a golfing resort especially designed to attract the tourists to Spain. All the tourist attractions are to be found there, even the un-Spanish activity of cricket.*

216

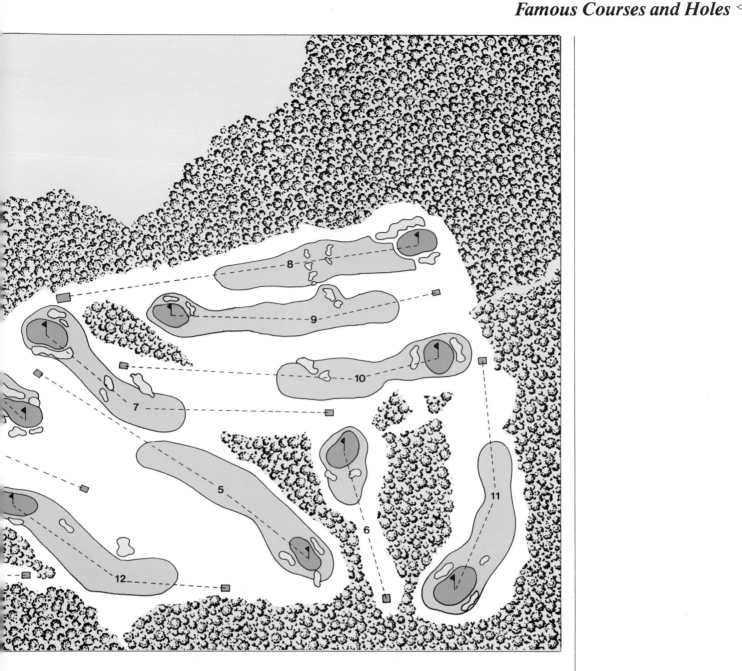

was opened in 1966 alongside its luxury hotel and has been a popular venue for golfers ever since. Cotton also created another course in the Algarve of an entirely different nature. Vale de Lobo, near Faro, was cut out of trees on rolling countryside which runs down to the cliff-tops. Here Cotton was able to build one of the most famous short holes in golf, the 200-yard 7th, which runs along the cliff-edge and where the tee shot has to carry some unnerving crevasses before the green is reached. Vilamoura and Quinta do Lago are two particularly fine courses in the region, which is a favourite for British visitors.

France

Golf in France is an exclusive and expensive sport which has never overwhelmed the population. Even so, the French Open Championship, founded in 1906, is one of the oldest in the world and has a list of distinguished winners from Vardon to Ballesteros. The majority of the country's top courses are situated in the Paris area,

Above: The beautiful 3rd hole at St Nom-la-Breteche, a championship course near Paris. France has rarely produced top-class men golfers, which is surprising considering courses like this.

Falsterbo

Falsterbo Golfklubb, Fack, Sweden

Out	3,100 yards	34
In	3,555 yards	37
Total	6,655 yards	par 71

Card of the course

No.		
1	448 yards	par 4
2	175 yards	par 3
3	530 yards	par 5
4	427 yards	par 4
5	399 yards	par 4
6	186 yards	par 3
7	317 yards	par 4
8	191 yards	par 3
9	427 yards	par 4
10	394 yards	par 4
11	153 yards	par 3
12	405 yards	par 4
13	574 yards	par 5
14	241 yards	par 3
15	525 yards	par 5
16	388 yards	par 4
17	377 yards	par 4
18	498 yards	par 5

with St Cloud and St Nom-la-Breteche being regularly used for tournaments, but the favourite of many players would undoubtedly be Chantilly. Set in a forest on gently rolling land, Chantilly provides a serenity and peace that is all too rarely captured. The holes are neatly separated by the trees so the player has the feeling of isolation which is so important to the concentration. The club was founded in 1908 and was redesigned in the 1920s by Tom Simpson. Some of his work was destroyed in the Second World War but the essence of it remains. It is a long and rugged test, stretching to over 7,000 yards from the back trees, with the 596-yard 18th providing a fitting finale to a second nine in which none of the par fours are less than 400 yards long.

Germany

Golf in Germany is like that in France in being the preserve of the well-to-do, although the recent exploits of Bernhard Langer have sparked an upsurge of interest which may well see other players of Langer's calibre emerge in the future. The outstanding course in the country is that of Club Zur Vahr at Bremen which ranks as one of the toughest in Europe. The course is laid out among tall pines and is no place for the timid or weak driver. Drives must be long and straight and, since many of the holes dog-leg, the placing of the tee shot is also important or a shaped second is necessary. Measuring over 7,000 yards, Club Zur Vahr tests the best.

Italy

Moving south towards Italy, the travelling golfer could pause to good effect to take in Crans-Sur-Sierre and its spectacular Alpine setting where the ball flies a very satisfactory distance through the rarefied mountain air, but then it would be on to Rome to the home of Olgiata, Italy's most famous and best

course. There are 27 holes at Olgiata, designed by the British architect, Ken Cotton, in 1961 and the main course spreads away from the clubhouse in two separate loops of nine holes. The greens are large and carefully, but not severely, bunkered. The rise and fall of the land keeps the player on his mettle and the size of the greens means that approach shots must be accurate. Olgiata was the site of the 1968 World Cup.

Holland

There are few classic links courses outside Britain but of those which do exist those at Kennemer in Holland and Falsterbo in Sweden are among the finest.

The historical connection between golf and the ancient Dutch game of *kolven* has been well examined without any irrefutable evidence that the game began in Holland and Kennemer itself provides no further leads since the club was only founded in 1910. The

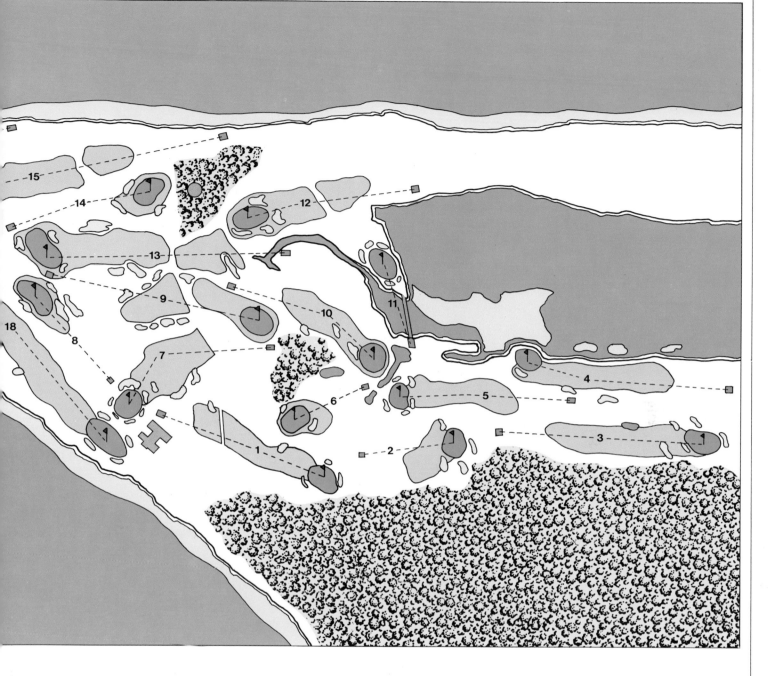

present course was constructed in the 1920s by Harry Colt and he made full use of the towering sandhills, undulating fairways and outcrops of pine trees. Colt made the fairways generously wide but provided extra teeth by narrowing them at the landing areas, and did the same with the entrances to the greens which follow the tradition of links greens by putting fast and true. Kennemer has staged many tournaments and championships and in 1976 saw the beginning of Severiano Ballesteros' madcap dance of youth across the fairways of the world when he won the Dutch Open title there.

Sweden

Far away on the southern edge of Sweden lies Falsterbo, set on a small peninsula with Denmark only 30 miles away across the Baltic Sea. Falsterbo retains all the natural charm usually associated with links courses and is, of course, prey to all manner of winds. The 4th, 5th and 11th run close by a large inlet which as well as existing as a potential home for errantly struck golf balls, is also a haven for thousands of migratory birds. The 4th and 5th both have water on the right to catch the slice while the 11th, a short hole of 153 yards, has water all the way up to the green and also on the right. From there on, the only water is the sea itself which washes up onto the beach around the last four holes.

In recent years, golf in Sweden has been approached with much the same fervour as in Japan and the Swedes have taken to producing national playing squads along the same lines as their tennis teams. So far, their success has been slower than that of their tennis-playing counterparts but a breakthrough did occur in 1986 when Ove Sellberg became the first Swedish professional to win a tournament on the PGA European Tour, followed by compatriots Mats Lanner and Anders Forsbrand in 1987.

Equipment and Clothing

The evolution of golf club and golf ball over the past 450 years has seen many radical changes. When the game first took root in Scotland, clubs were crude implements fashioned from indigenous woods while the ball was made from a leather sack stuffed with goose feathers. The emergence of a ball made from gutta-percha brought many changes to the design of clubs and heralded the introduction of clubs with steel heads. The next significant change occurred with the appearance of the rubber-cored ball and this signalled the first great golf explosion. Since the phasing out of hickory shafts in 1929, golf club and ball manufacture has become a highly technical industry with many companies battling for a share of a lucrative market.

Left: The workshop of Robert Forgan and Sons, in which were produced superior hand-crafted golf clubs from about 1856. Forgan was a pioneer of the use of hickory for shafts. In 1863 Forgan became clubmaker to the Prince of Wales, and by 1900 the firm had become the largest manufacturer in St Andrews.

In the early days when golf neither resembled the game as we know it today nor bore the same name, equipment was also rudimentary. With a simple stick and a stone was how certain precursory forms of the sport were played and no doubt other equally rustic equipment was used.

In those early days the materials adopted were to be found naturally. A stick was simply hewn from the hedgerow and shaped and styled, while as far as the ball was concerned those early players of the game turned to animals for such as leather, wool or feathers. It is known that the Romans played a game called Paganica with a ball filled with flock while in the 14th century in England something similar called Cambuca used a wooden ball.

Although little is known about the clubs adopted for either game, it is easy to see that the development of clubs and balls has been interwoven with improvements in one leading to changes in the other. During those early days the implements adopted for hitting the ball and the ball itself were extremely basic and of a rough nature. There were no such things as clubmakers at this stage. Those who played whatever pioneering form of the game simply improvised, creating their own clubs of whatever pattern or style they felt was right at the time.

Below: The development of golf clubs and that of balls have gone hand-in-hand, as an improvement in one has led to an improvement in another. The achievement of length off the tee has not been a priority, as this would clearly render out of date the course itself, which is more difficult to change. Therefore devices like this, which owes its invention to the imagination of Heath Robinson, have not been part of the history of clubmaking.

THE DEVELOPMENT OF CLUBS

The earliest record of someone being employed to fashion clubs — and it is somewhat tenuous to say the least — was in the early 16th century and concerned James IV of Scotland. He is believed to have bought certain 'golf clubbes' from a 'bower' or bowmaker in Perth around 1502. At that time the bowmaker was perhaps the only craftsman with the tools to fashion the clubhead and shafts needed. It is a fair assumption to make and it is also felt that the bowmaker's craft began to decline with the advent of guns and gunpowder so that he diversified into the business of clubmaking.

Perhaps the first acknowledged club-maker was indeed a bowmaker. William Mayne was described in the language of the day as a 'bower burgess' but his new-found trade was put squarely on the map when he was appointed Clubmaker to the court of King James I of England and VI of Scotland. Mayne, from Edinburgh, received his appointment in 1603 after the king took a distinct liking to knocking a ball around. Then, in 1628, thanks to another member of the gentry of the day, the Duke of Montrose, a certain James Pett of St Andrews, became a clubmaker of repute in the town. There are stories that there existed a close friendship between the Duke and Pett's daughter, but others discount that, supporting their view with the tale of his wedding to Magdaline Carnegie. The Duke is said to have rushed from the golf course to the church, and after the marriage rushed back again. This, say the doubters, proves he was no womaniser but a man devoted to the game of golf. Nevertheless he certainly set Pett up as one of the earliest clubmakers.

Not far down the Scottish coast at Leith, the Dickson family were also engaged as club and ballmakers. Thomas and William Dickson were certainly in business around the same time as Pett. In the following generation John Dickson was licensed to make golf balls by Aberdeen Town Council in 1642. Other Dicksons followed and the family line in the golf trade was maintained until 1787.

In the first half of the 18th century further Leith men, John and David Clephane, were mentioned as clubmakers from 1725 to 1750. John was a formidable golfer whose relative

Lukie ran the tavern in Kirkgate, Leith, a favourite haunt of members of the Honourable Company of Edinburgh Golfers and where they dined before their own Golf House was built. Around the same time there are records of an Andrew Bailey at Bruntsfield, Edinburgh, making clubs and balls, while at St Andrews there were David Dick and George and Henry Miln.

Bruntsfield and Leith, just a few miles apart, helped, at the time, to make Edinburgh a centre for club and ballmaking, and when James McEwan moved there from Stirling in 1770 that unofficial title was appropriate until the focus switched to Musselburgh around 1830. McEwan's move was significant as it marked the founding of a business that was to stamp its authority on clubmaking for over 100 years. James McEwan was a joiner or cartwright and he set up home adjacent to the Bruntsfield Links, obtaining his burgess ticket to the City of Edinburgh in 1775. His clubs earned a wide reputation and were all stamped with a thistle beneath which was 'J.MCEWAN'. Until that time there is no evidence of a ballmaker at Bruntsfield, but in 1780 a Douglas Gourlay came to the town and shared a shed with James McEwan, thereby providing golfers with a full facility under one roof.

The two families became linked when Douglas' daughter Jean married James' son Peter in 1802 and in turn their eldest son James was apprenticed to Gourlays before becoming a clubmaker in his own right. By the turn of the 19th century, the McEwan name had earned a glowing reputation, so much so that their clubs were being supplied to other hotbeds of golf such as Aberdeen, Montrose, Perth, and St Andrews, as well as south of the border to Blackheath in London, thereby creating a significant 'export' business. When James snr died in 1800, the 'J' was deleted from the stamp on each club and just 'MCEWAN' was used from then on.

Customized clubs

It seems that a personal service to golfers is nothing new. In those days, McEwans would send one of their men all the way from Leith to St Andrews, an arduous journey by ferry then horse and trap, each spring and autumn medal meeting to attend to the players' needs. But by 1847, with the golf societies moving out to the Musselburgh links because of increasing difficulties at Leith and Bruntsfield, McEwans opened a branch of their business at the new venue.

Even in those days there was a form of customizing in operation. When a customer made his requirements known, he took the clubmaker's advice although still having some say in the matter. A lot depended on whether the customer was an expert golfer or just a novice, but whatever the case a certain amount of coming and going with trials of the clubs would take place before the right formula was arrived at. Often the shape of

the head would be altered or the loft on the face while the amount of lead in the back of the head might be changed. There was also a possibility that the thickness of the grip or the shaft might require a change, but whatever alterations were made, the end product did, to all intent and purpose, suit the individual.

Early wooden clubs

Of course, until the introduction of iron clubs in the second half of the 19th century, all clubs were woods and mainly of the long-nosed, shallow-faced variety. They also had a very flat lie and somewhat slim neck, a design suited for getting a feathery ball off the rather thick turf. Many of those early clubs also appeared to have concave faces. They were not made that way but the centre of the face tended to be driven back through constant striking of the ball while the heel and toe consequently 'moved' inwards in the form of an arc.

Players must have needed to adopt an extremely flat type of swing to manipulate these difficult clubs but manipulate them they did. Of course, as with today's woods, the clubs were made with different degrees of loft but instead of being numbered, each club usually carried a name descriptive of its task, a much more colourful system. There were two types of driver, distinguished by the long tapering flexible shafts, the play club and the grassed driver. The former was for getting the game underway and the grassed driver — a driver with a slight loft — was what we would term a fairway wood. The term 'grassed' indicated loft.

Then there were the spoons, usually four — long spoon, middle spoon, short spoon and baffing spoon. The spoons were usually fitted with stiffer shafts and higher degrees of

Above: Perhaps the most personal club in a golfer's bag is the putter. The putter is the club most associated with the foibles and fancies of individual golfers. Consequently it is the most difficult club to manufacture. It is also a club which has retained its original name.

loft while the description long, middle, short and baffing referred mainly to the length of shaft, although still giving an indication of the loft of the face. The long spoon was the next in line to the grassed driver and was employed for longish shots while the middle spoon had that extra degree of loft for shorter shots as the player got nearer the green. The short spoon possessed even more loft and was used for making half strokes, what we would term closer to a pitch-and-run, or for extracting the ball from difficult lies. The baffing spoon possessed the greatest

Right: Eddie Davis, one of the last craftsmen to fashion clubs by hand. His workshop is at the ancient golfing stronghold of Westward Ho! Eddie is shaping the basic head of the club with a rasp.
Below: His apprentice is smoothing the wood with a plane and (bottom) is using a file to put the finishing touches to the shape of the head as required by the customer.

degree of loft and was used for skying the ball over a hazard on to the green when the shot required was too short for the others.

The term 'baffing' came from the noise emitted when the club struck the ground and ball simultaneously, or the ground fractionally before the ball. It was then said that the ball was 'baffed'. In some quarters the baffing spoon was also referred to as the 'cutty', but why is not fully clear. The obvious guess is because the ball was 'cut up' into the air but that has never been authenticated. While on this subject of names, the whole family of spoon clubs were so called because the clubface was gently spooned out in a concave style.

All these clubs were in their element while the feathery ball was in use because by its very nature the ball would readily rise into the air. But once the gutty ball was introduced around 1848 it spelt the demise of these long-nosed wooden clubs. The gutty was much harder in texture and therefore less easily made to rise by the spoons and they were in time replaced with iron-headed clubs.

Niblicks and brassies

Apart from putters, which we will deal with later, there was another club in the golfer's artillery at that time — the niblick. The wooden niblick resembled a spoon except that it had a much smaller head and the shaft was stiff. It was specifically designed to fit into a rut or hole in the ground where a short spoon or baffing spoon, with their much larger heads, would be unable to operate. It must be remembered that courses in those days were far from the manicured ones we know today, and ruts, holes and crevices were frequent. So the niblick was ideally suited to extract the ball. Yet it too became obsolete with the advent of the gutty, although the iron club used for a similar task also bore the niblick name until well into this century.

In the same family was the brassie, which was equivalent to today's No 2 wood. The brassie came into being around 1880 and its name derived from the brass sole plate that was screwed into the bottom of the club to protect it when used on hard surfaces. In the early days this brass plate covered the bone leading edge but later the bone was discarded and the brass plate was screwed directly to the bottom of the clubhead. However, not everyone was happy with the disappearance of the bone, because it was felt that with frequent use the clubface would get hammered back and consequently the forward edge of the brass plate would protrude and cut the ball.

The advent of irons

As stated earlier, it was the advent of the gutty ball that brought the introduction of iron clubs. At first they weren't called irons but cleeks, and they were made by cleekmakers. While the wooden clubs were made by craftsmen who were used to working in wood, there were no experts in golf who were used to working in metal. So it was left to blacksmiths to make the early iron heads under instruction from the clubmaker. When the finished article was returned the clubmaker would add the shaft and the grip. The early irons were somewhat crude with concave faces and no markings or grooves and they were generally used as a last resort when extracting the ball was beyond the capabilities of a wooden club.

Whenever they were used with the feathery ball there was always the fear that an iron club would burst it. So it wasn't until the gutty arrived that the iron or cleek came into its own. The iron head was fashioned from a piece of iron some seven inches (175 mm) long, two inches (50 mm) wide and about an eighth of an inch (3 mm) thick. When the iron was heated it was hammered into shape, the socket into which the shaft would fix being formed first. This was a pretty exacting task from a solid piece of metal. Then the angle of the head to the socket was formed, thereby giving the iron the appropriate lie.

Once that was achieved a further amount of hammering and twisting, using an anvil, was performed to give the necessary loft while the face would also be given a shape if that was ordered. Then a hole would be punched in each side of the socket at right angles to the line of the clubface. This would allow the clubmaker to fix a rivet when the shaft was added, while the top of the socket would be nicked or scored in order to help grip the shaft when it was driven in. Once the head had been filed to remove any rough edges, it was passed on to the clubmaker to complete the job. Later, when a pattern or grooves were added to the head, they were also done by the blacksmith. Sometimes the cleekmaker's name or mark was added to the back of the head as well as that of the clubmaker.

The clubmaker, on receipt of the finished head, had to ensure that the shaft was a good fit because this would affect the 'feel' of the club and its driving ability. Once a suitable shaft was cut and tapered to fit the socket, the clubmaker was careful to set the grain of the wood in the line of the shot which the club would make. That achieved he would begin shaping the shaft with sandpaper until the correct stiffness and whip was obtained. Furthermore, he had to think about the overall length of the shaft and what thickness would be achieved once the grip was added.

When the gutty ball was introduced, irons became very popular and there was a marked increase in the number produced. There was also a marked increase in the variety of iron clubs, so to cope with the demand some of the blacksmiths became cleekmakers only. They enlarged their workshops and took on more staff, adding apprentices to learn the art of making iron clubs. Additional tools and machines appeared including grinding wheels and polishers, while a special iron — Waverley Iron — was developed for the making of iron heads. This ever-increasing trend towards mechanization eventually led to the steam forge while each worker specialized in one facet of the operation as the process became a production line.

The process continued but in 1906 the American company Spalding opened a factory in London and introduced a new method of making iron heads known as drop-forging. This consisted of pouring molten steel into metal moulds and permitted large numbers of heads to be produced in a rapid space of time. The socket still had to be bored, but once that was done and the head polished on an emery wheel, you had your finished head and what's more, because all the heads were produced in a mould, they were all identical.

Today a set of irons progresses in numbers from one to nine or ten, but when irons were introduced each style had a name, such as track or rut irons, niblicks and mashies. As we saw with the wooden niblick, which was used for removing the ball from holes or ruts, so the rut iron was designed for the same task. The head was little bigger than the ball but it was invaluable for extracting the ball from small indentations or the like. The rut iron was also termed the rutter, track iron or rutting iron. They were often heavy, upright clubs with a lofted, concave face. Later these clubs were also used for approach shots but because the head was so small, the greatest accuracy was required.

The development of iron clubs

Young Tom Morris was a great and regular exponent of the use of iron clubs for approach shots and he was greatly responsible for the development of iron clubs. As soon as the qualities of the iron club were recognized, its development was rapid. Gradually different types of irons were introduced and all were graced with names far more descriptive and colourful than their modern counterparts. There were lofting irons, which were precisely that with their lofted and concaved blade which was thicker at the bottom than the top. They had strong, rigid shafts and superseded the baffing spoon.

There was the mashie, which is equivalent to today's 5-iron. It was a development of the lofting iron, but more lofted and with a deeper face while the upper and lower edges were almost parallel. It was used for pitching shots to the green and became universally popular after J.H. Taylor proved himself a master of the club when winning his first Open Championship in 1894. There were other forms of the mashie, like the driving mashie which had less loft than the cleek but retained the mashie length of head and depth of face. It was ideal for driving at 'long' short holes and for long approach shots to the green, something equivalent to today's 2- or 3-iron.

The mashie niblick had more loft than the mashie and was the forerunner of today's 7-iron. It also had a slightly deeper and longer face with a round toe and curved

Below: The basic materials for a hand-crafted club made to the customer's specifications. They include horn, which is fixed to the club head with hickory pegs, lead, which is poured in to weight the head and leather strips for the handle.

upper and lower edges. It was the introduction of this club that paved the way for such terms as 'socket' and 'shank' to become household words. The spade mashie was very similar to the mashie niblick, perhaps nearer our 6-iron, and was used for removing the ball from thick grassy lies.

Many of the clubmakers of the time introduced their own particular facets of clubs, mostly hybrids of the general style, but even then offset heads were not unusual. Today's modern sets of clubs have developed from those early implements apart perhaps from the sand wedge. Many credit American Gene Sarazen with its development in the late 1920s and early 1930s, when he soldered lead to the leading edge of a normal wedge to achieve the effect of the clubhead floating through sand instead of digging in. He may not have been the inventor, but he certainly enhanced its popularity.

Right: Irons with a cavity back design and heel and toe weighting. These irons are popular with handicap players as they help achieve height and the distribution of weight helps obtain accuracy with the shot.

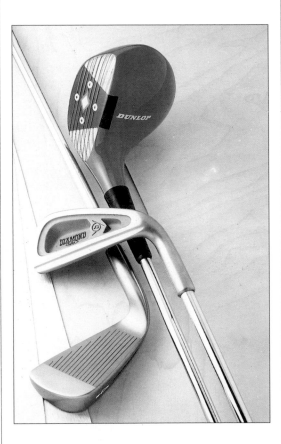

Putters and putting

While there have been many varied assortments of clubs down the centuries, the styles and shapes of putters have been incredible. Putting is a game within a game so it isn't difficult to understand why putters have become very personalized clubs to each player. Even the grip adopted for its use is different from those for the other clubs while many golfers pay particular attention to 'feel' with their putter and often remove their glove to improve this. Also the different materials used in the making of putters has been wide, and today you can buy a club made of steel, aluminium, plastic, glassfibre or wood.

Wood, of course, was the material for the early putters which were used for several different functions. Greens in the early days were nothing like today's finely cut lawns. They were rough patches of ground which often couldn't be distinguished from the fairway. The forerunners of today's clubs were not unlike the wooden-headed clubs of their day. Indeed, up to the early years of the 19th century there were three clubs recognized as putters: the driving putter, approach putter and putter. The driving putter has little to do with putting and was used to drive the ball low into the wind until it was replaced by iron clubs. The approach putter had a definite loft and was, as its name suggests, employed for approach shots where there were no hazards. The putter was not unlike the driver in shape but it had a shorter head with an upright lie and was somewhat heavier.

The wooden putters shaped like a driving wood were the first choice, and while iron and some aluminium putters were introduced, they didn't become popular until well into the era of the gutty ball. The early clubs were putting cleeks with a shallow face and less loft than a normal cleek. The shaft was shorter than the cleek and stiff. While the greens were still not flat, smooth surfaces, the lofted putter allowed the ball to be hit from doubtful lies while a certain amount of backspin could also be generated to stop the ball quickly. Gradually the cleeks were superseded by the more usual putter with deeper faces but they still had more loft than today's putters.

As the 19th century drew towards its close, an important invention credited to Willie Park jnr came about, namely the wry-necked putter. Its birth is somewhat shrouded in mystery and the story goes that his original putter fell under the wheels of a cart and became bent to that shape. More likely is that the shaft of his putter became warped so that the shaft was in front of the putter head. Whatever is the true version, this was a significant development.

The other deserving mention is the Schenectady, which was a centre-shafted putter introduced into Britain by the American Walter J. Travis and which helped him win the Amateur Championship at Sandwich in 1904. After that the Royal & Ancient banned centre-shafted putters as illegal which didn't endear them to the Americans. It was to be 50 years before the ban was lifted.

The types of wood used

Before moving off those early clubs, consideration should be given to the materials used in their construction. As previously stated, those materials were to be found naturally, but it should be remembered that the ball not only controlled the type of clubs but also the way they were made and what they were made of. To hit a comparatively soft feathery ball the timber had to be light in weight yet as hard as possible. The most widely used woods were hawthorn, apple and pear. Thorn was the most regular while apple tended to have small faults which could lead to a clubhead shattering.

With the arrival of the much harder gutty ball in the middle of the 19th century woods had to be sought to replace the more traditional types. Holly, hornbeam, dogwood and sometimes hickory were used, but the most popular by far was beech. But selection had to be right: too tight grained and it would be too heavy, too wide grained and it would prove too soft and liable to damage. However, another change came in the late part of the century when persimmon was discovered, while the gutty ball gave way to the rubber-cored. Persimmon proved perfect. It was hard, light and tough and ideal for use with a rubber-wound ball.

Hickory shafts

The earliest records suggest that hazel was the wood used as shafts with wooden clubs, but by the early part of the 19th century ash had taken over. This in turn was supplanted by hickory which, before the advent of steel shafts, is recalled as the finest possible material for shafts. Stories credit Russia as being the source of the first hickory to be used for shafts and its arrival in Britain came by accident as the wood was used as ballast in a ship. But this is not written down anywhere and is somewhat suspect. More likely the hickory came from America in the mid-19th century for other uses such as axe handles and pit props. Robert Forgan is believed to have been the first clubmaker to use hickory for shafts but the exact date is not chronicled. Its superiority over ash arose because hickory possessed a toughness yet a powerful springy quality without too much flexibility. These qualities were not in all hickory. A lot depended on where the wood came from and where exactly it was grown — at the top of a hill or in a valley. Most of the hickory came from Tennessee, but if it was cut from too near the top of the hill it was too brittle, while if it came from too far down it was too soft and didn't possess sufficient spring. Also hickory that was split with an axe along its grain proved to be better for shafts than hickory which has been sawn.

The experts could tell at a glance where a piece of hickory was grown, whether it faced the sun or was facing away from it or if it was grown high up the hill or lower towards the valley. Nevertheless, soon thousands of hickory shafts were being produced in America and shipped to Britain where the best clubmakers would round them off with scraper and sandpaper ready to fit them to a particular clubhead. But before such a selection was made, thought had to be given to the weight of the head and the use to which the club would be put. Often many shafts would be discarded before the right shape and weight of shaft was found suitable for fitting to a certain head.

Joining shafts to heads

The various ways of joining shafts to heads is worth considering, for many different ways were used down the years depending on the materials. Up to 1900 it was the scared or spliced joint. Scared is derived from 'scarf', which is an old joinery term meaning a straight glued joint. This spliced system seems to have been the accepted method of making a club for many years but in the 19th century many experiments were made to alter this type of joint. One combined the scare with a form of mortice and tenon but this was such an ingenious method that it required highly skilled craftsmen.

After 1900 the socket head was adopted from an original design by Anderson & Son of Edinburgh. Here the shaft is inserted through the head and wedged at the bottom, a comparatively easier task than making the scared join and neck but only possible when you could drill through the neck of the club. Andersons were the first to make clubs this way but soon others began making socket clubs. At first they pushed the shafts only part way into the head, not through to the sole, probably to avoid infringing the patent. Yet soon everyone was using the full socket when, ironically, Andersons had gone out of business. The socket method was a weaker fixing than the scare but with the softer ball it did not matter.

There were a few other joins but none that really lasted. One was a front scare, one a cricket bat type splice and another a proper splice. But the socket was a clear winner and remains to this day as the best joint for the task in hand.

Development of grips

At the other end of the club is the grip, which in the old days was made of leather and, in some of the earlier clubs, sheepskin. Later cowhide or horse was used. The early grips were thick and rough but this was partly so

Above: The wedge, a relatively new club in the golfer's armoury. Differing degrees of loft are available. For making short shots to the green, the wedge throws the ball high and imparts great backspin. They are useful for getting underneath the ball and digging it out from deep rough.

Above: A set of irons, from 3 on the left, to 9 on the right. The angle of the face, known as the loft, determines the length and height of the shot. Irons became popular with the gutty ball. In the old days many had romantic names, i.e. the 5-iron equivalent was a mashie, the 7-iron was a mashie-niblick.

that the club could be gripped in the palm of the hands rather than in the fingers. Another function was as a crude form of shock-absorber to lessen the jarring sensation when striking a gutty ball. Some grips were placed over rind, which were linen strips wound directly on to the wooden shaft. However, this tended to make the overall grip too thick and a few felt they resembled cricket bat handles instead of a slim and graceful play club.

There seems little doubt that leather made the best grips and even to this day leather grips, while in the minority against the rubber compounds, is regarded as the quality article, although it is more expensive and more difficult to keep in good shape. Grips, of course, came into their own when steel shafts became the norm. Steel shafts were in use in America around 1920 but they were not 'legalized' in Britain until 1929. The change was resisted here partly because it was felt that the steel shaft would propel the ball so much further that it would cost a fortune to extend the courses. Of course, the ball travelled little or no further, and when hickory began to go out of supply the change was forced. Few could argue that the change was not for the good with fewer breakages and a greater durability. Steel also made for another change in the way players swung the club, the swings becoming more upright, while the arrival of such great players as Walter Hagen, Bobby Jones, Henry Cotton and Ben Hogan led to a

completely new era of the game.

When Harry Vardon introduced his revolutionary new way of gripping the club, it was ideally suited to the move towards more upright clubs with slimmer grips, encouraging the hands to work as a complete unit. Also the stance narrowed and therefore the player stood more upright, a style portrayed by Jones. There is little doubt that he had one of the most graceful swings in the game and was one of the best exponents of hickory shafted clubs, which required a control of the torque or twisting action.

The arrival of steel shafts with a much smaller torque factor and less weight allowed the club and the back of the left hand to stay in plane during the swing, whereas with the earlier traditional swing with hickory clubs the cocking of the wrists went out of plane to counter the torque.

THE DEVELOPMENT OF THE BALL

It is not difficult to understand that the game of golf has progressed in direct consequence of the development of the ball. As with all such games, the ball is the focal point and as that has been gradually perfected so the rest of the equipment used to propel it has also improved and will go on improving. The one dictates the other, and while the early golf balls are a far cry from today's products of modern technology, the present day golfer probably knows as little about its production as did his predecessors.

It seems fair to assume that the first 'golf ball' was a small stone. It was almost certainly replaced by one made of wood, probably beech, then by a leather ball filled with wool, flock or feathers before rubber and the gutty came on the scene and more sophisticated methods produced composition gutty balls which were the forerunners of today's wound and two-piece balls. Not much is chronicled about wooden balls. Suffice to say that these do appear in paintings and illustrations of the 15th century and earlier, many from the Dutch school, which adds weight to claims that golf had part of its beginnings on the continent of Europe.

The feathery

However, we know a lot more about balls made of leather and feathers and their manufacture was a long, slow and expensive business. All were made by hand so not more than four or five could be produced by one man in a day. Tanned leather, either from cattle or horses, was cut into strips which were then softened by soaking in a solution of alum. The strips were stitched together then turned inside out, leaving just a small hole through which the feathers were stuffed. The feathers were usually from the breast of a goose, although chicken feathers were also used. The feathers were boiled to make them soft and workable and usually it took a top-hatful to fill each ball. Using a kind of awl called a brogue, the ballmaker would poke the feathers into the leather case until it was packed tight. Then the small hole would be sewn up and the feathery was complete.

As all the components had been soaked there was a drying process during which the feathers expanded and the leather shrank. This dual pressure of an expanding core and a shrinking cover produced a hard ball. Because the manufacturing process was rudimentary, the finished articles were not totally the same size from ball to ball despite the use of calipers. Yet they were still remarkably uniform, although there was no set size for a ball laid down until well into the 20th century. Once the ball had dried and was hard a form of waterproofing by rubbing with oil was carried out while scouring with chalk helped identification. Yet despite this, featheries were susceptible to weather conditions, growing heavier when it was wet while the stitching was inclined to break.

Because of the slow process and various unfortunate side-effects, the feathery was not cheap to buy. Also, the ballmaker's health wasn't enhanced by the inhalation of particles of feather causing asthma and lung disease. Yet despite all this the feathery lasted several hundred years, and making it would appear to have been a more remunerative and steadier job than that of the clubmaker. It certainly involved a long apprenticeship of around four years.

As with the early clubs, some ballmakers adopted the process of stamping their names on balls and the aforementioned Douglas Gourlay was one of the first with simply the word 'GOURLAY'. Over at St Andrews Allan Robertson, one of the many members of the Robertson family engaged in making feathery golf balls, stamped his golf balls 'ALLAN'.

The gutta-percha ball

The fate of the feathery was indeed sealed midway through the 19th century with the introduction of the ball made of gutta-percha from Malaya. Gutta-percha, literally translated from the Malayan, means 'tree sap' and it was indeed an early form of rubber. It was the milky juice from the gutta-percha tree but it was not collected, as other forms of obtaining rubber latex from trees, by simply making an incision — the gutta-percha trees were cut down, the bark stripped off and the liquid collected. This was somewhat counter-productive because not only did each tree produce less than 30 lb (13½ kg), but it was often contaminated, while huge forests were felled just to obtain a small amount.

The man generally credited with introducing gutta-percha to the Western world was a surgeon, William Montgomerie, who noticed on his travels to Malaya for the East India Company that the handles of knives, daggers and hoes were made of a hard substance which could be softened by immersion in hot water. Not that there was an immediate connection with golf but within three years the new material was in golfers' hands. Of course, people had been experimenting with

Below: A selection of old balls. The indentations on a golf ball improve its flight, a phenomenon originally discovered by chance. On the left is a hand-hammered gutta-percha ball. Later the indentations were mesh-marked in an iron press mould, as shown at the top. Such balls are shown at the bottom. On the right are two featheries. The seams on the leather improved the flight.

various forms of rubber from around the start of the 19th century, but none had come up with a satisfactory ball before 1848 when the first gutta appeared. There is documentary evidence that they were used at Blackheath and at Musselburgh that year, although the common denominator in both cases seems to have been Admiral Maitland Dougal, who played at both venues, although he had obtained the balls in London.

However, the arrival of the gutta-percha ball was a bitter blow to those making featheries. The ballmakers obviously feared for their future and Allan Robertson, the last of six generations of St Andrews ballmakers, did everything he could to fight the newcomer. First he derided its qualities, which at the time were certainly suspect, then he is said to have bought up every gutta-percha ball he could find and burned it. He also made Tom Morris, then in his employ having been apprenticed to him as a ballmaker, swear not to use the new ball. When Robertson learned Morris had used it a bitter row ensued and Morris departed the company.

The diehards were fighting a lost cause, although the end wasn't as clear cut as many might think now. The feathery didn't suffer an immediate death, more a slow lingering one as more and more golfers switched to the new ball. In fact, although the gutta-percha ball arrived in 1848, the feathery was still reported as being used as late as 1865. However, if there was some suspicion over the gutta-percha ball it was soon forgotten when golfers realized what they had to pay for it. It was certainly a boon to the golfer's pocket, being sold for less than half the price of the feathery.

But the newcomers' early years were not all plain sailing. At first the gutta-percha contained impurities which made it hard to bind. However, this was only a temporary problem and soon many of the traditional ballmakers were switching to the new material in ever-increasing numbers. At first the gutta-percha arrived in sheet form, was cut into pieces and, after being softened in hot water, was drawn out into ribbons, wound into a ball and pressed by hand until smooth. It was then heated again and pressed until it was as solid as possible. Although there were no moulds until later, the ballmakers could achieve a high degree of roundness before the balls were dropped into cold water to harden. Even then they had to be constantly moved because any part that broke the surface tended to swell out of shape. Balls were made in this fashion for several years but the invention of a smooth iron mould was a great advance.

It was found that the early gutta-percha ball tended not to travel through the air as well as the feathery, especially when new and smooth. However, a distinct improvement came when the ball became older and collected a few scuffs and grazes. At first, players were alarmed at these marks and were informed that the balls could be restored to their original smooth condition by putting them into warm water and rolling out the marks. However, once it was discovered that an uneven surface on a ball struck with backspin will result in setting up a higher pressure beneath and therefore lift it into the air, it became the practice for golfers to hack new balls until the surface was scored.

Soon the ballmakers were carrying out this function, the balls being placed into special moulds then hand-hammered to a regular pattern. It was Robert Forgan of St Andrews who claimed to be the first to hand-hammer patterns on balls but soon most ballmakers were following suit. The finest of the early gutta balls came from Forgan, Old Tom Morris and the Auchterlonies, while brand names began to appear from this trio, such as 'Henley', 'Al Black', 'Acleva' and 'Agrippa'.

While the making of the new balls was centred mostly in Scotland, it seems that Blackheath played a not insignificant part. Many members of the club were merchants in the City of London and therefore would have been well aware of the qualities of gutta-percha and of its importation. So the material would have been available to them, while nearby was the rubber works of S.W. Silver. In 1852 the company moved across the Thames to found Silvertown, and 30 years later produced the Silvertown range of balls which were followed by the famous Silver King. The Silvertown balls also carried printed on the box 'thoroughly seasoned'. This meant they had been left to mature, something peculiar to gutta and gutty composition balls, but why this procedure was adopted is unclear. One reason may have been connected with the painting, because the early gutta-percha balls didn't take paint well and some balls were sold unpainted. Another reason may have been to enable the balls to lose any water content. Possibly it was a combination of both. The painting also tended to fill the hand-hammered markings. It was to be many years before a suitable paint was developed or a white material was found for the cover.

The introduction of the gutta ball made it possible for anyone who could obtain the raw material to make their own. Quite a do-it-yourself operation grew up, and by 1880 a 'Home Golf Ball Kit' could be bought, consisting of a mould, some paint and a drying rack, although painting was a problem.

The gutty composition ball

Around 1870 machined golf balls began to appear and about the same time the gutty ball, a composition of gutta-percha and other components such as ground cork, leather, metal filings and an adhesive liquid, came on the market. A patent, the first ever specifically for a golf ball, was taken out by Captain Duncan Stewart RN of St Andrews.

Captain Stewart took out his patent in

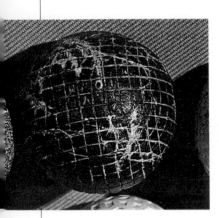

Above: A gutta-percha ball manufactured by the Silvertown Rubber Co. around 1895. The gutty was soon to be replaced by the Haskell ball.

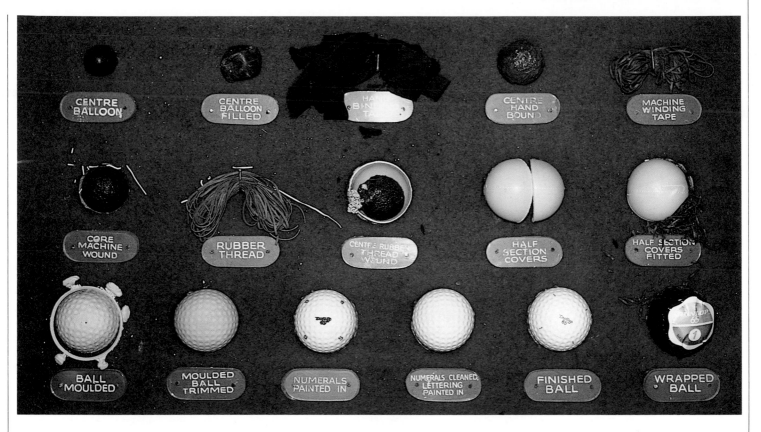

Above: A display at the R & A Museum at St Andrews showing the stages in the manufacture of a modern golf ball. From top left to bottom right the materials and stages are labelled: (top row) centre balloon; centre balloon filled; hand binding tape; centre hand bound; machine winding tape; (centre row) core machine wound; rubber thread; centre rubber thread wound; half section covers; half section covers fitted; (bottom row) ball moulded; moulded ball trimmed; numerals painted in; numerals cleaned, lettering painted in; finished ball; wrapped ball.

1876, yet five years earlier he had begun making a ball using the method of winding rubber thread then enclosing it in a cover of gutta-percha. It was on such a principle that the world-beating Haskell ball, produced some 30 years later, was based.

A year after Stewart's patent, another was taken out by William Currie of the Caledonian Rubber Works in Edinburgh, again for a composite ball which was moulded and vulcanized. This time canvas was laid inside the mould which stuck to the surface of the ball but, when later removed, left an indent or moulding. The ball was named the 'Eclipse'. An advertisement stated that these balls were almost indestructible, they couldn't be hacked or marked, they flew beautifully, retained their shape and could be driven further than the gutta-percha ball which they had superseded. Also, they ran quite true on the putting green. The Eclipse was quite successful for a number of years but by 1887 the Caledonian Rubber Works were experiencing trouble over manufacture.

The following year, 1888, saw the India Rubber Gutta-Percha & Telegraph Works Co Ltd, formerly S.W. Silver of Woolwich and now the Silvertown company, produce another theme on the composite ball which was much harder than anything before produced. It bore the name 'Silvertown No 4' and was to prove the forerunner of a whole range of balls, including the 'Silver King'. This extra hardness added weight to the increasing changes in the design of wooden clubs. The old long-nosed wooden clubs were on the way out while the effect of continuous striking of the gutty ball led to the faces of the other wooden clubs being protected and

strengthened by inserts of leather or vulcanite.

That extra hardness in the manufacture of balls was achieved by vulcanizing them in a tank of molten sulphur. But care had to be taken, for if a ball was left too long it could become brittle and tended to shatter on being hit. If such a thing happened then the player was allowed to put down another ball at the point where the largest piece of the shattered ball lay.

The number of ball patents taken out became something of a deluge in the 1890s. Among them were two from famous Scottish golfer Willie Park, for a diamond mesh ball in 1890, and six years later for the 'Royal', a ball with flat facings, designed to slow it up on the greens. Others were, in 1892, for the rifle mesh, designed so that the ball would fly like a projectile from a gun, and in 1895 for a gutta-percha ball with metal discs embedded in it. There was also an increase in the number of rubber manufacturers turning to making golf balls while the sale of balls were by this time being offered through golf professionals as well as sports equipment shops.

The Haskell ball

At the turn of the century a ball was introduced which was to have a stimulating effect on golf. Over in the United States, one Coburn Haskell dabbled in the bicycle-manufacturing business among other things before meeting Bertram Work of the Goodrich rubber plant at Akron, Ohio, who supplied him with cycle tyres. Together they came up with the idea of winding elastic thread around a core and covering it with gutta-percha. This was in 1898. At first the balls were wound by hand but this wasn't a success. Only when the process was mechanized using an inner core on which to wind the rubber was a modern type of ball produced. Each ball contained hundreds of feet of elastic. A drawback in those early days was that the outside covers were quite easily cut and the elastic thread laid bare. However, the new ball was a great advance.

The Haskell ball was found to fly some 20 to 30 yards (25 m approx) further than the earlier composite balls yet, like most new trends, it was treated with some suspicion by the professionals of the day. It failed to become an overnight success, especially in top-class golf where it had its disadvantages, being harder to control on and around the greens. In the United States it achieved limited success in 1900 and when it arrived in Britain a year later, having by then become known as the 'Bounding Billy', it was considered to confer an unfair advantage to the player using it in relation to someone who did not. However, in 1902 Sandy Herd practised at Hoylake for the Open Championship with one and was so impressed that he used it in the Championship itself, and won by one stroke from Harry Vardon and James Braid.

That single success, more than anything else, gave the Haskell ball the green light as far as Britain was concerned and even if, at the end, the ball had worn so much that the rubber threads were showing — Herd having played all four rounds with it — it was a great advertisement. Of course, these balls were not cheap and they were still prone to easy damage, cracking open if they were topped and thereby being unfit for play. Yet players were willing to take a chance and to pay anything up to £1.50 (about $2.50), a fortune at the time, to get their hands on one.

The top professionals of the day were divided in their opinions, but whenever the Haskell was pitted against the gutty in competition the newcomer usually came out on top. Such was the case in the final of the 1904 Amateur Championship, when Walter Travis of America, using the Haskell, beat Britain's longer hitter, Ted Blackwell, who stuck with the gutty. A couple of years later the Goodrich Company produced the Haskell 'Pneumatic' ball, composed of a rubber shell into which air was compressed. However, it was not a success because it required considerable hitting power while it was prone to deflate or even explode in flight or in a player's bag. In 1907 the Goodrich people tried something else, an improvement on the Pneumatic called the 'Silk Pneumatic' because silk strands were woven into the cover for added strength. The idea was 'stolen' from the manufacturing process used for motor tyres, but again it didn't prove a winner. The British were also experimenting with various systems but with little success.

As the first decade of the 20th century passed there was still a considerable school of support for the gutty and for its retention for championships and other major events. But in 1914 a contest, promoted by the magazine *Golf Illustrated*, was staged at Sandy Lodge Golf Club near London to decide once and for all which ball was best. Vardon, Braid and Taylor, the Great Triumvirate, together with George Duncan played a four-ball match using the two different balls, turn and turn about. The previous day a long driving contest had been held and, as expected, the Haskell won. Then, in the match, although all four men played brilliantly with the gutty, the big difference was length which had already been confirmed.

Although the Haskell or rubber-based ball had clearly come to stay there was always room for improvements and these will, no doubt, be an ever-present feature of the golf ball business. One of the earlier improvements concerned the toughness of the cover, an area which deserved the greatest attention because one mishit with an iron club could cut through the cover and thereby render the ball useless for further play. That, of course, meant these balls were expensive for an often short life. The composition of covers has been the subject of many experiments over the years, but it seemed little could prevent cutting if a ball was hacked with an iron club. Only in recent times have materials been developed giving greater insurance against cuts, or 'smiles' as golfers have grown accustomed to nicknaming them.

The advent of Surlyn, a durable cover for the average player, led to a longer life for the golf ball which, fortunately, was in proportion to the escalation in cost. However, Surlyn did not find complete favour with the better players, who preferred the balata cover for better control and 'feel' in their shotmaking. The other recent advance in terms of golf ball design and construction has been the two-piece solid ball. This has a hard, resilient core and a tough synthetic cover and has been popular, providing distance and durability.

The size and weight of the ball

There was a time when there was no limit to the size or weight of the golf ball. This freedom of choice led to many experiments with small, heavy balls as well as 'floaters' of various sizes and it was not unusual for a player to use different types of balls in a single round dependent on conditions. But that was not always a sound policy because if the right result was not obtained then there was always the feeling that the other ball should have been used.

All this became a thing of the past when the golf ball was standardized. This came in 1921 when a ball of not less than 1.62 inches (41.15 mm) and not more than 1.62 ounces (45.91 g) in weight was agreed upon, the equality of those two figures being coincidental. There was a certain amount of objection but it wasn't very serious and it meant that all players could be judged on a similar level. It also led to a greater standardization in play, with everyone learning to master the

Left: The golf ball from the feathery at the top to today's high-tec product. The Dunlop 65 is probably the best-known, as the ball with which Henry Cotton made his famous Open Championship score in 1934.

same type of ball, albeit not the same make.

Before the standardization there were also experiments with dimple markings on the surface of balls. As the earlier players found, surface markings meant greater aerodynamics. After the early method of scoring the cover, the trend was towards the bramble pattern, where the surface of the ball resembled a blackberry or a raspberry. This in turn led to the reverse pattern with a number of shallow cavities, usually circular in shape, covering the surface. The idea spread quickly to many manufacturers and is the design principle which has endured.

Modern balls

By the turn of the century golf ball manufacture had become a highly competitive market with the larger companies prepared to make not only their own brand of balls but to diversify their operations by making balls for others and stamping their names on them. Another move saw the point of sale of golf balls less monopolized by the club professional, with stocks being held by sports shops and major stores. Dunlop, a name that was to become synonymous with golf balls as well as sports equipment in general down the

years, entered the golf ball field in 1908. After the First World War Dunlop really came to the fore with its famous 'Maxfli', which is a name still appearing on today's modern ball. This period was a time of feverish activity on the golf ball front, with many makers producing a wide range of balls. Unfortunately, many of those companies have disappeared or been swallowed up by the bigger ones, so that today's manufacturers, while producing a much superior quality of ball, are less numerous than their predecessors.

Although there is a great deal of uniformity in modern golf ball design, for many years the sport was faced with the absurd situation of having two different sizes of ball in operation. This was because the Americans adopted the larger 1.68 inch (42.67 mm) ball because the smaller, British ball tended to sit deep in the American type of grass. By switching to the larger ball, which still weighed 1.62 ounces (45.91 g) and so conformed to the rules, the Americans advanced their game so much that they commanded the golfing stage for decades. It is generally agreed that the 1.68 ball was more difficult to play particularly in windy conditions, but once mastered it produced much more skilful players, a fact that has been proved beyond doubt in Britain and Europe.

However, the British were reluctant to switch from the 1.62 and for many years it was obligatory to play the small ball in major competitions and championships. But gradually these barriers came down. Players were allowed to play whichever ball they preferred, and as time went by more and more began to see the benefits of the 1.68. Slowly more and more manufacturers in Britain stepped up their production of the bigger ball as demand grew until in 1960 at Wentworth the first big-ball tournament took place. There was still a certain amount of opposition in various areas but once the professionals decreed it was for them, the 1.68 was on its way to becoming the universal ball. There is no doubt that British players were at a disadvantage when playing against the Americans, whose game had been honed to a fine degree on the bigger ball. Yet it wasn't until 1968 that it became the tournament ball in Europe and it took another six years before the 1.68 became compulsory in the Open Championship, the title having gone across

the Atlantic many times before then as the Americans proved their mastery. By the 1980s many amateur players had become convinced the bigger ball was also for them and after the 1.68 became compulsory for the British Amateur Championship also, many national, county and club competitions followed suit.

Over the period when the two balls were in tandem, many far-sighted people were calling for the switch in Britain in order that home players could match their American cousins instead of being also-rans whenever the two clashed. How right they were, and although it has been a long process, that gap has been narrowed if not closed completely and today the Americans no longer command a monopoly of any tournament wherever it is played. Many people took a lot of convincing but if they were still in any doubt about the wisdom of switching to the 1.68 ball then it came with home victories in the Open Championship in 1985 and 1987 (the first since 1969) as well as Europe's magnificent triumph in the 1985 Ryder Cup at the Belfry.

GOLFING DRESS

Today's natty fashions of the fairways are a far cry from the cumbersome costumes of the players of the early 19th century. In fact, they looked so cumbersome and restricting that it is difficult to imagine anyone swinging a golf club dressed in such a style.

Nevertheless play they did and while little study has been made of golfing dress it is a subject that deserves close examination. In the early days there were no special clothes for playing golf as there are today. Therefore many different styles could be seen, although as from early days golf was a rich man's game, the players were from the upper classes and therefore mostly well attired. The gentlemen players usually wore tall silk hats, swallowtail coats of many colours and tight trousers. These can often be seen in paintings with the spectators similarly attired, so that the players can only be identified by the clubs they are holding.

Shoes were elegant and probably didn't have studs in the soles so keeping a foothold could not have been easy. It would have been much easier for the working man whose boots would have had tacks or hobnails in the soles and therefore would have afforded him a much better grip. This would have given him a distinct advantage over his more well-to-do neighbour. Otherwise his dress was strictly workaday — a rough shirt, baggy corduroy trousers with braces or tied with string, and a cap or woollen hat. This was the style for the greater part of the 19th century.

When it came to formal occasions, however, the dress was red coats, white silk trousers and large hats. The red dress coat

*Below: The first Ladies'
Amateur Champion — and
a real lady at that, Lady
Margaret Scott, with the
trophy she won at St Andrews
in 1893. The long skirt was
probably her biggest handicap,
especially in the wind, but
this standard dress was
comparatively streamlined
compared to 20 years earlier.*

has passed the test of time, for today it is still the formal attire at certain golf club occasions and county functions. The red jacket performed a useful task back in the early part of the last century when many players dressed that way in order to signify to others using common land that they were striking a golf ball. This again has lasted to the present day in certain parts of Britain where golfers always play in red, albeit a sweater, to show they are playing golf.

Towards the middle of the 19th century, with the advent of the gutty ball, and more leisure time, many more of the working class took up the game so on-course dress became even more varied. Knee-breeches with stockings and a jacket tailored for freedom around the shoulders were introduced while others wore ordinary suits with bowler hats. About this time tailors were starting to become conscious of fashions for golf but it was still a long way from what we know today. Headwear included the Scottish Tam o'Shanter which was to spread south of the Border in ever-greater numbers, but caddies still dressed as the lowest of the low, often with nothing on their feet.

Towards the turn of the century the knickerbocker suit and tweed hat became the vogue for men, and Harry Vardon became the first professional to wear such a style for golf. These were the forerunners of the 'plus fours' which became the style early in the 20th century and which in many parts have lasted to the present day. Still the dress looked a little cumbersome, particularly as jackets continued to be worn together with a shirt and tie. This was still the style well into the 1920s and the jacket only gave way to the sweater towards the end of that decade. But ties continued to be worn for playing golf of the highest order. In fact, that great South African Bobby Locke still played in a tie up to his death in 1987.

Since the Second World War dress for golf has seen dramatic changes. It was the Americans such as Walter Hagen and Gene Sarazen before the war and Arnold Palmer and Doug Sanders after it who struck a blow for colour and the modern style, since when the game has been transformed as far as fashion is concerned. Today it is a multi-million pound industry.

When ladies' golf began in earnest around the 1870s the dress consisted of a long-skirted gown with a bustle. Swinging a golf club was virtually impossible, but at that time ladies' golf was almost entirely restricted to putting. Ladies also wore a bonnet which must have been a real handicap on windy days. It was against the social decorum of the day for ladies to swing a club above shoulder height so it was all quite genteel. However, 20 years later, and with social attitudes a little more relaxed, ladies' costumes still required a long skirt over buttoned-up boots, a blouse with leg o'mutton sleeves and a straw boater. The

full skirt could prove a problem in the wind until later an elastic garter was slipped around at knee level as a form of control. On wet days the skirt would be lifted just to clear the grass, but otherwise a shapely ankle was not to be seen.

After the turn of the century ankles were definitely in. Skirts were short enough to give a glimpse of that part of a lady's anatomy while shoes had replaced the laced boots. The complete outfit was taking on a decidedly tailored look with a full skirt providing sufficient room for a wide stance, while the jacket also allowed a free swing. The rest of the ensemble consisted of a white blouse with collar and box tie plus a wide-brimmed hat.

Gradually, over the years, women's golfing dress has become even more emancipated. Soon the jacket was discarded while the skirts afforded a more generous view of the ankle, although these were often under a pair of neat spats. The hat had become optional but the whole outfit before the First World War remained extremely cumbersome compared to today's fashions. Afterwards skirts shortened to just below the knee while a jumper or cardigan was worn over a blouse. There was still a hat but by now a cloche or bell-shape style. This fashion remained the same for some time, although the beret was the vogue in the 1930s.

It wasn't until after the Second World War that women's fashions, with a greater accent on colour, grew closer to the masculine style. Trousers were adopted by some and as the years have gone by shorts and culottes have been added to the fashion so that any such style can now be seen on the fairways of the world.

Above: Top-heavy hats and restricting jackets were the order of the day at the Troon Ladies' Open in 1904. These are the four semi-finalists. The winner was Lottie Dod, also the youngest ever winner of the Wimbledon tennis title, and an Olympic silver medallist at archery.

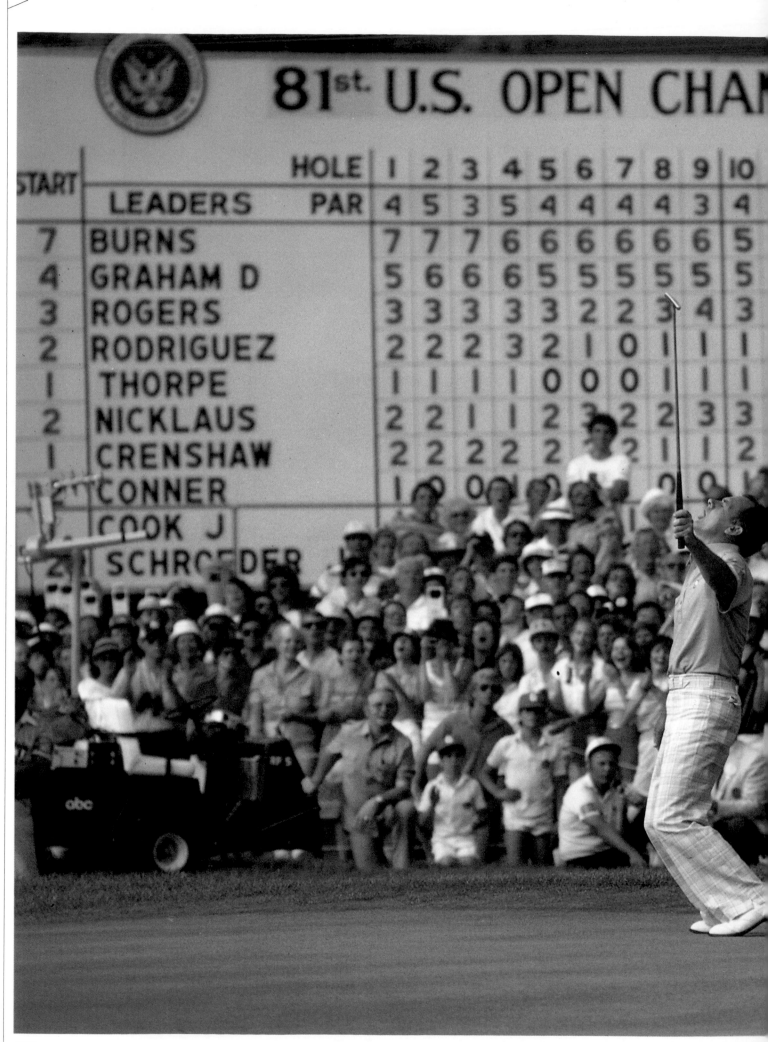

The Major Records

The question as to who won what, where and when often creates heated discussion among golfers. These differences are thoroughly resolved in this section by a comprehensive listing of winners, venues and scores of all the major championships, tournaments and international matches. A careful study of these records is recommended for any golfer who wishes to increase his or her knowledge of the game and its competitive history.

Left: David Graham of Australia frustrated at a putt which did not drop at the last hole of the US Open at Merion in 1981. The leader board shows he has shots to spare, however, and he won the title.

THE OPEN CHAMPIONSHIP
(Players from Great Britain or Ireland unless otherwise stated. *denotes an amateur)

YEAR	VENUE	WINNER	SCORE
1860	Prestwick	Willie Park	174
1861	Prestwick	Tom Morris Snr	163
1862	Prestwick	Tom Morris Snr	163
1863	Prestwick	Willie Park	168
1864	Prestwick	Tom Morris Snr	167
1865	Prestwick	Andrew Strath	162
1866	Prestwick	Willie Park	169
1867	Prestwick	Tom Morris Snr	170
1868	Prestwick	Tom Morris Jnr	157
1869	Prestwick	Tom Morris Jnr	154
1870	Prestwick	Tom Morris Jnr	149
1871	No competition		
1872	Prestwick	Tom Morris Jnr	166
1873	St Andrews	Tom Kidd	179
1874	Musselburgh	Mungo Park	159
1875	Prestwick	Willie Park	166
1876	St Andrews	Bob Martin	176
1877	Musselburgh	Jamie Anderson	160
1878	Prestwick	Jamie Anderson	157
1879	St Andrews	Jamie Anderson	169
1880	Musselburgh	Bob Ferguson	162
1881	Prestwick	Bob Ferguson	170
1882	St Andrews	Bob Ferguson	171
1883	Musselburgh	Willie Fernie	159
1884	Prestwick	Jack Simpson	160
1885	St Andrews	Bob Martin	171
1886	Musselburgh	David Brown	157
1887	Prestwick	Willie Park Jnr	161
1888	St Andrews	Jack Burns	171
1889	Musselburgh	Willie Park Jnr *(play-off with Andrew Kirkaldy)*	155
1890	Prestwick	*John Ball	164
1891	St Andrews	Hugh Kirkaldy	166
1892	Muirfield	*Harold Hilton *(championship extended to 72 holes)*	305
1893	Prestwick	Willie Auchterlonie	322
1894	Sandwich	J.H. Taylor	326
1895	St Andrews	J.H. Taylor	322
1896	Muirfield	Harry Vardon *(play-off with J.H. Taylor)*	316
1897	Hoylake	*Harold Hilton	314
1898	Prestwick	Harry Vardon	307
1899	Sandwich	Harry Vardon	310
1900	St Andrews	J.H. Taylor	309
1901	Muirfield	James Braid	309
1902	Hoylake	Alex Herd	307
1903	Prestwick	Harry Vardon	300
1904	Sandwich	Jack White	296
1905	St Andrews	James Braid	318
1906	Muirfield	James Braid	300
1907	Hoylake	Arnaud Massy *(France)*	312
1908	Prestwick	James Braid	291
1909	Deal	J.H. Taylor	295
1910	St Andrews	James Braid	299
1911	Sandwich	Harry Vardon *(play-off with Arnaud Massy)*	303
1912	Muirfield	Ted Ray	295
1913	Hoylake	J.H. Taylor	304
1914	Prestwick	Harry Vardon	306
1915-19	No competition		
1920	Deal	George Duncan	303

YEAR	VENUE	WINNER	SCORE
1921	St Andrews	Jock Hutchison *(US)* *(play-off with Roger Wethered)*	296
1922	Sandwich	Walter Hagen *(US)*	300
1923	Troon	Arthur Havers	295
1924	Hoylake	Walter Hagen *(US)*	301
1925	Prestwick	Jim Barnes *(US)*	300
1926	Royal Lytham	*Bobby Jones Jnr *(US)*	291
1927	St Andrews	*Bobby Jones Jnr *(US)*	285
1928	Sandwich	Walter Hagen *(US)*	292
1929	Muirfield	Walter Hagen *(US)*	292
1930	Hoylake	*Bobby Jones Jnr *(US)*	291
1931	Carnoustie	Tommy Armour *(US)*	296
1932	Prince's	Gene Sarazen *(US)*	283
1933	St Andrews	Densmore Shute *(US)* *(play-off with Craig Wood)*	292
1934	Sandwich	Henry Cotton	283
1935	Muirfield	Alf Perry	283
1936	Hoylake	Alf Padgham	287
1937	Carnoustie	Henry Cotton	290
1938	Sandwich	Reg Whitcombe	295
1939	St Andrews	Dick Burton	290
1940-45	No competition		
1946	St Andrews	Sam Snead *(US)*	290
1947	Hoylake	Fred Daly	293
1948	Muirfield	Henry Cotton	284
1949	Sandwich	Bobby Locke *(Sth Africa)* *(play-off with Harry Bradshaw)*	283
1950	Troon	Bobby Locke *(Sth Africa)*	279
1951	Royal Portrush	Max Faulkner	285
1952	Royal Lytham	Bobby Locke *(Sth Africa)*	287
1953	Carnoustie	Ben Hogan *(US)*	282
1954	Royal Birkdale	Peter Thomson *(Australia)*	283
1955	St Andrews	Peter Thomson *(Australia)*	281
1956	Hoylake	Peter Thomson *(Australia)*	286
1957	St Andrews	Bobby Locke *(Sth Africa)*	279
1958	Royal Lytham	Peter Thomson *(Australia)* *(play-off with David Thomas)*	278
1959	Muirfield	Gary Player *(Sth Africa)*	284
1960	St Andrews	Kel Nagle *(Australia)*	278
1961	Royal Birkdale	Arnold Palmer *(US)*	284
1962	Troon	Arnold Palmer *(US)*	276
1963	Royal Lytham	Bob Charles *(New Zealand)* *(play-off with Phil Rodgers)*	277
1964	St Andrews	Tony Lema *(US)*	279
1965	Royal Birkdale	Peter Thomson *(Australia)*	285
1966	Muirfield	Jack Nicklaus *(US)*	282
1967	Hoylake	Roberto de Vicenzo *(Argentina)*	278
1968	Carnoustie	Gary Player *(Sth Africa)*	289
1969	Royal Lytham	Tony Jacklin	280
1970	St Andrews	Jack Nicklaus *(US)* *(play-off with Doug Sanders)*	283
1971	Royal Birkdale	Lee Trevino *(US)*	278
1972	Muirfield	Lee Trevino *(US)*	278
1973	Troon	Tom Weiskopf *(US)*	276
1974	Royal Lytham	Gary Player *(Sth Africa)*	282

YEAR	VENUE	WINNER	SCORE
1975	Carnoustie	Tom Watson *(US) (play-off with Jack Newton)*	279
1976	Royal Birkdale	Johnny Miller *(US)*	279
1977	Turnberry	Tom Watson *(US)*	268
1978	St Andrews	Jack Nicklaus *(US)*	281
1979	Royal Lytham	Severiano Ballesteros *(Spain)*	283
1980	Muirfield	Tom Watson *(US)*	271
1981	Sandwich	Bill Rogers *(US)*	276
1982	Royal Troon	Tom Watson *(US)*	284
1983	Royal Birkdale	Tom Watson *(US)*	275

YEAR	VENUE	WINNER	SCORE
1984	St Andrews	Severiano Ballesteros *(Spain)*	276
1985	Sandwich	Sandy Lyle	282
1986	Turnberry	Greg Norman *(Australia)*	280
1987	Muirfield	Nick Faldo	279

Above: *One of the most exciting Open Championships of recent years was that at Turnberry in 1977 when Jack Nicklaus and Tom Watson, seen together on the tee , drew away from the rest of the field. Watson won by a single stroke.*

UNITED STATES OPEN
(Players from USA unless otherwise stated. *denotes an amateur)

YEAR	VENUE	WINNER	SCORE	YEAR	VENUE	WINNER	SCORE
1895	Newport, RI	Horace Rawlins	173	1906	Onwentsia, Ill	Alex Smith	295
1896	Shinnecock Hills, NY	James Foulis	152	1907	Philadelphia, Pa	Alec Ross	302
1897	Chicago, Ill	Joe Lloyd	162	1908	Myopia Hunt Club, Mass	Fred McLeod (play-off with Willie Smith)	322
1898	Myopia Hunt Club, Mass	Fred Herd (championship extended to 72 holes)	328	1909	Englewood, NJ	George Sargent	290
1899	Baltimore, Md	Willie Smith	315	1910	Philadelphia, Pa	Alex Smith (play-off with John McDermott and Macdonald Smith)	298
1900	Chicago, Ill	Harry Vardon (GB)	313				
1901	Myopia Hunt Club, Mass	Willie Anderson	331	1911	Chicago, Ill	John McDermott (play-off with Mike Brady and George Simpson)	307
1902	Garden City, NY	Laurie Auchterlonie (GB)	307	1912	Buffalo, NY	John McDermott	294
1903	Baltusrol, NJ	Willie Anderson (play-off with David Brown)	307	1913	Brookline, Mass	*Francis Ouimet (play-off with Harry Vardon and Ted Ray)	304
1904	Glen View, Ill	Willie Anderson	303				
1905	Myopia Hunt Club, Mass	Willie Anderson	314	1914	Midlothian, Ill	Walter Hagen	290

Above: Tom Watson in a purple patch in 1982, when he won the Open Championships of Great Britain and the USA. Here he celebrates a shot at the 17th at Pebble Beach on his way to the US title.

YEAR	VENUE	WINNER	SCORE	YEAR	VENUE	WINNER	SCORE
1915	Baltusrol, NJ	*Jerome Travers	297	1957	Inverness, Ohio	Dick Mayer *(play-off with Cary Middlecoff)*	282
1916	Minikahda, Minn	*Charles Evans	286	1958	Southern Hills, Okla	Tommy Bolt	283
1917-18	No competition			1959	Winged Foot, NY	Billy Casper	282
1919	Brae Burn, Mass	Walter Hagen *(play-off with Mike Brady)*	301	1960	Cherry Hills, Colo	Arnold Palmer	280
1920	Inverness, Ohio	Ted Ray *(GB)*	295	1961	Oakland Hills, Mich	Gene Littler	281
1921	Columbia, Md	Jim Barnes	289	1962	Oakmont, Pa	Jack Nicklaus *(play-off with Arnold Palmer)*	283
1922	Skokie, Ill	Gene Sarazen	288	1963	Brookline, Mass	Julius Boros *(play-off with Jacky Cupit and Arnold Palmer)*	293
1923	Inwood, NY	*Bobby Jones *(play-off with Bobby Cruikshank)*	296	1964	Congressional, Wash, DC	Ken Venturi	278
1924	Oakland Hills, Mich	Cyril Walker	297	1965	Bellerive, Miss	Gary Player *(Sth Africa) (play-off with Kel Nagle)*	282
1925	Worcester, Mass	Willie Macfarlane *(play-off with *Bobby Jones)*	291	1966	Olympic, Cal	Billy Casper *(play-off with Arnold Palmer)*	278
1926	Scioto, Ohio	*Bobby Jones	293	1967	Baltusrol, NJ	Jack Nicklaus	275
1927	Oakmont, Pa	Tommy Armour *(play-off with Harry Cooper)*	301	1968	Oak Hill, NY	Lee Trevino	275
1928	Olympia Fields, Ill	Johnny Farrell *(play-off with *Bobby Jones)*	294	1969	Champions, Tex	Orville Moody	281
1929	Winged Foot, NY	*Bobby Jones *(play-off with Al Espinosa)*	294	1970	Hazeltine, Minn	Tony Jacklin *(GB)*	281
1930	Interlachen, Minn	*Bobby Jones	287	1971	Merion, Pa	Lee Trevino *(play-off with Jack Nicklaus)*	280
1931	Inverness, Ohio	Billy Burke *(play-off with George von Elm)*	292	1972	Pebble Beach, Cal	Jack Nicklaus	290
1932	Fresh Meadow, NY	Gene Sarazen	286	1973	Oakmont, Pa	Johnny Miller	279
1933	North Shore, Ill	*Johnny Goodman	287	1974	Winged Foot, NY	Hale Irwin	287
1934	Merion, Pa	Olin Dutra	293	1975	Medinah, Ill	Lou Graham *(play-off with John Mahaffey)*	287
1935	Oakmont, Pa	Sam Parks Jnr	299	1976	Atlanta, Ga	Jerry Pate	277
1936	Baltusrol, NJ	Tony Manero	282	1977	Southern Hills, Okla	Hubert Green	278
1937	Oakland Hills, Mich	Ralph Guldahl	281	1978	Cherry Hills, Colo	Andy North	285
1938	Cherry Hills, Colo	Ralph Guldahl	284	1979	Inverness, Ohio	Hale Irwin	284
1939	Philadelphia, Pa	Byron Nelson *(play-off with Craig Wood and Densmore Shute)*	284	1980	Baltusrol, NJ	Jack Nicklaus	272
1940	Canterbury, Ohio	Lawson Little *(play-off with Gene Sarazen)*	287	1981	Merion, Pa	David Graham *(Australia)*	273
1941	Colonial Club, Tex	Craig Wood	284	1982	Pebble Beach, Cal	Tom Watson	282
1942-45	No competition			1983	Oakmont, Pa	Larry Nelson	280
1946	Canterbury, Ohio	Lloyd Mangrum *(play-off with Byron Nelson and Vic Ghezzi)*	284	1984	Winged Foot, NY	Fuzzy Zoeller *(play-off with Greg Norman)*	276
1947	St Louis, Mo	Lew Worsham *(play-off with Sam Snead)*	282	1985	Oakland Hills, Mich	Andy North	279
1948	Riviera, Cal	Ben Hogan	276	1986	Shinnecock Hills, NY	Ray Floyd	279
1949	Medinah, Ill	Cary Middlecoff	286	1987	Olympic, Cal	Scott Simpson	277
1950	Merion, Pa	Ben Hogan *(play-off with Lloyd Mangrum and George Fazio)*	287				
1951	Oakland Hills, Mich	Ben Hogan	287				
1952	Northwood, Tex	Julius Boros	281				
1953	Oakmont, Pa	Ben Hogan	283				
1954	Baltusrol, NJ	Ed Furgol	284				
1955	Olympic, Cal	Jack Fleck *(play-off with Ben Hogan)*	287				
1956	Oak Hill, NY	Cary Middlecoff	281				

241

UNITED STATES PGA CHAMPIONSHIP
(Players from USA unless otherwise stated)

YEAR	VENUE	WINNER (Match-Play)	YEAR	VENUE	WINNER (Stroke-Play)	SCORE
1916	Siwanoy, NY	Jim Barnes		*Championship changed to stroke play*		
1917-18	No competition		1958	Llanerch, Pa	Dow Finsterwald	276
1919	Engineers, NY	Jim Barnes	1959	Minneapolis, Minn	Bob Rosburg	277
1920	Flossmoor, Ill	Jock Hutchison				
1921	Inwood, NY	Walter Hagen	1960	Firestone, Ohio	Jay Hebert	281
1922	Oakmont, Pa	Gene Sarazen	1961	Olympia Fields, Ill	Jerry Barber *(play-off with Don January)*	277
1923	Pelham, NY	Gene Sarazen				
1924	French Lick, Ind	Walter Hagen	1962	Aronimink, Pa	Gary Player *(Sth Africa)*	278
1925	Olympia Fields, Ill	Walter Hagen	1963	Dallas, Tex	Jack Nicklaus	279
1926	Salisbury, NY	Walter Hagen	1964	Columbus, Ohio	Bobby Nichols	271
1927	Cedar Crest, Tex	Walter Hagen				
1928	Baltimore, Md	Leo Diegel	1965	Laurel Valley, Pa	Dave Marr	280
1929	Hillcrest, Cal	Leo Diegel				
1930	Fresh Meadow, NY	Tommy Armour	1966	Firestone, Ohio	Al Geiberger	280
1931	Wannamoisett, RI	Tom Creavy	1967	Columbine, Colo	Don January *(play-off with Don Massengale)*	281
1932	Keller, Minn	Olin Dutra				
1933	Blue Mound, Wis	Gene Sarazen	1968	Pecan Valley, Tex	Julius Boros	281
1934	Park, NY	Paul Runyan				
1935	Twin Hills, Okla	Johnny Revolta	1969	Dayton, Ohio	Ray Floyd	276
1936	Pinehurst, NC	Densmore Shute	1970	Southern Hills, Okla	Dave Stockton	279
1937	Pittsburgh, Pa	Densmore Shute				
1938	Shawnee, Pa	Paul Runyan	1971	PGA National, Fla	Jack Nicklaus	281
1939	Pomonok, NY	Henry Picard				
1940	Hershey, Pa	Byron Nelson	1972	Oakland Hills, Mich	Gary Player *(Sth Africa)*	281
1941	Cherry Hills, Colo	Vic Ghezzi				
1942	Seaview, NJ	Sam Snead	1973	Canterbury, Ohio	Jack Nicklaus	277
1943	No competition					
1944	Manito, Wash	Bob Hamilton	1974	Tanglewood, NC	Lee Trevino	276
1945	Morraine, Ohio	Byron Nelson				
1946	Portland, Ore	Ben Hogan	1975	Firestone, Ohio	Jack Nicklaus	276
1947	Plum Hollow, Mich	Jim Ferrier	1976	Congressional, Md	Dave Stockton	281
1948	Norwood Hills, Miss	Ben Hogan				
1949	Hermitage, Va	Sam Snead	1977	Pebble Beach, Cal	Lanny Wadkins *(play-off with Gene Littler)*	282
1950	Scioto, Ohio	Chandler Harper				
1951	Oakmont, Pa	Sam Snead	1978	Oakmont, Pa	John Mahaffey *(play-off with Jerry Pate and Tom Watson)*	276
1952	Big Spring, Ky	Jim Turnesa				
1953	Birmingham, Mich	Walter Burkemo				
1954	Keller, Minn	Chick Harbert	1979	Oakland Hills, Mich	David Graham *(Australia) (play-off with Ben Crenshaw)*	272
1955	Meadowbrook, Mich	Doug Ford				
1956	Blue Hill, Mass	Jack Burke				
1957	Miami Valley, Ohio	Lionel Herbert	1980	Oak Hill, NY	Jack Nicklaus	274
			1981	Atlanta, Ga	Larry Nelson	273
			1982	Southern Hills, Okla	Raymond Floyd	272
			1983	Riviera, Cal	Hal Sutton	274
			1984	Shoal Creek, Ala	Lee Trevino	273
			1985	Cherry Hills, Colo	Hubert Green	278
			1986	Inverness, Ohio	Bob Tway	276
			1987	PGA National, Fla	Larry Nelson	287

US MASTERS
(All played at Augusta National, Georgia. Players from the USA unless otherwise stated)

YEAR	WINNER	SCORE		YEAR	VENUE WINNER	SCORE
1934	Horton Smith	284		1967	Gay Brewer	280
1935	Gene Sarazen *(play-off with Craig Wood)*	282		1968	Bob Goalby	277
1936	Horton Smith	285		1969	George Archer	281
1937	Byron Nelson	283		1970	Billy Casper *(play-off with Gene Littler)*	279
1938	Henry Picard	285		1971	Charles Coody	279
1939	Ralph Guldahl	279		1972	Jack Nicklaus	286
1940	Jimmy Demaret	280		1973	Tommy Aaron	283
1941	Craig Wood	280		1974	Gary Player *(Sth Africa)*	278
1942	Byron Nelson *(play-off with Ben Hogan)*	280		1975	Jack Nicklaus	276
1943-45	No competition			1976	Ray Floyd	271
1946	Herman Keiser	282		1977	Tom Watson	276
1947	Jimmy Demaret	281		1978	Gary Player *(Sth Africa)*	277
1948	Claude Harman	279		1979	Fuzzy Zoeller *(play off with Tom Watson and Ed Sneed)*	280
1949	Sam Snead	282				
1950	Jimmy Demaret	283		1980	Severiano Ballesteros *(Spain)*	275
1951	Ben Hogan	280		1981	Tom Watson	280
1952	Sam Snead	286		1982	Craig Stadler *(play-off with Dan Pohl)*	284
1953	Ben Hogan	274		1983	Severiano Ballesteros *(Spain)*	280
1954	Sam Snead *(play-off with Ben Hogan)*	289		1984	Ben Crenshaw	277
1955	Cary Middlecoff	279		1985	Bernhard Langer *(W. Germany)*	278
1956	Jack Burke Jnr	289		1986	Jack Nicklaus	279
1957	Doug Ford	283		1987	Larry Mize *(play-off with Severiano Ballesteros and Greg Norman)*	285
1958	Arnold Palmer	284				
1959	Art Wall Jnr	284				
1960	Arnold Palmer	282				
1961	Gary Player *(Sth Africa)*	280				
1962	Arnold Palmer *(play-off with Gary Player and Dow Finsterwald)*	280				
1963	Jack Nicklaus	286				
1964	Arnold Palmer	276				
1965	Jack Nicklaus	271				
1966	Jack Nicklaus *(play-off with Tommy Jacobs and Gay Brewer)*	288				

Above: Seve Ballesteros on the 18th green after registering his fourth World Match Play Championship in 1985. Ballesteros is shaking hands with the beaten finalist Bernhard Langer.

WORLD MATCH PLAY CHAMPIONSHIP
(All played at Wentworth, Surrey)

YEAR	WINNER	YEAR	WINNER
1964	Arnold Palmer *(US)*	1978	Isao Aoki *(Japan)*
1965	Gary Player *(Sth Africa)*	1979	Bill Rogers *(US)*
1966	Gary Player *(Sth Africa)*	1980	Greg Norman *(Australia)*
1967	Arnold Palmer *(US)*	1981	Severiano Ballesteros *(Spain)*
1968	Gary Player *(Sth Africa)*	1982	Severiano Ballesteros *(Spain)*
1969	Bob Charles *(New Zealand)*	1983	Greg Norman *(Australia)*
1970	Jack Nicklaus *(US)*	1984	Severiano Ballesteros *(Spain)*
1971	Gary Player *(Sth Africa)*	1985	Severiano Ballesteros *(Spain)*
1972	Tom Weiskopf *(US)*	1986	Greg Norman *(Australia)*
1973	Gary Player *(Sth Africa)*	1987	Ian Woosnam *(GB)*
1974	Hale Irwin *(US)*		
1975	Hale Irwin *(US)*		
1976	David Graham *(Australia)*		
1977	Graham Marsh *(Australia)*		

AUSTRALIAN OPEN
(Players Australian unless otherwise stated. *denotes an amateur)

YEAR	VENUE	WINNER	SCORE	YEAR	VENUE	WINNER	SCORE
1904	The Australian	*Hon Michael Scott *(GB)*	324	1955	Gailes	Bobby Locke *(Sth Africa)*	290
1905	Royal Melbourne	D. Soutar	330	1956	Royal Sydney	Bruce Crampton	289
1906	Royal Sydney	Carnegie Clark	322	1957	Kingston Heath	Frank Phillips	287
1907	Royal Melbourne	*Hon Michael Scott *(GB)*	318	1958	Kooyonga	Gary Player *(Sth Africa)*	271
1908	The Australian	*Clyde Pearce	311	1959	The Australian	Kel Nagle	284
1909	Royal Melbourne	*Claude Felstead	316	1960	Lake Karrinyup	*Bruce Devlin	282
1910	Royal Adelaide	Carnegie Clark	306	1961	Victoria	Frank Phillips	275
1911	Royal Sydney	Carnegie Clark	321	1962	Royal Adelaide	Gary Player *(Sth Africa)*	281
1912	Royal Melbourne	*Ivo Whitton	321	1963	Royal Melbourne	Gary Player *(Sth Africa)*	278
1913	Royal Melbourne	*Ivo Whitton	302	1964	The Lakes	Jack Nicklaus *(US)*	287
1914-19	No competition			1965	Kooyonga	Gary Player *(Sth Africa)*	264
1920	The Australian	Joe Kirkwood	290	1966	Royal Queensland	Arnold Palmer *(US)*	276
1921	Royal Melbourne	A. le Fevre	295	1967	Commonwealth	Peter Thomson	281
1922	Royal Sydney	C. Campbell	307	1968	Lake Karrinyup	Jack Nicklaus *(US)*	270
1923	Royal Adelaide	T. Howard	301	1969	Royal Sydney	Gary Player *(Sth Africa)*	288
1924	Royal Melbourne	*A. Russell	303	1970	Kingston Heath	Gary Player *(Sth Africa)*	280
1925	The Australian	F. Popplewell	299	1971	Royal Hobart	Jack Nicklaus *(US)*	269
1926	Royal Adelaide	*Ivo Whitton	297	1972	Kooyonga	Peter Thomson	281
1927	Royal Melbourne	R. Stewart	297	1973	Royal Queensland	J.C. Snead *(US)*	280
1928	Royal Sydney	F. Popplewell	295	1974	Lake Karrinyup	Gary Player *(Sth Africa)*	279
1929	Royal Adelaide	*Ivo Whitton	309	1975	The Australian	Jack Nicklaus *(US)*	279
1930	Metropolitan	F. Eyre	306	1976	The Australian	Jack Nicklaus *(US)*	286
1931	The Australian	*Ivo Whitton	301	1977	The Australian	David Graham	284
1932	Royal Adelaide	*M.J. Ryan	296	1978	The Australian	Jack Nicklaus *(US)*	284
1933	Royal Melbourne	M.L. Kelly	302	1979	Metropolitan	Jack Newton	288
1934	Royal Sydney	W.J. Bolger	283	1980	The Lakes	Greg Norman	284
1935	Royal Adelaide	F. McMahon	293	1981	Victoria	Bill Rogers *(US)*	282
1936	Metropolitan	Gene Sarazen *(US)*	282	1982	The Australian	Bob Shearer	287
1937	The Australian	G. Naismith	299	1983	Kingston Heath	Peter Fowler	285
1938	Royal Adelaide	*Jim Ferrier	283	1984	Royal Melbourne	Tom Watson *(US)*	281
1939	Royal Melbourne	*Jim Ferrier	285	1985	The Australian	Greg Norman (54 holes)	212
1940-45	No competition			1986	The Australian	Rodger Davis	278
1946	Royal Sydney	Ossie Pickworth	289				
1947	Royal Queensland	Ossie Pickworth	285				
1948	Kingston Heath	Ossie Pickworth	289				
1949	The Australian	Eric Cremin	287				
1950	Kooyonga	Norman von Nida	286				
1951	Metropolitan	Peter Thomson	283				
1952	Lake Karrinyup	Norman von Nida	278				
1953	Royal Melbourne	Norman von Nida	278				
1954	Kooyonga	Ossie Pickworth	280				

BRITISH AMATEUR CHAMPIONSHIP
(Players from Great Britain or Ireland unless otherwise stated)

YEAR	VENUE	WINNER	YEAR	VENUE	WINNER
1885	Hoylake	A.F. MacFie	1957	Formby	R. Reid Jack
1886	St Andrews	H.G. Hutchinson	1958	St Andrews	J.B. Carr
1887	Hoylake	H.G. Hutchinson	1959	Sandwich	D.R. Beman *(US)*
1888	Prestwick	John Ball	1960	Portrush	J.B. Carr
1889	St Andrews	J.E. Laidlay	1961	Turnberry	M.F. Bonallack
1890	Hoylake	John Ball	1962	Hoylake	R.D. Davies *(US)*
1891	St Andrews	J.E. Laidlay	1963	St Andrews	M.S.R. Lunt
1892	Sandwich	John Ball	1964	Ganton	Gordon J. Clark
1893	Prestwick	Peter Anderson	1965	Porthcawl	M.F. Bonallack
1894	Hoylake	John Ball	1966	Carnoustie	R.E. Cole *(Sth Africa)*
1895	St Andrews	L.M.B. Melville	1967	Formby	R.B. Dickson *(US)*
1896	Sandwich	F.G. Tait	1968	Troon	M.F. Bonallack
1897	Muirfield	A.J.T. Allan	1969	Hoylake	M.F. Bonallack
1898	Hoylake	F.G. Tait	1970	Newcastle Co Down	M.F. Bonallack
1899	Prestwick	John Ball	1971	Carnoustie	S. Melnyk *(US)*
1900	Sandwich	H.H. Hilton	1972	Sandwich	T. Homer
1901	St Andrews	H.H. Hilton	1973	Porthcawl	R. Siderowf *(US)*
1902	Hoylake	C. Hutchings	1974	Muirfield	T. Homer
1903	Muirfield	R. Maxwell	1975	Hoylake	M.M. Giles *(US)*
1904	Sandwich	W.J. Travis *(US)*	1976	St Andrews	R. Siderowf *(US)*
1905	Prestwick	A.G. Barry	1977	Ganton	P. McEvoy
1906	Hoylake	James Robb	1978	Troon	P. McEvoy
1907	St Andrews	John Ball	1979	Hillside	J. Sigel *(US)*
1908	Sandwich	E.A. Lassen	1980	Porthcawl	D. Evans
1909	Muirfield	R. Maxwell	1981	St Andrews	P. Ploujoux *(France)*
1910	Hoylake	John Ball	1982	Deal	M. Thompson
1911	Prestwick	H.H. Hilton	1983	Turnberry	A.P. Parkin
1912	Westward Ho!	John Ball	1984	Formby	J.M. Olazabal *(Spain)*
1913	St Andrews	H.H. Hilton	1985	Dornoch	G. McGimpsey
1914	Sandwich	J.L.C. Jenkins	1986	Lytham St Annes	D. Curry
1915-19	No competition		1987	Prestwick	P. Mayo
1920	Muirfield	C.J.H. Tolley			
1921	Hoylake	W.I. Hunter			
1922	Prestwick	E.W.E. Holderness			
1923	Deal	R.H. Wethered			
1924	St Andrews	E.W.E. Holderness			
1925	Westward Ho!	Robert Harris			
1926	Muirfield	Jesse Sweetser *(US)*			
1927	Hoylake	Dr W. Tweddell			
1928	Prestwick	T.P. Perkins			
1929	Sandwich	C.J.H. Tolley			
1930	St Andrews	R.T. Jones Jnr *(US)*			
1931	Westward Ho!	Eric Martin Smith			
1932	Muirfield	J. De Forest			
1933	Hoylake	Hon M. Scott			
1934	Prestwick	W. Lawson Little *(US)*			
1935	Lytham St Annes	W. Lawson Little *(US)*			
1936	St Andrews	H. Thomson			
1937	Sandwich	R. Sweeny Jnr *(US)*			
1938	Troon	C.R. Yates *(US)*			
1939	Hoylake	A.T. Kyle			
1940-45	No competition				
1946	Birkdale	J. Bruen			
1947	Carnoustie	W.P. Turnesa *(US)*			
1948	Sandwich	F.R. Stranahan *(US)*			
1949	Portmarnock	S.M. McCready			
1950	St Andrews	F.R. Stranahan *(US)*			
1951	Porthcawl	R.D. Chapman *(US)*			
1952	Prestwick	E.H. Ward *(US)*			
1953	Hoylake	J.B. Carr			
1954	Muirfield	D.W. Bachli *(Australia)*			
1955	Lytham St Annes	J.W. Conrad *(US)*			
1956	Troon	J.C. Beharrell			

AMERICAN AMATEUR CHAMPIONSHIP
(Players from the USA unless otherwise stated)

YEAR	VENUE	WINNER	YEAR	VENUE	WINNER
	(Prior to organisation of USGA)		1958	San Francisco	C.R. Coe
1893	Newport RI	W.G. Lawrence	1959	Broadmoor	J.W. Nicklaus
1894	St Andrews	L.B. Stoddart	1960	St Louis, Mo	D.R. Beman
	(Under the auspices of USGA)		1961	Pebble Beach	J.W. Nicklaus
1895	Newport RI	C.B. Macdonald	1962	Pinehurst	L.E. Harris, Jnr
1896	Shinnecock	H.J. Whigham	1963	Des Moines	D.R. Beman
1897	Wheaton, Ill	H.J. Whigham	1964	Canterbury, Ohio	W. Campbell
1898	Morris County	Finlay S. Douglas	1965	Tulsa, Okla	R. Murphy
1899	Onwentsia	H.M. Harriman	1966	Ardmore, Penn	G. Cowan
1900	Garden City	W.J. Travis	1967	Colorado	R. Dickson
1901	Atlantic City	W.J. Travis	1968	Columbus	B. Fleisher
1902	Glen View	Louis N. James	1969	Oakmont	S. Melnyk
1903	Nassau	W.J. Travis	1970	Portland	L. Wadkins
1904	Baltusrol	H. Chandler Egan	1971	Wilmington	G. Cowan
1905	Wheaton, Ill	H. Chandler Egan	1972	Charlotte, NC	M. Giles
1906	Englewood	E.M. Byers	1973	Inverness, Toledo, Ohio	C. Stadler
1907	Cleveland	Jerome D. Travers	1974	Ridgewood, NJ	J. Pate
1908	Midlothian, Ill	Jerome D. Travers	1975	Richmond, Va	F. Ridley
1909	Wheaton, Ill	R. Gardner	1976	Bel-Air	B. Sander
1910	Brookline	W.C. Fownes Jnr	1977	Aronimink, Pa	J. Fought
1911	Apawamis	H.H. Hilton *(GB)*	1978	Plainfield, NJ	J. Cook
1912	Wheaton, Ill	Jerome D. Travers	1979	Canterbury, Ohio	M. O'Meara
1913	Garden City	Jerome D. Travers	1980	North Carolina	H. Sutton
1914	Ekwanok	F. Ouimet	1981	San Francisco	N. Crosby
1915	Detroit	R.A. Gardner	1982	The Country Club, Brookline	J. Sigel
1916	Merion	Chas Evans	1983	North Shore, Chicago	J. Sigel
1917-18	No competition		1984	Oak Tree	S. Verplank
1919	Oakmont	D. Heron	1985	Montclair, NJ	S. Randolph
1920	Engineers Club	C. Evans	1986	Shoal Creek	S. Alexander
1921	St Louis, Mo	J. Guildford			
1922	Brookline	J. Sweetser			
1923	Flossmoor	Max Marston			
1924	Merion	R.T. Jones Jnr			
1925	Oakmont	R.T. Jones Jnr			
1926	Baltusrol	Geo von Elm			
1927	Minikahda	R.T. Jones Jnr			
1928	Brae Burn	R.T. Jones Jnr			
1929	Del Monte	H.R. Johnston			
1930	Merion	R.T. Jones Jnr			
1931	Beverley	F. Ouimet			
1932	Baltimore	C.R. Somerville *(Canada)*			
1933	Kenwood	G.T. Dunlap			
1934	Brookline	W. Lawson Little			
1935	Cleveland	W. Lawson Little			
1936	Garden City	J. Fischer			
1937	Portland	J. Goodman			
1938	Oakmont	W.P. Turnesa			
1939	Glenview	M.H. Ward			
1940	Winged Foot	R.D. Chapman			
1941	Omaha	M.H. Ward			
1942-45	No competition				
1946	Baltusrol	S.E. Bishop			
1947	Pebble Beach	R.H. Riegel			
1948	Memphis	W.P. Turnesa			
1949	Rochester	C.R. Coe			
1950	Minneapolis	S. Urzetta			
1951	Saucon Valley, Pa	W.J. Maxwell			
1952	Seattle	J. Westland			
1953	Oklahoma City	G. Littler			
1954	Detroit	A. Palmer			
1955	Richmond, Va	E. Harvie Ward			
1956	Lake Forest, Ill	E. Harvie Ward			
1957	Brookline	H. Robbins			

EISENHOWER TROPHY
(Men's world amateur team championship)

YEAR	VENUE	WINNER
1958	St Andrews, Scotland	Australia 918
1960	Merion, USA	United States 834
1962	Fuji, Japan	United States 854
1964	Olgiata, Italy	Gt Britain 895
1966	Mexico City	Australia 877
1968	Royal Melbourne, Australia	United States 868
1970	Puerto de Hierro, Spain	United States 857
1972	Olivos, Argentina	United States 865
1974	Campo de Golf, Dominica	United States 888
1976	Penina, Portugal	Gt Britain 892
1978	Pacific Harbour, Fiji	United States 873
1980	Pinehurst No 2, United States	United States 848
1982	Lausanne, Switzerland	United States 859
1984	Royal Hong Kong	Japan 870
1986	Caracas, Venezuela	Canada 860

RYDER CUP

YEAR	VENUE	RESULT
1927	Worcester, Mass	US 9½, GB2½
1929	Moortown, Leeds	GB 7, US 5
1931	Scioto, Ohio	US 9, GB 3
1933	Southport & Ainsdale, Lancs	GB 6½, US 5½
1935	Ridgewood, NJ	US 9, GB 3
1937	Southport & Ainsdale, Lancs	US 8, GB 4
1939-45	No competition	
1947	Portland, Ore	US 11, GB 1
1949	Ganton, Yorks	US 7, GB 5
1951	Pinehurst, NC	US 9½, GB 2½
1953	Wentworth, Surrey	US 6½, GB 5½
1955	Palm Springs, Cal	US 8, GB 4
1957	Lindrick, Sheffield	GB 7½, US 4½
1959	Palm Desert, Cal	US 8½, GB 3½
1961	Royal Lytham, Lancs	US 14½, GB 9½
1963	Atlanta, Ga	US 23, GB 9
1965	Royal Birkdale, Lancs	US 19½, GB 12½
1967	Houston, Tex	US 23½, GB 8½
1969	Royal Birkdale, Lancs	US 16, GB 16
1971	St Louis, Mo	US 18½, GB 13½
1973	Muirfield, Scotland	US 19, GB 13
1975	Laurel Valley, Pa	US 21, GB 11
1977	Royal Lytham, Lancs	US 12½, GB 7½
1979	Greenbrier, W Va	US 17, Europe 11
1981	Walton Heath, Surrey	US 18½, Europe 9½
1983	PGA National, Fla	US 14½, Europe 13½
1985	The Belfry, West Midlands	Europe 16½, US 11½
1987	Muirfield Village, Ohio	Europe 15, US 13

WORLD CUP

YEAR	VENUE	WINNER
1953	Beaconsfield, Montreal	Argentina 287
1954	Laval sur le Lac, Montreal	Australia 556
1955	Columbia, Washington, USA	United States 560
1956	Wentworth, England	United States 567
1957	Kasumigaseki, Tokyo	Japan 557
1958	Club de Golf, Mexico City	Ireland 579
1959	Royal Melbourne, Australia	Australia 563
1960	Portmarnock, Dublin	United States 565
1961	Dorado Beach, Puerto Rico	United States 560
1962	Jockey Club, Buenos Aires	United States 557
1963	St Nom la Breteche, Paris	United States 482
1964	Royal Kaanapali, Hawaii	United States 554
1965	Club de Campo, Madrid	South Africa 571
1966	Yomiuri, Tokyo	United States 548
1967	Club de Golf, Mexico City	United States 557
1968	Olgiata, Rome	Canada, 569
1969	Singapore Island	United States 552
1970	Jockey Club, Buenos Aires	Australia 544
1971	PGA National, Palm Beach, USA	United States 555
1972	Royal Melbourne, Australia	Taiwan 438
1973	Golf Nueva Andalucia, Spain	United States 558
1974	Lagunita, Venezuela	South Africa 554
1975	Navatanee, Bangkok	United States 554
1976	Mission Hills, Palm Springs, USA	Spain 574
1977	Wack Wack, Manila	Spain 591
1978	Princeville Maka, Hawaii	United States 564
1979	Glyfada, Athens	United States 575
1980	El Rignon, Bogota	Canada 572
1981	No competition	
1982	Acapulco, Mexico	Spain 563
1983	Pondok Indah, Indonesia	United States 565
1984	Olgiata, Rome	Spain 414
1985	La Quinta, California, USA	Canada 559
1986	No competition	

Left: The first victory in the Ryder Cup by a team representing Europe being celebrated at The Belfry in 1985 by Spaniard Seve Ballesteros nearly drowning Welshman Ian Woosnam in the traditional champagne.

WALKER CUP

YEAR	VENUE	SCORE	YEAR	VENUE	SCORE
1922	National Links, Long Island	US 8, GB & Ireland 4	1965	Baltimore, Md	US 12, GB & Ireland 12
1923	St Andrews, Scotland	US 6½, GB & Ireland 5½	1967	Royal St Georges, Sandwich	US 15, GB & Ireland 9
1924	Garden City, NY	US 9, GB & Ireland 3	1969	Milwaukee, Wis	US 13, GB & Ireland 11
1926	St Andrews, Scotland	US 6½, GB & Ireland 5½	1971	St Andrews, Scotland	GB & Ireland 13, US 11
1928	Chicago GC, Ill	US 11, GB & Ireland 1	1973	Brooklyn, Mass	US 14, GB & Ireland 10
1930	Royal St Georges, Sandwich	US 10, GB & Ireland 2	1975	St Andrews, Scotland	US 15½, GB & Ireland 8½
1932	Country Club, Brooklyn, Mass	US 9½, GB & Ireland 2½	1977	Shinnecock Hills, NY	US 16, GB & Ireland 8
1934	St Andrews, Scotland	US 9½, GB & Ireland 2½	1979	Muirfield, Scotland	US 15½, GB & Ireland 8½
1936	Pine Valley, NJ	US 10½, GB & Ireland 1½	1981	Cypress Point, Cal	US 15, GB & Ireland 9
1938	St Andrews, Scotland	GB & Ireland 7½, US 4½	1983	Royal Liverpool, England	US 13½, GB & Ireland 10½
1940-46	No competition		1985	Pine Valley, NJ	US 13, GB & Ireland 11
1947	St Andrews, Scotland	US 8, GB & Ireland 4	1987	Sunningdale, England	US 16½, GB & Ireland 7½
1949	Winged Foot, NY	US 10, GB & Ireland 2			
1951	Royal Birkdale, Lancs	US 7½, GB & Ireland 4½			
1953	Kittansett, Mass	US 9, GB & Ireland 3			
1955	St Andrews, Scotland	US 10, GB & Ireland 2			
1957	Minikahda, Minn	US 8½, GB & Ireland 3½			
1959	Muirfield, Scotland	US 9, GB & Ireland 3			
1961	Seattle, Washington	US 11, GB & Ireland 1			
1963	Turnberry, Scotland	US 14, GB & Ireland 10			

BRITISH WOMEN'S OPEN
(Players British unless otherwise stated)

YEAR	VENUE	WINNER	SCORE
1976	Gosforth Park	Jenny Lee-Smith	299
1977	Lindrick	Vivien Saunders	306
1978	Foxhills	Janet Melville	310
1979	Southport & Ainsdale	Alison Sheard (Sth Africa)	301
1980	Wentworth East	Debbie Massey (US)	294
1981	Northumberland	Debbie Massey (US)	295
1982	Royal Birkdale	Marta Figueras-Dotti (Spain)	296
1983	No competition		
1984	Woburn	Ayako Okamoto (Japan)	289
1985	Moor Park	Betsy King (US)	300
1986	Royal Birkdale	Laura Davies	283

CURTIS CUP

YEAR	VENUE	RESULT
1932	Wentworth, Surrey	US 5½, GB & Ireland 3½
1934	Chevy Chase, Md	US 6½, GB & Ireland 2½
1936	Gleneagles, Scotland	US 4½, GB & Ireland 4½
1938	Essex CC, Mass	US 5½, GB & Ireland 3½
1940-46	No competition	
1948	Royal Birkdale, Lancs	US 6½, GB & Ireland 2½
1950	Buffalo, NY	US 7½, GB & Ireland 1½
1952	Muirfield, Scotland	GB & Ireland 5, US 4
1954	Merion, Pa	US 6, GB & Ireland 3
1956	Prince's, England	GB & Ireland 5, US 4
1958	Brae Burn, Mass	GB & Ireland 4½, US 4½
1960	Lindrick, Yorks	US 6½, GB & Ireland 2½
1962	Broadmoor, Colorado Springs	US 8, GB & Ireland 1
1964	Royal Porthcawl, Wales	US 10½, GB & Ireland 7½
1966	Cascades, Hot Springs, Va	US 13, GB & Ireland 5
1968	Royal County Down, Ireland	US 10½, GB & Ireland 7½
1970	Brae Burn, Mass	US 11½, GB & Ireland 6½
1972	Western Gailes, Scotland	US 10, GB & Ireland 8
1974	San Francisco, Cal	US 13, GB & Ireland 5
1976	Royal Lytham, Lancs	US 11½, GB & Ireland 6½
1978	Apawamis, NY	US 12, GB & Ireland 6
1980	St Pierre, Chepstow, Wales	US 13, GB & Ireland 5
1982	Denver, Colo	US 14½, GB & Ireland 3½
1984	Muirfield, Scotland	US 9½, GB & Ireland 8½
1986	Prairie Dunes, Kansas	GB & Ireland 13, US 5

US WOMEN'S OPEN
*(Players from US unless stated. *amateur)*

YEAR	VENUE	WINNER	SCORE
1946	Spokane, Washington	Patty Berg (match-play)	5&4
1947	Starmount Forest	Betty Jameson	300
1948	Atlantic City	Mildred Zaharias	300
1949	Prince Georges	Louise Suggs	291
1950	Rolling Hills	Mildred Zaharias	291
1951	Druid Hills	Betsy Rawls	293
1952	Bala	Louise Suggs	284
1953	Rochester	Betsy Rawls	302
1954	Salem	Mildred Zaharias	291
1955	Wichita	Fay Crocker	299
1956	Northland	Kathy Cornelius	302
1957	Winged Foot	Betsy Rawls	299
1958	Forest Lake	Mickey Wright	290
1959	Churchill Valley	Mickey Wright	287
1960	Worcester	Betsy Rawls	292
1961	Baltusrol	Mickey Wright	293
1962	Dunes Golf & Beach Club	Murle Lindstrom	301
1963	Kenwood	Mary Mills	289
1964	San Diego	Mickey Wright	290
1965	Atlantic City	Carol Mann	290
1966	Hazeltine National	Sandra Spuzich	297
1967	Hot Springs, Virginia	*Catherine Lacoste (France)	294
1968	Moselem Springs	Susie Berning	289
1969	Scenic Hills	Donna Caponi	294
1970	Muskogee	Donna Caponi	287
1971	Kahkwa Club	JoAnne Carner	288
1972	Winged Foot	Susie Berning	299
1973	Rochester	Susie Berning	290
1974	Le Grange	Sandra Haynie	295
1975	Atlantic City	Sandra Palmer	295
1976	Rolling Green	JoAnne Carner	292
1977	Hazeltine National	Hollis Stacy	292
1978	Indianapolis	Hollis Stacy	289
1979	Brooklawn	Jerilyn Britz	284
1980	Richland	Amy Alcott	280
1981	La Grange	Pat Bradley	279
1982	Del Paso, Sacramento	Janet Anderson	283
1983	Cedar Ridge, Tulsa	Jan Stephenson	290
1984	Salem, Mass	Hollis Stacy	290
1985	Baltusrol, NJ	Kathy Baker	280
1986	Dayton, Ohio	Jane Geddes	287
1987	Plainfields, NJ	Laura Davies (GB)	285

BRITISH WOMEN'S AMATEUR
(Players British unless otherwise stated)

YEAR	VENUE	WINNER
1893	St Annes	Lady Margaret Scott
1894	Littlestone	Lady Margaret Scott
1895	Portrush	Lady Margaret Scott
1896	Hoylake	Amy Pascoe
1897	Gullane	Edith Orr
1898	Yarmouth	L. Thomson
1899	Newcastle, Co Down	May Hezlet
1900	Westward Ho!	Rhona Adair
1901	Aberdovey	Molly Graham
1902	Deal	May Hezlet
1903	Portrush	Rhona Adair
1904	Troon	Lottie Dod
1905	Cromer	B. Thompson
1906	Burnham	Mrs Kennion
1907	Newcastle, Co Down	May Hezlet
1908	St Andrews	M. Titterton
1909	Birkdale	Dorothy Campbell
1910	Westward Ho!	Mrs Grant Suttie
1911	Portrush	Dorothy Campbell
1912	Turnberry	Gladys Ravenscroft
1913	St Annes	Muriel Dodd
1914	Hunstanton	Cecil Leitch
1915-18	No competition	
1919	Cancelled	
1920	Newcastle, Co Down	Cecil Leitch
1921	Turnberry	Cecil Leitch
1922	Prince's, Sandwich	Joyce Wethered
1923	Burnham	Doris Chambers
1924	Portrush	Joyce Wethered
1925	Troon	Joyce Wethered
1926	Harlech	Cecil Leitch
1927	Newcastle, Co Down	T. de la Chaume *(France)*
1928	Hunstanton	Nanette Le Blan *(France)*
1929	St Andrews	Joyce Wethered
1930	Formby	Diana Fishwick
1931	Portmarnock	Enid Wilson
1932	Saunton	Enid Wilson
1933	Gleneagles	Enid Wilson
1934	Royal Porthcawl	Helen Holm
1935	Newcastle, Co Down	Wanda Morgan
1936	Southport & Ainsdale	Pam Barton
1937	Turnberry	Jessie Anderson
1938	Burnham	Helen Holm
1939	Portrush	Pam Barton
1940-45	No competition	
1946	Hunstanton	Jean Hetherington
1947	Gullane	Babe Zaharias *(US)*
1948	Royal Lytham	Louise Suggs *(US)*
1949	Harlech	Frances Stephens
1950	Newcastle, Co Down	Vicomtesse de St Sauveur *(France)*
1951	Broadstone	P.G. MacCann
1952	Troon	Moira Paterson
1953	Porthcawl	Marlene Stewart
1954	Ganton	Frances Stephens
1955	Portrush	Jessie Valentine
1956	Sunningdale	Margaret Smith
1957	Gleneagles	Philomena Garvey
1958	Hunstanton	Jessie Valentine
1959	Ascot	Elizabeth Price
1960	Harlech	Barbara McIntire *(US)*
1961	Carnoustie	Marley Spearman
1962	Royal Birkdale	Marley Spearman

YEAR	VENUE	WINNER
1963	Newcastle, Co Down	Brigitte Varangot *(France)*
1964	Prince's, Sandwich	Carol Sorenson *(US)*
1965	St Andrews	Brigitte Varangot *(France)*
1966	Ganton	Elizabeth Chadwick
1967	Harlech	Elizabeth Chadwick
1968	Walton Heath	Brigitte Varangot *(France)*
1969	Portrush	Catherine Lacoste *(France)*
1970	Gullane	Dinah Oxley
1971	Alwoodley	Michelle Walker
1972	Hunstanton	Michelle Walker
1973	Carnoustie	Ann Irvin
1974	Royal Porthcawl	Carol Semple *(US)*
1975	St Andrews	Nancy Syms *(US)*
1976	Silloth	Cathy Panton
1977	Hillside	Angela Uzielli
1978	Notts	Edwina Kennedy *(Australia)*
1979	Nairn	Maureen Madill
1980	Woodhall Spa	Anne Sander *(US)*
1981	Caernarvonshire	Belle Robertson
1982	Walton Heath	Kitrina Douglas
1983	Silloth	Jill Thornhill
1984	Royal Troon	Jody Rosenthal *(US)*
1985	Ganton	Lillian Behan
1986	West Sussex	Marie McGuire *(NZ)*
1987	Royal St David's	Janet Collingham

ESPIRITO SANTO TROPHY
(Women's world amateur team championship)

YEAR	VENUE	WINNER
1964	St Germain, France	France 588
1966	Mexico City CC	United States 580
1968	Victoria GC, Australia	United States 616
1970	Club de Campo, Spain	United States 598
1972	Hindu CC, Argentina	United States 583
1974	Campo de Golf, Dominica	United States 620
1976	Vilamoura, Portugal	United States 605
1978	Pacific Harbour, Fiji	Australia 596
1980	Pinehurst No 2, USA	United States 588
1982	Geneva, Switzerland	United States 579
1984	Royal Hong Kong	United States 585
1986	Caracas, Venezuela	Spain 580

Index

Page numbers in *italics* refer to illustration captions. Those in **bold** refer to main entries.

Acknowledgements

The author wishes to thank David Hamilton for his editorial assistance.

Artworks

All plans of courses by Simon Roulstone.

Pictures

Action Photos: 56, 61. Aldus Archive: 234, 235. Allsport: 2, 79, 89, 90, 98, 100, 108, 113, 119, 126, 129, 134, 137, 138, 141, 158, 162/3, 165, 166, 185, 188/9, 199. Associated Press: 150(b), 151. Associated Sports Photography: 54. Australian Tourist Commission: 209. BBC Hulton Picture Library: 18(b), 21, 25, 26, 30, 32, 34, 35, 48(t), 73, 80(t), 91(t), 109, 110(t), 111, 122. Bridgeman Art Library: 8/9. Central Press/The Photo Source: 39(tl), 103, 115, 150(l), 156. Colorsport: 76, 104, 123. Gerry Cranham: 41, 80(b), 125. Peter Dazeley: 39(b), 40, 44/5(t), 70, 71, 81, 88, 99, 101, 102, 106, 107, 117, 121, 127, 128, 132, 135, 159, 160, 161, 162, 164, 177, 207, 239, 243. Dunlop Slazenger International: 226, 227, 233. Mary Evans Picture Library: 10, 11, 29. Paul Felix: 224, 225. Fox Photos/The Photo Source: 153, 154. Su Gooders/T. Hoskison: 20. Ray Green: 39(tr), 74(b). Sonia Halliday: 6/7. James Holden: 230. Ed Lacey: 110(b), 118, 131. Lawrence Levy: 142/3. Mansell Collection: 16/7, 47, 91(b), 144, 145, 146, 147, 148/9. Bert Neale Collection: 42, 48(b), 49, 50, 51, 69(t,b), 94, 97, 157. Phillips Fine Art Auctioneers: 229. Popperfoto/UPI: 60(t,b), 62, 130, 152. Press Association: 33, 46. Courtesy Royal Lytham & St Annes Golf Club: 31. Phil Sheldon: 4/5, 13, 14, 15, 19, 22/3, 44/5(b), 52, 52/3, 55, 57, 58, 58/9, 63, 64/5, 66, 67, 68, 72/3, 77, 78, 78/9, 82, 83, 84, 85, 86/7, 92, 105, 168/9, 170/1, 174/5, 176, 181, 189, 192/3, 196, 197, 200, 202, 203, 214, 215, 216/7, 218, 231, 236, 240, 242, 244, 249. Sothebys: 222 courtesy of the estate of Mrs J.C. Robinson, 223 'The Putt' by Charles Edmund Brock. Sport & General: 114, 155. St Andrews University Library: 220/1. Sunday Times: 38. Syndication International: 37, 75, 93. Transworld Feature Syndicate: 112.